D1054788

THE HISTORY OF
PLAYING CARDS

The hero prostrated

M.ʳ Turner & his patron

TWO CARICATURE CARDS FROM A PACK FORMERLY
BELONGING TO THE LATE COUNT D'ORSAY.

THE HISTORY
OF
PLAYING CARDS

with Anecdotes of their use in
Conjuring, Fortune-Telling
and Card-Sharping

edited by
Rev. Ed. S. TAYLOR, B.A.
AND OTHERS

John Dewey Library
Johnson State College
Johnson, Vermont 05656

CHARLES E. TUTTLE COMPANY
Rutland, Vermont & Tokyo, Japan

Representatives

Continental Europe: BOXERBOOKS, INC., *Zurich*
British Isles: PRENTICE-HALL INTERNATIONAL, INC., *London*
Australasia: PAUL FLESCH & CO., PTY. LTD., *Melbourne*
Canada: M. G. HURTIG LTD., *Edmonton*

688.754
T213R
54-1105

Published by the Charles E. Tuttle Company, Inc.
of Rutland, Vermont & Tokyo, Japan
with editorial offices at
Suido 1-chome, 2-6, Bunkyo-ku, Tokyo, Japan

© *1973 by Charles E. Tuttle Co., Inc.*

All rights reserved

Library of Congress Catalog Card No. 72-89739

International Standard Book No. 0-8048-1026-5

First edition, 1865 by John Camden Hotten, London
First Tuttle edition, 1973

TABLE OF CONTENTS

PART THE FIRST.

LIST OF PLATES.

PUBLISHER'S FOREWORD

—oo✦❀✦oo—

Cards deal their peculiar brand of magic to the millions
of shufflers the world over. They have amused and
often confused all classes of society for several centuries. Fortunes have been won and lost on the cut
of a card. Countless lovers have leaped to their deaths,
or been transported to the heights by a pair of hearts
or diamonds, and great battles have been lost because
of a bad shuffle. To philosophize a bit, one might say
that fate deals the decisive hand—therefore the
fascination with cards.

Books about playing cards also deal into this fateful
game, and are more popular today than ever. This
History of Playing Cards is a quaint but popular
compendium of facts, figures, and anecdotes. Added
to this enlightening exposition are fifty priceless
illustrations, a Cruikshank masterpiece, and several
facsimiles of old cards from the Print Room in the
British Museum. The connoisseur is thus assured of
coming up with a winner. The publisher is proud to
reprint this winning combination as a contribution
to world peace and pastime.

The Rev. Ed. S. Taylor, B.A., a historian in the true

sense, and a person whose curiosity was matched only by his writings, contributed many curious and timely articles to the popular mid-nineteenth-century periodical *Notes and Queries*. In his *History of Playing Cards* he dealt posterity an invaluable heritage of curious and fascinating lore.

PREFACE.

—∞∘❀∘∞—

FIVE years ago I purchased from an eminent French publisher some tasteful wood-engravings, illustrative of the History of Playing Cards. These, with the small work in which they originally appeared, were placed in the hands of the late Rev. ED. S. TAYLOR, of Ormesby St. Margaret, Great Yarmouth, as material for a *History of Playing Cards, English and Foreign,* which he had offered to undertake for me. The readers of *Notes and Queries* will remember this gentleman as the valued contributor of many curious articles to that useful periodical. His knowledge was wide and varied, although his tastes were of that peculiar kind which delights in the careful exploration of the bye-ways, rather than the high roads, of learning.

The first part of the work was soon in the printers' hands, but ill-health followed, and the book proceeded slowly up to the time of the Editor's decease, two years ago. It was deemed necessary to mention this fact, as some of the references are to matters long since passed, although they are stated as of the present day.

To the French Illustrations have been added several facsimiles of old cards from the Print-room in the British Museum, and other sources.

The third and last division of the work—that treating of Card-Conjuring, Fortune-Telling, and Card-Sharping—might have been extended to a much greater length, but it was found that the size of the work, as projected, had already been much exceeded ; and so the writer was necessarily compelled to omit much that he had collected upon these curious subjects.   Hereafter a small volume, entirely devoted to their consideration, may probably see the light.

With these explanations the present book is given to the world, not as an exhaustive treatise upon the subject, but rather as a popular compend of facts and anecdotes relating to a pastime which has amused all classes of society for many generations.

One more statement—this time in our own behalf—is, perhaps, necessary.   The student or the antiquary, acquainted with the larger works of Breitkopt, Singer, and Chatto, writers who have so elaborately treated our subject, is reminded that many facts and particulars, unknown to those learned enquirers, may be found scattered through our pages.

J. C. H.

PICCADILLY, W.

Playing Cards.

PART THE FIRST.

THE HISTORY OF CARDS.

I.

INTRODUCTION.

CARDS AND GIPSIES — FRENCH CLAIM TO INVENTION OF CARDS
UNFOUNDED — TAROTS.

THE present age is remarkable for a more accurate
spirit of historical research than that of those
which preceded it; and the result has been far
greater success in the treatment of numerous
historic difficulties which had baffled the ingenuity of former writers. A more skilful and
systematic investigation of facts has detected the
idle conceits with which a fanciful but less accurate research had invested them. Nevertheless,
there still remain some, not only of the more
recondite and unusual subjects of enquiry, but even
of matters of every day attention and the occur-
rences of common life, which await a satisfactory
solution.

We have, for instance, scattered about on the

earth, sojourning awhile in the busy centres of life and activity, or wandering at will in the more secluded districts, a strange and peculiar race, going their own ways, and persistent in habits and customs differing from all around them, caring little for the world's opinion, and nothing at all for the elaborate theories which the learned have propounded as to their origin. It need hardly be said, we refer to the Gipsies—that inexplicable, vagabond, half-ruffianly, and yet provokingly interesting people, of whom the French ditty asks in words which may be rendered in English—

> "Sorcerers, jugglers, sharpers, say
>   Where do you come from, Gipsies gay?"

And what is their answer?

> "Where do we come from?   Nobody knows :
>   The swallow free,
>   Whence comes it hither o'er land and sea?"

Not a very suggestive one certainly, but yet the only one they can or care to give. Research has failed to discover with any degree of certainty the cradle of their race.

Now, precisely the same obscurity hangs over the origin of our ordinary playing-cards. Gipsies and cards, who does not know them? But what do we know about them? Absolutely nothing.

These two difficulties, however, fortunately for our purpose, are intimately connected, and whoever shall succeed in resolving the one, will have at his command the means of unravelling the other.

We shall be met here by the objections of those who, relying on the statements of ordinary works of reference, have accepted as a fact the traditionary invention of cards by a miniature painter named Gringonneur, attached to the court of Charles VI. of France. This notion, however, we shall demonstrate to be erroneous; and our neighbours across the channel must be content to forego their claim to cards as an invention solely French, devised with a view of amusing Charles VI. during the period of his imbecility.*

At the same time, we may add, as a salvo to

---

* Père Menestrier, who lived about the close of the reign of Louis XIV., was the author of this belief. While searching among the records of the age of Charles VI., he found a notice of Gringonneur the painter, and of certain cards illuminated by him, which, in a memoir on the subject, he erroneously assumed to be the first examples. Since Menestrier's time, however, cards far more ancient, or, at any rate, traces of their existence, have been discovered; but the knowledge of these is confined to the few who have made cards their especial study, for Menestrier's account still obtains general credence among the public at large.

their *amour propre*, that no European nation
whatever is in a better position in this respect
than themselves; and that France has, in adopt-
ing a foreign invention, as in numerous other instances, made it to a great extent her own, and,
so to speak, popularized it, by infusing into
it that grace and spirit which is characteristic
of her genius.

The truth is, that cards, like chess, are an
importation from the East, and their origin is to
be sought for in the most remote antiquity. Of
the accuracy of this hypothesis we hope to adduce
satisfactory evidence. Moreover, it is to the
Gipsies that we owe their introduction into
Europe, which took place about the end of the
thirteenth century, and their existence in southern
countries has been ascertained, before the French
had anything to do with them.

It must not, however, be imagined that these
very ancient cards, derived from a quarter so
remote, bore much resemblance to those now in
use, which are mainly, in point of fact, of French
origin. They bore emblematical figures, mys-
teriously grouped in accordance with the lore of
Ind, and were doubtless employed rather for the
fancied interpretation of the will of the unseen
God, than for the amusement of the profane.

Very different is the office of our cards.

Unfortunately, no specimens of the original cards, as first introduced into Europe, have come down to us; and we can only form an idea of them from certain emblematical cards of a similar character, the use of which, though confined to a few localities, is not yet obsolete.

These cards are called *tarots*,* and are still extant in Switzerland and Germany, and in some parts of Alsace and Franche Compté. They are unknown, except as curiosities, to the Parisians and to ourselves; but they are, nevertheless, the sole representatives of the original cards which the Gipsies brought with them into Europe. Some day, perchance, the archæological investigations, which are being prosecuted with so much success in Asia, will bring to light remains of ancient art, which will furnish us with data hitherto unsuspected, for the history of what we may call the *heroic* epoch of the game of cards. At present, however, this is a mere matter of conjecture, and

* The derivation of the word tarot is exceedingly obscure. In France, cards which are figured on their backs with a kind of grisaille or diaper pattern, are called "Cartes Tarotées," which led Lacroix to derive the word from τερειν, *trouer*, as representing pierced work. The incorporated Card-makers of Paris, in their statute of 1694, call themselves *Tarcotiers*. Probably, however, it is a corruption of Tarocchi, by which name the emblematic cards were commonly known.

our better course is to avoid losing ourselves in a
maze of untenable speculations.   The utmost we
can hope to arrive at is a portion of the truth,
and this we will endeavour to establish on sure
grounds.

It is not of much moment to determine
the exact form of cards in use in Asia during
the unrecorded period of their adoption.   Our
most remote researches go no further back than
their appearance contemporaneously with the
Gipsies ; and their reliable history can only consist in a recital of their adventures on European
soil.

II.

ORIENTAL ORIGIN OF CARDS.

THE GIPSIES IN INDIA—THEIR EXPULSION, AND ARRIVAL IN
EUROPE—DESCRIPTION OF TAROT CARDS—THEIR ORIENTAL
CHARACTER—LIVRE DE THOTH—CHINESE AND PERSIAN
CARDS — INDIAN CARDS — NOTICES OF CARDS BEFORE
CHARLES VI. OF FRANCE—NAIBI—RETENTION OF THE
ANCIENT DIVINATORY USE OF CARDS BY THE GIPSIES.

WE have asserted, then, that cards are of Eastern
origin, and that it was by the instrumentality of
the Gipsies that they were first introduced into
Europe. These statements, before entering further into the subject, we must proceed to verify.

It will not be necessary, however, to inflict on
the general reader the mass of abstruse, weari-
some, and often contradictory evidence, by which
this conclusion is arrived at. It will suffice to
give a brief outline of the leading facts, and the
most rational, if not the only possible explanation
of which the various accounts are susceptible. At
the same time, references will be found in the foot
notes, for the information of those who desire to
investigate the subject more thoroughly, to those
authorities who have written more fully on

the subject, than the limits of these pages will allow.*

Doubtless, the opinion which assigns the origin of cards to the far East is a correct one, and their connection with the Gipsies necessitates us to seek for the traces of both in one and the same quarter. The Gipsies themselves have no tradition to help us—we are therefore driven to philological and ethnological affinities. These in the case of the Gipsy and Hindustani languages have been long remarked. There is every reason, moreover, for believing that the Gipsies were originally some one of the Paria or lower castes of the Hindu race,† and being swept on before some Thibetian or Mongolian irruption,‡ after making the country of the Zingani, below Multan, their first asylum, were again driven forth, precipitated on Persia and Arabia, and continuing their onward march arrived in Egypt, from which

* Marsden, Pallas, Bernouilli, Rüdiger, Grellmann, &c.

† Bombay Transactions, 1820. Some of the lowest castes in Beloochistan have a great resemblance in manners and physique to the Gipsies. They evince a great fondness for carrion, which is also characteristic of the Gipsy race.

‡ This was possibly the great wave of Mohammedan invasion under Timur Beg. There is a tribe near the mouths of the Indus called Tchinganes, and Sind is one of the names the Gipsies give themselves. *Vide* Grellmann, *Versuch über die Zigeuner.* Göttingen, 1787.

they found their way into Europe.* Here they established themselves to some extent after the manner of the Jews and Armenians, forming part of the floating population in every country, but avoiding all unnecessary intercourse with the natives.

The Gipsies, moreover, have retained ever since their nomadic habits, and present to this day the singular spectacle of an Oriental people, surrounded, yet almost entirely unaffected by the civilization of Europe.

In France, they have received the name of Bohomians, either from an early sojourn in that country, or from *Böem*, an old French word denoting a sorcerer; the English call them Gipsies (quasi *Egyptians*): but these are only fanciful appellations, and have no resemblance to their real title.

In Italy, they are Zingari; in Germany, Zigeuner; both evident corruptions of *Zingani*, the name they are supposed to have borne in India.

* Pasquier, in his *Recherches Historiques*, says, that they first appeared at Paris in the character of pilgrims, or penitents, in August, 1427, in a troop of more than one hundred, under some chiefs, who styled themselves Counts, and represented themselves as Christians driven out of Egypt by the Moslems, with a view, no doubt, of exciting sympathy, and obtaining a footing in the country under false pretences.

A French artist, M. Théodore Valerio, has lately published a series of sketches of Gipsy physiognomy, collected during a tour on the Danube, Moldau, and Theiss, which give one a vivid notion of the distinctive features of this singular race. The heads are positively splendid; especially those of their women, whose large dark eyes, and tresses of a bluish-black lustre, command admiration, in spite of the rags and tatters which scantily supply to them the place of clothing. M. Valerio denominates them *Tsiganes*—a name which we are at a loss to interpret, but which is, nevertheless, their proper epithet—the ancient name of their race, and perhaps of the allies which accompanied them in their flight. These Tsiganes or Zinganes, Zigeuner or Zingari, these Bohemians or Gipsies, if you prefer it, were the introducers into Europe of the tarot cards of the East.

And if we consider the existent habits of the people, as we encounter them in our daily intercourse, we shall see a further corroboration of our hypothesis. For, allowing that the tarots are the predecessors of our present cards—these tarots which we have seen were devised for divinatory purposes—who but the Gipsies, we may ask, are still the fortune-tellers, the card-conjurors of the world *par excellence*? The trade is

PLATE I

IIII

LANPEREVT

THE EMPEROR.
(Paris Tarot Pack, *circa* 1500.)

PLATE II

THE WORLD.
(Paris Tarot Pack, *circa* 1500.)

PLATE III

ACE OF DENIERS.
(Ace of Diamonds, Tarot Pack, *circa* 1500.)

PLATE IV

QUEEN OF SWORDS.
(Queen of Spades, Tarot Pack, *circa* 1500.)

PLATE V

KNIGHT OF CLUBS.
(Extra Coat Card, Tarot Pack, *circa* 1500.)

PLATE VI

KNAVE OF SWORDS.
(Spades, Tarot Pack, *circa* 1500.)

inherent in their very blood, and cards are the Gipsies' patrimony.

Assuming, then, that the Gipsies are from India, and that they are in all probability identical with the Parias we have mentioned, we have before us the first germ of the origin of Cards. It would not affect our argument to any great extent if the cards themselves presented no internal evidence of Indian civilization, but fortunately nothing is more apparent.

If we examine attentively a pack of tarots, either such as cartomancers or fortune tellers use, or such a one as may be still met with on the banks of the Rhine or the Upper Danube, we shall perceive a wide difference between them and our modern game. Among our illustrations will be observed ten of these cards, detached examples from several packs of tarots, which will give us a general idea of the entire set. Six of these belong to a pack manufactured at Paris, about the year 1500. They represent "the Emperor" and "the World," both emblematical figures, then an ace, a queen, a chevalier or knight, and a valet or knave, all distinguished by symbols totally differing from our marks of suits, hearts, diamonds, spades, and clubs.*

* Plates I.—VI.

Plate VII. is a copy of one of the cards of a small tarot pack of rather earlier date ; it represents "the Lover" (*L'Amoureux*), or Cupid himself (*L'Amour*), a regular emblematic picture ; and "the Sun," belonging to an Italian pack of the sixteenth century, may be classed under the same category. The next is comparatively modern. It is still "the World," but the design is modified after the fashion of the tarots of the present time. Plate X., of Italian make, is the *Fou*, Fool or Clown.

These cards will repay our trouble if we attentively consider them; they will serve to evince the peculiarities of the tarot pack, which is, as may be perceived, no myth, excessively mythological though it be.

The drawing of these ancient specimens may be seen at a glance, to have nothing very finished about it. Occasionally even, there is in the figures an absolute deformity, and yet from their simplicity they are very far from displeasing.

The representation of the Sun in Plate VIII. is so distinct that no one can fail to recognise him. The woman spinning below, and who has very much the appearance of a S. Geneviève keeping sheep, is merely a fantastical accessory. The

PLATE VII

THE LOVER.
(Tarot Card, Italy, Sec. xvi.)

PLATE VIII

THE SUN.
(Tarot Card, Italy, Sec. xvi.)

PLATE IX

THE WORLD.
(Modern Tarot.)

PLATE X

THE FOOL.
(Tarot, Recent Italian Pack.)

meaning of the *second* design, representing "the World," is not so self-evident. The antique symbol explains itself,—the modern has pretensions in a philosophic direction, which do not help us in the explanation of the allegory.

The comparative absence of distinctive character in the remaining example is remarkable, for usually the "Fool" of the tarot series bears the stamp of thorough idiotcy—a complete simpleton. The length of the card is also unusual.

As was before observed, these are merely detached specimens of a pack of tarots. At first sight, perhaps, they are calculated to surprise those who have lived under the impression that there are no cards in existence, but kings of hearts, knaves of clubs, eights of diamonds, aces of spades, and so on. It is for all that a regular game,—a game which is played still; and more than that, it is just about such a pack of cards as has existed in Europe since the very first period of their introduction.

An entire pack of this kind is composed of of seventy-eight cards : viz., the *Fou*, which is reckoned separately, and performs the same office as the functional zero in the Arabic numeral system—that is to say, it has no independent value, but increases that of any card which may be combined with it; twenty-one *atouts*,* having a particular value of their own, and bearing emblems, the different combinations of which give a zest to the game of a far more varied and lively nature than is possible with our own picture cards; and lastly, fifty six cards perfectly analagous to those in present use, although distinguished by signs of a different kind,—these are, forty pip cards, the ace to the ten, in four suits, four kings, four queens, four chevaliers (or knights, as in chess), and four valets.

The " Fou," as before stated, has a method of action of his own.

The twenty-one emblematic atouts are generally such as the following :

TAROTS PUBLISHED AT PARIS ABOUT A.D. 1500.	TAROTS OF RECENT DATE.
I. The Bateleur, or Juggler.	The World.
II. The Papess (Pope Joan)	The Last Judgment.
III. The Empress.	The Sun.
IV. The Emperor.	The Moon.
V. The Pope.	The Star.
VI. L'Amoureux.	The Devil.
VII. The Chariot	Temperance

* According to M. Duchesne, the word *atout* denotes that such cards are of higher value than the rest : " Ces cartes sont dites *a tutti*, à tous, c'est à dire, superieures à tout autre, et n'appartenant à aucune couleur." Ordinarily, atout means *trump*.

VIII.	Justice.	Death.
IX.	The Hermit	The Maison de Dieu.
X.	The Wheel of Fortune.	Le Pendu.
XI.	Fortitude.	Fortitude.
XII.	Le Pendu, a man hung by one leg.	Fortune
XIII.	Death	The Priest.
XIV.	Temperance.	Justice.
XV.	The Devil.	The Chariot.
XVI.	The Thunderbolt.	L'Amoureux.
XVII.	The Star.	Jupiter.
XVIII.	The Moon.	Juno.
XIX.	The Sun.	The Emperor.
XX.	The Last Judgment.	The Empress.
XXI.	The World.	The Juggler.
XXII.	The Fool.	The Fool.

The order in which these figures are numbered is not always the same, but this is unimportant.

A wide field of speculation is open to those who may desire to examine more fully into the meaning of these emblematic atouts,* and much

---

* *Vide* Court de Gebelin, *Le Monde Primitif*, vol. viii., for an extraordinary article on the subject, at the end of which, is a memoir more extraordinary still. In 1781, Court de Gebelin became a violent advocate of the Oriental origin of cards. The miscellaneous dissertations of this original scholar, which are remarkable for the admixture of sentiment with the most profound philosophy, were published by subscription under the title of *Le Monde Primitif*, and it is from these that the best arguments in favour of the Oriental theory of tarots are derived.

He commences thus: "If we heard it announced, that a work of the ancient Egyptians was in existence, a book of theirs, which had escaped the conflagration which destroyed their magnificent libraries, and which contained their teaching in an incorrupt state, on subjects of the most interesting nature, beyond

no doubt connected with them of a curious
and valuable nature remains to be discovered.
The opinion which assigns to cards in general, an antiquity much higher than had been

a doubt every one would be eager to become acquainted with a
book of so extraordinary a description; most certainly this
would be the case. Well, then, this book of ancient Egypt is
the game of tarots,—we have it in *cards*." He has not a doubt
on the subject.

We can perfectly avail ourselves of these arguments which
go to prove that cards are the offspring of the learning of Egypt,
and at the same time keep to our own hypothesis of their
Asiatic origin—from India, in fact—along with the Gipsy immi-
gration. There is no contradiction involved here. Egypt is the
East all the same, and every one knows there is a family connection between these venerable civilizations of the past—those
of Egypt and India. In the ancient legends of Egypt, the science
of cards is connected even with their divinities. Thus Plutarch
relates, quoting an Egyptian fable (Treatise on Isis and Osiris),
that the Sun having discovered the illicit intercourse of Saturn
and Rhea, desired that she should have no opportunity to bring
forth, *in any month* or *in any year*. Mercury, who was enamoured of the same goddess, played against the Moon, and
won from her every seventieth part of the time she was above
the horizon ; the god joined all these portions of time together,
and so made five days, which were added to the year, which
before that consisted of only three hundred and sixty days.

In admitting, however, to a certain extent, the affinity
between *ancient* Egypt and India, while discussing the history of
the Gipsies, we must keep it altogether distinct from an apparent similarity in the names ; for between the Gipsies and the
Copts and Fellahs of modern times there is no resemblance
whatever in appearance, manners, or language. The name
Gipsies, however it may invite us to look for traces of them on
the banks of the Nile, originated with the false statement they
themselves put forth on their first appearance in Europe.

hitherto assumed, was first broached about the close of the last century, and was propounded with some show of research. And it is exactly the examination of the cards of a pack of tarots, which has helped to substantiate these new conjectures. Since that time the obscurities of the question have been very much cleared up ; but the public have not been made acquainted with the fact.

It is evident that the tarots, altered as they are, nay, perverted from their original design, still retain the impress of a civilization which is by no means European.

This clown, these kings and knights, are all pieces of a game of chess, which is an Indian affair. This property of the Fou, analogous to the function of the zero in the Arabic digits, is it not a proof of an Oriental origin ? The emblem entitled La Maison de Dieu, represents a house shattered by the lightning stroke, and falling into ruins. Remove the inscription, which is evidently a modern perversion,—what is this but Desolation, the symbol of a catastrophe, a card of evil omen.

Take again the card of Death, numbered XIII. in the series of symbols. The idea of ill-fatedness attached to the number XIII. is essentially Oriental, and the fact that the emblematic *atouts* are numbered so to speak, from low to high, just as certain Asiatic alphabets are written from right to left, may conceal a similar interpretation.*

Some would explain the word Tarocchi, or Tarot, as meaning the " Royal Road of Life," and assert that the word is compounded of the word TAR, signifying *road*, and Ro, Ros, or Rog, which means *king*—*royal*, an etymology quite as probable as the following, though not a whit more satisfactory.

"This book (this book of destiny—this sacred game) appears to have been denominated A-ROSH from A, *i.e.* doctrine, science, and ROSCH, Mercury, and this combined with the article T, signifies the synopsis of the Mercurial doctrine ; but as *rosh* has also the meaning of *commencement*, this word *ta-rosh* was especially devoted to his cosmogony ; in the same manner as the *Ethotia* (History of Time) was the title of his astronomy ; and possibly Athotes, who has been taken for one of the kings and the son of Thoth, is only the offspring of his own imagination, and denotes in reality the history of the kings of Egypt."†

* *Vide* plates of Tarocchi cards in Singer, *Researches into the History of Playing Cards*, p. 202.

† Extract from a paper, drawn up by a general officer, entitled *Recherches sur les Tarots, et sur la Divination par les Cartes*

Passing over these very apocryphal interpretations, another question suggests itself. How comes it about that the tarot series seems based on the combinations of the number *seven*—the sacred number of the East? There are seventy-eight cards in the pack : put the " Fou " on one side, and there remain seventy-seven (11 × 7). These seventy-seven cards are further divided into two classes,—the twenty-one emblematic atouts (3 × 7), and the fifty-six cards embracing the kings, queens, knights, valets, and pips (8 × 7). This may possibly be accidental, but it may also be an indication of a religious origin.

The distribution of the fifty-six cards, properly denominated *numerals*, has likewise a signification peculiar to itself. We perceive that they are classed by suits, and these suits, four in number, have each their proper emblem—vase, money, sword, baton—which, though possibly receiving some modification in the course of time, have all the appearance of denoting the four castes into

des Tarot, which Court de Gebelin has appended to his own dissertation. The tarot pack used by the modern *cartomanciennes* at Paris and elsewhere, for fortune-telling, is called by them "Livre de Thot." Thoth was the Egyptian Mercury, said to be one of the early kings, and the inventor of the hieroglyphic system and its attendant mysticism. *Vide* Henri Delaage, *Le Monde Occulte*, fourth edition, p. 26.

which the community was anciently divided, as well on the banks of the Ganges as those of the Nile. The vase denotes the priest; the sword, the warrior; the piece of money, the merchant—the artizan; and the baton or club, the tiller of the soil.*

So far, all seems tolerably conclusive as to the connection of Egypt, India, and Asia, with the history of cards; but we need not stop here.

In the vocabulary of the modern game of tarots, we have certain terms preserved, which afford us fresh proofs—the word *mat*, for instance,

---

* Read Court de Gebelin. What we content ourselves with hinting at, he boldly developes, details and all. Some of his conjectures are entirely baseless, others are deductions of very questionable accuracy. He sees Egypt throughout—even in the cross and globe which surmounts the sceptre of the king, and which, without the slightest hesitation, he pronounces to be the sacred Tau.

The Pope he calls High Priest and Chief of the Hierophants, and accounts for the Papess (figured on some tarots) by reminding his readers that the Egyptian priesthood were *Benedicts*. "Otherwise," says he, "what can be meant by this figure of a woman? As for the sceptre, with its triple cross, that is a relic exclusively Egyptian—see it in the Table of Isis in the character T.T., which is connected with the licentious symbol which they used to parade in the celebrated festival of the Pamylies, rejoicing over the recovery of Osiris. It was in the Egyptian symbolism an emblem of the reproduction of vegetable life, and of Nature in all her phases.

Two Taus placed sideways form an ⊢⊣, which, surmounted by a third, is the triple Tau ⊥. In the old Hebrew character also, the Tau is represented in the shape of *a Latin Cross*.

by which the *Fou* is designated, and which means prostrated, dead, cracked; the word *pagad* again, which is the appellation of the *Bateleur* or Cup Juggler,* and which, derived from *pag* master and *gad* fortune, seems to mean Master of Fortune. The juggler master of fortune! here's a philosophy for you! The Orient with a vengeance!

These scraps of Eastern speech—these assumed combinations which centre round a sacred number —these names of certain figures,—assuredly all this, taken as a whole, must be something more than mere speculation.

It is asserted that the groundwork of a game analogous to these tarots which are now under discussion, has been discovered in China. All the parts of this game are based upon the number seven; and there are in all seventy-seven tablets inscribed with incomprehensible characters.

If this be a fact, nothing is more reasonable to suppose than that cards, in China, were an importation from India, and that they received

* *Fr. joueur de gobelet.* The Bateleur is represented with his cup and balls in Singer's plate, p. 202, No. 1. Here we probably have again an unsuspected trace of the East, the Hermes-goblet of Egypt.

there considerable modifications, exactly as has
in fact taken place in Europe. The Chinese
cards of the present day do not offer the same
points of resemblance. It is necessary to remark,
however, that our knowledge of them is exceedingly imperfect; and what we have expressed on
the subject, has reference only to some few uncon-
nected examples.*

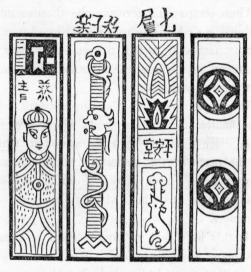

* There are some specimens in the Imperial Library, at
Paris. These cards are of an oblong shape, about 2 inches or
2¼ long, and a little more than half an inch in breadth. On
some there are only patterns of which nothing can be made,
while the figures on others seem explained by the legends. One
would take the engravings of them to represent cakes of ink.

When the " Son of Virtue" has completed the destruction of the Mongol dynasty—an event which seemed at one time anything but unlikely— we shall see, perhaps, the barriers removed which environ the secrets of the Celestial Empire, and then, and not till then, will these hitherto un-known regions supply something more definite than mere conjectures for the history of cards.

Meanwhile, we may take it as a fact that the Chinese were acquainted with the use of cards as early as A.D. 1120 ; and if so, we need go no further for proof that cards in Asia are of far more ancient date than our own.*

An account appeared in the pages of the *Magasin Pittoresque* of a number of Persian tarots, which were purchased at Cairo by a M. Prisse. These were of ivory, rather diminutive in size, and of rectangular form, with devices painted on them in miniature, of turbans, swords and helmets, crowns and hieroglyphic symbols of

* It is a Chinese scholar, M. Abel de Rémusat, who has affirmed this on the authority of Chinese MSS. Though we are not in a position to verify this precise date, it cannot possibly be fictitious. M. Remusat's remarks, however, do not neces-sarily point to a Chinese *invention*. The date he gives is probably that of the introduction of the Indian game, or, rather, he intends to denote the period when China manufactured for herself the tangible materials of the sacerdotal and philo-sophical game of the Pantheistic races of Hindustan.

which the signification is as yet undiscovered.
The Persians, although Mohammedans, are
addicted to card playing, as they belong to the
Shiite sect, which rejects the 7,000 traditions
of the prophet.

India, too, has its cards, and, moreover, the
modern Hindustani game is precisely that which
presents the most striking analogy with the ancient
tarots of Europe.*   Their pieces are of oblong or
circular shape, in gold and mother-of-pearl, or
else painted on pasteboard in gold and colours.
They are divided into a certain number of suits,
seven or eight, each one being composed of a
king, a vizir (no queen or knight), and ten pip
cards.

Each suit has its distinctive emblem,—a sword
or sabre, a small bell, a piece of money, an ivory
ball, a flower, a cabalistic legend or talisman,
a pagoda or small ivory figure, a harp, &c.
Besides these cards there are emblematic figures,
atouts in fact, the proper number of which has
not been ascertained.

Now we have seen that the sword and piece
of money, are two of the marks which serve

* Mr. Singer has collected several specimens, as has also
M. Leber. They are by no means complete, but they suffice for
the direction of the analogies of which we are in search.

in the European tarots to distinguish the suits
of numeral cards, as our hearts, diamonds,
clubs, and spades, denote the suits in the
common game.

This correspondence is worthy of notice. As
to the *grelot*, or hawk-bell, which forms one of
the distinctive emblems of the Indian cards, it has
also figured, and it figures still, on some of the
European tarots.

In Germany, the marks of suits, which in the
the South, as in Spain and Italy, have been confined to the vase, sword, denier, and baton, have
been subject to several variations. There are
some German cards on which beasts, birds, and
flowers appear; others have leaves on one of the
suits—an idea essentially German, all redolent of
spring, like one of their forest lays; and on
others, both ancient and modern, is the mark
of the *bell*.

At the present day even, likely as is the
pack of our present type to become of uni-
versal acceptance, the Germans, instead of our
marks, constantly use bells, hearts, leaves, and
acorns, to distinguish their suits. As, therefore, we see the sword and the money of the
Hindustani packs, on the tarots of Southern
Europe, so we have the Indian bell on the

tarots, and even on the modern playing cards, of Germany. The sword, money, and bell are alike Oriental emblems.

A very little acquaintance with the usages of the East, will make us cognizant of the fact that the bell is there one of the insignia of rank and magnificence. With them the Hindus deck their idols, and ornament the dresses of their dancing girls. They are mentioned in Holy Scripture itself; for Aaron the priest was enjoined to wear golden bells on the hem of his sacerdotal garments.* The Arabs also have adopted them, and use them for a similar purpose.

We may say, moreover, of this particular symbolic ornament, that though, as we have seen, it is essentially Asiatic in character, we may detect traces of it nearer home. In Europe, before it jingled on the fool's cap and bauble, it was, from a very early period, a mark of dignity. A bell tied to the falcon's neck was a necessary adjunct of knightly sport; and it was one of the insignia of rank before the epoch of heraldic distinctions.

A symbol it is—derived, like every other sym-bol, from poetic Asia—from the clime where men devote themselves to dreamy voluptuousness, rapt

* *Vide* Exodus xxviii. 35, and xxxix. 25.

in the romantic associations which invest their ideas of aught that is new and strange.

The Fou, again—the Fou of the tarots—have we not here the jester of the East, cherished alike by people and by prince, a quasi-divinity ? for in the lands where the fanatic flings himself with unnatural eagerness under the wheels of the car which bears his god in triumph, the imbecile bears a sacred character.

The fool of our mediæval courts, was the representative of an Asiatic idea ; and this clings to him, no matter what the associations connected with him. The Fou of these cards, for instance, has a mode of action of his own, just as he has his oblique and peculiar move in the Indian chess game.

We cannot be far wrong then, in assuming that these two noble games have originated among the same people.*

Of course, we must bear in mind throughout, that the modern playing cards, such as are used

* The bishop in chess was anciently styled *anfyn*, which is conjectured to be a form of the Arabic *al fil*, or elephant, that being the piece which corresponds with our bishop in the Indian game of chess [*Vide* Ducange s. v. *Alphinus*]. Of this the French *fol* or *fou* is by some writers considered a corruption, as *Vierge* is of Ferze or Vizir, which in both games became eventually *dame* or queen.

for whist, piquet, lansquenet, &c., offer no such
means of comparison as those we have described.
These are merely the offspring of others of
earlier date ; and these even we may expect to
see bye-and-bye superseded by other cards, which
have been deduced from them in a similar
manner.

To the observations we have already propounded, drawn from the fundamental principles
of the ancient tarots, viz., the order and arrangement of a pack, and the symbols and
figures depicted thereon, it is well to add a
remark of quite another description. Is it not
a singular fact, that at the very period which
most nearly approaches the epoch ordinarily assigned to the introduction of cards, writers who
mention them do not by any means allude to
them as a recent invention !

Aretino assigns the discovery of them, like
chess, to Palamedes, in the Grecian camp before
the walls of Troy, and by way of enhancing the
idea of their antiquity says, the Sun himself, if he
could speak, would confess their origin was beyond his ken.

Others believe that a mention of cards is to
be found in an obscure passage of one of the works
attributed to S. Cyprian.

Lambert Daneau, a French writer of the sixteenth century, insists that the figures on the
most ancient cards represented idols; this is, in
fact, a kind of foreshadowing of the quaint conceits of Court de Gebelin.

These notices are valuable only as showing
the notions current at the time, and would have
been entirely lost sight of and forgotten, but for
some isolated scholars.* Most certainly, if cards
had been put forth as an absolute discovery in the
time of Charles VI., contemporary writers would
have challenged the invention, and in the succeeding century there would have been no place for
speculations as to their antiquity.

The whole matter becomes perfectly intelligible, if we bear in mind the distinction between

* In the last century, before Gebelin, and Singer and
Breitkopf—both of whom are timid to a fault—Beneton de
Peyrins in the *Mercure* had turned his attention to the East.
He even believed, and gave reasons for his belief, that cards of
Eastern origin were known to the Romans in their decadence: a
by no means impossible supposition. In other places besides
France—in Italy, for instance—the antiquity of cards was never
disputed. A Bolognese gentleman, Innocentio Ringhierri, in
describing the extraordinary game called *Jeu du Roi*, speaks of
them in the following manner, about the year 1551:—"This
game is derived from the game of cards, invented in days of
yore by an industrious and, in my opinion, a very learned person." (. . . *tratto dal jiaoco delle carte, già ritrovato da
industrioso (come io credo) e molto savio inventore.*)

the four-suit or modern cards, and the more
ancient kind which preceded them.

Moreover, we have seen that besides the
antiquity, the Oriental derivation of cards was
also admitted at this early period. Proofs at
that time were in existence and everywhere met
with, entirely indisputable. These we only light
upon now by mere accident.

The engraving which forms our twelfth illustration will demonstrate the value of this sort
of evidence.

It is a king of diamonds (*carreaux*), one of a
pack which certainly dates as far back as Charles
VII. of France*—that is, about 1425. It is, then,

---

* The plates which accompany this history of cards are
copied as far as outline goes with the most scrupulous exacti-
tude. In general, the exact size is preserved. Occasionally,
however, a card has occurred among those which we required for
illustration of larger size than the rest, and these it has been
necessary to reduce a trifle, to bring them within the compass
of our pages. Here and there the figures will be found slightly
shaded, although the original may not; but the originals are
in most cases coloured, and the colouring gives an effect which
could not be reproduced in a wood-cut outline.

It is for this reason that a little shading has been introduced
to give the effect of the colour. The major part of the drawings
have been made from the Cabinet des Estampes, at Paris, by
M. E. Coppin, and selected both from the ordinary portfolios
of the collection and from those more choice and precious
examples, which the curator, M. Duchesne, kindly permitted
to be selected.

PLATE XI

KING OF DIAMONDS.
(Pack of Charles VII., *circa* 1425.)

PLATE X

KING OF DIAMONDS
(Deck of Charles VII, about 1440)

more than 400 years old—in fact, we have no more ancient example.

This king of carreaux (the French marks of suits had by that time come into use) bears the name of COURSUBE. And who is Coursube? Coursube is the name of a Saracen—a hero of one of the old romances; and APOLLIN, the king of spades (*piques*), is another worthy of the same race. We may easily see to what an important extent this bears on our argument, for the Saracen is the type of the Asiatic—the Moor, the Bohemian, the Egyptian—Europe's antagonist in all ages, from the Crusades of old in Palestine to their more recent naval conflicts around the walls of Rhodes and Malta, the rocks of the Balearic Isles, and the coasts of Spain.

Nor need we suppose this to be an isolated specimen, and useless for our purpose; for far from being a chance discovery, it is a *bona-fide* record, which receives a confirmation from a totally independent source.

In a history of Viterbo, by Feliciano Busi, published in 1742, we find quoted a statement of one Covelluzzo, which affirms that the game of cards called *Naib* was introduced into that city in 1379, from a Saracen source. " Anno 1379, fu recato in Viterbo el gioco delle carte, *che venne*

de Seracinia e chiamasi tra loro NAIB." This
is evidently a link in the chain of evidence, and
goes far to prove the truth of our position. The
use of the term Naib in Italy for cards, is one of
the strongest proofs of their introduction into
Europe by the Gipsies. To this day they are
called in Spain, *Naypes*, which is clearly a
corruption of the Arabic *Nabi*, a prophet; and
we have, therefore, the significant fact that cards
have been, and are still called in Spain, by
a title which fortune-tellers —Gipsies, in fact—
might easily be supposed to claim.*

The ancient examples of European cards bear
the impress of a civilization of remote date. This
civilization is Oriental. It matters nothing
which you suppose it to be, Indian or Egyptian,
for the further you go back into the history of
these two races, the more intimate do their
relations appear. What can be more clear then,
than that it is the Gipsies, or, to speak more
correctly, these emigrants from India, who have,
in the guise of a mystic volume, brought with

---

* The Hebrew word נָבִיא (Arabic نَبِيّ *Nabion* or *Nabi)*
signifies (1) *an interpreter*, or *mouthpiece (cf.* Exod. iv. 16, with
vii. 1) ; (2) a *prophet*, in which sense it occurs in almost every
instance in the Old Testament. Both these words are derived
from a root the primary meaning of which is, to *announce,
declare, predict*, &c.

them the tarots into Europe; and much as this volume has changed its destiny, the wandering Gipsy-woman is even now true to the traditions of her country, when she fingers her cards, not for the purpose of play or amusement, but to learn the course of destiny.

To ourselves cards serve as a mere pastime; but their Asiatic inventors had a far different object in view, aiming rather at a means of instruction and consolation, than of amusement and recreation.

The Oriental of the present day is passive and unprogressive as of old, in his apathetic adoration, and in his slavish dread of the unknown; but there was a time in the history of the East, when its nationalities were in their infancy, when no action was performed which had not in it something of a religious import, and when everything in the way of civilization was enveloped in mysticism. Life was an aimless progress to dissolution. The priest ruled as king, the priest directed the whole machine : in the matter of public instruction, and the administration of justice and government, he was supreme. Everything had its mystic side. Their ancient game was a series of interrogations addressed to Fate, and not a pastime like our own. They were the

Sibylline books of the dreamers of the East, who, fondly looking upon combinations accidentally formed, as oracular responses, and unceasingly bowed down under their fear, and the influence of a blind faith, were content to distract their attention from the present, by invoking the oracles of the future.

In Europe, it was only at the outset that cards appeared in this character.

The race of Japhet, rejoicing in a cooler sky, is by nature strong-minded and energetic, vigorous in action, and emulous of freedom. Ever on the move, these DO and invent, instead of brooding over impossibilities. They have, therefore, preferred to devise a new plaything, rather than to plague themselves everlastingly with symbols, and out of the Eastern tarots they have constructed the European *cards*.

In due course followed a host of other combinations of a light and amusing character; and with a view to simple recreation, or to minister more agreeably to a long existent instinct, and certainly with not the slightest admixture of a serious or mystic sentiment, they seat themselves gaily, these more practical children of the West, some around tables covered with green cloth, others astride a bench, or squatted round a drum, and, since the period we have alluded to, in time of peace and in time of war, have, one and all, betaken themselves to ombre and piquet, whist and écarté—their little ones, to beggar-my-neighbour—and so, in one word, have become card-players.

Be not hard, therefore, on the Gipsy and his cards. Cold in temperament, and indolent in action, his imagination, yet, at the distance of five or six centuries, dwells on the sunlit land of his ancestors. He no longer possesses the olden game; the modern version is his only substitute. But if the mystic emblems are no longer his, there is yet the feeling in his mind that cards are profaned by the sacrilegious nations of the West; he deems himself a priest, a seer, and the interpreter of the Unknown upon earth; his very existence is bound up with these traditions, therefore is he a fortune teller.

III.

INTRODUCTION OF CARDS INTO SOUTHERN
EUROPE.

ROUTE OF CARDS INTO EUROPE—GERMANY, ITALY, OR SPAIN
—THE MOORISH INVASION—NATIONAL STYLES OF PLAY—
PRIORITY OF THE SPANISH GAME.

LET us assume the fact that cards were of
Oriental origin and of Gipsy introduction; it is
clear that neither France, nor England which
is generally supposed to have received them from
her, can have been the country where they were
first known.

This follows as a matter of course, since the
question resolves itself into the fact of an importation.   Before   reaching   France,   Cards
must have been introduced from the South
through Italy or Spain, or else through the Germanic territories direct from the East.   It
remains, therefore, to ascertain which of the three
countries, Italy, Spain, or Germany, was first
acquainted with the game.   There is no lack of
erudite patriots, who, in behalf of one or the

other, have sought to demolish the claims of their rivals.* The Italians, the Spaniards, and the Germans have possessed alike the knowledge of tarots. They have used them from a very early period, and they use them still; and even although France has furnished them with cards of a fresh description, they have been by no means forward in accepting them, and have impressed on them some of the features of the older cards.

France, on the other hand, has had but a slight acquaintance with the antique tarot, and the little she had was only for a short period, and obtained for it no general acceptance or popularity. From these considerations alone, we may decide that Italy, Spain, and Germany must have preceded her in the adoption of cards. Now, of these three nations, which has the appearance of having most scrupulously adhered to the tradi-

---

* It will be enough to adduce Bettinelli as an advocate for the Italian, and Heinecken for the German claim. Spain has also had supporters of her pretensions, the most able of whom is a Frenchman, the Abbé La Rive. France has on her side, apart from the erroneous assertion of Menestrier and the disquisitions of Père Daniel, the advocacy of Bullet. MM. Depping, Paul Lacroix, Peignot, the elder Duchesne, and others, have also investigated the question, but without disposing of it. M. Leber, perhaps, has formed the clearest notion of any; but his perspicuity is to some extent neutralized by his timidity.

tions of the past? Decidedly, Italy and Spain
have here the advantage over Germany, for in them
the distinctive marks of suits—vase, sword, denier,
and baton—have been more generally adhered to;
and the name under which cards were anciently
known there is still more conclusive. The Oriental card game is essentially an affair of divination—the game of the fortune-teller—of the *Nabi*.
Now, the Italians have long given to their cards
the name of *Naïbi*, and they are still known
among the Spaniards as *Naypes.** This is quite
enough to place their pretensions at the head of
the list.

Besides, to establish the fact that Germany had
adopted cards before Spain and Italy, it must
first be assumed that they have arrived through
the passes of the Caucasus in the train of the
Sclavonic irruptions, and this would necessarily
involve a Tartaric or Mongolian origin, of which
there is not the slightest trace. There is, there-

* Some of those etymology-hunters, who impose on the
credulity of the public, have put forth a peculiarly absurd explanation of *Naïbi*, on the ground that the Greek word νήπιος
signifies *infant*—one who cannot speak νὴ·ἔπος: they assert
that *Naïbi* is the *infants' game*—a game of pictures. It is difficult to see what light this eccentric derivation throws on the
question. Fortunately, however, there is an etymology far more
simple, evidently correct, and incontestably of importance in a
historical point of view: it is that we have given.

fore, nothing in this to invalidate our theory of
the importation of cards from India by the
Gipsies, who, in order to reach Europe, would
naturally follow the track opened by the Moors
and Arabs along the African coast to Tangier,
from which there would be a ready access to
Spain.

The issue, then, can only subsist between Italy
and the former country, and it is Spain which
seems to possess the best title.*

In the first place, Spain is the country whose
history in the middle ages was most involved with
that of Eastern races. The Moor set hostile foot
on her shores, and soon held undisputed sway

---

* This is not by any means a universally received opinion.
The main support of the Spanish claim is the authority of
the Abbé La Rive, who has been the subject of endless attacks.
The majority of modern scholars are inclined to award the
priority to Italy. M. Depping, for instance, believes he can trace
an Italian acquaintance with cards up to the time of the Crusades. M. Duchesne the elder puts in a plea for Florence or
Venice, and, in the face of all probability, on the ground of their
commercial relations with the Greeks.[1] M. Leber hesitates, of

[1] M. Duchesne, who has examined the argument, has made the objection
that the Spaniards, in mediæval times, were not sufficiently skilful artists
or manufacturers to have fabricated cards before Italy. Nevertheless, this
objection seems to have very little weight. Of what import is the industrial
condition of a people in such a case? Construct an electric telegraph in the
centre of the Iroquois country—100 years after, locate another in China.
The Iroquois have no notion of imitation; they would never multiply the
telegraph; whereas the Chinese would make twenty copies of it. Would one
assume afterwards that China was acquainted with the electric telegraph
before the Iroquois?

in the smiling Granada, in Cordova the proud, and the love-inspiring Seville, in the green and balmy Huerta of Valencia, and the towns on the Tagus.

Italy, it is true, has been subject to Saracen invasion, but it was never subjugated by them; and if even ancient Italian records were to afford evidence of the introduction of cards into certain parts of that country by the Saracens, there would still be no ground for the assumption that the Moors had located the Gipsies on the coasts of Italy prior to their settlement in Spain.

The rage for play has been the same in both countries—no inference can be deduced, therefore, on that score.* The style of play, however, materially differs. The Italians have been the inventors of almost all the games of pure chance;

course: he is on the scent,—he knows the fact, but dares not say so. As for the others, they merely compile, with no sort of desire to make clear what they copy. M. Paul Lacroix, for instance, is well enough, as far as the Oriental origin goes, but he gives this strange etymology of tarot: "*Tarot* is derived from *Taro*, a province of Lombardy (a name still in use), or from φθορα, corruption, or from τερειν, to pierce."

* Much has been made of the enthusiasm the Italians have ever evinced for play. The Spaniards are not a whit behind in this respect.

The following extract from the *Recherches Historiques* of Bullet, proves that their passion has been the same in all ages:

"The Spaniards have a great taste for cards. Paschasius Justus, who travelled in this kingdom in the sixteenth century, says, the Spaniards, on the contrary, affect none but those of a dignified character. Their national game—Ombre, "the game of Man"—a modification of the earlier game of Primero—is, of all modern games, that which most resembles the ancient tarot. We may conclude, therefore, that it is the earliest of existing games, and upon that assumption, that the Spaniards were the earliest card-players.

A last reason, and the best of all, remains in support of all the rest. So far as we are acquainted with them, there are no queens among the numeral cards of the Indian game; neither are there, or have there been, any queens in the Spanish pack. Of all European nations, therefore, we assign to the Spaniards the first place in the annals of cards.

that he had often travelled leagues in that country without being able to procure bread, wine, or any necessary of life; but no matter how sorry might be the village, and however miserable the hamlet, they had always cards for sale.

"The Spaniards took with them to the New World their passion for cards. When in the island of S. Dominique, they found themselves destitute of cards to play with, they actually manufactured some out of the leaves of a tree called copey. [*Histoire des Voyages*, tome xlvi. p. 180.]

" From Spain, cards were introduced into Italy. The Italians called them at the first *naïbes*, which is identical with *naïpes*, a clear proof that from the Spaniards came both the name and the thing signified."

IV.

DATE OF INTRODUCTION OF CARDS.

STATUTES OF THE BAND, A.D. 1332—EDICT OF JOHN I. OF
CASTILE, A.D. 1387—ALLEGED INTERPOLATIONS—DOCU-
MENTARY EVIDENCE IN FAVOUR OF ITALY—ORDER OF
THE INTRODUCTION OF CARDS—SPAIN AND ITALY, GER-
MANY, FRANCE, AND ENGLAND.

ALTHOUGH it is impossible to fix the precise epoch
of the introduction of cards into Europe, there is
every probability that the use of them was known
ever since the commencement of the fourteenth
century, and perhaps even from the end of the
thirteenth.*

Alphonso XI., king of Castile, founded in
1332, an order of chivalry denominated *the
Band*.

Don Antonio de Guevara, bishop and chap-

* The Abbé la Rive, who is desirous to fix the invention of
cards on Spain [and who, for want of observing the distinction
between tarots and cards of the modern description, has resorted
to a derivation of the term *Naypes* from N. P. the initials of
Nicolas Pepin, who, in an old Castilian Dictionary is named
as the inventor of cards], has examined the chronological
question with great care. Unfortunately, the passages he has
adduced have been decided to be more or less equivocal. In
spite of this, we are of his opinion, and this opinion, albeit open
to criticism, is in perfect accordance with the probable truth.

lain to Charles V., has given in his epistles a copy of the statutes of this order, and in the French translation of these by Dr. Gutery, we find a passage to the effect, that none of the knights of the Band were to play at *cards* or dice. (*Comandoit leur ordre que nul des chevaliers de la Bande, n'osast iouer aux* cartes *ou dez*.)

It is said that the word *cartes*, is a mistranslation of Gutery's, and that it is not to be found in the original version; but there is no positive proof of such an interpolation ; and there is, therefore, no obstacle to the assumption, that cards were prohibited in Spain by the statutes of an order established in 1332.

This exact date, however, cannot be regarded as that of their first introduction into Spain, for they must have been introduced there, at any rate, a few years before. They were again forbidden in 1387, by John I. of Castile.*

* It has been even attempted to show, that this prohibition of cards by John I. is an interpolation of the editor who printed in 1640 the *Recopilacion de las leyes destos regnos, &c.*, from the fact that the word *naypes* is not to be found in the collection entitled *Ordenanças reales de Castilla*, which appeared at Medina del Campo in 1541.

Prudence would therefore demand that we should not draw deductions too precise from disputed passages, but we may still contend for the possible existence even, of contested facts. Without laying more stress on these passages than they will fairly bear, cannot we see in them, at any rate, a shadow of

After all however, every one understands that the mere absence of written evidence by no means invalidates the authority of facts which are sufficiently established by reason. And even if two countries dispute the honour of an invention, it is better not to come to a hasty decision, because it is within the range of possibility that a record may eventually turn up in favour of the claims of the one, earlier by several years than anything hitherto discovered in support of the other.

Were we to base our argument simply on the inferences to be gleaned from manuscript documents, Italy would to a certainty bear away the palm from Spain, a conclusion we can never admit. Notices of cards in Italy date actually from the thirteenth century.[*]

testimony? La Rive could have had no interested motive in adducing a passage in one of the laws of Spain, which had no real existence save in the brain of a translator.

[*] It is, in fact, an Italian work which seems to bear the most ancient testimony as to the existence of cards; but if even it does exhibit the earliest epoch of their introduction, it does not, for all that, establish the claim of Italy. This document goes back thirty years earlier than the doubtful version of the statutes of the order of the Band in Spain. It is a MS. of Pipozzo di Sandro, having for its title *Trattato del governo della famiglia*. Tiraboschi, who cites it in his *Histoire de la Littérvture Italienne* (vol. v. part ii. p. 402), assures us that its date is 1299; and Taxi, author of a *History of Copper-plate and Wood Engraving*, while wholly believing that it is by some years more modern, does not detract much from its

The conclusion to which we are irresistibly impelled, is, that cards, originally devised in the East, and migrating with the Gipsies, were known in Europe about the beginning of the fourteenth century, and that the channel by which they arrived was Spain.

antiquity.   We find in it this sentence : " *Se guicherà di danari o cosi o alle carte, gli apparuchierai la via* "—" if he play for money in this manner, or at cards, you must facilitate the means of his doing so."   The word *carte* appears already in the language.   In Spain, as we have said, the term *naypes* has been too long and too deeply rooted to be so easily eradicated.

This would have been a date to depend on, and to be considered apart from all vexatious and irrelevant discussions, but a certain Abbé Zani has started the objection that even if Pipozzo di Sandro wrote in 1299, the transcript of his MS. cannot be assigned to a date anterior to 1440.   According to this, here is another case of interpolation.   It cannot be, however, that every date we have given is erroneous.   If 1299 in Italy, and 1332 in Spain, are intentionally forged, the Viterbo date of 1379 is at least true.   Can it be a mistake again that cards are mentioned under A.D. 1361, in the Chronicle of Provence?   (*Vide* Nostradamus *Hist. et Chron. de Provence*, *Lyons*, 1614) or is the Pastoral of the Bishop of Wurtzburg, which Breitkopf and the Germans adduce in support of their national claims, a falsification?   Singer mentions one of the miniatures of a very ancient MS. of the *Roman du Roi Méliadus*, which depicts the king cards in hand ; and although one of the two or three MSS. of the poem of *Renart le Contrefait*, completed in 1341, contains no allusion to cards, yet another distinctly mentions them.

> Si comme fols et folles sont
> Qui pour gaigner . . . .
> Jouent aux dez, *aux cartes*, aux tables (trictrac),
> Qui à Dieu ne sont délectables.

Their introduction into Italy was, probably, almost contemporaneous; for a brisk commerce was in existence at that time with Spain, and being like that country a promontory of Europe, it had a seaboard equally exposed to Moslem invasion.

Germany, from her direct communication with Italy, would be the next in order, and would naturally receive them before France. There is every probability, from geographical as well as historical considerations, that this was the case; and the fact, that the ancient game has prevailed most in Spain, next in Italy, and then in Germany, fully bears it out.

Once arrived in France, cards received an entire transformation; and though other nations may successfully assert a priority of adoption, in that country, the national genius has almost rendered them a new creation. Their extension into our own country will be discussed in a separate chapter.

Such, then, ought in future to be the account

Of course, this is alleged to be an interpolation of the transcriber; as was said of the statutes of the "Band;" of the MS. which Tiraboschi has quoted; and of the letter of the Bishop of Wurtzburg : but in spite of all, the weight of testimony goes to prove that cards in Europe date from the thirteenth century, or, at any rate, from the commencement of the fourteenth.

given of cards in all dictionaries, historical, etymological, and artistic; for though not at present amounting to an absolute scientific certainty, it must, on rational grounds, be eventually accepted as the basis of a general opinion.

V.

INTRODUCTION OF CARDS INTO FRANCE.

THE ERA OF AGINCOURT—EXPEDITION OF DUGUESCLIN, A.D.
    1366—GAME OF BRELAN—EDICT OF CHARLES V.—CON-
    FORT D'AMY — CARDS PROHIBITED, 1397 — JACQUEMIN
    GRINGONNEUR.

From the view we have taken of our subject, it
will be seen that here we are on entirely new
ground. Before, however, we commence the discussion of the cards we have spoken of, that is
to say, the European version of the old Oriental
type, it will be desirable to ascertain the earliest
trace of the existence of cards of any kind
in France. And first, although we have on
sufficient grounds assumed that the Spaniards,
Italians, and Germans, preceded the French
in the adoption of cards, there is no necessity
to suppose a whole century intervened before
they were known to the latter people. Under
the form of tarots, the Gipsy cards were in
general use all through the South of Europe and
in Germany, and most likely, ombre in Spain,

and some games of chance in Italy were already in existence, early in the fourteenth century.

At that epoch, the amusements of the French people, it appears, consisted in playing at nine-pins, tennis, and dice.

France had little intercourse with the South; she was engaged in continual strife with England; and her attention was, in consequence, mainly occupied by the North.

This helps us to indicate the time when, in due course, France received her cards by the way either of the Pyrenees or the Alps.

Now this could hardly be before the latter half of the fourteenth century—that is to say, in the reign of Charles V.—the exact date being probably coincident with the foray of Duguesclin into Spain, nominally to combat with the Saracens, but in reality to take service with Henry of Transtamare.

Duguesclin's expedition took place in 1366. His troops were those formidable companies of veterans, which spread terror and devastation wherever they went, and, in passing near Avignon, compelled even the Pope to pay them black mail. Adventurers in the fullest sense of the term, and precursors of the *condottieri* and *lanzknechts* of a later date, these ruthless soldiers were the agents of the introduction of the new game into France, and, at the same time, the authors of its incipient modification.

With them, on the return of the expedition, cards passed the frontier. No doubt, the vulgar, at first, saw in them only strange figures and emblems, as yet beyond their comprehension ; the higher classes would pay them very little attention; while the soldiers who brought them, would soon reject the tedious and solemn game of ombre, for more stirring and lively variations.

The *brelan* in its most simple form most probably originated in their camps.

This notion is not only extremely feasible, but is also to some extent susceptible of proof.

Charles V., by his edict of 1369, prohibited all games of chance, and even of skill. By the terms of this *ordonnance* were interdicted dice, tables (chess or trictrac), tennis, skittles, quoits, soule (football), and billiards. The prohibition is excessively rigorous. That, however, is not so much to be noted as the absence of all mention of *cards*. Evidently, had cards been then in general use, they would have been included in so stringent and comprehensive an enactment.

Again, in an exhortation addressed to this king by a French poet, Guillaume de Machau, entitled

Confort d'Amy (Solace of the Soul), Charles V. is dissuaded, at his accession to the throne, from playing at dice, but there is not a syllable on the subject of cards.

Moreover, to adopt the excellent argument of Bullet, we see nothing in the shape of cards represented on the bas-reliefs, paintings, and tapestries, belonging to an earlier date, though dice, dice-boxes, chess, and draughts are common.

The silence of all writers and monuments of antiquity up to the fourteenth century, attains the force of positive proof, when we consider that from the end of that century, the edicts of councils, ecclesiastical authorities, and princes, never condemn games which are not expressly designated games of cards. The Provost of Paris, by an *ordonnance*, dated 22 January, 1397, was the first to prohibit men engaged in business from playing on working-days at tennis, dice, *cards*, and ninepins.

Cards were therefore unknowr in France in 1369, or if known at all, they were only in circulation as mere pictures, and had as yet evoked no prohibitory enactment on the part of the legislature; and this corresponds with the fact, that the expedition of Duguesclin had only taken place three years previously.

John Dewey Library
Johnson State College
Johnson, Vermont 05656

On the other hand, the edict of the Provost
of Paris proves that card playing had attracted
notice in 1397. It is, therefore, between these
two dates that we must assign the period of the
introduction of cards into France ;* and the one
most likely to be correct would coincide with the
close of the reign of Charles V.

As to their existence in Charles VI.'s time,
there is no room for doubt, and it is with the very

* Bullet attempts to arrive at a date still more precise, from
an examination of costumes on cards, and other considerations, weak enough, but all fortified by a great display of
erudition. He fixes the probable date in 1375 or 1376. In this,
decidedly, he goes too far.

He certainly quotes, in support of his assertion, a passage of
the *Chronique du Petit Jehan de Saintré*, where the pages of
Charles V. are mentioned as playing at dice and cards. And,
no doubt, this passage proves something, but then it is attacked
like the others, and declared, as they have declared ten other
quotations, to be an interpolation of the transcriber. Nevertheless, this disputed passage is found in all the old printed copies
of the Chronicle, and in one of three MSS. of it in the Imperial
library.

Supposing, however, we admit the possibility of this extraordinary chance, it is enough for our purpose that cards were unknown in France in 1369, but no longer so at the time when
Charles VI. became imbecile. The extract from the Chronicle
of Petit Jehan de Saintré serves only to confine the field of
uncertainty between narrower limits, *i. e.* 1369 and 1380, which
is the date of Charles the Fifth's death. Thus there would be
an interval of eleven years. Let us extend this by all means, if a
passage affected by a doubt is inadmissible ; but the fact remains,
that shortly after the commencement of the second half of the
fourteenth century cards were well known among the French.

period of his imbecility that so many efforts have
been made to connect the whole question. The
mistake originated with Menestrier, who was somewhat given to blundering, and whom nothing
would suit but the extraction from a sentence of a
sense beyond what it would bear.

The worthy Jesuit stumbled on an account
rendered by Charles Poupart (or Charbot Poupart, to speak after the manner of Monstrelet),
argentier, i.e. the king's treasurer.

"Donné à Iacquemin Gringonneur, peintre,
pour trois ieux de cartes à or et à diverses couleurs,
de plusieurs devises, pour porter devers le dit
seigneur roi, pour son ébattement, cinquante-six
sols parisis."*

It is easy to see that this item of an account
is no proof at all that the *invention* ought to be
ascribed to the painter; on the contrary, the
mention of cards is as of a well-known article,
and by no means as a diversion specially contrived
with a view of amusing poor Charles VI.

Neither Froissart, nor Monstrelet, nor any
other chronicler speaks of any similar invention,
though they enter sometimes, as may be seen in

---

* "Paid to Jacquemin Gringonneur, painter, for three packs
of cards in gold and colours of divers devices, to present to the
said lord the king for his amusement, 60 sols parisis."

the collections of Le Laboureur, into the most minute details on the subject of the diversions which served to distract the royal imbecility.*

It follows, then, that the common opinion, based on the erroneous suppositions of Père Menestrier, falls to the ground of itself; and, on the other hand, all the indications of truth con- verge to one point, viz., that France received the knowledge of cards from Spain, about the time of Duguesclin's expedition, and that they were generally known among the French during the last years of Charles V.

* Moreover, the malady of Charles VI. only dates from the year 1392, and as there is no reason for supposing that at the very outset, cards were put into the hands of the poor imbecile, there is nothing which gives Père Menestrier the right to fix exact date of that which, in *his* opinion merely, is the era of the invention of cards.

VI.

THE CARDS OF CHARLES VI.

HAVING pursued the history of cards thus far, it
will be proper to remind our readers, that the
examples we have been discussing are by no means
identical with the playing cards of the present day.
It was as yet only the game prevalent at that
period in southern Europe—the tarot.

When a fresh element is introduced into the
every day pursuits of a nation, it retains for some
time its normal impress. It is not all on a sudden
that the genius of a people takes full possession
of a novelty to effect an alteration. Thus cards,
as we have seen, were known in France towards
the end of the fourteenth century, and their
original form would at the outset be adopted with
them. It was essentially the game of tarots which
Charles VI. played during the prostration of his
intellect; the pictures amused him; the emblems

caused him a little meditation; but he was not even capable of playing a close game at piquet or whist. Besides, neither piquet, nor of course whist, was then in existence; at the most, with the pip cards, they might have invented the *brelan*, but the only pack with which they had to do, was of tarots.

We have seen of what sort of cards these tarots consist. They form, when complete, a series of emblematical figures, which, in all probability, are the creation of the East. There are also four suits of numeral cards, each distinguished by peculiar signs, which savour also of Oriental origin, but whose identity has not been so well maintained.

We may easily imagine that cards, since their first appearance in Europe, considering the variety of the countries which adopted them, would necessarily have undergone many and important modifications of arrangement and design—modifications which, in other respects, would not alter the game to the extent that the subsequent alterations which are attributable to the French have done—and, consequently, that these veritable tarots, already modified in a slight degree, were the actual form in which cards were first introduced to the notice of that people.

Cards of the ordinary modern or French type were not invented before the middle of the fifteenth century; and thus, from the time when they were imported from the South, to the date of their alteration in character, a considerable interval existed—almost a century, indeed—during which the cards then used in France were in every respect analogous to the foreign examples, tarots in fact, a game possessing little attraction, and which can have only obtained a mediocre amount of success. We are in possession of proof that, at the end of the fourteenth century, this description of cards was exclusively used.

There exists a very curious miniature* in a French MS. entitled *Le Roman du Roi Méliadus*, once in the library of M. de Lamoignon, and subsequently in the Roxburgh collection, from which it passed to the possession of Sir Egerton Brydges; in this, the monarch is depicted playing at cards with three nobles of his court. The game, being a four-handed one, has not the appearance of one of the ancient games of France. Bataille and piquet, which were probably among the earliest French varieties, require but two players.

Singularly enough, it is possible to distinguish

* *Vide* Singer, *Researches into the History of Playing Cards*, p. 67 ; and note, p. 45. *supra*.

clearly upon the cards which are dealt, *money* and *batons*, as the marks of suits.

There is one defect exceedingly difficult to avoid, and that is the singular attachment one feels for a bit of testimony when it happens to be almost unsupported. This reservation, or rather this avowal being made, may we not infer that at the end of the fourteenth century, the date of the MS. in question, the cards employed in France were of the southern type? If the alterations had already been effected, the distinctive colours or marks invented, and the French style of play introduced, undoubtedly the miniaturist would have so represented it.

It may be urged: The miniaturist was possibly not a Frenchman; and although France had already the class of cards peculiarly hers, he would naturally depict the cards of his own country. Fortunately, however, we are able to supplement our argument by another example.

This is the very pack once belonging to Charles VI., the pack which Jacquemin Gringonneur painted, and for which Charles Poupart paid the bill.

These precious cards, or, at any rate, seventeen of them, are preserved in the Imperial Library at Paris. There is no written evidence of their genuineness, and no record has preserved the details of their history, but the traditionary account of their execution is accepted as a fact, and, if we are to believe M. Duchesne, upon very satisfactory grounds.

These cards came from the collection of M. de Gaignières, assistant tutor of the grandchildren of Louis XIV.

They are painted with great care, as M. Duchesne tells us, and even in a talented manner, on a golden field relieved with an ornamental dotted pattern faintly impressed on the ground over which the gilding is laid. The border is in silver, bearing likewise the dotted ornament, the same being repeated on all the cards, and intended to represent a ribbon wound round a cylinder. Some portions of the embroidery on the dresses are heightened with gold, the arms and armour being represented in silver, oxidised to a great extent by time, like that on the border.

No inscription, letter, or number, indicates the manner in which the cards were to be arranged.

They occur in the following order :

I. Le Pape—the Pope.
II. L'Empereur—the Emperor.
III. L'Ermite—the Hermit.
IV. La Maison de Dieu—the Hospital.
V. Le Fou—the Buffoon.
VI. Un Valet—a Squire on horseback.
VII. Les Amoureux — the Lovers.
VIII. Le Pendu—a man hanging by one leg.
IX. Le Chariot—the Chariot.

X. La Lune—the Moon.
XI. Le Soleil—the Sun.
XII. La Justice—Justice.
XIII. La Force—Fortitude.
XIV. La Tempérance —
Temperance.

XV. La Fortune—Fortune.
XVI. La Mort—Death.
XVII. Le Jugement—the last
Judgment.

The sumptuousness of these miniatures seems in accordance with their traditional history. It is the veritable pack of Charles VI., or, if not, it is a pack which sound criticism would by no means assign to a fifteenth century date, for the style most assuredly belongs to the fourteenth.

In these seventeen cards, our readers will at once distinguish sixteen *atouts* of the old tarot series (including the *Fou*), and a valet.

This valet, therefore, remains as the only specimen extant of the fifty-six numeral cards which accompany the twenty-two emblematical ones. It is by a rare chance that it has been preserved, showing as it does, that the game of tarots as then arranged was completely identical with that in present use in some countries.

There are, besides, at Venice, seven cards which are believed to have formed part of the same pack. The following description is by one who has personally inspected them.*

" The Marchese Girolamo at Venice, has

* *Dictionnaire de Beaux Arts,* by A. S. Millin.

PLATE XII

KNAVE.
(Gringonneur's Pack, *temp*. Charles VI.)

specimens in his possession of playing cards of these remote times. They are larger than the ordinary cards of the present day. They are very thick, and resemble the cotton paper of the ancient MSS.

" The figures are impressed on a golden field, and consist of three kings, two ladies, and two valets, one of whom is on horseback; each figure has a baton, a sword, or a piece of money. The drawing approaches very nearly that of Jacobello del Fiore; the design appears to be impressed, and the colours applied by a species of wood-block."

If, indeed, these cards were really detached from the pack above-mentioned (which however, we do not assume for certain), we see at once that these seven specimens preserved at Venice, are figures which do not belong to the *atout* series, but are kings, ladies, valets, and knights of the numeral suits.

Spain, as we are aware, has never admitted ladies into her game—ladies being found here therefore, proves that it is not a Spanish pack; and if it is a pack of French execution—the identical cards painted by Gringonneur—the presence of ladies is a fact of great significance.

The French would not have as yet invented

their national cards, the ordinary cards of the regular European pack, but they would have already introduced ladies into their game, a modification due, in all probability, to the *galanterie* of that people.

In the time of Charles V., then, the tarot game was imported into France from Spain; under Charles VI., the queens took their place beside their lords; but it was the reign of Charles VII. which gave to the French their true national or *piquet* cards.

VII.

INVENTION OF THE FRENCH CARDS AND GAME OF PIQUET.

WE are now come to a period when the history of cards is more a matter of detail, and when,
for the first time, we have to do with such as bear
the especial impress of French ingenuity.

In itself, the French invention is neither a
great display of ability, nor a total antithesis of
the tarots. It is a simplification of the apparatus
of the game—a measure of order—an elimination.

If we examine a pack of modern cards, whether
of the full number, or reduced,* we perceive that
they consist of four suits or series, each one containing three court cards, and a set of "pips,"

* The number of cards employed in the several foreign
games varies from 36 to 52, the low cards being rejected in
different proportions, as described at page 64.

varying in number, but not exceeding ten in any case.

The tarot has furnished the elements of these packs : first, the symbolic *atouts* went at one sweep, it being very justly concluded that the mystic and philosophic element was altogether out of place in a game designed for mere amusement, and might with great propriety be handed over to the professors of the black art. There then remained the fourfold series of the ancient tarot—fifty-six cards, according to the tarot pack as now existing, which contains kings, queens, knights, and valets, with ten pip-cards—fifty-two, rejecting the queens—or even forty-eight, if we assume, which is far more probable, that the primitive tarot had only a king and a valet as the honours of each suit, or, in other words, the Sovereign and a subordinate.*

To these forty-eight cards were annexed the queens; and then, by the rejection of the low cards (the two, three, four, five, and subsequently the six), was formed a reduced pack of thirty-six or thirty-two cards, less complicated, and therefore

---

* This card is called by the Germans, *unter* or *untermann* (the next superior card, answering to our queen, being the *ober* or *obermann*); by the French, *valet;* by the Italians, *fante;* and by the Spaniards, *soto :* names all denoting a servant or underling. We shall refer to this again in discussing the English *knave* or *jack.*

more easily managed, with no trace of elaborate symbolism; and on this, by the invention of various figures, colours, and marks of suits, were based the various French games, the most original of which is *piquet*.

This was the metamorphosis effected in France in the fifteenth century.

It was complete towards the close of that century, as may be inferred from a satirical print, dated 1499, and entitled *le Revers du Jeu des Suysses*, in which are represented all the crowned heads of Europe playing at cards, the distinctive emblems of which, are all according to the French style.

At the precise moment of this transformation, cards were by no means so much in vogue as they afterwards became. The earlier cards were, to all intents and purposes, *miniatures*, and therefore luxuries of an expensive kind. The invention of wood-engraving introduced a new era and a fresh growth; and this marks the period when, it becoming possible for cards to be in everybody's hands, France took possession of them; and her practical genius, always brilliant in idea and intelligent in execution, and ever on the watch to minister to the requirements of the times, was the instrument of a total alteration in their character.

The new cards made their appearance at a most convenient juncture. No sooner had Germany invented engraving, than France dismembered the old tarot, abolished the symbols, and simplified a game whose destiny was to be popular. We shall see shortly, in what manner.

The fifteenth century marks the invention of the genuine engraving on wood and copper, by which a design of any kind could be multiplied, by means of copies, to any extent. The discovery of wood engraving heralded that of printing. In 1455 appeared the famous Bible—the first and earliest of books, properly so called, and which was printed with wooden types. In 1457 we have the Psalter of Mayence. The art of engraving had been invented some time before, and the most ancient impression, the St. Christopher, is dated 1423; but before the production of the St. Christopher, it is certain that other prints had been engraved, and many impressions struck off. These prints were *cards*.

Germany, therefore, bears a most important part in the history which forms the subject of these pages; to her we owe the process by which the production of copies was effected, and she may therefore claim the invention of *printed* cards.

The exact date is, of course, impossible to be

ascertained ; but, at the same time, no one doubts the existence of these first essays of the graver.

It is the production of engraved cards of the German tarot, which is the earliest dawn of an art to which the world owes the invention of printing. Competent judges, Baron Heinecken at their head, are unanimous in their opinion on this point.

Since then, the facility of multiplication of copies has caused cards to be disseminated in all quarters, and with their multiplication and diffusion, a change in their character soon followed as a matter of course. Before this, they could scarcely have been accessible to any but the rich ; and as far as the mass of the people were concerned, they could only have been known as a manual of divination for the sole use of the prophets of the streets. Now, they became a game for every one to know. It was imperative to discard their antique guise, so that their meaning might be generally comprehended, and use made of them without unnecessary trouble.

The progress of the transformation, which from the card of ancient times produced the modern playing-card, was accelerated by this multiplication of examples.

If we knew the exact date when cards were

first engraved, the solution of our chronological difficulties would be easy. In default of this, we must rest content with an approximate calculation. The St. Christopher is of the date 1423;* and from the style of its execution, we may infer that it was not long subsequent to the discovery of card engraving.

Possibly only a few months intervened between the appearance of the first engraved card and that of the first wood-cut. But, to keep within limits, let us infer from this only the probability, that from the first commencement of the fifteenth century, cards printed on paper and coloured were in existence.

Charles VI. died in 1422, the same year with his rival, Henry V. of England, who had subjugated the whole of France north of the Loire, and had been declared heir presumptive of the kingdom, to the prejudice of the dauphin, Charles

* This specimen, which is supposed to be the earliest dated wood-cut, was discovered pasted within the cover of a MS., bequeathed to the convent of Buxheim, in Suabia, about 1435. The date *Millesimo cccc° xx°tercio* is a part of the engraving. Another wood-cut, probably contemporary (subject, the Annunciation), was also contained in the same volume, and both passed into the collection of Earl Spencer. A fac-simile of a third cut, of the still earlier date of 1418, is given in the *Athenæum* of the 4th of October, 1845, but the numerals present some appearance of having been tampered with. It was discovered at Mechlin, and is preserved in the Royal Library, at Brussels.

VII. During this struggle, which only ended in 1453, the disorganization which prevailed, increased by domestic dissensions, renders it futile to expect any indications of cards or their history. We pass over, therefore, a quarter of a century, a period of twenty-five years, during which the German cards would have an opportunity of diffusion, and it is then that the notion of their simplification and reformation must have arisen.

Now, if the regular French cards did not exist at the commencement of the fifteenth century, they certainly existed towards the close of the reign of Charles VII., and even before that.

One of those persons who pass their lives in the search for curious historical relics, M. Hénin, espied one day, at Lyons, an old book, the cover of which presented an appearance which attracted his attention. This cover turned out to be an agglomeration of playing cards. He purchased the MS., removed the cover, and separated the cards. They made the round of the amateurs, and eventually found their way into the Cabinet des Estampes, where they became an object of great curiosity.

The following is the account of them drawn up by M. Duchesne:

" These cards are of French manufacture,

since the inscriptions and names are all in that language.

"The figures are engraved on wood, printed with a pale ink of a brownish tint, and afterwards coloured with a stencil in the usual manner.

"The kings' crowns are formed of *fleurs de lys*, and the costumes are those of the period of Charles VII.

"On these grounds, and moreover from the colour of the ink, and the character of the drawing, we assign them almost certainly to the second quarter of the fifteenth century."

"They are arranged in two rows in the following order:

A   B   C
VALET, KING, and QUEEN of Clubs [*Trèfle*].

D   E
KING and QUEEN of Diamonds [*Carreau*].

F   G   H
VALET, QUEEN, and KING of Spades [*Pique*].

I   J
QUEEN and KING of Hearts [*Cœur*].

A. Valet or Knave of Clubs, holding a battle-axe in his right hand. He bears the name of 𝕽𝖔𝖑𝖆𝖓, one of Charlemagne's knights.

B. King of Clubs, carries a sceptre in his right hand, and holds a flower in the other. The inscription is faut sou, which doubtless signifies *Lackpenny*.

C. Queen of Clubs, a sceptre in her left hand, and holding a ring with her right, an emblem of conjugal fidelity, which, taken in connection with the legend Tromperie, deceit, seems to be a bitter satire upon marriage.

D. King of Diamonds, holding a sword in his left hand. He bears the name of Coursube, which, in the old romances, is the name of a Saracen king. [Plate XI.]

E. Queen of Diamonds. She holds a sceptre in her left hand, and with the other a sort of toy in goldsmith's work. The inscription is en toi te fie—that is to say, "*Trust in none but thyself.*"

F. Valet or Knave of Spades. His left hand on the pommel of his sword, and holding in his right a large torch. At his feet is the imperial globe. The inscription appears to be ctarde, to which I can attach no sense.*

G. Queen of Spades: her left hand on her hip, and holding with her right a flower. The meaning of the legend on this card, ie aut dict, is also obscure.

H. King of Spades, holding with both hands a tilting lance, and bearing the name of Apollin, which is the name of an idol attributed to the Saracens in the romances of that period.

I. Queen of Hearts: her right hand on her hip, and with a sceptre in her left. Legend, la foi est pdu—*la foi est perdue*, faith is lost.

J. King of Hearts, holding a sceptre in his left hand. In this card the inscription is cut off."

* Mr. Chatto, in 1841, singularly enough, was also the discoverer of four knaves of a pack precisely similar to these in date, character, and execution, in the covers of an old black letter volume, formerly in the Cathedral Library, at Peterborough. In these, the name of the knave of diamonds is *Rolant*, and that of hearts *Valery*, with an *f* appended. M. Paulin Paris, in a letter to Mr. Wright, suggests the hero represented by the last to be *Erard de Valery*, the famous companion of Charles of Anjou, at the battle of Tagliacozzo. Mr. Chatto, therefore, very ingeniously, and with every appearance of probability, submits that the *ctarde* on M. Henin's knave of spades would probably, on a careful examination of the original, turn out to be *Erarde*, and so both specimens would commemorate the same individual. These four cards are now in the print-room of the British Museum.—*Facts and Speculations on the Origin and History of Playing Cards*, 1848, p. 219. [Frontispiece.]

M. Leber, in his *Etudes Historiques*, differs
from M. Duchesne in reading the inscription on
the queen of spades, *Leaute due*, loyalty due,
and so engraves it.

The description of these ten specimens is a
most important contribution towards the history
of playing cards, inasmuch as they form part of
the earliest example we possess of a French pack
of the fifteenth century.

On them, for the first time, are perceived our
present marks of suits; and to them, if need be,
we shall resort for the confirmation of some of our
conjectures.

The imperial globe which is placed at the feet
of the knave of spades is an evident indication of
a recent introduction of the German engraved
cards into France, while the names of Coursube
and Apollin can be nothing else than a reflex of
the originals of the game itself.

This evidence in our possession, we can
resolve the problem which was set us. Here are
French cards for piquet, in existence somewhere
about 1450,* with marks of suits, at any rate,

---

* M. Leber fully appreciates the value of this testimony,
and has devoted much attention to its examination. It is a pity
that a dissertation so full and useful should be so wanting in
perspicuity and arrangement. He calls them the pack of Charles

identical with our own, if the figures on the court-
cards are different ; but the modern figures almost
immediately replace those which are here described, and these serve, therefore, as a transition
between the relics of the ancient tarot and the
allegories of the existing pack.

Now, are these an example of cards modified
for the game of piquet? and is piquet anterior, or
is it subsequent to them ? How did the invention
of that game come about ? and what is the history
of the modification which has been effected in
France in cards derived from a foreign source,
and used for a game of an entirely new description?

It will be impossible to answer these points
if the answer is to be decisive. Failing the attain-
ment of absolute certainty, we have a few remarks
to make, not entirely devoid of interest.

Were we to believe the worthy *savants* of the
past century, nothing would be simpler than the
resolution of this agglomeration of problems.

To believe them, the painter Gringonneur was
the inventor of cards, and forthwith the court of
Charles VI. devised the different games, which
different nations hastened to adopt, along with the

VII.; but to avoid giving an erroneous impression, and not to
incur the charge of too rash a definition, it would be better to
speak of them as *the pack of the time of Charles* VII.

very cards whose appearance and character they were about to transform. Père Daniel has taken still further pains, and draws up a dissertation in due form, with a view of tracing the history of the game of piquet, to the property of which the French nation in general claim a prescriptive title.

This game, in his view, is a figurative representation of the French monarchy under Charles VII., and with the ordinary pack of cards in use in that country before him, he strings together his deductions in the following manner:

The knave of hearts is called La Hire. This is Stephen de Vignolles, the La Hire who was the devoted adherent of Charles VII.

The knave of diamonds is Hector of Troy, the traditionary ancestor of the kings of France, or perhaps Hector de Gallard, another officer of Charles VII., and at a later period captain of the royal guard under Louis XI.

The knave of spades, Ogier, is one of the peers of Charlemagne, Ogier the Dane.* The kings (still according to Père Daniel) present to

---

* This hero was a grandson of Pepin d'Heristal, the great grandfather of Charlemagne, and the nephew of St. Hubert, the hunter's saint. His epithet, *le Danois*, marks him as a native not of Denmark proper, but of the *Dane-marche*, the march or border land between the Danish settlement and France, now called the Ardennes.

us the four most illustrious sovereigns of antiquity, viz., Alexander, Cæsar, David, and Charlemagne. The ladies are Pallas, goddess of war,
Rachel the Israelitess, Judith, and Argine. By
Pallas is denoted Joan of Arc. " Charles VII.,"
it appears, " who was certainly indebted to her for
the recovery in his affairs, which were in a well
nigh desperate state when she put herself at the
head of his troops to relieve Orleans, and compel
the English to raise the siege, wished to give her,
by way of memorial, her place in this military
game." One need be gifted with a great amount
of credulity to swallow these assertions.

Argine is an anagram of *regina*, queen, and
represents Mary of Anjou, wife of Charles VII.
The fair Rachel is no other than Agnes Sorel,
who, although in the equivocal position of the
king's mistress, exercised a happy influence over
his reign. Judith is the empress, consort of
Louis le Débonnaire, but under the name of this
atrocious woman, P. Daniel pretends that Isabel
of Bavaria, the mother of Charles VII., is in
reality intended.

These speculations are hazarded by Père
Daniel with the greatest assurance; as, for instance, when he writes, "There is a great apparent
probability that this game of piquet was originally

enacted at some *carrousel*, or masquerade, in four companies or quadrilles, according to the four ensigns of *piques*, *carreaux*, *cœurs*, and *trèfles*. Although I can adduce no fact in history, a science which hardly descends to details, by which I could substantiate this hypothesis, I shall still avail myself of the idea in order to state the plan of this game."

Most certainly it would be vain indeed to look for historical support of his astonishing imaginations ; but he makes himself perfectly easy, and continues without the slightest compunction :

"*Maxim the First.* Money is the sinews of war; this is denoted by the four Aces. Ace or *as* being the Latin for the pound weight of copper which the Romans at the first used as money."

I should be glad to know upon the same construction, what the four tens, the four nines, &c., denote.

Maxim the Second. It is anything but prudent for a prince to take the field with his army till there is forage to be had. This is what is designed by the *trèfle*, trefoil or clover plant."

The same convenient process furnishes M. Daniel with a representation of the munitions of war in the *piques* and *carreaux*, *i. e.*, pikes and quarrels, a kind of heavy square-headed arrows, and in the hearts, the symbol of courage, as necessary to the soldier as the trefoil (*forage*) and the quarrels for the cross-bows.

A whole host of charming conceits follows the specimens given above, some more than usually elaborate; as, for instance, the following:

"Female intrigues are oft-times perilous in courts; a clear proof of this is to be found in the example of Queen Isabel of Bavaria and the Empress Judith, who is her representative in the piquet cards. The ladies, however, require to be managed with great consideration; for the commotions which happened at this time were all the effect of this very queen's vengeance, excited by the sequestration of her jewels and a large sum of money by Charles VII., when Dauphin, for the purpose of carrying on the war against the English, and which she had lodged in different churches in Paris and its environs, for security."

These absurdities are in no way instructive. As well might we admit the explanations of another worthy father (Menestrier), who will have it that the kings, queens, and valets or knights, represent the nobility; the hearts (*cœurs*) are the ecclesiastics, whose place is in the choir (*chœur*); the pike (*pique*), the military; the *carreau*, one of the senses of which is a paving tile, the citizens, whose houses are paved with brick, and the trefoil (*trèfle*,) the labourers and country folk.*

* So thoroughly ridiculous are all these explanations that Bullet quotes them with the utmost reluctance. It is a pity he did not devote his attention to demolishing them instead of

It would be very desirable to have it in our
power to substitute for these vagaries some reliable
account of the first stage in the introduction of
cards of the ordinary sort, and of the game of
piquet, which seems to have originated at the same
time.

Unfortunately no precise evidence of the kind

discussing such trifles at all, though, to do him justice, he only
adopts their general outline with a view to the details which
he, with his extraordinary Celtic or Breton predilections, supplies after his fashion, with the most imperturbable *sang froid*.
On the ordinary cards of the seventeenth century, the queen of
hearts is called, not Judith, but Judic. Neither Menestrier nor
Daniel saw anything extraordinary in this; but here Bullet
makes a grand discovery. Argine is a compound of two Celtic
words, *ar* and *gin*, which signify *La Belle*, while *Judic* is from
jud, queen, and *dyc*, twice; and this he takes for a certain
proof that these two names were selected to indicate Anne of
Bretagne, who was a beauty, and moreover twice queen of
France. Twenty pages of dissertation, profusely annotated,
are occupied in developing this burlesque idea. At the end of
these, Bullet has devoted ten others to show that P. Daniel has
been wrong in seeing in the name of King David an evident
allusion to the reign of Charles VII.

Among this rubbish one good remark is to be found. In
one of the ancient packs examined by Bullet, the imperial
eagle represented by the side of the king of hearts, Charlemagne, has but one head. Now, the first seal of the Germanic
empire, which bears the double-headed eagle, is fully as ancient
as the close of the reign of Sigismund [1411-37]. There is a
deed dated 1417, which proves this. The figure of the king of
hearts, therefore, was originally designed at an epoch anterior
to this, or, at any rate, it could not have been much after. This
rather makes for the chronology we have attempted to establish.

is within our reach, and even the very name of the game awaits a satisfactory derivation.*

Whatever may be the true state of the case, thus much is certain, cards with the distinguishing marks of *cœur, carreau, pique,* and *trèfle* were undeniably in existence in the reign of Charles VII., and do not appear to have been even known as early as Charles VI.

More than this, the formation of the game of piquet seems connected with the epoch of Charles VII. in more ways than one.†

It seems hardly possible to conceive that the game and the cards with which it was played were

---

* According to Bullet, the word *piquet* is derived from the Celtic (it is always the Celtic with him) *piquo,* signifying to choose, the application of which does not seem very evident. What he says of *pic* and *repic* is more curious. These, in Celtic, have the sense of *doubled* and *redoubled,* which is tolerably in accordance with their meaning in the game. Bullet goes on to say, that the "point" was anciently called *Ronfle,* which is compounded of two Celtic words *rum,* a gathering together, and *bell* (in composition *fell*) a combat; hence *rumfell, rumfle, ronfle,* an assemblage of cards of the same suit. *Capot,* he says, signified in Celtic, *balked of one's expectation;* but this is unnecessarily far fetched, capot being very naturally derived from a well-known German word which signifies, *completely destroyed —annihilated.*

† Play was greatly in fashion under Charles VII. Pasquier, *Recherches,* p. 721, speaks of a certain monk in this reign, whose persuasive eloquence decided the Parisians one fine day to burn all their cards.

invented all at once. The heart, called by the
Germans *Roth*, or red, has been also adopted by
that people as one of their marks of suits, which
are hearts, leaves, acorns, and bells.

There must have been some hidden relation
between the games of all European nations, and
one of the inferences which suggest themselves
to those who have taken pains to investigate the
subject thoroughly is, that during the hundred
years between 1350 and 1450 more than one
modification of the ancient cards must have
escaped us. Things arrive at maturity by slow
degrees. The system of steam navigation must
have passed through the hands of ten mechani-
cians before it resulted in the employment of
the screw. Therefore, what is more likely than
that in another species of discovery, many attempts would have been made, always supposing
the nature of things to remain the same, before
they would have completed the dismemberment
of the framework of the old tarot, and that
with the new game, they would have con-
cocted the rules and regulations of the French
system.

It is the opinion of some, that there existed
an intermediate game between the Southern or
German tarot and the French piquet; but of this

there are no traces, just as none exist of the process by which the invention of piquet was completed.*

It will not do to say, therefore, with M. Paul Lacroix, that we owe the game of piquet to La Hire, or rather to one of his subordinates, who is personified by the valet of tréfle, the only valet without a title. This card at an early period bore the name of Lancelot, which was only omitted when the cardmakers of France were required by an *ordonnance* of Louis XIII. to put their names upon their cards, and they adopted the custom of signing them upon the valet of trèfle.

It will not do, in fact, to accept any longer the pretended explanations of the learned of the last century, which are, in general, nothing else but wretched guesses.†

* This is no reason, however, for believing with Grosley, that the game of piquet was the invention of a mathematician of Troyes, who lived in the reign of Louis XIII., and whose name was Picquet. M. Louis Albach has sanctioned this opinion in an article in the *Revue de Paris*. It is easily disproved by a comparison of the piquet or *cent* mentioned by Rabelais.

† The arguments which have been built on the costumes of the figured cards, to determine the approximate date of the invention of the French game, are designedly omitted. It would be necessary, before commencing any useful discussion on this point, to be able to refer to a specimen altogether of the primitive sort. None such, however, exist.

Menestrier, Bullet, Daniel, and others, have simply selected

It would be, in all probability, at the fêtes at Chinon, where Charles VII. so gaily ruined his kingdom; or at Paris, when victory once more smiled on him, and in the joy of triumph, that the gallant and warlike court of this king, rescued by Joan of Arc, would have devised and worked out the new system of cards.

Further than this we hesitate to go, and let us be content with being able to give the *résumé* which follows, as a legitimate conclusion.

France was acquainted with the tarot in the second half of the fourteenth century. The first

for study the common piquet pack of their own times. This, of course, is not the original type in its integrity. It would be far better to take the cards of the time of Charles VII., described above, which are the most valuable materials for comparison we possess. At the same time, one may deduce from the consideration of these costumes a certain amount of probability, which it may be well not to disregard. Bullet has availed himself of it. He takes, for instance, one of these cards, no matter which, which he declares were invented in the time of Charles V. (an erroneous notion, for even the cards of Charles VI. were tarots), and he sees on them no shoes *à la poulaine*. Now, Charles V., in 1365, had prohibited the use of these absurdities, because the French had exaggerated the fashion to the extent of having them three feet in length. After his death, the fashion reappeared. Bullet thereupon jumps to the conclusion, that since there were no cards before 1369, but that they did exist in Charles V's time, and these long-pointed shoes did not, therefore, the invention of cards is to be fixed between 1369 and 1380, or at most between 1365 and the last date. All this is perfectly gratuitous.

variation she effected was probably the introduction of queens.

It was only after the muliplication of examples
to any extent became possible, by means of engravings, for which we are indebted to Germany,
that the use of cards became general; and it was
then that France set herself to assimilate these
cards to her peculiar genius, a task which resulted
in the invention of piquet, by a simplification of
the original elements. The marks of suits, and
the number of the cards, as well as the enactment
of the fundamental laws of this game, date from
the middle of the reign of Charles VII., which
coincides with the middle of the fifteenth century.

It is at this exact period that the history of
cards is involved in the greatest obscurity, although the invention of the French game is the
most important element in it. From the period
of this interval, the ancient cards lose by little and
little their influence. Fashion and reason combined to diffuse through Europe the opportune
invention and intelligible principles of the new
game, which is a game in reality, and no longer
a mythological symbol. The tarot cards exist,
but no longer have the pre-eminence, and the
rules which regulate them have become less
complicated and obscure. Those who play at it

yet, in districts where the use of it lingers, play no longer in the fashion of times past. The wandering gipsy alone preserves its traditions. She refuses to part with the mysterious volume which speaks to her of occult mysteries, the oracles which gain for her her daily bread. The tarot, at the present moment, is no longer met with in France, except among the cartomanciers; and in Europe, it only struggles for existence in secluded spots, as in the cabin of the peasant of the Black Forest, or of the Estremaduran or Calabrian bandit. The cards at this time in general use are the cards of France, and that is her share in the matter.

VIII.

CARDS IN ENGLAND.

HAVING traced thus far the progress of cards in France, and their gradual dissemination in Continental Europe, we must now proceed to investigate the scanty materials at our command for their early history in this country. The evidence deduced from these as to their first introduction being of a stamp rather negative than positive, renders the approximate date even, much more a subject of speculation than a matter in any degree approaching to certainty.

There appear no sustainable grounds for supposing that the ancient tarot cards were ever used or known in England.

The term *Alea*, which was employed with considerable latitude in various ordinances and prohibitory decrees of early date, to denote games of chance, cannot with any foundation be taken to include cards. In fact, by some writers they are expressly distinguished from each other.*

Ducange, indeed, who quotes in his *Glossary* under the term "Ludi," the 38th Canon of the Council of Worcester, held in 1240, which enjoins persons in holy orders neither to take part in disreputable games or sports, "nec sustineant ludos fieri *de Rege et Regina*—nor to allow the games of King and Queen to take place in their presence," suggests that a game of cards is thereby intended; but he has overlooked the fact that no queen is to be found either in the Indian game or in the earliest European cards; and the phraseology of the canon rather indicates a spectacle of no very delicate or edifying a character.†

There have not been wanting others who have sought to claim for cards a high antiquity in England.

---

* Cardani *Opera*, tom. i. *Liber* de Ludo Aleæ, cap. xxiv. Singer, *Appendix*, *No.* 10.

† There was, however, a Christmas game in the time of Queen Elizabeth, called King and Queen, and we have mention of it moreover, in connection with cards. John Heywood, the great epigrammatist, according to Camden, " used to say, he did not love to play at *king and queene* but at Christmasse, according to the old order of Englande,—that few men plaied at cardes but at Christmasse, and then, almost all, men and boyes" (*Remains*, p. 378). Perhaps chess was meant.

Mr. Anstis, in his *History of the Garter* (vol. ii., p. 357), cites a passage from the Wardrobe Rolls of the 6th Edward I. [1278], which he conjectures is a reference to cards : "Waltero Sturton ad opus regis ad ludendum *ad quatuor reges*, viii^s. v^d." The Hon. Daines Barrington, in confirmation of this conjecture, suggests, with great plausibility, that Edward, who served five years in Syria before his accession to the throne, might have been taught this game during his expedition in that country.*

It is also certain that cards were well known in England by the name of the " Books of the Four Kings," if not so early as the date of the passage in the Wardrobe Rolls, yet certainly long before it appeared in Anstis' *History of the Garter*.†

* See *Archæologia*, vol. viii. Mr. Gough's objection to this, that the crusaders had too much on their hands to admit of their turning their attention to so trivial an employment, is quite overruled by the preservation of a very curious edict, which shows the state of gaming in the Christian army, commanded by Richard I. and Philip of France, during the crusade in the year 1190. By this it was enacted, that " no person in the army is permitted to play at any sort of game for money except knights and clergymen, who, in one whole day and night, shall not, each, lose more than twenty shillings, on pain of forfeiting one hundred shillings to the archbishop of the army. The two kings may play for what they please."

† Chatto gives several proofs of this, *e. g.*, Sir Thomas Urquhart, *Translation of Rabelais*, chap. xxii., book i. Also an article in *Fraser's Magazine* for August, 1844.

Or again, taking it for granted, as we do, that cards were of Oriental origin, and that Europe first obtained the knowledge of them by the way of Spain, and by the intervention of the Saracens in their invasion of that country, perhaps about the end of the thirteenth century, the supposition appears possible, that Edward may have learned the game from his queen, Eleanor of Castile, especially as there are certain peculiarities in the names of two of the suits of our English cards, as compared with the marks, which seem to indicate that our first acquaintance with them might be connected in some way with Spain.

Much, however, as we should desire to adopt hypotheses so tempting, in aid of our theory as to the channel by which cards were disseminated in Europe, the silence of the statutes in which various games are enumerated and prohibited, and of the writers who have particularized the amusements of the people, among which cards are not included, seems conclusive against their existence in England at so early a period.

From Sir William Jones's essay on the Indian game of chess, printed in vol. ii. of the *Asiatic Researches*, in which, moreover, the affinity between chess and cards very clearly appears, there can scarcely be a doubt, that the game of the

"four kings," played at by Edward I., was chess, and that this name was a literal translation of the Sanskrit word *Chatur-anga*, or, closer still, *Chaturaji*—the four rajahs or kings. " This game," he says, "seems to have been immemorially known in Hindustan by the name of ' *Chatur-anga*,' that is the FOUR *angas* or members of an army, which are said in the Amaracosha to be elephants, horses, chariots, and foot-soldiers ; and, in this sense, the word is frequently used by epic poets in their descriptions of real armies."*
This particular game seems known only by tra-

---

* Chaturanga was corrupted by the ancient Persians into *Chatrang*, and by the Arabs into *Shatranj*, as they had neither the initial nor the final letter in their alphabet ; and this becoming the modern Persian form, found its way back into the dialects of India, and thence, by successive changes in different languages, became *exedras*, *scacchi*, *echecs*, chess, with which are also connected *check*, *chequer*, and *exchequer*.   Mr. Chatto derives the title of the sister game of cards from the same root, by the following process :   The common word for cards in India is *Taj* or *Tas*, a leaf, and figuratively a diadem or crown, the emblem of kingly dignity ; and as chahar or chatur signifies four (Lat. *quatuor*), *chahar-taj* or *chahar-tas* would be suggestive of nearly the same idea as the " four kings," and be almost identical in sound with the Latin *chartæ*, cards.

Singularly enough, in ancient French works, the word is sometimes written *quartz* or *quartes*, as if, in the mind of the writer, it was rather associated with the idea of *four* than *paper*, though χαρτης (Lat. *charta*) paper, may also contain the notion of a square (*quarré*) of paper, in contradistinction to a roll or volume. Compare also the French *cahier* or *cayer*, a quire of paper.

dition; but Sir William gives a description of another very ancient Indian game, also called *Chaturanga*, but more frequently *Chaturaji*, since it is played by four persons, representing as many princes, two allied armies combating on each side.

Here we have the notion of the *four* suits, a number which is in other ways associated with cards, for in each suit there are four honours, reckoning the ace as is done in some games, not to mention the old game of all-fours, which seems connected with winning in each of the four divisions, now called high, low, jack, and game.

From the notices we possess of the game of chess, it is evident that its introduction took place prior to that of cards. We know from Boccaccio, who lived in the fourteenth century, that it was common at Florence in his time. Lydgate mentions a game of chess, in which a queen drove the king into a corner of the board, and he even introduces the term *mate;* and Froissart, who is silent on the subject of cards, relates a game of chess between Charles V. of France and the Duke of Burgundy. In an ancient MS.,* in the

* Harl. MS., 4690:
    "And Kyng Rychard stode and playe
      At the chesse in his galley."

British Museum, Cœur de Lion even, is represented as diverting the tedium of the voyage to
Palestine by the same means.

Among the moneys issued from the Exchequer
28th Edward I. (A.D. 1300), are some payments
to the Prince of Wales for his use in playing at
different games (ad ludendum ad *creag'* et alios
ludos per vices, 10s.) Among these, however,
cards are not specified, unless indeed *creagium*
may be supposed to denote any game of the
kind.*

There seems to be every probability that
cards made their way into England by way of
France; but, considering the extensive footing
which our kings possessed on the soil of that
kingdom, and which, dating from the marriage
of Henry II. with the heiress of Guienne, cul-
minated in the coronation of Henry VI. as king
of France, in 1430, there does not appear equal

* Halliwell and Wright both explain *creag'* by " ninepins."
Krijgertje spelen, in Picard's Dutch Dictionary, is to play at
prison bars. Both are connected, probably, with the German
krieg, war. There is an ancient Italian card game, denominated
cricca, which is considered to be related to our gleek. Berni, in
his *rifaccimento* of Bojardo's *Orlando Inamorato,* compares two
of his combatants to two players at this game, because they are
fighting with clubs.

> Sembran Costor due giocator' di cricca
> Ch' abbian il punto tutti due in bastoni.

reason for the assumption that we received them necessarily from the French *people*.*

It was as prince of Guienne, that Edward I. was affianced to his Castilian bride, and it was in the same capacity, that the Black Prince, in aid of Peter, king of Castile, defeated at the battle of Najara, that very Henry of Transtamare whom the constable Duguesclin led his bands to assist.† If, therefore, the soldiers of Duguesclin, as we have ventured to affirm, were the agents of the introduction of the cards of Spain into France, is it not reasonable to suppose, that by similar means they may have become known in the English possessions in the south-western part of that country? For the causes which led to the adoption of cards by the allies of one Castilian prince, would surely have a tendency to propagate them among the partizans of the other.

The port of Bourdeaux would afford to cards a ready means of access to England; but no traces of any have come down to us which we might safely assign to this locality and period.

There exists indeed a pack of cards for which

* The English possessions in France were Normandy, Guienne, Poictou, Saintonge, Touraine, Anjou, and Maine. Of these the kings of England were in real or nominal possession for nearly 300 years.

† *Vide suprà*, p. 49.

was claimed an English connection, and at the same time an antiquity superior to the French account of their invention and use under their king Charles VI.

These cards were brought under the notice of the Society of Antiquaries, Nov. 9, 1763, by Dr. Stukeley, having been taken from an old edition of Claudian, printed before 1500, of which they formed the covers, a leaf or two of Erasmus' adages being pasted between the layers of cards.

The entire series has been engraved by Singer, from which it may be perceived that the suits consisted of bells, hearts, leaves, and acorns; and a king, knight, and knave, made the court cards. There were no queens or aces, and on every deuce was the cardmakers' arms, two crossed mallets, with which the doctor supposed they *stamped* the cards, whereas the French cards of Charles VI's time were drawn or coloured by hand, and thence called *tabellæ* or *pagellæ pictæ*.

But the circumstance from which he inferred the extreme antiquity of these cards, and the probability that they were so far from being an imitation of the French, that there seemed reason to consider them of English invention and of much older date, was, that on the deuce of acorns, besides the cardmakers' arms, was, what he took to be, a white hart couchant, the well-known badge of Richard II.

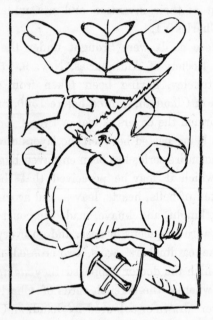

It is evident, however, that these conjectures are entirely erroneous ; for, even supposing them to be of the required antiquity, the marks of suits refer them unmistakeably to the German type, and the material of which they are composed disposes at once of the possibility of their being of English manufacture, as paper-making was unknown in this country in the fourteenth century.

The doctor's hart, too, has much more the appearance of a *unicorn*, and he contradicts himself in claiming for them a date antecedent to that of Charles VI. of France, inasmuch as the imbecility of that prince and the era of our Richard II. (1377—1399) were coincident.

It has been objected by Mr. Gough, that had cards been introduced into England prior to the reign of Richard II., Chaucer, who died in 1400, would have made some mention of them; yet, in speaking of amusements, he only says—

> They dancen and they play at ches and tables.
> *Franklin's Tale I.*, 11,212.

And this is an objection which deserves much consideration.

Bullet, in insisting that we derive our knowledge of cards from France, remarks, that our use of the term *knave* to designate the valet, proves that the game was unknown to us until the latter term came to signify in France a servant. Chaucer,* however, and Wiclif employ the term

---

* *Man of Lawes Tale I.*, 5,135, where it is said of the king of Northumberland, "On hire he gat a knave-child anon."— See Tyrwhitt's *Glossary*, *in voce*. So *knabe*, in German, in the same sense. The term Valet (*Valettus Regis*, *Vassalettus*) appears both in England and France to have been usually applied to young persons of distinction before they attained the distinction of *scutifer*, esquire or knight. In 1327, the

knave-child to designate a boy; and Anstis considers it a proof of the antiquity of the game, as denoting a youth whose place was next to the king and queen, and being as it were their son, in which sense that term was used.

Whether, therefore, cards were known in England from a very early period of their introduction into Europe, and whether we obtained them from Eastern sources in common with our neighbours, or received them from the Spaniards or French—whether, in fact, the English were in possession of cards of the earlier type or not, certain it is, that until the latter part of the fifteenth century, we find no absolute historic certainty of the existence of English cards properly so called; and while Spain, Italy, Germany, and France, were each in possession of their national modifications of the original tarot, it is only at a comparatively recent period that we

poet Chaucer, being then in his 39th year, received from King Edward III. a pension of twenty marks. In the patent, he is called by the above title. In his 44th year he is styled scutifer. Neither knave nor valet, therefore, appear primarily to have denoted a person of servile condition, but the third honour in the ancient game of which the king was the first, and the Phers, the general or chief officer (before the name was changed into *fierge, vierge,* and *dame*), the second. The subordination was of age or military rank. Mr. Chatto, however, considers the low condition of the knave an evidence of the Spanish origin of our English cards.—*Facts and Speculations,* pp. 230—235.

are found to have followed the example of other
nations, in inventing a game of a totally distinct
character, and peculiar to ourselves.

The reigns of Henry VI. of England, and
Charles VII. of France (1422—1460), though a
period of incessant and obstinate conflict between
the two nations on the soil of France, was yet, as
we have seen, the epoch of the appearance of the
four-suit or piquet cards. During a large portion
of this period, the English retained possession,
with varying success, of the fairest provinces of
France. In 1430, Henry VI. was crowned at
Paris, according to treaty, as king of that country; and, although Charles VII. obstinately re-
sisted the claim, it was not till 1450 that Guienne
and the English possessions in the south-west of
France were finally wrested from them, after a
contested occupation of nearly 300 years. If,
therefore, cards, during this interval, had obtained
any very general circulation in France, it is
impossible to believe but that the knowledge of
them would have extended to a people who had
long occupied so large a portion of its territory.*

Certain specimens of a pack, moreover, are in
existence, which, by assuming a small portion of

* Singer produces evidence that cards were in use in England
in the reign of Henry VI. In the Chester plays or mysteries, a

French licence, might be taken not only to belong to this period, but also to contain indications of a connection with England.

The same source which has, as we have seen, afforded so many xylographical discoveries, especially in the matter of ancient examples of playing cards, viz., the covers of an ancient volume—disclosed to Mr. Chatto, in 1841, four squares of paper, one containing the valets of clubs and spades, with the names Lancelot and Hogier; and another, the valets of diamonds and hearts, Rolant and Erard de Valery* twice repeated. The other two squares consisted of "pips" of diamonds and hearts, which were so arranged that each piece of paper might be cut into four cards : the low cards on one square being the nine, four, five, and seven of diamonds ; and those on the other, the ten, four, five, and eight of hearts.

The character of these cards is in singular accordance with M. Duchesne's description of the

copy of which is preserved among the Harleian MSS., in the British Museum, an old ale-wife or brewer is introduced in a scene of hell. She is consigned to the taunts and torments of three devils, one of whom thus addresses her :

" Welcome, deare darlinge, to endless bale,
Useinge *cardes*, dice, and cuppes smale,
With many false other, to sell thy ale,
Now thou shalt have a feaste."

Researches, p. 250.

* *Vide* note *suprà*. p. 71.

" Coursube " pack, *temp*. Charles VII., discovered
in a similar manner by M. Hénin, at Lyons, the
outlines of the figures having been engraved on
wood, printed in a brownish tint, something like
Indian ink mixed with bistre, and the colours
filled in with a stencil plate.

The volume from which these cards were taken,
was a small quarto, formerly belonging to the Cathedral Library of Peterborough, containing the
sermons of S. Vincent de Ferrer, a Spanish friar
of great repute in his day, who died in 1419. The
probable date of the book was 1490—1500, but both
title page and last leaf were unfortunately missing.

There is a general resemblance, moreover,
between these and the French cards, in the names
and costumes of the figures, and, though of slightly
better execution, it is agreed they belong to about
the same date.

Now, on the card which bears the name of
Valery, the shield of this hero is charged with the
Red Rose crowned,* a symbol essentially English.

We have, then, these two points in favour of
the English origin of these cards—that they were
discovered on English ground, in the covers of a
book which had belonged originally to an English

* See Frontispiece to this book, or Chatto, *Facts and Speculations*, p. 214,

monastery, at a time when monks were their own bookbinders, and used any materials at hand to construct their boards ; and, secondly, that they bear the well-known badge of a line of English sovereigns especially connected with French history, and that, too, at a period singularly coincident with the date we have ventured to assign to the corresponding French examples. Mr. Chatto even says, that the features, expression, and bodily proportions of the figures are more characteristic of Englishmen than Frenchmen.

Without venturing, however, to appropriate these cards as exclusively English, may we not at least say, that they constitute just such a pack as we might expect would be fabricated during the last years of the English rule in France, that is to say, prior to 1450 ?*

Quitting now the field of speculation for that

---

* True it is that Mr. Chatto, from an examination of costume, &c., assigns these cards to a period shortly after the accession of Henry VII. (1485), when the Red Rose of Lancaster had obtained the ascendancy ; nor does he allow a higher antiquity to those which bear the names of Coursube and Apollin. But as he himself remarks, conclusions drawn from the costume displayed on cards are not of much weight in the determination of a date, seeing that persons supposed to be well acquainted with the subject of costume have not been able to determine from that alone the date of any old drawing, even within fifty years. The badge, moreover, of Henry VII. after his marriage with Elizabeth of York, was the Tudor Rose,—quarterly, *gules* and *argent*.

of certainty, we have documentary proof that cards were in use in England some time previous to 1463, for in the Parliament Rolls of that year, 3 Edward IV., among other articles the importation of which was prohibited, are mentioned "dyces, tenys balles, *cardes for pleiying*," in contradistinction to "*cardes for wolle*, or whitewyre,"* &c. ; and this prohibition, which was made upon the petition of the English artificers generally, would seem to indicate that they had not only been commonly imported from foreign parts, but that cards of English manufacture were then in existence; this act, according to Anderson (*History of Commerce*, vol. i., p. 483), being passed in consequence of the manufacturers and tradesmen of London and other parts of England having made heavy complaints against the importation of foreign manufactured wares, which greatly obstructed their own employment, and injured the home market.

About 1484, cards, whether of English or foreign manufacture, occur familiarly as a common Christmas game, at any rate among the

* In the 1 Edward IV. Hugh Cardmaker was prior of S. John Baptist, at Bridgenorth. If, however, his name was derived from the occupation of an ancestor, it is no proof that a maker of *playing* cards was intended.

upper classes.   In that curious and valuable collection, the *Paston Letters,* Margery Paston thus writes to her husband, John Paston:

"Ryght worschipful husbond, I recomaund me onto you; plese it you to wete, that I sent you^r eldest Sunne to my Lady Morlee, to have knolage wat sports wer husyd in her hows in Kyrstemesse next folloyng, aftyr the decysse of my Lord her husbond; and sche seyd, that yer wer non Dysgysyngs, ner harpyng, ner lutyng, ner syngyn, ner nō lowde dysports; but pleyng at the tabyllys, and schesse, and *cards;* sweche dysports sche gave her folkys leve to play and nō odyr. You^r Sunne dede hese heyrne (*errand*) ryght wele as ye shal her aftyr yis. I sent you^r yonger Sunne to the Lady Stabylton, and sche seyd acordyng to my Lady Morlees seyng in that; and as sche hadde seyn husyd in placs of worschip yer as sche hathe beyn."* (Dated Friday, 24th of December, 1484, 2 Richard III.)—Vol ii., p. 333, edit. 1778.

In the eleventh year of Henry VII. (1495-6), cards are first mentioned among the games pro-

* William Lovel, Lord Morley, died July 23, 1475. By "*places of worship,*" are not meant, of course, houses of prayer, but the houses of worshipful people, lords, knights, and persons high in office.

hibited by the law, and at that time they seem to have been very generally used; for the edict, (2 Henry VII., cap. 2) expressly forbids the practice of card-playing to servants and apprentices, excepting during the Christmas holidays, and then only in their master's houses, under the penalty to the householder of six shillings and eightpence for every offence. We learn from Stow (*Survey of London*, p. 79) that these holidays extended "from All-hallows evening to the day after Candlemas-day, when," says the historian, "there was, among other sports, playing at cards for counters, nailes, and points, in every house, more for pastime than for gain."

It would appear that these games, cards included, were not forbidden from any peculiarly evil tendency in themselves, but because they engrossed too much of the leisure and attention of the people, and diverted their minds from pursuits of a martial nature.*

Indeed, the amusement of card-playing must

* See Strutt's *Sports and Pastimes of England*, Introduction p. lxi.; Hone's edition. An old Scotch writer, author of an anonymous poem of "Covetice," cited by Warton, *Hist. Eng. Poet.* ii., 317, laments that horse racing was falling into disrepute through the prevalency of games of chance.

> "Halking, hunting, and swift horse running
> Are changit all in wrangus, wynning;
> There is no play but cartes and dyce," &c.

have been greatly in fashion at the court of
Henry VII., for among that monarch's privy
purse expenses are three several entries of money
issued for his majesty's losses at cards; and in
1502, his daughter Margaret, aged 14, was found
engaged at cards by James IV. of Scotland, on
his first interview with her, after her arrival in
Scotland for the purpose of being married to
him.* James himself is said to have been greatly
addicted to card-playing; and in the accounts of
his treasurer there are several entries of money
disbursed on account of the game. On Christmas
night, 1496, there are delivered to the king at
Melrose, to spend at cards, "thirty-five unicornis,
eleven French crowns, a ducat, a ridare, and a leu,"
—in all forty-two pounds. On the 23rd of August,
1504, when the king was at Lochmaben, he
appears to have lost several sums at cards to
Lord Dacre, the warden of the English marches;
and on the 26th of the same month, there is an
entry of four French crowns given "to Cuddy,
the Inglis luter, to louse his cheyne of grotis,

* Leland's *Collectanea*, Appendix iii., p. 214. "The kynge
came prively to the said Castell (New bottle) and entered
within the chammer with a small cumpany, whare he founde
the queene *playing at cardes*."—See the Hon. Daines Barrington, *On the Antiquity of Card-playing in England.*—
Archæologia, vol. viii., p. 137.

quhilk he tint at the cartis"—to redeem his chain
of groats which he lost at cards.*

From the whole of the evidence before us, there
would appear to be merely a bare possibility that
cards were known in England, soon after the
second Crusade, at the latter end of the thirteenth
century, it being certain that the slender grounds
for this conjecture are better referred to an early
form of the game of chess; and there is only
a probability that their introduction to the
English was coincident with their extensive
occupation of the French territory in the
fourteenth or fifteenth.

The earliest existing examples of cards, however, which bear any trace which can be construed
to denote an English origin, are of the French
type, and of about the same date as their first
piquet, or four suit cards; but we have tangible
proof that cards, both of English and foreign
manufacture, were known here at least for some
time previous to 1464; and though it is very
probable they were not in common use at their
first introduction, but confined to the court, and
the houses of the great, it is certain that long

* *Vide* Chatto, *Facts and Speculations, &c.*, p. 98; and a
notice of the private life of James IV. of Scotland, in *Chambers'
Edinburgh Journal*, Nos. 9 and 10, 1832.

before the end of the fifteenth century they were
used for pastime by the idle of all classes.

It is singular that the use of cards should
have been made a subject of legislation in
France a hundred years earlier than in England,
but the respective habits of the two nations may
perhaps account for the difference.

IX.

HISTORY OF TAROTS, AS TOLD BY THEMSELVES.

HAVING related the successive stages by which the
French arrived at the invention of their national
cards, and discussed the speculations which have
been made as to the manner and time of their
introduction into this country, which, however,
as we have seen, was an accomplished fact before
1464; it is time to recur to our old acquaintances
the Oriental tarots, whose *début* in Spain, Italy,
and Germany, was so evidently successful.

It is natural to expect that modifications
should take place in these; and even in the cards of
the French type, the earlier packs would present
in all probability, considerable variations. It is
these modifications and variations, which we now
propose to investigate in detail.

The importance which attends the determination of the date of the invention of engraving, has been already pointed out, for the earliest efforts of the art in Germany were most certainly devoted to the production of cards. As a measure of caution, we have hitherto carried this date no higher than the early part of the fifteenth century. This, however, is certainly below the mark, and there appear good reasons for assigning the invention of card-engraving to the middle of the preceding century, or about 1360; so that there might have been printed cards in Germany, at an epoch when it is anything but certain that cards of the earlier miniature style had been yet introduced to any extent into France.

It is an acknowledged fact, that the German card-makers were the earliest wood-engravers in Europe.* Their original marks of suits were

---

* See those who have written on the subject; Heinecken, Bartsch, Breitkopf, Jansen, Zani, Singer, &c., whose names will be found in the Bibliographical appendix. Some attribute the impressed cards to Laurence Coster. Heinecken makes them invented at Ulm. They were called there *Briefe*,[1] implying nothing more than "papers," but subsequently became also known as *Karten*,—perhaps after they began to be manufactured for exportation. "It was before 1376," says Jansen (i. 87), "that they have been in use in this country (Suabia); and it is even said, in a book called *Das Gulden Spil* (the Golden Game), that the game of cards had begun to make progress in Germany in 1300."

[1] It is singular that cards constructed on a cheating principle are called in cant phraseology, *Briefs*.

Schellen, grelots or hawk-bells; *Roth,* red, or *Herzen,* hearts; *Grün,* green (leaves); and *Eicheln,* acorns; supposed respectively to denote the nobility, the clergy, the gentry, land-owners or farmers, and the labourers: the application of this last is not so evident, but the other emblems are thoroughly German in idea. We have already (p. 25) adverted to the bell as the distinctive emblem of the class of kings and nobles, in corroboration of which Breitkopf gives a plate which he calls "*Alte-Deutsche-Furst-Schellen-tracht*"—that is to say, Ancient German princely bell-costume—containing four figures, of dates between 1138 and 1218, all adorned with small bells.

The notion of hearts, as the seat of the affections and impressions, in connection with the office of the clergy, is just as likely a connecting link as the French derivation from *Chœur* (p. 77). In the room of these, the cards of the Southern type have *Copas,* or chalices, as more symbolical of the order.

The similarity, as far as outline goes, between the marks of the other two suits and the French *pique* and *trèfle* is remarkable.

Even at this early period, the printed cards were coloured, and indeed they would hardly have made their way without it. Those who cut the blocks were called *formschneiders,* and the artists who illuminated the impressions *brief- mahlers.** There was no attempt at shading, or, where any existed, it was merely a series of lines as strong as those which formed the outline.

The city of Ulm was the centre of the card manufacture, and the Suabian cards had for a long time—fifty years, at least—a considerable run: this was in the first half of the fifteenth century.

It was these which decided France, who was about to remodel the design of her cards, to betake herself to a game very different from the dice and nine-pins of earlier times.

It was Italy, however, above all other countries, which furnished the grand outlet for the com- merce of Ulm.† At a later period she accepted with equal readiness the cards of France.

The game in vogue at that time in Italy was

---

* It is necessary to observe, that these words mean simply *block-cutter* and *card-painter ;* for a certain author, of no mean reputation, has gravely supposed engraved cards to be the invention of a person named Briefmahler. As well might it be said, that the typographic art emanated from a *Mr. Printer.*

† Heinecken found in the library of the Stadt-house at Ulm, an old MS. Chronicle of that city, finished in 1474, in which was written the following memorandum : " Playing-cards were sent in large bales into Italy, Sicily, and other parts by sea, getting in exchange spices and other merchandize. By this it may be seen how numerous the card-makers and painters dwelling here must have been."—*Idée Générale,* p 244.

*Trappola.** Of the method of playing it nothing is known, and, besides, this is not the place to discuss it. It was the ancient game of Italy, derived, say some, direct from the Saracens, though others detect in the name the root of an Italian verb, signifying to *deceive or inveigle*. The early Italian cards bear the same marks of suits as the Spanish pack, possibly the original Eastern emblems: *spade* (swords), *coppe* (cups or chalices), *denari* (pieces of money), and *bastoni* (clubs or sticks); and each of these suits had three figured cards—*Re, Cavallo, Fante*, (king, knight or horseman, and valet or knave). According to Singer, the pack consisted, like the piquet series, of thirty-six cards, and he remarks on the analogy between this and the Indian game of chess. Garzoni speaks of it as the common game, and *Tarocco*, the new invention, for which he quotes the authority of Volaterrano—the latter

* The game of Trappola seems to be the first exemplar of the games of pure *hazard;* all these have among them an evident relationship, and succeeded each other according to the taste of the day; *e.g.*, lansquenet, fiorentini, hocca, bassa, faro (*pharaon*) bouillotte, &c., which are at bottom, all one and the same game. In general, games of hazard may be set down as originally Italian; games of intricate construction, as Spanish; while the lively and merry varieties may be safely referred to France. For specimens of the so-called Trappola cards, *vide* Chatto, p. 227 ; Singer, p. 199.

game, however, as we have before stated, was of a more complex description, and was played with a greater number of cards. (See p. 14.)

The influx of German cards at this period, consequent on the new invention, met with a ready acceptance.* Baron Heinecken, whose patriotic energy in the matter of cards is something wonderful, brings forward numberless proofs of this. He has raked together a mass of evidence from chronicles, MSS. registers, &c., from every possible source, to demonstrate that Ulm, at this triumphant period, was despatching cards of German manufacture to all quarters.

The examples which could give us any definite information as to the character of the first engraved and painted cards are very rare. Such as belong to this period, and have survived, are

* As might be expected, however, a clashing of interests took place, and great complaints were made in consequence. The native cardmakers were in danger of being starved, and we find in a letter of Temanza to Count Algarotti (*Lettere Pittoriche*, t. v., p. 321) the text of the petition which the Venetian cardmakers presented to the Senate of that city, Oct. 11, 1441. They complain that "the art and mystery of manufacturing cards and printed figures which they practised at Venice, had been totally ruined by the great quantity of playing cards and painted printed figures *(carte e fegure depente stampide)* imported into that city from other parts," and they demand the monopoly; moreover, they obtained it—another example of the vicissitudes in which cards have figured alternately as victims and public benefactors.

PLATE XIII.

PLATE XIII

KNAVE OF LEAVES.
(Early German Pack.)

generally in the miniature style, owing to these last having been got up with a view to greater durability.*

Nevertheless, a comparison of the various European collections would probably furnish a very instructive series.

In the print-room of the British Museum is a portion of a pack of very early cards with the German marks of suits, which Mr. Chatto considers, from the character of the figures and the manner of their execution (being evidently *stencilled*, and not printed or "rubbed off" from wood-blocks after the Chinese fashion) to be of as early a date as 1440. He is, moreover, of opinion, from the costume of the figures, and the occurrence of the lion of S. Mark on more than one of them, that they are the production of a Venetian card-maker. These also were taken from the covers of an old book, and were sold to the Museum by Mr. D. Colnaghi. They are of rather larger size, but resemble, in many respects, the curious German pack described by Mr. Gough in the eighth volume of the *Archæologia*, and already alluded to in the preceding chapter.

* *Vide* Plate XIII, an engraved card of the earliest date, and of evident German design. The design reminds us at once of the miniatures in mediæval MSS. There are some very similar in the library at Angers, gracefully executed by King Réné.

This resemblance is most strikingly seen in the king of bells, the design of which, in both packs is nearly identical (see Chatto's plate No. 1., p. 88). The number of "pips" appears also to have been the same, with the same "coat," or court-cards, King, Knight or Superior officer, and a Knave or Inferior, or, as Mr. Chatto expresses it, King, Jack, and Jack's man.

Singer and others have considered Mr. Gough's cards to be among the earliest known

Knave of Bells.

specimens; and the dress and character of the figures indicative of a date not later than the early part of the fifteenth century. To quote his own words : " They are just what it might have been imagined the earliest printed cards would be, rude outlines daubed over with one or two simple colours ; those used in the present instance appear to have been red and green." " It may be as well here to observe," he continues, " that the cap and dress of the knave in the above card, bears a strong resemblance to that of Abner in the eighteenth cut of the *Speculum*."

Speculations, however, as regards date founded on costume, are, as has been elsewhere observed, very often fallacious, as any type, once become conventional, might continue in circulation for a considerable period, and this too, in different countries.

It is after all very possible that the estimated antiquity of these cards may be erroneous, for we have before us, examples of a pack answering in every respect the description given above, and at p. 93, and corresponding exactly with the plates in Singer, save that the cardmakers' arms on the deuces is wanting, and on the nine of hearts the date 1546 is legibly impressed in Arabic numerals, and in addition to the colours before mentioned, yellow is employed for the bells and the king's crowns.*

In France, there are some undeniably ancient specimens both in the collection of the *Bibliothèque Impériale*, and also in that of M. Leber, at Rouen.

M. Leber's catalogue describes, under the number x., a four of *grelots*, on which is a Saint Anthony, placed between four little bells. This print appears to belong to about 1450, like the so-called "Pack of the time of Charles VII." which has been so much under discussion. There are one or two other examples of fifteenth century date, affording evidence that already fantastic designs were beginning to appear; of this the Saint Anthony and his four bells is a sufficient proof.

This notion once introduced, would soon make itself evident. Fancy is of too enterprising a character to be easily brought to a stand-still, and it is, as it were, a law of human nature, that after a discovery it should kick up its heels for a bit, and commit all manner of extravagancies, in token of exultation.

* These cards, which have been kindly lent us for inspection by Mr. Quaritch, bookseller, 15, Piccadilly, consist of three honours, the king and knave of leaves, and the king of bells, and ten numeral cards, and were found complete, in demolishing a house in the Fürstenwalde, in 1797; the remainder of the pack was stolen by the workmen at the time.

PLATE XIV

KNAVE (P) OF THE "MASTER."
(Paris, 1466.)

Hard upon the discovery of card-engraving, there followed cards upon cards, pack upon pack, the pencil and the graver untrammelled in their efforts, scattered to the winds a thousand follies. Good bye to the antique devices! what need now to be fettered with the conventionalities of the past? The ancients limited themselves to four distinctions of suits,—in one country, swords, &c., in another, bells and leaves, and so forth, always the same thing: but the new mania must have fresh symbols and fresh designs. Give the artist scope for his fancy, the play will be neither better nor worse. As a natural result, ensued a perfect shower of quaint figures and capricious emblems. The main principles of the pack, (i. e. of the *tarot*, which is still in vogue as well in Germany as in Italy) remain the same; but in place of bells, leaves, hearts, and acorns, came a succession of novelties — figures of men, animals, birds, and flowers, each one in its turn being superseded by another. The Imperial Library at Paris possesses a very beautiful pack of this description. The name of the engraver is unknown; but they are believed to be the work of the German artist, usually called by collectors "the Master of 1466." We engrave one as a specimen. They are remarkable for a peculiarity in their execution, pointed out by M. Duchesne, several copper-plates being employed to print them,—the five of Flowers, for instance, requiring as many pieces of ir-regular form, which were fixed evenly in a matrix, and the impression then taken off in the usual manner.*

There is also a very curious pack of cards, of a circular shape, described by Bartsch and Singer, which are of rather a later date. Several of them are engraved in Strutt's *Sports and Pastimes*, and four in Singer's work, from the collection of Mr. Douce. The suits, five in number, are hares, parrots, pinks, roses, and columbines. There are four picture cards to each suit, king, queen, and as is usual on some German cards, two *lanzknechte* or knaves.

* *Vide* Pl. XIV., and Bartsch, vol. x. p. 100. In the *Catalogue Raisonné of the Select Collection of Engravings of an Amateur* (Thomas Wilson, Esq.), there is a description of twenty-nine cards, also assigned to " the Master of 1466." These were subsequently purchased, and added to the collection in the Bibliothèque Impériale. They appear to have consisted, when complete, of fifty-two pieces, each of the four suits—human figures, bears and lions, deer, and birds—containing four coat, and nine numeral cards. Fac-similes of thirty-seven specimens of the pack are given in the *Jeux de Cartes Tarots et de Cartes Numerales*, published by the Society of Bibliophiles François. Four, beautifully engraved, may also be seen in Mr. Chatto's book. These cards are of extraordinary size, being 5⅞ inches long, by 3½ in breadth.

Mr. Douce's specimens were accompanied by the original wrapper, on which were engraved three crowns, and upon a scroll, SALVE. FELIX. COLONIA., so that they were probably executed by a German or Flemish artist in that city; and it has been supposed that they were of as early a date as 1470.* Mr. Singer supposes the entire pack to

Circular Cards.—Ace of Columbines.
(*Cabinet des Estampes.*)

* These cards have been ascribed to Martin Schön or Schöngauer, but it is believed erroneously. The ace of roses is engraved in Strutt, and that suit was possibly substituted occasionally for another, to give variety to the game.

have consisted of seventy cards, the increased number of suits being indicative of their Oriental derivation. Certain it is also, that the circular shape is Eastern in character, and symbolic of pantheism. Europe has uniformly preferred her cards to be square.

Another pack of circular cards in the Paris collection wants the suit of roses, and has no tens; M. Duchesne, however, considers it complete. The kings and queens are on horseback, the other two figures on foot. Though very similar to the former, it is the work of a different hand.

The execution of these cards is very artistic, as may be seen from the above specimen. The engraver is unknown, but T. W., probably his initials, appears on the borders. On the ace of hares, is an inscription in Platt-Deutsch, the interpretation of which, must be left to the ingenuity of our readers:

AVE MI DRINT ME VIN
DAEROM MOT IC EN LEPUS SIN.*

* A proposed modern Dutch version of this couplet has been forwarded by a correspondent (Dr. Andrews):

Hebbende mij, drinkt men wijn,
Daarom moet ic een Lepus zijn,—

and this is strongly corroborated by the last stanza of an old

The cards are not cut up, but are just as they left the printer's hands ; and on the plate containing the aces, they profess to read the date, 1477.

There are other antique specimens in the *Cabinet des Estampes*, kept in a portfolio by themselves ; but as it may be doubted whether they are fairly classed as cards, we need not now stay to notice them.

We pass on, therefore, to the beautiful Florentine engravings, which have been attributed to no less celebrated an artist than Andrea Mantegna, and are known to the Paris dealers as *Cartes de Baldini*. Of these there are two series, one being supposed to be a copy of the other. Each has had advocates of its originality, but the best executed specimens are probably the earliest. Of these

German song, on the calamitous life of a hare, for a transcript of which we are indebted to Mr. N. Trübner :

> Die grossen Herrn und ihre Gäst',
> Die heben mich auf bis zu allerletzt,
>   Bei allen Tractamenten,
>   Da thun Sie mich anwenden;
> Auf mich, *da trinken Sie den Rhein'schen Wein,*
> Ach! bin ich nicht ein armer Häsulein ?

Dr. Bell suggests with great probability that a *double entendre* of some kind is aimed at, from the use of the word *Lepus* instead of *Hase*, and that some old derivative of *laufen, loopen* (hence our North-country word *lop*, a flea), to leap or run, resembled lepus in form and sound.

there is a complete set in our National Collection, as also in the Bibliothèque Impériale at Paris, for which was given, at the sale of M. Pallière's collection in 1820, no less a sum than 2,000 francs. Eighty pounds for a pack of cards!

This so-called pack of Mantegna is composed of fifty pieces, of which the following is a list:

Jeu de Mantegna.

I. MISERO—a Beggar.
II. FAMEIO—a Valet.
III. ARTIXAN—a Goldsmith.
IV. MERCADANTE — a Merchant.
V. ZINTILOMO—a Gentleman.
VI. CHAVALIER — a Knight.
VII. DOXE—the Doge.
VIII. RE—a King.
IX. IMPERATOR — an Emperor.
X. PAPA—the Pope.

XI. CALLIOPE.
XII. URANIA.
XIII. TERSICORE. (*Terpsichore*).
XIV. ERATO.
XV. POLIMNIA (*Polyhymnia*).
XVI. TALIA. (*Thalia*).
XVII. MELPOMENE.
XVIII. EUTERPE.

XIX. CLIO.
XX. APOLLO.

XXI. GRAMMATICA— Grammar.
XXII. LOICA—Logic.
XXIII. RHETORICA — Rhetoric.
XXIV. GEOMETRIA — Geometry.
XXV. ARITHMETICA— Arithmetic.
XXVI. MUSICHA—Music.
XXVII. POESIA—Poetry.
XXVIII. PHILOSOFIA — Philosophy.
XXIX. ASTROLOGIA— Astrology.
XXX. THEOLOGIA—Theology.

XXXI. ILIACO—Astronomy.
XXXII. CHRONICO — Chronology.

PLATE XV

C | ARITMETICA · XXV · | ZS

ARITHMETICA.
(Jeu de Mantegna, Brit. Museum.)

ARITMETRICA · XXVI ·

ARITHMETIC
(Der da Montagna, Belt. Mitando)

XXXIII. Cosmico—Cosmology.

XXXIV. Temperancia—Temperance.

XXXV. Prudencia—Prudence.

XXXVI. Forteza — Fortitude.

XXXVII. Justicia—Justice.

XXXVIII. Charita—Charity.

XXXIX. Speranza—Hope.

XL. Fede—Faith.

XLI. Luna—the Moon.

XLII. Mercurio — Mercury.

XLIII. Venus—Venus.

XLIV. Sol—the Sun.

XLV. Marte—Mars.

XLVI. Jupiter—Jupiter.

XLVII. Saturno—Saturn.

XLVIII. Octava Spera — the 8th Sphere.

XLIX. Primo Mobile — the Chief Agent.

L. Prima Causa—the First Cause.

We are here a long way removed from the symbolic figures of the ancient tarot. These savour of the philosophy of Campanella and Vanini, and no longer of that of ancient Egypt. The Eighth Sphere! the First Cause! — these certainly are something new in a game of cards. But the delicacy of their execution is no less remarkable than the strangeness of their designs. It has been said they are too beautiful and therefore too dear, too large moreover, and evidently not intended for colouring, and therefore not playing cards at all. But what are they then? M. Leber considers them merely a "Jeu de Fantasie," a capricious effort of artistic genius, one of the many which followed the discovery of printing. They are beautiful designs suggested by the tarot pack, and nothing more.

M. Duchesne hazards a guess, which, guess as it is, should not be passed by.* "There are five classes," he says, "in these cards: the different grades of society, from I. to X. inclusive; the Muses and Apollo, from XI. to XX. the Sciences, from XXI. to XXX.; the Virtues, from XXXI. to XL. (one would think from the list, however, that the three first items should be included in the former category); and the Planets, from XLI. to L. Here we have the primitive *naïbi*—the ancient tarot in all its simplicity—a unique specimen of the primitive type of packs of cards."

They are, however, quite significant of the period—a perfect reflex of the philosophy of the time.

Of the cards of a more recent date, and which bring us more towards the sixteenth century, are those engraved on copper by Virgil Solis. These have no knights, but have the pip cards from the ace to the ten. There was no lack of astonishing

* In other respects M. Duchesne displays much acuteness in his remarks. He gives us the date of these cards, 1485, which he has discovered on the title of one of the copies—which, however, is called by Bartsch (t. xxii., p. 720) the earliest—bearing the figure named Arithmetica. In the other series, which is the more ancient (perhaps as early as 1470), the corresponding figure appears to be counting money. (*Vide* Plate XV.)

PLATE XVII.

PLATE XVI

KNAVE OF LEAVES.
(German Pack in Paris Library, *circa* 1511.)

conceits in those fantastic times : some were
more or less indelicate, some grave and decorous,
others utterly unintelligible. The marks of suits
were equally various. Those which Solis adopted
were lions, parrots, apes, and peacocks. In some
packs, the knights are entirely missing; but, in
almost all, the ladies supply their place, with
the sole exception of the Spanish.

No. xiv. of M. Leber's catalogue describes
thirty cards, wood-cut outlines, and painted
in gold, silver, and colours, of an Italian tarot
pack of the sixteenth century, whereon are personified the four great monarchies of antiquity,
according to Bullet's notion.

No. xviij. contains an account of certain
German cards of the first half of the same
century. It is a complete pack of forty-eight
pieces, with the usual German marks : king,
queen, two valets, and eight numeral cards in
each suit, there being neither aces nor tens.
These also are wood-engravings, and form part
of a German satiric poem against card-players,
published at Strasburg in 1545.

Of a very similar character, and with the same
suits, is a pack of which we engrave three examples (Plates XVI., XVII., and XVIII.), originally
consisting of fifty-two cards. Thirty-six of these

are preserved in the Bibliothèque Impériale, and facsimiles are given in the *Jeux de Cartes Tarots et de Cartes Numerales*, fol. 92—95. Chatto, who engraves two other specimens, says that their date is 1511, and that on the deuce of acorns are the letters F. C. Z., the two first being probably the initials of the artist who made the designs (*zeichnet*). On the deuce of leaves are two shields suspended from a tree; the one bearing two swords in saltire, and the other the arms of the house of Saxony, as they are frequently found on the productions of Lucas Cranach, whose style indeed, the figures, which are drawn with much spirit and freedom, resemble.*

The three of bells (Plate XVII.) is a good specimen of the grotesque spirit of the time. These two Xantippes, in all the engrossing excitement of a scratching-match, forcibly recall to us the style of the old caricatures.

Plate XVIII., according to Singer, represents the itinerant barber, accompanied by his squirrel, and bearing about him the implements of his pro-

* On a third shield, at the bottom of the same card, are a pick-axe and mallet in saltire, resembling that on Dr. Stukeley's cards (*vide suprà*, p. 93), and probably the mark of the card-maker.

PLATE XVII

THREE OF BELLS.
(Saxon Pack, Paris Library, *circa* 1511.)

PLATE XVIII

KNAVE OF HEARTS.
(Saxon Pack, Itinerant Barber, 1511.)

fession.* His costume is rather more gay and
fantastic than that of our knights of the shaving-
brush, but it should seem to have been the common one of his fraternity at that period, for in
the curious and beautiful *Book of Trades* by Jost
Ammon, published at Frankfort, in 1564, is a de-
lineation of a barber's shop, in which the principal
operator is attired in a similar manner.†

Some confusion is apt to arise from the adoption of the word *tarot*, when it is applied, as it is
by Leber, to packs which contain no *atouts*, which
are, nevertheless, the especial characteristics of a

* One of the specimens of this pack given by Chatto—the
second coat-card of the suit of leaves—represents another trade,
that of a scribe. Hence Mr. C. infers that they were designed to
answer a double purpose, not only as an amusement, but also as
vehicles of instruction as *prints*,—an idea more fully developed
by Murner, as will be seen in our next chapter.

† The best of all the German fanciful cards of the sixteenth
century, are those engraved on wood from the designs of Jost
Ammon. These were published at Nuremberg, in a small quarto
volume, in 1588, and seem to have been designed to inculcate
the superiority of industry and learning over idleness and drunkenness. The subjects are treated for the most part humourously,
the four suits being books, printers' balls, wine-pots, and drinking cups, with Latin and German verses by H. S. de Gustrou.[1]
Singer has engraved and described specimens of the most interesting of them, and there is a copy in the British Museum.

[1] In the *Bibliotheca Universalis* of Conrad Gesner, Tiguri, 1548, under
the article *de ludis*, mention is made of cards with sentences from the
ancient poets, and of others with French verses, and with sentences from the
Bible in German, as being sold by Wechel at Paris.

tarot pack properly so called.   The example lately
quoted, with its double valet, and which, though
evidently complete, contains neither ace nor ten, is
to all intents and purposes, a pack of the modern
sort.   The new principle introduced by the French
was becoming general, but, as may be easily imagined, would not at that time, be subject to fixed
laws of any kind.

Pattern, number of honours, materials even,
were all a matter of uncertainty.   Breitkopf possessed a piquet-pack of silver plates, on which the
designs were chased and gilt.   Of these, he says:
" To judge by their style, these were the production of an artist in the Low Countries, in the sixteenth century."   And he adds: " De La Vega,
in his *History of the Conquest of Florida*, tells us
that the soldiers in that expedition played with
leathern cards."

The use of the word *Trappola* (which is properly the title of a game), by some writers, is also
liable to misconception.   In the British Museum,
there is nearly a complete pack of the cards which
Breitkopf, in his *Enquiry*, &c., calls " German
Piquet Cards of the fifteenth century with Trappola characters;" by which he apparently means,
such as have the Southern marks of suits, in the
same manner as our present cards are often dis-

tinguished as French Piquet Cards. The complete pack appears to have consisted of fifty-two,
each suit containing king, queen, and valet or
knave, with ten numeral cards. They are generally ascribed to Israel Van Mecken, a native of
Bocholt, in the Netherlands; and the substitu-
tion of the suit of *pomegranates* in them for that
of money, is possibly in compliment to the Spanish dynasty, which assumed the *Granada*, or
pomegranate, as one of its badges, on the conquest of the kingdom and city of that name by
Ferdinand and Isabella in 1497.* The pomegranate also appears as a mark of a suit, with
roses, leaves, and flowers, on a pack which bears
the monogram of Erhardt Schön, who flourished
about 1530. Specimens of these are given by
Singer in his *Researches*, from Mr. Ottley's collection, bearing fantastic groups of figures, but
they are of inferior execution to the pack of 1511.
Leber, also, describes certain German fanciful
cards of the earlier half of the seventeenth century, with the suits of leaves, acorns, pomegranates, and roses.

* See four beautiful copper-plate facsimiles in Chatto, *Facts
and Speculations*, p. 226. The baton on one of these resembles
the heraldic bearing called the " ragged staff," but in the later
examples, it is more like that borne by a beadle or a London
footman. For the local names of these cards, see chap. xii.

The so-called Trappola cards of this period present none of the grotesque imagery which is characteristic of the German style. None are known of earlier date than the sixteenth century, and these are coloured with the same simplicity as the early German cards, the colours being red and green, and laid on by means of pierced patterns or stencils, in a similar manner. Some, from the collection of Mr. Douce, are described by Singer as being composed of three pieces of paper pasted together, that forming the back being wider than the others, so that the edges when brought over the front, formed a border. The reverse bears some device, or is simply *tarotté* or diapered.* The marks of suits, cups, or rather chalices, of elegant form, batons and swords, grouped or interlaced, and coins, are the same as in the numerical cards of the modern tarots, and probably identical to a great extent with those of the original type: but the number of cards follows the French reduction, the principle of which remaining unaltered in the country of its invention, speedily superseded in Italy, during this century, not merely the German

* The ace of *danari* in this pack bears a legend, unfortunately partially illegible, IESI . FECE ...... ANTONIO ZA ..., but which is probably the name of the artist, and place of manufacture.

importations, but even the miniatures of Florentine and Venetian art.

Much more might be said, in continuing the
history of the more recent career of the ancient
type to our days—of its connection with the
science and art and international relations of the
period, in which direction the subject is capable
of almost infinite extension; but the limits we
have set ourselves compel us to abstain from
giving any part of it more than its due promin-
ence. We shall content ourselves therefore, with
giving, for the consideration of such of our readers
as may desire to look further into the subject, a
brief description of some peculiar varieties of
these later cards, which, as they present some
curious and suggestive facts, it is well not to
omit, but interspersing our own remarks as sparingly as possible, for fear of wearying the patience of the rest.

1. German Cards, (Century XVII.), with Southern
   or Trappola marks of suits, but with Roses
   substituted for Deniers or Money.

   These cards were brought from Germany by Mr. Quaritch; when complete, they were fifty-two in number—
   king, knight (on horseback), and valet, and ten numeral
   cards in each suit. The colours are red, blue, green, and
   yellow; costumes pseudo-classic, and of very inferior execution. On the backs of some which have lost the stiffening

layers, are honours of the bell and acorn suits in outline, of far better execution, and in the costume of the time; but when perfect, the reverse of each card was *tarotté*.

The ace of batons bears a scroll with the imprint, GEDRVCKT .. VON MICHAEL SCHMIT IN BVCHHOLZ.*

2. Tarots, presumed to be Bohemian, Cent. XVII.

Complete pack (less two) of seventy-eight coloured cards. On one of the numerals is the word PRAGUE; the designs and emblems are nevertheless, indicative of an Italian origin.

The envelope bears a German inscription, of which the following is a translation: " Scarce pack of tarots, No. 2. of which, bears the satirical figure for which its author was beheaded." This figure is the *Papess*, or Pope Joan, who, notwithstanding this, is to be found on some modern packs —aye, even in Italy itself. (Leber's *Catal.*)

3. Italian Tarots, Cent. XVIII.

Usual marks of suits. Sixteen honours, kings, queens, chevaliers, and valets, with titles in *French*. This pack, incomplete, is in the possession of Mr. Quaritch, but as the *atouts* which remain correspond exactly with those described by Court de Gebelin, there was no doubt the full number of seventy-eight. The costume is of the early part of the eighteenth century. The backs are printed in blue, with a figure of Diana with hound and javelin. Imprint, FAB . IN TRIESTE.

---

* This can hardly be identical with Bocholt, mentioned p. 129 in connection with Israel Van Mecken. On the wrapper of these cards is a MS. note in German, to this effect: "From information obtained from the cardmaker Peterjan, in Annaberg, who is almost the only one of this trade there, we learn that in the year 1654 Heinrich Michael Schmidt, sen., and in 1675 Michael Schmidt, jun., were admitted as members into the cardmakers' guild; but there have been none of the name since. The pattern is singular and unknown both in Buchholz and in Annaberg, while the cards made in an earlier period, correspond exactly with those in common use."

4. Italian Cards. Maker's name, Guillaut, Naples.

Same marks of suits as preceding. Complete pack of forty. Twelve honours, kings, chevaliers, and valets : no queens, in the Spanish fashion. Twenty.eight numeral cards, ace to seven inclusive. (Leber's *Catal.*)

5. German Tarots, double-headed.

French marks of suits: *hearts*, &c. This is very remarkable in a pack of the German tarot. Twenty-two atouts, &c., full number. (*Id.*)

6. Swiss Cards. Maker's name, Hunter, Schaff-hausen.

Marks of suits, German mixed : acorns, bells, coats of arms, and flowers. Twelve honours, kings, valets, and clowns. Twenty-four numeral cards: ace, deuce, six, seven, eight, and nine. This remarkable pack consists of thirty-six cards, complete. (*Id.*)

7. German Proverb-Cards, manufactured at Leip-sic.

German marks of suits : kings, valets, and clowns. Twenty-four numeral cards : deuce, six, seven, eight, nine, and ten. (*Id.*)

8. Catalan Tarots, manufactured at Barcelona.

Southern marks of suits : *swords*, &c. Twelve honours, kings, knights, and knaves ; no queens. Thirty-six numeral cards: ace to the nine. These are incorrectly termed tarots in M. Leber's *Catalogue*. It is a pack on the French principle, of which the elimination of the symbolic atouts is the main characteristic, but with the costumes and emblems belonging to the ancient type, which is remarkable.

9. Portuguese pack.   Cent. XVII.

Specimens of these, which appear to have been executed in 1693, are preserved in the Bibliothèque Impériale. Chatto, who has engraved the four knights, which are respectively marked CB, CC, CD, and CS, for *Caballo* of *Bastone*, *Coppe*, *Danari*, and *Spade*, remarks, that the attributes and general appearance are of a very Oriental or Indian character. Twelve honours—kings, *queens*, (the Portugal of that time was gallant, it seems), and knights,—no valets ; forty numeral cards, ace to the ten ; making in all fifty-two pieces. This, also, is a remarkable pack.

These few notes will sufficiently display the changes which in the course of time have taken place in the original type.   The following are some additional notes on some curious modern specimens in the Cabinet des Estampes, by M. Boiteau d'Ambly.

10. " Tarots fins faites par J. Jerger, fabriquant carts à Besançon," seventy-eight pieces complete.

It is a list of the atouts of this pack, which was given at our first mention of the tarot subject (p. 14, col. 2). The orthography of the legends is in accordance with that of the title, e.g. *l'Etoille, le Jugemant, la Roux de Fortune, le Charioz, l'Imperatris*. Perhaps, as the game is not in use among the French, and the cards were manufactured for exportation, the worthy *cartier* judged it a work of supererogation to initiate foreigners into the niceties of his own language. The back of these cards is rose-marbled. This, and all other ornament on the reverse of modern cards, is now styled *le tarotage*.

11. A similar pack, by Jean Noblet, of the faubourg Saint-Germain, Paris.

The orthography of this pack is so abominable, that it has somewhat the appearance of a trick played off by the maker upon foreign buyers.

12. Another specimen, which bears the following:

On the ace of deniers: " Pere sainct faît moy yustice de ce vielart ma . E . Baga . amoureux . de ceste . Dame . qvy . soit crye . a son de trompe . par tout le monde de par le Pape la Papesse Lanpereur Linperatrice le Soleil." On the deuce of cups, " La Lune, les Etoilles, la Foudre. Prins a Force qvy soit pendu et . trauvay au Diable." On the deuce of deniers, " IAQUES VIEVIL, à Paris."

The meaning of this unintelligible stuff we cannot possibly divine.

13. Spanish pack, manufactured at Paris.

The envelope is of a very ornate character, and of a delicate rose tint. On the label are the excise stamps:

INTÉRIEUR   and on the left   PORTRAIT / ETRANGER   32.

Future historians, if at least they turn their attention to cards, will construct some wonderful hypothesis upon this. Listen to the advertisement of the maker: *Juego Completo Naypes superfinos de la Fabrica S^{RA} Vindad Morin* (the *Senora* Morin indeed!) *Pasadizo de la Trinida Patio de los Azulejos par la Calle Greneta, No.* 33, *communicando par la Calle Saint-Deonis, No.* 268, *en Paris.*" Amazingly precise directions these, to find so villanous a locality!

14. Italian Tarot-Pack, marked *Matteo*.

The ace of deniers is a coin with this inscription: *Filippus, Dei gratiá, Hispaniarum Rex.*

15. Pack of Tarots, with the Southern marks of suits.

Swords are here replaced by sabres. The value of the honours is indicated by letters, as in No. 9. R.C. (*Roi de Coupes*), R.D. (*Roi de Deniers*), R.B. (*Roi de Bâtons*), R.S. (*Roi de Sabres*), &c. This nomenclature is indicative of French manufacture.

16. Pack of Tarots, with the address, Jehan Hémau, Æspinal.

Marks of suits, acorns, fruits, flowers, shields of arms. The figures are very fantastic.

17. Tarots, with the arms of Bavaria, printed by And. Ben. Gool. Date, early part of XVIII. century.

These cards are longer and of more graceful form than those in common use, and are evidently designed for the cabinets of *virtuosi*. They bear a set of little groups, spiritedly coloured, and the subjects, as far as may be, explained by inscriptions in German. It is difficult to describe them otherwise than generally, as chariots all garlanded with foliage and flowers, with ribbons and spangles of all sorts, in which a host of miniature characters are drinking and singing, habited in the Louis Quinze style, with chubby faces, lips of scarlet, and eyes of transparent blue. These make up the twenty-one symbolic atouts. Our old friend the fool is at the head of the game. The figures of the numeral cards are wanting.

The only conclusion to be arrived at, in addition to what has been already advanced, may be thus briefly stated :—From the moment of the invention of the French game, the elder variety, losing its pre-eminence, became the sport of fancy. It exists—but altered in every possible way, and constantly losing ground.

The French game, on the contrary, has continually attained an increasing degree of regularity and success.

X.

MODERN HISTORY OF FRENCH AND ENGLISH CARDS.

WE return now to the history of the French cards, which, as presenting greater affinities with those in common use, will be more interesting to the general reader. It will be understood that what we include under this title, is that reduction of the original tarot-pack which was first invented in France, and subsequently adopted in some other countries, that is to say, the series formed by the four suits, the distinctive marks of which, though differing in name, are identical in form and colour with our own. Each of these suits, or colours, as the French call them, is composed of three figured cards—king, queen, and valet or knave—and a number of " pip " cards which varies, but is never less than five—the ace, ten, nine, eight, and seven —as in the piquet game now played ; and not exceeding ten, which is the number required for the original piquet in use up to the eighteenth century, including the six, five, four, trey, and deuce. In all, thirty-two cards at least, fifty-two at most.

The custom of giving names to the figured cards is peculiar to France ;—those anciently conferred are as follows ·

Suit.	Kings.	Queens.	Valets.
Cœur (Hearts)	Charles or Charlemagne	Judith	Lahire
Carreau (Diamonds)	Cæsar	Rachel	Hector
Trefle (Clubs)	Alexander	Argine	Lancelot*
Pique (Spades)	David	Pallas	Hogier

and though not uniformly observed, they have been reimposed in modern times. The four kings are supposed to represent the four ancient monarchies of the Jews, Greeks, Romans, and Franks ; and the queens, Wisdom, Birth, Beauty, and Fortitude. In some packs, Esther, as an impersonation of piety, is substituted for Rachel.

The adoption of this entirely novel organization, necessarily involves the idea of a new game.

* See p. 81.

The French would hardly have effected such an alteration in the implements of play, unless a corresponding reform in the method of playing had been already in progress. It is assumed, therefore, that the alteration was consequent on the invention of *piquet*, and for this reason the cards we have described are distinguished by writers on the subject, as Piquet, or French piquet-cards, to which variety we have now to confine our remarks.

It is unfortunate that we have so few examples of sufficiently early date for our guidance. Of the insignificant packs of the eighteenth century, we have an abundance; but only very few of the seventeenth, and hardly any which approach in importance the valuable relic which we have designated as the " Pack of the time of Charles VII."

To the English features of certain cards nearly allied to these last, we have already drawn attention; but whether the French type maintained its position continuously and uninterruptedly in this country, to the latter part of the sixteenth century, to the exclusion of other varieties, is difficult to decide.

The Hon. Daines Barrington, in his paper in the eighth volume of the *Archæologia* on the " Antiquity of Card-playing in England," maintains the probability, that cards of the Spanish type, and bearing the marks of cups, money, clubs, and swords (of the Spanish names of the last two, *Bastos* and *Espadas*, our clubs and spades are certainly, of the one, a translation, and of the other, a corruption), preceded the adoption of French cards in this country; and he endeavours to connect them with the arrival of Philip II. and his suite, though an equally plausible argument might be founded on the marriage of Henry VIII. with a Spanish princess, Catharine of Arragon, of whom it is recorded by Sir William Forrest,* that in her youth

> " With stoole and with needyl she was not to seeke,
> And other practiseinges for ladyes meete,
> To pastyme at tables, tick tacke, or gleeke,
> Cardis and dyce," &c.

Mr. Chatto, in support of this assumed priority of the Spanish cards, remarks, that the knave or jack of our popular game, the meaning of which he defines to be " a servant of low condition," has more affinity in character with the Spanish *sota*, or the Italian *fante*, than with the French *valet*, which in the earliest French cards always bears the name of some person in romance or history. This sense of knave however, which

* Warton, *History of English Poetry*, vol. iii., p. 311.

is curiously parallel to the modern sense of *valet*, like the still earlier one of "man-child," soon became obsolete,* and the word came to be used exclusively to donote a cheat or dishonest person. According to the same author, the original of the English term Jackanapes was in all probability JACK-A-NAIPES, *i. e.*, *a buffoon in a particoloured dress*, like a knave on cards.†

We shall hereafter discuss the notices of games of the sixteenth century which occur in ancient writers, among which *primero* and other Spanish games are included ; but it by no means follows that these games were necessarily played with Spanish cards. We have evidence indeed, of a contrary practice, for Barrington describes a

---

* Compare note, p. 95. The use of the word knave as a term of reproach, may be traced as early as the time of Queen Mary, as in the following curious quotation from the *Description des Royaulmes d'Angleterre, par Estienne Perlin*, in 1558: " Les gens de ceste nation hayent à mort les Françoys, comme leur vielz enemis, et du tout nous appellant *France chenesve* (knave), *France dogue*, qui est à dire, maraultz François, chiens François, et autrement nous appellant *or-son* (whoreson) *villains*, filz de putains."—See an article " On the Costume of Coate Cards," by J. Adey Repton, in the *Gentleman's Magazine* for November, 1843.

† See a very interesting discussion in his *Facts and Speculations*, p. 230. The earliest use of this appellation occurs in a ballad in the British Museum, date about 1450, where Jac Napes is applied as a term of reproach to the unfortunate Duke of Suffolk, then lately murdered.

picture by Zucchero, formerly belonging to Lord Falkland, representing the great Lord Burleigh playing at cards with three other noblemen, in which the incident attempted to be described, is the winning point in the game of primero, and he expressly states, that their cards are marked as at present, and differ from those of more modern times only by being narrower and longer.

It is certain, however, that at a later period, the cards used in England, as also our modern cards, were derived from the French type.

John Northbrooke, in his *Treatise against Dicing, Dauncing*, &c., published about 1577, writes thus: "And therefore to conclude, I say with that good father, St. Cyprian, the playe at cardes is an invention of the deuill, which he found out that he might the easier bring in ydolatrie amongst men. For the kings and coate cardes *that we vse nowe*, were in old times the images of idols and false gods, which they that would seeme christians, have changed into Charlemaine, Launcelot, Hector, and such lyke names, bicause they would not seeme to imitate their idolatrie therein, and yet maintaine the playe itselfe the very inuention of Satan, the deuill, and woulde so disguise the mischeife vnder the cloake of such gaye names."*

In the curious satirical poem, *The Knave of Harts his Supplication to the Card-makers*, by Samuel Rowlands, 1612, the knave complains of the old-fashioned attire to which he and his fellows were condemned, and expressly attributes its origin to the French:

> " All other knaves are at their owne free-wille
> To brave it out, and follow fashion still
> In any cut, according to the time ;
> But we poore knaves (I know not for what crime)
> Are kept in pie-bald suites, which we have worne
> Hundreds of years ; this hardly can be borne.
> The idle-headed Frenche devis'd us first,
> Who of all fashion-mongers is the worst ;
> For he doth change farre oftner than the moone ;
> Dislikes his morning suite in th' after-noone.
> The English is his imitating ape,
> In every toy the tailer's sheares can shape,
> Comes dropping after as the divell entices,
> And pulleth on the Frenchman's cast devices :
> Yet wee (with whom thus long they both have plaid)
> Must weare the suites in which we first were made."

The terms of this "Supplication" would certainly seem to apply only to cards manufactured in England, but the relative proportions of these

---

* The treatise *De Aleatoribus*, anciently, though erroneously, attributed to S. Cyprian, is of too high antiquity to refer to cards. A contemporary French writer is quoted above, p. 29, as holding the same opinion.

in use, and of the imported foreign cards, is like
the nationality of the latter, by no means
certain.

There is evidence, we have seen, of the existence of both descriptions as early as 1463, and
from that time, and especially between the reign
of Henry VIII., when there is abundant testimony that they were everywhere used from the
palace to the cottage, and 1615, when a stricter
prohibition against the future importation of cards
was issued, (as the art of making them was then
brought into perfection in this country), large
quantities must have been brought over from
foreign parts, for which the vicinity of the
French coast afforded great facilities. * Herbert
notices "a patent to Raffe Bowes and Thomas
Beddingfield, Esquires, to import playing cards
into this kingdom," A.D. 1571, and Barrington gathers from a proclamation of Elizabeth,
and another of her successor, that they did

Singer, p. 223, &c. Up to 1558 Calais remained an English
port, and Henry VIII in his thirty-second year, appointed an
officer to regulate Plays there, among which cards are expressly
mentioned.—See Rymer, *Fœdera*, xiv., 707. The importation
of cards, however, being always illegal here, and their export,
even from France, forbidden by an *ordonnance* of 1605 ; the
continuance of the trade shows it to have been contraband, but
winked at by Government for reasons of its own.—See the
discussion on Sir R. Coningsby's patent, *infra*. p. 162.

not make many cards in England at that period.*

Whether home-manufactured, however, or imported, we may conclude that the cards in use in the time of "bluff king Hal," were not very superb performances, if we may judge from the price they sold at, which we find specified in a very curious passage of Roger Ascham's *Toxophilus*, first printed in 1545 : " A man no shoter, (not longe agoo) wolde defende playing at cardes and dise, if it were honestly used, to be as honest a pastime as your shotinge : for he layed for him, that a man might pleye for a litle at cardes and dyse, and also a man might shote away all that euer he had. He sayd a payre of cardes cost not past ij.d, and that they neded not so moche reparation as bowe and shaftes, they wolde neuer hurte a man his hande, nor neuer weare his gere." And the Continental "figure" would appear to have been equally reasonable, for Albert Durer in the journal which he kept during his visit to the Netherlands in 1521, notes that he bought there half a dozen packs for seven stivers.

* There is, nevertheless, in the Society of Antiquaries' Library a patent to Edward Darcy for cards, at the close of Elizabeth's reign, as also a copy of the prohibition, and the Lord Treasurer's letter for 5s. to be paid to him for every gross of cards, dated October 29, 1615.

The grotesque representations of the human figure which occur on the French and English court cards, ancient and modern, are evidently derived from the rude illuminations and woodcuts of the fifteenth and sixteeenth centuries. It would be vain, however, to attempt to fix by costume only, the exact date of any particular example, as the design would probably be often intentionally archaic, and might present considerable anachronism in its details.

The " Valery " knave in our Frontispiece, reminds us forcibly, of the Squire in the Canterbury Tales, who is described by Chaucer, as wearing a short gaberdine, with sleeves long and wide, of the kind probably, which Camden calls a *court-pie* ; his dress was also embroidered,

> "As it were a mede,
> Alle fulle of freshe flowres white a rede."

These sleeves, commonly called *pokys*, were worn alike by masters and servants, and are frequently satirised by the writers of the day. The Monk of Evesham says they were denominated the "devil's receptacles," for what ever could be stolen was popped into them. As a similar nuisance has prevailed in our day, it may be as well to mentions that the Monk complains, that as the servants were bringing up pottage, sauces, &c.,

"their sleeves would go into them and have the first taste." Occleve, who flourished in Henry IVth's time deprecates their use by servants, for

> "What help shall he
> Whose sleeves encumbrous so side trail
> Do to his lord,—he may not him avail ;
> In such a case he is but a woman ;
> He may not stand him in stead of a man
> His arms two have right enough to do,
> And somewhat more, his sleeves up to hold."

The flat bonnet, frequently plumed, and notched or embattled on the edge, and having an under cap of embroidered velvet fittting close to the head, with which Mr. Chatto's four knaves, as well as those of our modern suits are decorated, is common about the end of the fifteenth century, in the illuminations of the time.

The nether habiliments of these personages, the disparity of which, renders the term *pair* wholly inadmissible, afford a good illustration of the lamentation which Chaucer puts in the mouth of the parson, concerning the "horrible disordinate scantiness of clothing, as be these cut slops or *hanselines*," (apparently a punning German rendering of *jack-et*) that through their shortness, he says, and the "wrapping of their hose, which are departed of two colours, white and red, white and blue, white and black, or black and red, make the wearer seem as though the fire of S. Anthony, or some such mischance, had cankered and consumed half their bodies."*

That this fashion of Chaucer's time was retained on cards two hundred years later, is evident from Samuel Rowlands' *Knave of Harts*, before quoted, who complains in the same strain :

" My sleeves are like some morris-daucing fellow,
    My stockings, idiot-like, red, greene, and yellow :
    My breeches like a paire of lute-pins be,
    Scarce buttock-roome, as every man may see.
    Like three-penie watchmen three of us doe stand,
    Each with a rustie browne-bill in his hand ;
    And Clubs he holds an arrow, like a clowne,
    The head-end upward and the feathers downe."†

The lappets which fall on each side of the face of the Queens, the gowns cut square at the neck, and the rich girdles with long pendants in front, are in fact a rude representation of the dress of the ladies of the reign of Henry VII., and remind us in some particulars of the fashions of the last few years.   The crown, or coronet, however, as being placed at the back of the head, may

* See Planché. *History of British Costume*, p. 194, &c.
† See the illustrations in the Percy Society's reprint of *Rowlands' Tracts*, edited by E. F. Rimbault, Esq., 1843 ; a comparison of which with Mr. Chatto's knaves, will demonstrate the period during which this particular type was in existence.

be traced, according to Mr. Repton, as late as the reign of Elizabeth or James.*

Plate XIX. is a copy of one of the French figured cards of the sixteenth century,—it represents the queen of hearts, Judith, here called Judic, or on other specimens, Juclie. She holds a flower in her right hand, like the *dame de pique* of the pack of Charles VIIth's time.

This is one of the rare early cards of the manufacture of Le Cornu, which are the prototypes of those in present use. The extent indeed, to which the ancient features have been preserved is remarkable; the same quaint antiquity of costume, and the same large and clumsy figures, so clumsy as to suggest to some a Chinese origin. The faces only have been a little modernized, which is a great mistake, for our kings and queens, with their trim physiognomies, carry off their conventional attire with far less propriety and character than the ancient examples, in which, all is in harmony, costume and countenance alike.

The Judith here represented is certainly a very different personage from her of the Jewish history; a flower replaces the uplifted blade,

* See paper before alluded to, *Gentleman's Magazine*, vol. xx. new series, p. 471.

PLATE XIX

QUEEN OF HEARTS.
(French "Coat" Cards, Sec. xvi.)

PLATE XX

QUEEN OF SPADES.
(Crescent Pack, of Ancient Date.)

with which she slaughtered Holofernes. [Vid. Pl. IV.]

Plate XX. offers a design possibly more ancient, but there is nothing characteristic, beyond its unusual simplicity and want of distortion, by which to fix its exact date. It belongs to a pack in which *crescents* are substituted for the diamond suit, a variation for which no explanation has been attempted.

The most celebrated of the French card-makers of the sixteenth century, is Jean Volay, who practised his art at the close of the reign of Francis I. (1515-47). Specimens of his cards are extant both in M. Leber's collection, and in the Bibliothèque Impériale, the figures clumsy and ugly, and their design barbarous in the extreme. Like Julien Rosnet, Pierre Leroux, Guillaume Guérin, Claude Astier, J. Gayrand, and other card-makers of this period, his productions embraced both varieties, piquet cards, and tarots, or cards of the Southern type.* A great deal of unnecessary discussion might have been spared, by attention to this fact, in the

---

* To these names of old French card-makers, we may add those of Pierre de Trois, R. Le Cornu, David Dubois, and Blatteron, who manufactured cards in the sixteenth and seventeenth centuries. Cards of Louis XIIIth's time, bear the maker's names Leblond, François, and P. Delettre.

matter of a curious relic of this maker, first
described by Barrington in the *Archæologia*.
This was a wood-block, with which he had been
furnished by Mr. Astle, and which had evidently
been designed for the purpose of stamping the
envelopes of cards for the Spanish market. The
impression bears on the edges, the arms of
Castile and Leon, and the four emblems, club,
sword, cup, and money, which are characteristic
of the South. The inscription is a compound of
Spanish and old French, and reads thus, 𝕮𝖆𝖗𝖙𝖆𝖘
𝖋𝖎𝖓𝖓𝖆𝖘 𝖋𝖆𝖎𝖈𝖙𝖊𝖘 𝖕𝖆𝖗 𝕵𝖊𝖍𝖆𝖓 𝖁𝖔𝖑𝖆𝖞, in coarse black
letter characters, and below, in ordinary letters,
the name of " Edward Warman," probably the
English vendor of the cards, an insertion into
the original block.

Barrington, of course, instantly seized on this,
as proof decisive of his Spanish hypothesis,
and by a strange blunder in reading the conclu-
ding sentence, "Je. Hauvola y Edward Warman,"
arrived at the conclusion that this supposed *firm*
could not dispose of their cards "to advantage in
France, unless there was some appearance of their
having been originally brought from Spain,"
the name of Edward Warman being inserted at
a later period, in the room of a supposed former
partner of Jean Hauvola. Singer somewhat

gratuitously suggests, that the block is an English fabrication.*

The varieties of the French cards at this period, are indicative rather of the aspect of the times, than of the old conventional designs. The valets often appear in armour, and have generally a bellicose appearance. Little attention is paid to orthographical accuracy. Judic, (which was quite a windfall for Bullet, see p. 78) and Juclie appear indifferently, for Judith, Sezar for Cæsar, and Hector de *Trois*. It was a season of perpetual and bloody wars, and the persecution of the Huguenots was about repeating in France the religious contests which were then convulsing the rest of Christendom. Orthography would naturally be at a discount, and the card-knaves

---

* See *Archæologia* viii., p. 143; also Mr. Gough's paper, *Ib.*, p. *168, which states on the authority of Mr. Herbert, that a person of the name of Warman kept a stationer's shop in Bishopgate Street, or Norton Falgate, about fifty years before the date of his paper, that is about 1737 ; but that he, or any other person of that name, attempted to sail under false colours by manufacturing this block, or using it in his trade, upon the supposition that Spanish cards were at that period most in fashion for play, is disproved by the " Advertisement," quoted by Singer himself, p. 223, which shews that at the very commencement of the century, they were regarded merely as articles of curiosity :—

" Spanish cards lately brought from Vigo. Being pleasant to the eye by their curious colours and *quite different from ours,* may be had at 1s. a pack, at Mrs. Baldwin's, in Warwick Lane." *Postman, Dec.* 12-15, 1702.

must don the cuirass like the rest. See for example the valet, Plate XXI., who, from the monogram on the shield, and on the blade of his halbert, is a creation of this Maitre Jean Volay, all bristling in his iron shell, like some of the specimens of the crab-*genus* one sees in the cabinets of the curious; his eye glares under the brim of his helmet; evidently he has scented a Huguenot; that grip on the sword-hilt has a meaning,—blood will flow presently, to a certainty.

Charles IX. it appears, whose character is best described as one of their own authors has described the French nation to be,—half ape, half tiger,—was a poet; Charles IX., the *hero* of the massacre of St. Bartholomew, wrote verses to Ronsard; Ronsard was a pedant; a pedantic nomenclature became therefore the order of the day, and the long buried personages of the dead languages revived on cards.

The kings were called Augustus, or Constantine: sometimes Clovis or Solomon. The following is a pack of this period; Kings,—Jupiter, Bacchus, Priapus, and Crœsus; Queens,—Juno, Ceres, Flora, and Diana; Valets, — Mercury, Sylvanus, Æsculapius, and Actæon. Turn to Plate XXII., and behold the last. Possibly our readers are aware what has gained him that

PLATE XXI

KNAVE OF CLUBS.
(Jean de Volay, 1515-47.)

PLATE XXII

ACTE
ON.

KNAVE OF SPADES.
(From a Pack of the time of Charles IX.)

ornament of stag's horns on his head. Let not those, however, who are ignorant of mythology, arrive at too hasty a conclusion. *Honi soit qui mal y pense.* The classic authors tell us he was so unfortunate as to surprise the chaste Diana and her nymphs at the bath, whereat the enraged goddess forthwith changed him into a stag, and he was devoured by his own dogs!

The card-makers of Charles IXth's time have compensated the luckless hunter, for they have made him Diana's valet, without taking her opinion into consideration.*

In a pack of French cards of the time of Henry IV., (1589-1610), in the Bibliothèque Impériale, which bear the initials of Vincent Goyraud, all the court-cards are habited in the costume of the period. The kings are, Solomon, Augustus, Clovis, and Constantine; and the

* Plate XXII. The hunting-spear borne by this figure is very peculiar, it is, nevertheless, similar to that which one of Mr. Chatto's four knaves, Roland, carries in his hands. Both figures have also hunting-horns, and a rabbit appears in both as part of the design, in the one case issuing from a burrow, but here squatted in the figure of the *pique*, though one would have thought the *trèfle* more to his taste. This identity of details is remarkable. The portrait of Jean Volay's knave is evidently copied on one of four old English cards, which Singer engraves, p. 223. On the original card Actæons' robe is red, and all the rest yellow. His air is that of a simpleton, but as a work of art, this design is far above the average.

Queens, Elizabeth (Plate XXIII.), Dido, Clotilda, and Penthesilea. The four valets are engraved and described in Mr. Chatto's work, from which it appears that they are called respectively: Valet de Court, Valet de Chasse, Valet de Hedi (d'eté), and Valet de Noblesse. The first has his hat under his arm, the second a dog in a leash, the third bears a large flower, and the fourth a hawk on his fist.

A modernised costume appears to have been also adopted on the English cards, about the same date, for in Rowlands' *More Knaves Yet*, published after his *Knave of Harts*, the knaves of spades and diamonds express their acknowledgements in the following manner :

> " As now the honest printer hath bin kinde,
> Bootes and stockins to our legs doth finde,
> Garters, polonia heeles, and rose shooe-strings,
> Which, somewhat, us two knaves in fashion brings ;
> From the kne downeward legs are well amended,
> And we acknowledge that we are befrended,
> And will requite him for it as we can :
> A knave sometime may serve an honest man."

and the tract has a woodcut exhibiting the speakers in their improved habiliments.

In the seventeenth century, during the reign of Louis XIII., further alterations were introduced in the French cards, and in a more marked

PLATE XXIII

QUEEN OF HEARTS.
(Elizabeth, Pack of Henry IV., 1589-1610.)

PLATE XXIV

QUEEN OF HEARTS.
(Roxane, Louis XIII., Sec. xvii.)

manner under Louis XIV. The designs of the past century were banished, and the august personages of ancient history began to reappear, but with costumes of an entirely novel description. The Queens are habited in the fashion of Marie de Medicis—see, for example, "Roxane," the queen of hearts, in Plate XXIV.;—at a later period, they assumed the costume of Madame de Montespan, the violent and variable mistress of Louis XIV. The general design of the pack is preserved, but there is plenty of variety in the names, and in the devices superadded. On a dainty little pack of fifty-two pieces is the motto,

> " Vive le roy,
> Vive la reine,
> Et la cour ;
> J'éme l'amour."*

* This seems to have been a favourite device. Chatto mentions a similar pack of the reign of Louis XIII, engraved in the *Jeux de Cartes Tarots et de Cartes Numérales*, published by the Society of Bibliophiles Français, in which the names given to the kings, queens, and valets, are: *Cœur*—Alexandre, Pentasilee, Roland ; *Carreau*—Cirus Major, Roxane, Renault ; *Pique*—Jule Cæsar, Pompeia, Roger ; *Trèfle*—Ninus, Semiramis ; the name of the valet wanting, for the reason given above, p. 81, but bearing the mark and name of the card-maker, P. de Lestre. Each of the aces is surrounded with an ornamental border, and at the bottom of each, a portion of a slightly different version of the motto on our pack :

> " Vive le Roy,
> Vive la Reyne,
> J'ayme l'Amour,
> Et la Court."

John Dewey Library
Johnson State College
Johnson, Vermont 05656

Louis Quatorze, whose fastidious taste could not endure " les magots de Teniers," would hardly be more tolerant of the monstrosities of the old-fashioned cards — the Judiths, with naked cutlasses, and physiognomies of fish-wives ; and kings, whose rugged aspect would better befit an encampment of savages, than the court of the *Grand Monarque*. Equally abhorrent to this spirit of refinement, would be the packs fabricated in Flanders, on the model indeed of the French, but with characters coarsely reproduced from the canvas of Adrien Brauwer or Craësbaecke. You may see them assembled in miniature in the plates of the Amsterdam edition of the *Académie des Jeux*. In a pack of this kind, the queen of spades is called Barbara. The king of clubs, though wanting the mien, bears the name of K. David, the K. being of course the initial of Koning (king). The knave is a Dutch-built fellow with the rotund proportions of an old-fashioned Rotterdam skipper : his title is Pieter Mefferdt (Pl. XXV.), possibly the name of the card-maker, though the supposition of its being his own property is borne out by the cognate appellation of the king of diamonds, Capit. Melu.

For a long time we have lost sight of the miniature-painted cards. At court, and among

PLATE XXV

KNAVE OF CLUBS.
(Early Dutch Pack.)

PLATE XXV

KNAVE OF CLUBS

the aristocracy, a new style was introduced, in order to differ as widely as possible from the cheap cards in use by the vulgar.

In Henry IInd's time (circ. 1550) there was a pack embroidered on white satin, enriched with silver, at Florence, after the manner of those for which one of the Visconti of Milan paid 1500 pieces of gold, a *chef d'œuvre* of art, though slightly indecent in design; and under Louis XIV. they had cards engraved on mother-of-pearl, like those in the Leber collection, which were taken from a reversis-box in the saloons of Versailles.

Contemporaneously with these cards, transformed, or *deformed*, if you like, the old standard pack would no doubt maintain its ground with some few people, just as a professedly fantastic invention of a waggishly inclined card-maker would meet with an occasional purchaser. A pack exists, the figures of which bear the distinctive emblems of the card on their *stomachs*. It is ugly enough in all conscience. The aces are rendered in a very droll manner: that of Hearts, by a fencing master; Diamonds, by Lantimêche;* Clubs, by some other odd fish; and

* Lantimêche is a kind of goblin character among the French, who is accused of putting out candles, &c.

Spades by Thomas Diafoirus, the whimsical lover
in Moliere's comedy, *Le Malade Imaginaire*.
This pack is of rather modern date. *Vide* Pl.
XXVI.

The usual devices adopted in the fancy packs
were flowers grouped and garlanded among the
hearts and diamonds; the embellishments of
this nature were endless. An eight of *trèfle*, for
instance, might be formed by eight thistles, with
a little trefoil-leaf at the bottom to indicate the
suit, and a cock in the middle of the thistles,
to indicate————nothing at all.

Such innovations as these, would in all probability, lead the cardmakers by degrees to a
considerable departure from the original type,
were it not that old associations on the part of
the public, and the regulations which were from
time to time enacted, and the revival of the
statutes of their own brotherhood, would combine
to keep up the attachment to the ancient model.
Of the vagaries which did appear, passing events
would be the prompters,—the news of a victory,
the capture of Charleroy, for instance,—in the
twinkling of an eye some enterprising *Cartier*
would produce a patriotic commemoration, in
the shape of a pack of cards. As a specimen ;—A four of spades bears as many cannon

PLATE XXVI

KING OF HEARTS.
(Modern Comic Pack.)

PLATE XXVI

KING OF HEARTS.

furiously bombarding a fortress. In another pack, hearts are replaced by trumpets and drums; the diamonds, by flowers; clubs, by the lilies of France; and the spades, by standards and helmets.

The famous embassy of the pretended King of Siam in 1686, that mystification with which the courtiers of Lous XIV. so politely contrived to feed his vanity, has left its traces on the history of cards, for a pack exists signed G. D. *à Paris, rue de l'Arbre Sec*, which is adorned with the portraiture of the King of Siam. This pack however, is not contemporary, but a subsequent fabrication.

It is asserted in the *Naval History of Great Britain*, (8vo, 1779) that the right of importing foreign cards into England, notwithstanding the prohibitions against it, was a Government monopoly in the reign of Elizabeth; and this is to some extent corroborated, by a petition of the card-makers, date about 1614, in which they complain " of the innumerable masses of foreign cards that are daily suffered to be brought in, through the negligence of the executing of those statutes, by which, for 200 years past, was prohibited the bringing in " of all such made wares, chaffers, or merchandise, as the subjects of this realm could of themselves, make, furnish, and prepare," playing cards included, and they petition to have a seal or mark, and a keeper thereof, to whom they "desire in such sort to contribute, as neither the commodity shall be advanced in price, nor themselves hindered or grieved, as heretofore of late by some ...... *Patent or monopolist* we have been;" and in case of any cards being sold without this seal or mark, to have them forfeited, one half to the king, and the other to the discoverer, to the great benefit both of themselves, "as likewise the carvers, collar makers, paper-makers, starch makers, and sundry others which depend on this mystery."*

In 1629, the trade would seem to have attained sufficient importance for the establishment of a

* Accordingly, by a warrant dated 24 Nov. 1615, it appears that a patent was granted to Sir Richard Coningsby, Knt., Gentleman Usher to the King, by which, in consideration of £1800 due to him from the Crown, the surrender of letters-patent for the sole transportation of tin, granted him by the late Queen for true and faithful service, and the payment to King James of £200 rent, he was appointed to the office of viewing, searching, and sealing all cards made in the kingdom, and to receive five shillings for every gross, as had been offered by the card-makers, any cards proving false to be forfeited. This was made a great grievance by the haberdashers or dealers in small wares, who making common cause with the Company of French merchants, upon whom, in prejudice of the treaty as they pretended, a charge of five shillings was likewise levied on every gross brought in (making the whole duty seven shillings), obtained by petition to the Lords, a reference to the Judges, who reported that as

company, which was incorporated, by letters-patent of King Charles I., dated 22nd of October, under the title of "The Master, Wardens, and Commonalty of the Mistery of the Makers of Playing Cards, of the City of London,"* but two years later, according to Macpherson, (*Annals of Commerce*, i. 679), that needy monarch created a monopoly of playing cards, purchasing all of the Company, and selling them out at a much higher price, which probably greatly lessened their advantages over the foreign cards.

In 1638, it was ordered by proclamation that the latter, after the Michaelmas next, should be sealed at London, and packed in new bindings

the importation of cards was forbidden by the ancient statutes, the grant to Coningsby was illegal. The Lords thereupon suspended the patent, and ordered that the Lord High Treasurer do direct his letters to the farmers and officers of the port of London to give liberty to the said French merchants to take up such cards as they have now brought out of France, and are either at the custom house or on shipboard in the river, upon former and usual duties. Sir Richard however petitioned also, and the privy council being instructed by the King to take order for the maintenance of the prerogative, the further report of the judges pronounced against the opposition, and declared the king's grant maintainable by law.—*Lansdowne MSS.*, Brit. Mus. 160, No. 90, fol. 288-300, and 487, No. 27, p. 366.

* Singer, p. 226, *Rott. Pat.*, 4 Car. i. p. 22, No. 6. Maitland, *History of London*, p. 603, fol. 1739, says, "This corporation is governed by a master, two wardens, and eighteen assistants, but have neither livery, nor hall to transact their affairs in."

or covers; and in July, 1643, upon the complaint of several poor card-makers, setting forth that they were likely to perish by reason of divers merchants bringing playing cards into the kingdom contrary to the laws and statutes, they were again absolutely prohibited, by a committee appointed by Parliament for the Navy and Customs, and order given that the officers should seize all such cards, and proceed against the parties offending.

The era of the Civil war would naturally afford few materials for the history of playing cards; men's minds were intent on a sterner game, which is sufficiently described in the title of a pamphlet of the time, "*The Bloudy Game at Cards, as it was played by the King of Hearts and the rest of his suite, against the residue of the pack, shuffled at London, cut at Westminster, dealt at York, and played in the open field.*" Cutting and dealing were indeed in fashion, but it was a matter of hard blows and cloven heads, rather than passages of skill on the arena of a card-table.

The Roundheads of course, professed to eschew such carnal vanities; but with the characteristic hypocrisy of the times, a compromise was effected, by the invention of various descriptions of the "Scientiall Cards," which, though ostensibly devoted to the advancement of knowledge and good learning, would yet apparently enable the timeserver to enjoy a taste of the old leaven, while keeping up appearances with the party in power.

At the Restoration, the Puritan incubus being removed, cards regained their sway, with an increased accession of force, and a desperate rage for gambling, which has constituted the chief argument against their use ever since. The "Merry Monarch" and his licentious court spent their time in playing, drinking, and merry-making, as if these were the sole objects for which they had been sent into the world, and their motto was—

Pone merum et talos, pereat qui crastina curat !

There was, however, a large and influential class, who strove to arrest the profligacy which the example of the Court was spreading through the land ; and evidence of this spirit may doubtless be found in the attempts to popularize and extend the use in this country, of the Historical, Geographical, Heraldic, and other instructional cards, which we shall see, in the next chapter, had been introduced in France a little before this time. Though well meant, these could have made little impression on the demand for the ordinary packs ;

for the influx of foreign cards again compelled the
Cardmaker's Company to petition, in consequence
of which, a proclamation was issued, in the last
year of King Charles II. (1684), reiterating and
enforcing the prohibitions and penalties of former
statutes ; and for the better encouragement of the
English manufacture, an office was erected in
Silver Street, Bloomsbury, pursuant to His
Majesty's Letters Patent, for surveying and
sealing all cards of English fabric, that frauds in
their making might be prevented, and contraband
importations discovered.

The price of the cards was to be put upon
each pack, and the very best sort was to be *fourpence* a pack, as sold in London by the last
retailer, the others cheaper in proportion.*

Our limits will not allow us to enter upon
anything approaching a detailed description of
the political, satirical, and fantastic cards which
appeared in this century; but as indications of
the spirit of the times and connected in some

* See *Gazettes* for 1684-5, quoted by Singer, p. 228. By an
advertisement in one of them, it appears that there were
occasional sales of playing cards "by inch of candle," duly sur-
veyed by Richard Whitfield, Master Cardmaker ;—" the prises,
viz., the mattriss at 10s. 6d. per gross; fine mattrisses at 12s.
per gross; fines at 16s. per gross; and superfines at 21s. per
gross ; the bidder to advance 6d. per gross upon each bidding."
Ib. note, p. 229.

measure with our subject, it might disappoint many of our readers to omit all mention of them; we say in some measure, because they are by some considered merely as amusing prints, arranged as cards to suit the popular taste. They are marked with the usual suits, and form the complete number of a pack, but it is unlikely they were actually used for the purposes of play, as their devices would have a tendency to distract attention from the game.

Sir Joseph Banks, in 1733, exhibited to the Society of Antiquaries a pack of this kind, containing a history of the Spanish Invasion; and in the Journal of the Archæological Association for 1853-4, is a full and copiously illustrated account by Mr. Pettigrew, of another, especially satirizing the members and proceedings of the Rump Parliament, and the private actions and conduct of several of the individuals most conspicuous during the Commonwealth.* One card, the seven of hearts, will serve as an example. On the top is a heart, and VII. to denote the number of the

* *Journ. Arch. Assoc.*, IX., pp. 121—154, and 308—329. These were purchased at the Hague, by the late Mr. Prest, of Connaught Place, for 35 guineas, and believed to be unique. Mr. P. thinks that they were executed in Holland, and that they formed a source of amusement to the Royalists at the Hague, during the residence there of Charles II. They are engraved on copper, and of very spirited execution.

suit; below this is a soldier running away, an army in the distance, and at the bottom, "*Nathaniel Fines, whereby hangs a tale.*" This is of course intended to represent Colonel Fiennes who undertook to hold Bristol for the Parliament, but after one day's siege surrendered it to the Cavaliers.

In the first number of "*Mercurius Domesticus, or Newes both from City and Country*, Fryday, Decemb. 19, 1679," a pack of cards is advertized as newly published, containing "*An History of all the Popish Plots that have been in England; beginning with those in Queen Elizabeth's time, and ending with this last damnable plot against His Majesty Charles II. Excellently engraven on Copper Plates with very large descriptions under each card. The like not extant. Sold by Randal Taylor, near Stationer's Hall, and Benjamin Harris, at the Stationer's Arms, under the Royal Exchange, in Cornhill. Price One Shilling each pack.*" No example of this, however, appears to have turned up; perhaps it proved a failure, and the public disapproved of what was apparently hinted at in a postscript, to make the reception of it a test of protestantism. A pack, however, so nearly answering this description, that Chatto considers it possibly identical, is described by him in his *Facts and Speculations, &c.*, — date about 1680—as on the four of clubs is represented the trial of Sir George Wakeman and three Benedictine Monks, on an indictment for high treason, 18th July, 1679, for conspiring to poison the king. Only the events of Oates' and Bedloe's plot (1678), however, are commemorated, and these on three of the suits, while the other is entirely occupied by the murder of Sir Edmondbury Godfrey. The ace of hearts has the Pope with three cardinals and a bishop at a table, and the devil underneath, with the description "The Plot first hatcht at Rome by the Pope and Cardinals, &c."

To the same reign belongs another pack, relating apparently to the Rye House Plot, but only four cards have been discovered, the designs of which are described by Mr. Chatto: queen of hearts — "Thompson, one of ye Conspirators, taken at Hammersmith;" knave of diamonds—"Rumbold, the Malster," with label *They shall dye;* ace of clubs — "Keeling troubled in mind," label, *King-killing is damnable;* ace of spades—"Hone taken prisoner at Cambridge."

The "Warming-Pan Plot," and the events

connected with the Revolution of 1688, afforded, as might be supposed, abundant incidents for packs of this kind, in which the Romanizing James and his Queen are severely handled.

There were, moreover, numerous sets of prints or cards of a fantastic description, published at various periods of the seventeenth and eighteenth centuries. Mr. Chatto has described a pack, neatly engraved on copper, which had been in the possession of the family of a Mr. Heywood upwards of a century, relating entirely to the subject of *Love*. The ace of spades, which has a red stamp, showing that the pack was manufactured and sold for the purpose of play, has a Cupid plucking a rose, and the inscription,—" In love no pleasure without pain,"—with some explanatory verses.

A similarly arranged pack, in excellent preservation, is in the British Museum, considered to have been published about 1730, also engraved on copper, and satirising the vices and follies of the day. Each card has an indifferently executed design, something in Hogarth's style, with a couplet at the bottom ; and the number and suit are indicated by a small card placed at the left-hand corner. As in the other pack, the ace of spades has the excise mark. The ace of diamonds has a gipsy-woman telling a lady's fortune, and the lines—

> How can you hope this gipsey drabb should know
> The Fates decrees, and who was made for you?

Fortune-telling must then have thriven apace. On the ace of clubs is another female, consulting an astrologer, who sits in a robe and chain, with a round, broad-brimmed hat on his head, and points to a paper with a triangle on it. A sphere stands at his left hand. Beneath is the couplet—

> Vain are their hopes who to magicians go,
> Decrees of Fate and Destiny to know.

The king of the same suit, displays a man and woman dancing to a fiddle; in front is a table, with an overturned jug and glass:

> "A well matched pair, they'l never freet,
> For a pound of greif woint pay an ounce Debt."

The designs and verses on the other cards are, if anything, duller and more stupid than these.

Another pack, of the time of Queen Anne or George I., is mentioned by Mr. Pettigrew as having been laid before the Archæological Association by Mr. Palin—simple in its design, having no specific object, and probably executed as a mere work of fancy. "The South Sea bubble, also," he adds, "formed the subject for a pack of cards; and the Missisippi scheme was in like manner recorded in Holland."

The cards in actual use by *players* during these centuries presented a general resemblance to our modern specimens, and have, in common with them, the same awkward bulky figures for honours, which we have remarked in the French, but they must have been smaller and meaner than ours, for, according to a state paper, quoted by Mr. Chatto, of the reign of Queen Anne, nine parts out of ten of the cards then made, were sold at from 6s. to 24s. per gross, and retailed out at an average of three halfpence a pack.

The French cards of the eighteenth century appear to have been to little or no extent affected by political events, until the approach of the Revolution, when every thing, from cards to the almanac, was turned topsy-turvy. As far back as Louis XVIth's time, coming events were casting their shadows before. In 1792 some satirical cards were issued, bearing the portrait of the unfortunate king, which they entitled *la partie de cartes du roi et du sans-culotte*.

The tenth of August upset Royalty, and what fate could be expected for the poor old cards of the *ancien régime*, with their courtly impress, and their crowns and fleurs de lys, and heraldic blazon, and the names of kings and queens of ancient renown?

The card-talk too, sanctioned as it was by three or four centuries of court use, and the entire complexion of the game, all must go down before the stream. Here they revolutionized without an idea of reform; at the very outset, the card makers were enjoined to abolish every thing which savoured of what they called in those days *le parti cher à Pitt et Cobourg*. Two master-cardmakers, Urbain Jaume, and Jean Démosthène Dugoure, had promptly asserted in the *Journal de Paris**that no republican could possibly make use, even at the card-table, of expressions which recalled so forcibly the former despotism and inequality of position, and they transmogrified, in their manufactory in the Rue Saint-Nicaise, the kings into Genii—the genius of *cœur*, or of war—of *trèfle*, or of peace—of *pique*, or of arts—of *carreau*, or of commerce; the queens became Liberties, the valets, Equalities, and the aces, Laws.

These absurd attempts to chime in with the new revolutionary spirit which reigned abroad, produced at first nothing but confusion. They succeeded in effacing whatever of the old features was

* See Edm. et Jules de Goncourt, *Histoire de la société Française pendant la Révolution*, ch. xi. p. 289.

possible to be effaced, but not in gaining countenance for the new. The artists did their best;
and a few of their more striking efforts obtained
some amount of patronage. These were line
engravings : the ideas good enough in their way,
but in a style rather too severe. For example, in
one of these packs, for the kings they have Sages;
—M. P. Cato the elder, Solon, J. J. Rousseau,
and L. J. Brutus. For queens are substituted
Virtues — Prudence, Justice, Union, and Fortitude; and in the place of valets appear the four
" Braves," Horatius Cocles, Hannibal, Decius,
and Scævola. The marks of suits, and the pip-
cards, remain unchanged.

One can hardly imagine the ridiculous effect
which would occasionally be produced by this
nomenclature. Other packs offer fresh series of
notabilities. In the following, which, like the
former, was engraved by Chossonnerie and Gayant,
in 1793-4, the philosophers—Molière, La Fontaine,
Voltaire, and Rousseau, stand for kings*; Virtues
as before, but with Temperance [Plate XXVII.]
substituted for Union; while the knaves are represented by four republicans, a pikeman, an
infantry soldier, an artillery-man, and a dragoon,

* Another selection of characters, not particularly well
matched, was Voltaire, Buffon, Racine, and Bayard.

PLATE XXVII

TEMPERANCE.
(Republican Pack, 1793-4.)

all anonymous. The rest of the pack is very tolerable, and the last-named characters are the only sanguinary traits in it. The drawing is exact, and the prints are coloured by hand. The most *outré* variety of any, is that just alluded to of the Fabrique de la Rue Saint Nicaise. These were designed by the painter David, and in a very formal style. The four kings, hitherto erect, were replaced by seated figures, with Phrygian caps, and surrounded by their attributes. These represented the Genii of War, Commerce, Peace, and Arts. The queens give place to four females vested *à l'antique*, symbolical of the Liberty of Religions, of Professions, of Marriage, and of the Press; while four males sitting, in civil or military costume, personified the Equality of Rank, of Colour, of Rights, and of Duties. These were the valets.†

† Chatto quotes from Peignot, *Analyse de Recherches sur les Cartes a Jouer*, a minute description of this extraordinary pack. The card which takes the place of the king of hearts, bears a winged genius seated on a cannon, a sword and wreath of laurel in his right hand, and in his left hand, a shield, with the inscription, *Pour la République Française.* At his feet is a bomb, a lighted match, and a heap of bullets. On the right, vertically from the top, is the word *Force*, and below, *Par brevet d' invention Naume et Dugonec* (sic) *au Génie de la Rep. franç.* The aces are surrounded by four fasces, with the words *La Loi Rép. franç.*, the whole coloured blue. In spite of its accordance with the spirit of the times, it seems to have met with no favour. The same may be said of an American pack, described at the

A pack with names belonging to the Gallo-Roman period, superseded these preposterous productions, and was extensively used up to the time of the Empire. Under the Imperial *régime*, the personages on cards have the proper costumes of the period in which they lived. Eminent artists did not disdain to design them. The old kings reappeared, but their queens, it would seem, did not accompany them. Instead, we find Hildegarde, Statira, Calpurnia, and Abigail. The valets were Ogier, Parmenion, Curio, and Azäel. We give Ogier as a specimen, Plate XXVII.

A change in the *colouring* of these cards is observable, the carmine and rose predominating, to the exclusion of the old red tint, but the majority of them display a grace and spirit quite as agreeable to the eye, as any of the older packs or those of the present day. The tradition, however, of four centuries was against them. No standard pattern was adopted under the Empire, and more than one rival pack disputed the palm

same page; makers name, R. Sauzade, probably a Frenchman. Instead of kings it has Washington, John Adams, Franklin, and La Fayette: for queens, Goddesses; Venus, Fortuna, Ceres and Minerva, the first "modestly concealing her charms with a mantle, in accordance with the American notions of delicacy:" the knaves, four Indian chiefs. These are coloured copperplates, and the pip-cards are the same as the English.

PLATE XXVII*

KNAVE OF HEARTS (OGIER).
(First French Empire.)

PLATE XXIX

KNAVE OF DIAMONDS.
(First French Empire.)

of elegance, according to the then notion of it, at any rate. The valets were denoted sometimes by charming little pages, attendant on high-born damsels of the merry times of yore, with velvet caps and floating plumes, in accordance with the taste affected at that time for the romances and lays of the age of chivalry. Double-headed honours, like the knave of diamonds, Pl. XXIX. (a fashion retained now on the cheaper cards), began to be common. A queen of spades of this kind, bearing the name of Pallas, by Gubitz, a German artist, is given by Singer; and in a Russian pack with double-headed honours, the queen of hearts is represented by a *negress*. The Russian cards, by the way, in general differ only from the French, in having the marks of suits taller and thinner.

The Spanish cards remain unaltered in respect of the absence of queens, and the retention of the symbols of the ancient tarot, but like those of other nations at this period display an occasional eccentricity. Pl. XXX., though of Parisian workmanship, is a Spanish knave of clubs, under the form of a Peruvian with a crest of blue and scarlet feathers. Singer says that the Spanish Government maintains a monopoly of cards, but we have besides this, another proof of that country being supplied from other quarters, in the Senora Morin,* who we have seen, made *naypes* for the Spanish market, at Paris, in the Rue Grenéta, and immense quantities of cards are produced in London, many of which have the suits of cups, money, clubs, and swords, those intended for the Spanish settlements being actually marked *de la Real fabrica de Madrid, para las Indias!*

After the fall of the Empire, the ancient cards in France regained their position, but not without struggles. The *Cartiers* of the Restoration in vain put forth substitutes, which they tried to make look very attractive, some having the ladies' tresses trussed up high behind, like the prints on a hair-dresser's advertisement. Of these attempts none excel the cards designed by Gatteaux, in 1817, for their coquettish simplicity. Mr. Chatto, and M. Amanton, in Peignot's *Analyse*, are lavish in their praises of the cards of Armand Houbigant, licensed for general use by Louis XVIII., in 1818, under the name of *Cartes Royales*. The coat cards, delicately coloured, display the costume of the French court at four different periods: spades—Charlemagne, Hildegarde, and Roland :

---

* Jean Volay also fabricated Spanish Cards at Paris ; no doubt these were preferred in all ages, from the greater skill evinced in their manufacture.

PLATE XXX

KNAVE OF CLUBS.
(Spanish Pack, of French make.)

diamonds—Louis IX, " *Sainct Loys ;*" his mother
Blanche of Castile, and his biographer, the Sire
de Joinville : clubs — Francis I, Marguerite de
Valois, and Bayard, with his motto *Sans peur
sans reproche :* hearts — Henry IV, his mother
Jeanne d'Albret, and his minister, the cautious
Sully, holding in his hand a paper inscribed,
Economie Roy. Although the details of these
cards are most carefully attended to, the faces
being actual portraits, and even the inscriptions
given in the proper character of the time, neither
they, nor the equally artistic productions of
Gatteaux, could stand their ground against the
old deformities, and owe their very existence to
having been preserved as curiosities.

Germany has revived her ancient *penchant* for
fancy cards. The *Karten Almanach* of Cotta, the
bookseller of Tübingen, first appeared in 1806,
the plates being entirely in the fashion of fanciful
cards, with the marks of suits ingeniously introduced into the subject, as in some English examples
we shall presently mention. In one of these
Almanacs, the figures on the coat cards are derived
from Schiller's *Joan of Arc*, and are attired in
their appropriate costumes.* In a German pack
which Mr. Chatto mentions, published at Frank-

* See Chatto, p. 259—60.

fort, in 1815, commemorating the events of the great Continental struggle in 1813-14, our " Iron Duke" figures as a Card-hero, the knave of diamonds, and his veteran comrade Blucher, as the knave of clubs.

Of the Dutch cards we have only to say, as of the Belgian, that they follow the style of their French neighbours. Who the *Aardige Piet*, the " pretty little Peter" of Plate XXXI. may be, we have no means of guessing, as it is the sole specimen we have been able to consult; but he is a very different Peter from the Peter of Plate XXV. In a pack in our possession, of *Cartes Déposées*, 52 in number, with double-headed honours, by Daveling of Bruges, the kings of diamonds, hearts, spades, and clubs, bear respectively the names of Richard Cœur de Lion, Charles V., Charlemagne, and Pepin le Bref. The queens and knaves are nameless, but the costume attempted is contemporary, very neatly drawn, and brilliantly coloured, in the modern style : the latter bear scutcheons of the arms of Holland, Flanders, Luxembourg, Nassau, &c., not very correctly represented ; and the aces, garlands of leaves and flowers.

Packs in imitation of Cotta's picture-cards soon made their appearance both in England and France. Two, apparently by the same artist, were

PLATE XXXI

FOUR OF HEARTS.
(Modern Dutch Pack.)

PLATE XXXII

SIX OF DIAMONDS.
(Vienna Pictorial Pack, 1818-19.)

PLATE XXXIII

ACE OF CLUBS.
(Vienna Pictorial Pack, 1818-19.)

PLATE XXXIV

FOUR OF CLUBS.
(Vienna Pictorial Pack, 1818-19.)

published in 1811, but neither of them intended for play .

Plates XXXII—IV. are specimens of " Pictorial Cards," designed by a Viennese artist, and published, four at a time, in the *Repository of Arts* for 1818-19, and as a pack afterwards, two editions of which are in the Paris Library. We should need the entire set to be engraved, to give a full idea of the variety of the very original and fantastic designs on these cards ; knights in armour, eastern warriors, figures of the classic mythology, scenes from modern tales and dramas,† costumes of every age and clime, well drawn, and displaying great versatility of talent, but with no apparent order or object, and crowded with accessories of every conceivable kind, in which the marks of suits are introduced in the most ingenious manner possible. The descriptions in the original work, are by the late J. B. Papworth, Esq., architect, from which we extract the one explanatory of Plate XXXII. " The six of diamonds represents the characters of a panto-

* See Chatto, p. 259—60.—One of these was published by S. and J. Fuller, Rathbone Place, London ; the other by Jones, Repository of Arts, Market Hill, Cambridge. On both packs is printed, on the wrapper, " METASTASIS. Transformation of Playing Cards."

† *e.g. Gil Blas*, the German drama of *Zielke*, and a tale called *The Fracas*, especially in the spade suit.

mime, and the several personages of the scene will be easily recognized. The emaciated and decrepit debauchee is still assuming the gallant, and mixing the habiliments of the soldier with the airs and manners of a youthful *petit maitre ;* he is gazing on a distant lady, while she, whom he vainly fancies he possesses in perfect security, is bestowing her favours on the first idiot that solicits them. The female is wantonly attired, and holding in her right hand a mask, the emblem of her duplicity, and from the other arm suspends a ridicule, the type of her condescensions. The diamond forms an ornament to a fan, ridicules, and the furniture of the apartment." The descriptions of the two succeeding, contain no more than the *prints* them selves will suggest. Only the marks of suits are coloured, and even this hardly redeems them from the charge of being too indistinct for use.*

* Another set, very facetious, and characteristic of the time, was published by Fores, of Piccadilly; the year is omitted in the imprint, but it was toward the end of George IVth's reign, as the king of hearts is represented by a caricature of that monarch, with a cupid offering him a basket of hearts. In vol. i. also, (1852) of a cheap periodical called the *Home Companion*, is the commencement of a series of prints representing cards, in which, though preserving the shape of the marks, the spades, clubs, &c. are made to form part of a variety of humorous designs, which tell their own tale far better than those in Ackermann's *Repository*. The publishers announce their intention to publish them at Christmas, as a pack of cards, at a moderate price.

About the same date there appeared a cleverly drawn satirical pack, at Paris, with the marks of suits introduced as in the above. These were called *Cartes à rire*, and were excessively severe on the party of the then Government, whom they stigmatised as *Immobiles*. Mr. Chatto, who had the opportunity of examining a pack of these cards, has described them in his excellent work, to which we must refer our readers.

From Mr. Chatto, also, to whom we confess so many obligations, we must abridge an account of a somewhat more pretentious pack than ordinary. These were called " Eclectic Cards," and were published by Baker and Co., in 1813, who, in a descriptive pamphlet, declared their intention to be, to relieve the monotony of the ancient figures, by substituting for the honours, a selection from those eminent characters who have rendered themselves conspicuous in the history of the United Kingdom, and making the other forty cards descriptive of the local and national emblems of the four nations. Clubs, or rather acorns, which are substituted for them, are assigned to England, hearts to Ireland, diamonds to Scotland, and spades to Wales. Knaves, as unsuitable to their plan, they replaced by knights ; and the latter suit bore what they pretended was a real *spata*, or two-edged falchion of the ancient Britons, and not a coal-heaver's spade.*

It is an endless task, to enumerate the manifold attempts which have been made to effect a reformation of the established designs. In 1830, some tricolor cards were brought out by a Parisian maker, J. A. Steinberger, as have been others, with emblems appropriate to the stirring periods of their history; and even while we write, a pack has appeared under the title of *Cartes de l'Ere Impériale*, each card of which, represents some remarkable fact connected with the history of Napoleon I. or III. All the figures are of the same period; the costume is perfect, and remarkable for the execution and brilliancy of the colours. In place of kings and queens, there are the four Napoleonic Emperors, including the Prince Imperial, and four Empresses, including the Empress-mother, and in place of knaves, four Bonapartes, brothers of Napoleon I. For aces, there are four islands, viz., Martinique, where the Empress Josephine was born, the island of St. Croix, Elba, and St. Helena.†

These are probably, like other attempts

*Mr. C. sneers at this; and it certainly has the appearance, as he says, of a heavy cast-metal article, new from the Carron Foundry, and of modern gothic design.

† *Times* of April 16, 1860.

of the kind, destined to a mere ephemeral existence, while the old conventional types, both in this country and in France, maintain their ancient popularity, and instead of improving with everything else in this improving age, have, except in material and manufacture, actually retrograded, and exhibit at the present day, figures and attributes ruder in design, than many of the earlier examples.*

The only parallel to this singularity, which we can call to mind, is in the religious hieroglyphic *formulæ*, which occur on the Egyptian tombs and temples, the series of which, though evidently faithful copies of each other, vary much in execution ; and the ruder examples were supposed to be indicative of a date so remote, as to invalidate the Scripture narrative. Subsequent researches, however, have shown that the exquisite

* The costume and attributes of our modern court cards vary slightly in different packs, though they have a general similarity. The knave of clubs (see p. 149) still holds his arrow, now distorted into a bed-post, with the "head end upward," but with the feathers gone. It has been suggested that the instrument held by some knaves of spades, is a kind of *spring-fork*, formerly used by constables to catch runaway offenders. Hearts has the "rustie browne bill," and diamonds, apparently what Falstaff (*Shaksp.*, Hen. IV. Pt. I. Act ii. Sc. 4.) calls a *Welsh Hook*, which Mr. Knight says, was a pike, with a hook placed at some distance below its point, like some of the ancient partisans.

early forms were continually reproduced in a coarser style, as art decayed in the country ; but as the same reason cannot be assigned in the case of cards, their rude and antique fashion remains an isolated fact, which we leave to philosophers to explain.

XI

THE APPLICATION OF CARDS TO SCIENCE.

THE ABBE GUALTIER—MURNER—LOGICAL CARDS—THE GAMES
OF DESMARETS, HISTORICAL, GEOGRAPHICAL, ETC.—DE
BRIANVILLE'S HERALDIC CARDS—ENGLISH AND SCOTTISH
HERALDIC CARDS — SCIENTIALL CARDS —ASTRONOMICAL
AND FORTUNE TELLING CARDS. — GERMAN ASTROLOGICAL
AND GEOGRAPHICAL CARDS.

GAMING and time-killing, are by no means the
only ends to which cards have been devoted.
The attempt to combine instruction and amusement in this direction, for the benefit of the young
especially, has been often made, and repeated in
our days. We have before observed, that the
German emblematical packs may have furnished
the first idea of making cards capable of commu-
nicating instruction, though it is, at the same time,
not impossible that some such notion may have
been involved in their earliest conception.*

* Not to mention the speculations of Court de Gebelin and
other Egyptologists with regard to the connection of cards with
astrology, which we shall have occasion to notice hereafter,
Gough expressly states that the Italian game called *La Menchiata*, which was played with the ancient tarot cards, was
invented at Sienna, by Michael Angelo, to teach children Arithmetic (*Archæol.* vol. viii.* 172.)

The well-known cards invented by the Abbé Gualtier, for the purpose of conveying, by means of a game, the elementary knowledge of history, geography, &c., are but a modification of the early philosophic packs, which were designed to assist the memory, by giving locality to ideas, upon the principle of association.

The first actual application of the system however, was more ambitious; this was the *Chartiludium Logicæ*, or cards for instruction in the Art of reasoning, of Dr. Thomas Murner, the opponent of Luther, printed at Cracow, in 1507, for the use of his pupils.

So astounding was the success of these, that the people first marvelled, and then wanted to set fire to the author, as was often the case in those days, with the inventor of any novelty that was more wonderful than intelligible.

The University however, on examination, pro-

---

* Murner was also the author of *Eulenspiegel*, (which after 105 Continental editions, has at length appeared, worthily edited, in English form, by Kenneth R. H. Mackenzie, F.S.A.,) and of several works in the style of Sebastian Brandt's *Ship of Fools*. He visited England in 1523, and ingratiated himself with Henry VIII. by writing a tract, "*Ob der Kunig usz Engelland ein lügner sey, oder der Luther?* Is the King of England a liar, or Luther?" Sir T. More, in a letter to Cardinal Wolsey, calls him "a frere of Saynt Francise, one of the chiefe stays agaynst the faction of Luther, and a man for wryting and preching, of great estimation in his cuntre."

nounced the invention something superhuman, and Murner, emboldened by his success, further applied the system to jurisprudence and the Institutes of Justinian.

The Logical cards are fifty-two in number, but have nothing else whatever in common with ordinary cards or cardplaying; indeed, in his preface to the book, Murner expressly disclaims all connection with it.

The cuts in the work are divided into sixteen suits, distinguished at the top of each, by as many varieties of emblems—bells, crayfish, acorns, scorpions, &c.—answering after a peculiar method to the different technical terms used in the science at that period, as "The Exception," "The Syllogism," "The Supposition," &c. Each subject, taken as a whole, is supposed to impress on the mind of the student, by a combination of symbols, the different ideas and terms necessary to be remembered in connection with it.

If this was the result achieved, and considered at the time worthy of such a display of ingenuity, we think the readers of our day at least, will deem it a good illustration of the rhyme:

> Logicus araneæ potest comparari,
> Quæ subtiles didicit telas operari,
> Quæ suis ex visceribus vult consummari
> Est pretium *musca*, si forte queat laqueari.

In 1650, according to Singer, Père Guichet, a Minorite friar, also published an Art of Logic, in the form of a pack of cards; but whether this was a re-impression of Murner's book, or a new one on the same model, he does not know.

Under Louis XIV., Desmarets, a well-known academician, with the assistance of the engraver La Belle, or Della Bella, revived in a new form the invention of the Polish Cordelier. The idea is said to have been suggested by Cardinal Mazarin, as a means of instruction for the youthful king, then only eight years old; the bare profession of which, would necessarily stand these new instructional cards in good stead, in commanding the attention of the public.

On the 9th of April, 1644, letters patent were issued in the king's name, to "Jean Desmarests, Conseiller, Secretaire, et Controlleur general de l'extraordinaire des Guerres," granting him the privilege and monopoly of having executed, in wood or copper-plate, engraving or etching, the figures of the games of cards of the history of the kings and queens, of illustrious men and women, fables, geography, ethics (morale), politics, logic, physic, and generally, of all other games of any art, science, history, or fable, which he has invented, or shall hereafter invent,

PLATE XXXV

PLATE XXXV

Arion

*Excellent musicien fut jetté dans
la mer par des marchands pour
auoir son bien, et ayant joüé de sa
lyre auant que d'estre jetté, un dau
phin le recoit et le mit au bord.*

1

ED. COPPIN.   BISSUN CUTTARD

ACE OF CLUBS.
(French Game of Fables, 1644.)

and forbids their sale by any one else, under a penalty of 3,000 livres, and confiscation of the articles.

The first of the series was the *Jeu de Fables*, containing, as the preface tells us, all the fabulous deities, and all the fables, or at least such as relate to metamorphoses. There are fifty-two in the pack, which is divided into the usual suits, the cards answering to the king, queen, and knave of each being as follows: hearts — Jupiter, Juno, and Mars; clubs — Neptune, Pallas, and Mercury; spades — Pluto, Diana, and Bacchus; and diamonds — Saturn, Venus, and Apollo.

Each card contains a picture, the value being denoted by a numeral, and the mark of the suit; thus—Niobe, with a X and a spade, is the ten of spades; and the ten of hearts is Actæon. The Nine Muses, with a X and a club, is the nine of clubs; and Arion, marked with an I and a club, is the ace. (Plate XXXV.)

Desmarets, encouraged by the protection he received, which also relieved him of the usual tax on cards, and by the reception which attended these really artistic designs, next produced a *Jeu de l'histoire de France*, which possessed some very original features. There are neither marks of

suits, nor the ordinary divisions. The list of the
kings is proof enough of its singularity. These
are arranged in six divisions : — good kings,
simple-minded kings, cruel kings, faithless kings,
luckless kings, and kings neither good nor bad.
Under this last category are included Charles the
Bald, Francis II., and Louis the Stammerer. In
all, there are sixty-five prints, after the manner of
Plate XXXVI. The last represents Louis XIV.
as an infant, in a carriage drawn by his mother,
with this note appended ;—

"Louis XIV., a prince long looked for, and who, granted by
the Almighty to the prayers of a good and wise queen, and of an
entire people, causes the expectation that he will be gifted with
all regal virtues, and that his reign will be indeed auspicious,
since it has commenced with the battle of Rocroy, and the
capture of Thionville."

After this appeared another, of a similar
description, very prettily designed, and delicately
coloured. This was the *Jeu des Cartes des
Reines renommées*. It contains fifty-two cards,
and could therefore be used for the purposes of
play. The queens are classed as follows : four
saintes—Clotilde, Baudour, Blanche, and Anne of
Austria, (the last, no doubt, being sanctified by her
secret marriage with a prince of the Church !);
these four occupy the place of kings in the
ordinary pack : next are four celebrated—Semiramis, Tomira *(Thamyris)*, Dido, and Zenobia ;

PLATE XXXVI

FRENCH HISTORICAL CARD.
(From Desmaret's Pack, *circa*, 1644.)

PLATE XXXVII

S   *galante*

Poppée Sabine

Femme de l'Empereur Neron, et aupauauant femme d'Otthon, qui fut contraint de la repudier pour la laisser a Neron, dont elle auoit gagné le cœur par ses attraits.

LD. COPPIN.   B.ISSGR.COTTARD.

FIVE OF CLUBS.
(Historical Game [Women] *circa*, 1644.)

these are the queens : four valiant, represent the valets; four pious, the tens : four wise, four cruel, four queens who were good women, (Alcestis, Evadne, Penelope, Artemisia), four unchaste, four *galantes*, four clever, four capricious, four unhappy, and four happy, complete the set.

These cards have the suits designated by *colours*—gold, silver, green, and the tint called "columbine," which is a delicate rose, a little inclined to buff. Desmarets has added notes like the following :

"Jeu particulier pour le *Hoc.**

" . . . When a '*capricieuse*' is led, one is paid to the game for him who makes the last Hoc. An '*impudique*' pays two, and a '*cruelle*' three."

A regular gradation observe — cruelty, unchastity, and inconstancy,—reckoned in the proportions of three, two, and one !

The beautiful *Jeu de Cartes de la Géographie*, also by Desmarets, followed the other three. The four quarters of the world form the four suits, and stand also for the aces; under each, are enumerated twelve divisions, making up fifty-two ; a native of one of the countries being represented on each card in his national costume, a peculiarity

* Hoc, a game supposed to be introduced into France by Cardinal Mazarin. See further notices of it in the second part of this work. The Cardinal was said to be privately married to the mother of Louis XIV.

which adds greatly to its interest, and an inscription explanatory of the design is appended. A description of the cards of the " golden" suit, will give an idea of the geography of the time; in fact, both this and the next mentioned pack, would form valuable materials for a history of the progress of that science in France. The king is Europe; the queen, France, of course; Spain is the valet, on account of Anne of Austria. After these, follow the numeral cards in order : Sicily Dalmatia, Greece, Servia, Hungary, Poland, Scandinavia, Great Britain, Germany, and Italy.

The invention took; a certain M. Duval, a little later, in 1677, published some Geographical Tables, arranged as a pack of cards, and dedicated to the Dauphin. In the British Museum, also, is a pack of fifty-two Geographical Cards, published at London, about 1680, on a similar, but more ingenious plan. As in the French pack, the four quarters of the globe form the suits, but having the usual marks—hearts, Europe; diamonds, Asia; spades, Africa; and clubs, America. The king of hearts bears a medallion portrait of Charles II., with an account of his dominions — " The British Isles contain, &c." The queen and knave have portraits of " RHEA SILVIA," and " A GREEK," with an account of

"Portugal and Algarve," and "Turky in Europe."
The numeral cards are thus arranged, to correspond with the internal divisions of each country
represented :

    I.—" Europe hath, &c. ;"—the different states
        enumerated.

    II.—" Denmark hath ii. kingdoms," &c.

    III.—" Moscovy, or the Great and White
        Russia, is triply divided into kingdoms,
        Dutchies, and Hoords or communities
        of Tartars," &c.

And so on, with the remainder of the pack.

The diamond suit has for honours, " VANLIE "
(*China*), STATIRA (*Persia*), and " A JANISARY "
(*Turkey in Asia*); the spades, " ZAGA CHRIS."*
(*Abyssinia*), CANDACE (*Nubia*), and " A NEGRO "
(*Negroland*) ; and the clubs, " JOHN IV., OF POR-
TUGAL" (*Brazil*, first discovered by the Portuguese),
ELIZABETH (*the English Plantations*, founded by
the English queen), and " A CANIBAL " (the *Carri-
bee Islands*); all with medallion portraits, in the
style of the first-named suit, with their titles
included in the circle. The latitude and longitude
of each country, with their divisions and princi-

    * See " Une Relation Véritable de Zaga-Christ, Prince
d'Ethiopie," in a curiously illustrated work called *La Terre
Sainte*, 4to., Paris, 1664.

pal towns are printed in small type, and the *speci-mens* given as court cards, are very fairly executed.

The coincidence in number, between the English counties, and the cards in a pack, appears to have suggested the construction of another game of this kind, also of the reign of Charles II., the title of which is given by Mr. Chatto; "The fifty-two counties of England, geographically described in a pack of cards, whereunto is added the length, breadth, and circuit of each county; the latitude, situation, and distance from London, of the principal cities, towns, and rivers, with other remarks; as plaine and ready for the playing of all our English games as any of the common cards." The heads of the kings are shown at the top of the maps of Hereford, Monmouth, Middlesex, and Yorkshire: the queens ornament those of Durham, Huntingdon, Radnor, and Worcestershire; and the knaves, Anglesey, Gloucester, Leicester, and Rutland. "If the deviser," (he remarks) "had any particular meaning in the assignment of the coat cards, it is not easy to be discovered; though it may be 'shrewdly guessed at' as respects Monmouth and York."

The afore-mentioned Duval, further signalised his ingenuity, by inventing a new game, which he called *Le Jeu des Princes de l'Empire;* the suits of the pack being distinguished by the crown imperial, the electoral bonnet, the chapeau of the Free Towns and the ducal coronet.

These heraldic distinctions bring us to the consideration of Heraldry in connection with cards, a science, which more than all others, appears to have been deemed susceptible of being imparted by this means. A pack of heraldic cards, by M. Claude Ozonce Finé *dit* de Brianville, with a small 12mo. volume as a guide, was published at Lyons, in 1659, probably executed for Desmarets, as in a later edition, there is printed as an appendix, together with the letters patent before-mentioned, a transfer of his privilege, dated 13th May of that year to Benoist Coral, Marchand Libraire, at Lyons, in so far as relates to the " *Cartes de Blason.*" The title of this edition, which is the only one we have been able to consult, is " *Jeu d'Armoiries des Sovverains et Estats d'Europe, pour apprendre le Blason et la Géographie, et l'Histoire curieuse.* A Monseigneur le Dauphin. Par M. de Brianville, Abbé de S. Benoist le Quinçay lez Poitiers. A Lyon, chez Benoist Coral, rue Merciere, a la Victoire, 1672. Auec Privilege du Roy."* The author com-

* We are indebted for the loan of this rare little work to the valuable heraldic Library of A. W. Morant, Esq , C.E., of Great

mences with an advertisement to the reader, in
which, after professing his obligations to Menestrier and others, for their assistance and advice,
he gives the following remarks and instructions
on the method of play. " The method of playing
this game does not differ from that adopted with
the ordinary cards, there being the same number
of cards, and the same points. The only change
made, is that of valet and ace into *prince* and
chevalier, which is done to prevent any miscon-
struction (*pour éviter tout equivoque.*)* The games
of Hère, Malcontant, or Coucou, are the most
suitable, because being the easiest, they are not
so likely to divert the attention needed for the
Blazonry, Geography, and History. The players
range themselves around a table covered with a
map of Europe, and after the cards are dealt and
exchanged to every one's satisfaction, the lowest
pays according to the laws of *Hère.* He who is

Yarmouth. Notices of other editions will be found in the
Bibliographical Appendix. In these, De Brianville is otherwise
styled *Mont-Dauphin*, and *Conseiller et Armoirier du Roy*. The
third edition, 1665, is dedicated, " *a son Altesse Royale de
Savoye.*"

* An explanation of this expression, very characteristic of
the times, is given by Singer. The aces and valets, it appears,
bore in the first edition the arms of certain princes and nobles.
This being considered offensive to their dignity, the plates were
seized by the magistrates, and only restored on condition that
princes and knights should be substituted.

first, then describes the blazonry of the card* he holds, forfeiting one, if he makes an error, either to the player who corrects him, or to the bank, if there is one. The next highest then follows suit, and so on through all the rest. The first round being completed, they then proceed to the second, describing this time the geography of each card, and forfeiting points for mistakes, as before. At the third round, they take the history in the same manner." He recommends that at first only the blazon should be attempted, as the game can be played in each division separately, as well as in all three collectively.

The cards are divided into the four suits, *cœurs*, *tréfles*, *piques*, and *carreaux*, distinguished respectively by the armorial bearings of the kingdoms, provinces, and great dignitaries of France, Italy, the North (*le Nort*), and Spain. The honours of course contain the most exalted, the King of Great Britain appearing as the prince (*knave*) of the spade or Northern suit. We present our readers with the trey of this suit, containing the arms of the seventeen provinces of the Low Countries, as one of the least intricate

* As this could not be done without considerable acquaintance with heraldry, a M. Gauthier devised, in 1686, a new pack of heraldic cards, to serve the purpose of a kind of grammar of the science. See *Bibliogr. App.*

(Plate XXXVIII.), with the accompanying lesson in blazonry, rendered into English heraldic
language :

1. *Flanders.*—*Or*, a lion rampant, *sa.*, armed and langued,
gu., the shield held by a lion sejant, his head concealed in a
tilting helm *à l'antique*, and crested with a lion's head, *sa.*,
between a pair of wings, *or.* 2. *Brabant.*—*Sa.*, a lion rampant,
or. 3.—*Limbourg.*—*Arg.*, a lion rampant, *gu.* 4. *Luxembourg.*
—Barry of 10, *arg.*, and *az.*, over all a lion rampant, *gu.*, armed,
langued, and crowned, *or.* 5. *Gueldres.*—*Az.*, a lion rampant
crowned, *or*, *contourné*, impaling *Juliers*,—*Or*, a lion ramp.
sa., crowned. 6. *Arras (Artois).*—Semé of *France*, a label of
three points, *gu.* each charged with three towers, *or.* 7.
Hainault.—Quarterly, *Flanders* and *Holland.* 8. *Namur.*—
Flanders, over all, a bendlet, *gu.* 9. *Holland.*—*Or*, a lion rampant, *gu.* 10. *Zeeland.*—Per fess, wavy, in chief, *or*, a lion
naissant, *gu*, in base, *az.*, two bars wavy, *arg.* 11. *Zutphen.*—
Or, a lion rampant, *arg.* 12. *Antwerp.*—*Gu.*, three towers
in triangle, joined by walls, the whole *arg.* masoned *sa.*, in the
dexter and sinister chief, a hand *apaumée ppr.*, one in bend,
the other in bar, the whole surmounted by a chief of the *Empire.* 13. *Mechlin.*—*Or*, three pales, *gu.*, over all, an escocheon
of the *Empire.* 14. *Utrecht.* — *Tranché*, *gu.*, and *arg.* 15.
Groningen.—The *Empire*, but according to the *Armorial Uni-
versel*, with a chief, *az.*, charged with three estoiles, *arg.* 16.
Friesland.—*Az.*, semé of billets, *couchées*, *or*, two lions passant
in pale of the same. 17. *Overyssel.*—Holland, debrised by a
bar wavy *az.*

The geographical and historical lessons are
very concise and comprehensive, the former
giving the latitude, boundaries, chief towns, &c.,
and the latter entering minutely into the descent
of the house whose arms are represented.

One can easily see that the *utile* in games like

PLATE XXXVIII

THREE OF SPADES.
(French Heraldic Pack, 1672.)

this, predominates very materially over the *dulce*, and it was doubtless deemed a very sorry recreation, by the royal urchin for whose edification it was devised. Nevertheless, the game found imitators ; in 1678, Antoine Bulifon, a Lyons bookseller, having established himself at Naples, published an Italian edition of these cards, and a society was even formed under the name of *Academici Armeristi*, for the express purpose of playing at Blazon.* In 1682, a pack containing the arms of the Venetian Nobility, was presented to the Doge and Senate of that city, by D. Casimin Freschet, who acknowledges, in his preface, that they were formed upon the model of the heraldic cards of De Brianville. Menestrier himself published more than one heraldic game of cards ; indeed, the good Jesuit seems so enchanted with these ingenious card-devices, that he thinks no other game affords such means of blending amusement with instruction.†

In England also, a pack was published, which,

* *Singer*, p 218. Chatto states on the authority of Menestrier, that the *Armeristi* were established by Don Annibal Acquaviva, and had a map of Europe for a device, with the motto, " *Pulchra sub imagine Ludi.*" The British Museum possesses a copy of the Neapolitan edition, dated 1692, translated and enlarged by B. Giustiniani.

† *Singer, Ib.* For notices of Menestrier's games, see our *Bibliographical Appendix.*

as far as we can judge from Mr. Chatto's description, was almost a reproduction of that of De Brianville. The knaves are expunged, and the letter P. for Prince appears instead, but they do not appear to be equally fastidious in the case of the aces, which remain. The heart and spade suit change places, in order to give the English sovereign the place of honour, as king of hearts. Another contemporary pack, relating exclusively to English heraldry, is mentioned by Mr. Chatto,* which, from its title-page or wrapper, preserved in Bagford's collections in the British Museum, appears to have been regularly licensed as an heraldic affair, by the Duke of Norfolk, as Earl Marshal of England. In this they get over the difficulty of the knaves, by dispensing with them altogether. Mr. C. gives the following summary of the distribution of the arms: " The king and queen of hearts were respectively represented by the arms of England, and of the Duke of York ; of diamonds, by the arms of Ireland and of Prince Rupert ; of spades, by the arms of France, and of

* Probably the same as that of which Singer quotes the advertisement from the *Observator*, No. 239, for Feb. 12, 168⅘, " Cards containing the arms of the Kings, and all the Lords spiritual and temporal, of England. Printed for John Nicholson, and sold by E. Evets, at the Green Dragon, in St. Paul's Church Yard." *Qy.* by Gregory King, Somerset Herald ? See Watt, *Bibl. Brit.* and our appendix, *s. v.*

PLATE XXXIX

QUEEN OF CLUBS.
(Scotch Heraldic Pack, 1691.)

PLATE XL

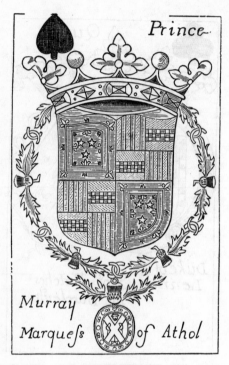

PRINCE OF SPADES.
(Scotch Heraldic Pack, 1691.)

PLATE XLI

TWO OF DIAMONDS.
(Scotch Heraldic Pack, 1691.)

PLATE XLII

ACE OF HEARTS.
(Scotch Heraldic Pack, 1691.)

the Archbishops of Canterbury and York; and of clubs, by the arms of Scotland, and of the Dukes of Norfolk, Somerset, and Buckingham. The arms of the earls were distributed among the sevens, eights, nines, and tens; the viscounts furnished the sixes; the bishops were quartered on the fives; and the baron's coats armorial clothed the nakedness of the lower orders, from the fours to the aces,—the aces in the heraldic game being low." Precisely similar to these, are a pack of Scottish heraldic cards, described in a paper in the fifth volume of the *Norfolk Archæology*, by the Rev. G. H. Dashwood, F.S.A., who has kindly permitted the use, for this work, of the four cuts which illustrate the series (Plates XXXIX —XLII). They exhibit the armorial ensigns of the nobility of Scotland in the year 1691. The king of hearts is represented by the arms of Scotland, and the other three by those of England, France, and Ireland. The four queens bear the shields of as many dukes, and the princes, those of the Marquises of Douglass, Graham, and Athol; he of diamonds being compensated by the coats of three earls. The other earls, sixty-five in number, occupy the tens, nines, eights, sevens, and sixes; and eighteen viscounts and fifty-three barons are distributed among the smaller cards. The wrapper displays, in two compartments, the official seal of Sir Alexander Areskine, or Erskine, of Cambo, Knight and Baronet, Lyon King at Arms, and the arms of Edinburgh, with the title "*Phylarcharum Scotorum Gentilicia Insignia illustrium a Gualtero Scot Aurifice,** Chartis lusoriis expressa. Sculpsit Edinburgi. Anno Dom. CIƆ.IƆC.XCI.

Plate XXXIX. is an extraordinary variation from "Quarterly 1 and 4, France quarterly England; 2, Scotland; 3, Ireland; all within a bordure compony *arg.* and *gu.*, charged with eight roses seeded and barbed, *ppr.*," the coat granted 30 Sept., 1675, to Charles Lennox, Duke of Richmond and Lennox, the illegitimate son of Charles II. and the fair and frail Louise de Kerouet, Duchess of Portsmouth. Scottish national vanity has in this instance, reversed the positions of England and Scotland in the shield.

* We have been favoured by John Stuart, Esq., Hon. Sec. of the Society of Antiquaries of Scotland, with a copy of a note by the late Sir Walter Scott, in the Abbotsford copy of the *Phylarcharum Insignia,* by which it appears that a Walter Scott, Goldsmith, in Edinburgh, was admitted a member of the Incorporation in 1686, and another, using a similar signature in 1701. One of these Walters, probably the engraver of the *Insignia,* must have been dead 28 August, 1706, on which day a daughter of *umquhile* Walter Scott was appointed to the Trades' Maiden Hospital. Walter Scott was elected deacon of the Incorporation, for the two years 1706-7, and 1707-8.

The games of De Brianville were adopted also in Holland, for in a catalogue of books printed by an Amsterdam firm in 1728,* are not only the heraldic and geographical games, and the game of "Celebrated Queens," but other *jeux* entitled respectively the " Four Quarters of the World," Illustrious Kings, Kings of France, "the Metamorphoses of Ovid," the game of War, the game of Fortifications, and the game of Boufon, —all having an explanatory guide book to accompany them.

According to Chatto, a pack of military cards, with instructions for playing the game, devised by the Sieurs des Martins, and dedicated to " Son Altesse le duc de Maine, Colonel-general des Suisses," appeared in 1676. This was the son of Louis XIV., and Madame de Montespan, and at that time of the mature age of six !

The same author notices, that while in France the class of cards we are discussing appear to have been devised for the exclusive use of the nobility and gentry ; their adaptation in England is " to the meanest capacity," and connected with far less exalted subjects.

The Commonwealth had produced the " Scien-

* J. Covens et C. Mortier, Marchands Libraires sur le Vygendam. App. to *Académie des Jeux*, p. 397.

tiall Cards" before alluded to, published by
Baptist Pendleton, in 1651, of which the long-
winded title alone is preserved in the Harleian
MSS., No. 5947, in the British Museum, by
which, while representing in all points and suits
"your vulgar or common cards," "the perfection of
the grammar principles," the author professes,
" may hereby be easily attained unto, both with
much delight and profit."

In 1656 was also published a little book
entitled the "*Schollers Practicall Cards*," by F.
Jackson, M.A., containing instructions by means of
cards, how to spell, write, cipher, and cast accounts,
together with many other excellent and necessary
rules of calculation, without either almanack or
ephemeris."

The author's proposed object is to convert the
cards in common use, to the purposes of knowledge and good learning, and remove "the scandall
and abuse, which every tinker that can but tell his
peeps (*pips*) exposeth them unto," but he lets the
truth out, when he refers to the games of "Gleek,
Ruff, Post and Pair, Saunt, Lodam, and Noddy,"
in his instructions, for no one, unless considerably
au fait at these games, could possibly make any
use of his absurd and complicated contrivance.*

* Chatto, *Facts and Speculations*, p. 140.

Some of the scientific cards of Charles IInd's time appear to have been got up by tradesmen, with a view to advertise their own wares, as well as instruct the public.

In 1676 was published "*The Use of Astronomical Playing Cards, teaching any ordinary capacity by them to be acquainted with all the Stars in Heaven, to know their place in Heaven, Colour, Nature, and Bigness ; as also the Poetical Reasons for every Constellation ; very useful, pleasant, and delightful for all lovers of ingenuity.* By Joseph Moxon, hydrographer to the King's most Excellent Majesty." The cards which accompany this treatise have not fallen in our way, but they are advertised to be sold with all manner of instruments, sea-plates, and books, by the author, " on Ludgate Hill, at the Signe of Atlas."

The mystery of this notable invention, appears by the instructions, to have consisted simply in setting down on each of the cards a constellation, together with the day of the month on which it rises at sunset, and the point of the compass it rises on, by which it might be recognized in the heavens when the day came round, by its resemblance to the diagram, and the fortunate possessor might "see (for himself) in what part of the constellation each particular star lies, and of what

nature, coulour and magnitude it is." The marks
of suits, spades, hearts, diamonds, and clubs, are
in the left hand corner of each card, with the
kings, queens, and knaves in the centre, on
the honours, and the numerals I, II, &c., to
X on the pips, and correspond with the four
colures, vernal, æstival, autumnal, and hyemnal,
or, spring, summer, autumn, and winter.

To the description of "puffing cards," belongs
also a mathematical pack, mentioned by Mr.
Chatto, as being published in the reign of either
Charles II., or James II., by Thomas Tuttell,
"mathematical instrument maker to the King's
most excellent Majesty." They were designed
by Boitard, and engraved by J. Savage, and
represent various kinds of mathematical instruments, together with the trades and professions
in which they were used, and are evidently got
up as an advertisement.

The idea of astronomy, and even mathematics,
was in those days intimately connected with
astrology and fortune-telling. The first lunar
tables which were constructed on the Newtonian
theory, were designed to assist the calculation of
nativities, and we need not therefore wonder to
find packs of cards devoted to those so-called
sciences. By the courtesy of the Rev. G. A.

Burnaby, Rector of S. Peter's, Bedford, we are enabled to instance a pack of the fortune-telling kind, of which, as it will be fully described in that portion of our history specially devoted to "Cartomancy," it will suffice here to observe, that the imprint states them to be "sold by Iohn Lenthall, stationer, at the Talbot, over against St. Dunstan's Church, London," who carried on business there from 1665 to 1685, and that as they resemble in design the political cards engraved in the *Journal of the Archæological Association*, and which we have described at p. 167, they were probably issued about the same period, that immediately succeeding the Restoration. Lenthall professed to be related to William Lenthall, the speaker of the Long Parliament, but this did not prevent him from figuring "one eyed Hewson," as the knave of clubs, accoutred in a leather apron, in allusion to his original trade of a cobbler, the subject of many a satire in the songs of the Cavaliers.*

> " And here are old Noll's brewing vessels,
>   And here are his dray and his slings :
> Here are Hewson's awl, and his bristles,
>   With diverse other odd things."

" *The Sale of Rebellious Household Stuff.*"   Percy's *Reliques*, II, B. iii. 14.

* For more, see " Huson the Cobbler," as the nine of hearts,

There is a very curious Astronomical, or rather Astrological pack of thirty-six cards in the British Museum, with the German marks of suits, and of the supposed date 1680, each suit consisting of König, Ober, Unter, *Daus*, (as is usual with German packs, no ace,) and pips from six to ten, coloured and arranged in a row on the top of each card. No allusion seems intended in the selection of the honours, the cards are numbered from I. to XXXVI., and contain a figure or diagram, its title in Latin, and a four-line stanza in German. The first eleven represent the ancient Solar systems of Ptolemy, Plato, Porphyry, Anaximander, Martian, and Plutarch, and the Egyptian, Tychonic, Semi-Tychonic, Copernican and Cocceianic. No. XII. depicts the twelve Houses of heaven, or astrological divisions of the firmament, by the position of the signs and planets in which, good or ill fortune is predicted, according to their mystic

in the pack described by Mr. Pettigrew. Granger mentions a portrait of Sir John Hewson, in which he is depicted in a buff coat, and says that " he once wore a leathern apron, and from a mender of shoes, became a reformer of government and religion." He was a colonel at the time of the death of Charles I., was one of his judges, and signed his death warrant. Subsequently he rose to be governor of Dublin, and one of Cromwell's lords of Parliament. He died in exile, in 1662.—*Journal of Archæol. Association*, vol. ix., p. 316, significations, which are concisely expressed in the couplet;

"Vita, Lucrum, Fratres, Genitor, Nati, Valetudo,
Uxor, Mors, Pietas, Regnum, Benefactaque Carcer."

In this diagram, Aries occupies the East or ascendant; Capricorn, the South, or Mid heaven; Libra, the West, or descendant; and Cancer, the North, or *Imum cœli*.

The next two give further illustrations of the system of calculating horoscopes and nativities, and the xvth is a design with which the readers of old almanacs are familiar, a naked figure surrounded by the Signs of the Zodiac, from which rays are directed to that part of the body, over which each is supposed, as the moon passes through it, to exert a peculiar influence; for the bearing in mind of which valuable information, old Gadbury supplies us with the following homely rhyme, each member being headed with its presiding sign, beginning with Aries;

"Head, Throat, Arms, Brest, Heart, Belly, Reins do greet
The ——, Thighs, Knees, Legs, and the active Feet."

Ephemeris, 1695. See *Merlinus Anglicus* for the same year, and another different in that of 1699.

No. xvi. is the signification of comets according to the Rabbins (*per dodecatemoria*), and the rest of the figures represent the different as-

tronomical phenomena as then understood, before
the Newtonian discoveries,—methods of dialling,
diagrams of eclipses, &c., intermixed with astrological fooleries, which though an attempt was
made to accomodate them to the new system, received their actual death-blow by the discovery of
Copernicus.* To the shame of the intelligence of
the nineteenth century however, be it spoken,
astrology is still professed by charlatans, who issue
works from their garrets, which are greedily read
by the credulous, and the rustic is still awed by
the " Figura Cœli," and portentous hieroglyphic
of his " Old Moore," and other popular almanacs,
and until very lately, was sceptical of the effect of

* All the systems before Copernicus, suppose the earth to be
the centre, and the Sun, moon, and planets revolving round it in
various ways. Ptolemy of Alexandria, wrote A.D. 130—150 ;
his book, called by the Arabs *Almagest*, was the basis of all astrological calculations. Martianus Capella, A.D. 470, in his
Satyricon, supposed Mercury and Venus to move round the Sun,
this is reported to have turned the attention of Copernicus to
the improved system named after him. The semi-Tychonic
system (*Tycho Brahé*, 1560—1609) admitted the *diurnal* motion
of the earth on its axis, but like the Tychonic denied its *annual*
revolution. The circles in which the heavenly bodies moved were
called orbs or spheres, and they were supposed to move in such
harmony, that Plutarch feigned each to have a Syren seated on
it, discoursing music to the whole universe ; hence the notion of
"*the Music of the Spheres*." The Eighth sphere, mentioned p.
123, was that of the fixed stars, and the farthest removed from
the earth.

PLATE XLIII

ASTROLOGICAL CARDS

PLATE XLIII

ASTROLOGICAL CARDS.
(From a German Pack, *circa*, 1680.)

necessary medicine, not administered when the *stomachic* " sign " was in the ascendant.

The verses on the cards seem merely descriptive, those on Pl. XLIII., which we give as a specimen, may be thus rendered in English :—

" How deep, with them of old, in superstition,
   They have progressed, whose mystic erudition
   Seeks in its creed the signs of life and death to know,
   These cards, and this the last of all, will show."

Mr. Quaritch has a German Geographical pack, in which the marks of suits are arranged in the same way as the above, in a row at the top, but of the French order and pattern ; König, Dame, Knecht, and Asz, and the full number of pips. The ace of spades is entitled " *Typus Orbis Terrarum* " and contains a map on Mercator's Projection, the longitude calculated from Ferrol. It bears the designers' and engravers' names, I. H. Seÿfrid, and Wilhelm Pfaun. Each card has a coloured map of one of the countries of Europe, without apparent preference, except that the ace of hearts is Europe, and the king, Germania. The cards are of larger size than the ordinary sort, their backs marbled, and the edges gilt. As Livonia is not included in " Muscovia," and St. Petersburg not mentioned, they are probably of the latter part of the seventeenth century, and anterior to Peter the Great. In short, "it would be difficult" says M. Leber, in a passage we take the liberty of reproducing from the author we have so often quoted,* "to name an elementary book of science or art, which had not a pack of cards as an auxiliary; Grammar, Rhetoric, Fable, Geography, History, Heraldry, the principles of Morals and Politics,—all these things and many others besides, were to be learnt through the medium of play. The game of cards had served for the amusement of a royal lunatic; and similar games were comprehended in the plan for the education of one of our greatest kings. Though France had a large share in the dissemination of such treasures of knowledge, England showed herself not less diligent in working the same mine; if to us she owes the game of piquet, it is from her own proper resources, that she has endowed the culinary art with a game of a different kind, yet highly interesting considered in its relation to the *play of the jaws*, the most ancient and highly esteemed of all play. It was in December, 1692, that the London papers first announced to the world, the invention of the game of Carving at Table. This precious announcement is conceived in the following terms: ' The genteel house-

* Chatto, *Facts and Speculations*, p. 155.

keeper's pastime, or the mode of Carving at the
Table, represented in a pack of playing cards, with
a book by which any ordinary capacity may learn
how to cut up, or carve in mode, all the most
usual dishes of flesh, fish, fowl, and baked meats,
with the several sauces and garnishes, proper to
each dish of meat.   Price 1s. 6d. Sold by J.
Moxon, Warwick Lane.' "We are further informed
that, " in these cards the suit of clubs is occupied
by fish; hearts, by flesh; diamonds, by fowl, and
spades, by baked meats.   The king of hearts pre-
sides over a sirloin of beef; of diamonds over a
turkey; of spades over a venison pasty; and
clubs over a pickled herring."   On the ace of
spades is a red stamp with the word " Sixpence,"
rather a high duty considering the price of the
pack.

With this we conclude our "History of
Cards," like Moxon and his games we have descended from Heaven to earth, from the credulous
superstition which regards them as the oracles of
the Divine will, to the matter of fact notion which
connects them with creature comforts, but of this
we may be sure, that all idea of instruction in
connection with cards, would be eschewed as a
bore by regular players, while as royal roads to
knowledge, their utility is very questionable.

XII.

CARD MISCELLANIES.

LEGISLATION—NOMENCLATURE—MANUFACTURE.

I. LEGISLATION. Considering the propensity which seems innate in man, to risk the loss of what he at present possesses, on the chance of acquiring something more valuable which is another's, it is not surprising that the abuse of this in relation to games should have led, first, those charged with the moral guidance of the people, and then the legislature, to denounce the practice of *gaming*, that is, the playing at games of chance for the purpose of *gain*, as prejudicial alike to the moral principle of individuals, and the general well-being of the State. "Many fierce declarations" says Jeremy Taylor, "from ancient sanctity, have been uttered against cards and dice, by reason of the craft used in the game, and the consequent evils, as invented by the Devil." "Cardes and dyce," however, was so general an expression among these writers, that they very often apply it, in their appeals to ancient invectives against gaming, to periods when cards were not invented, or not included in the condemnation of dice.*

The earliest special prohibition of card-playing is one we have had to mention in our investigation of the probable date of the introduction of cards into Europe, that of Alphonso of Castile to the Chevaliers of the Order of the Band in 1332, the genuineness of which is disputed. The French edicts of 1254 (article 35), 1319, and 1369 against gaming contain no mention of cards, and that of 1397, which mentions them, merely prohibits their use, with that of games in which no chance is involved, to working people on working days. In Germany, the earliest enactment is contained in an ancient code of the city of Nuremberg, the date of which Von Murr fixes between 1380 and 1384, by which the following games are under certain circumstances, exempted from the penalties of gaming; "horse-racing, shooting with cross-bows, *cards*, shovelboard, tric-trac, and bowls, at which

---

* Northbrooke for instance, "Juvenall counteth dice play among those vices that easiest corrupt a whole household, and is the worst example that can be in a well-governed house, saying :—

> ' If ancient folks, before their youth
> doe play at *cardes or dice*,
> Their youth will frame to doe the like
> and imitate their vice.' "

a man may bet from twopence to a groat." Under 1397, however, there is a statute against them in the "Red Book" of Ulm, and the German town-books in the first half of the 15th century are full of regulations, prohibiting indeed, the general and inordinate use of cards, but granting in many instances indulgencies for play, on stated occasions. The jolly burghers indeed, would seem to have needed a little regulation of their amusements if we may judge from a bye-law of the "Schuffliker," or Shoemakers' Guild of Bamberg, in 1491, which imposes a fine of half a pound of, not *cobbler's*—as Mr. Chatto facetiously remarks—but *bees'* wax, for a candle to burn before their patron saint, upon any brother who should throw the back-gammon pieces, cards, or dice out of the window.

No license however, was allowed to the Clergy, for by the canon " de Ludis Prohibitis " promulgated by the Synod of Langres, in 1404, all Ecclesiastics are strictly prohibited, and principally those who are in holy orders, (as opposed to the *minor* orders of the Roman Church), and above all, priests and curates, from playing at dice, at tric-trac, and at *cards*.

In 1430, according to Menestrier, gaming of all kinds for money, was forbidden in the territories of Savoy, by Duke Amadeus VIII., though his subjects were allowed to amuse themselves at certain games, provided they play only for meat and drink. With respect to cards they are forbidden; nevertheless, they are allowed to women, with whom men may also play, provided that they play only for *pins*,—" *dum ludus fiat tantum cum spinulis*," by which, however, Mr. Chatto understands only something of small value.

In 1463, we have already stated, their importation was forbidden in England, and they are not included in the act against gaming till the 11th Hen. VII. (1495-6).

In 11th Hen. IV., *anno* 1409, an act had passed directing the infliction of six days imprisonment on persons offending against a statute of 12th Rich. II., cap. 6., *anno* 1388, enjoining on the labouring class archery practice on Sundays and holidays, instead of " coytes, dyces, casting of the stone, (*gettre de pere*) keyles, *et auctres tielx jeues importunes*," which were forbidden. The 18th Edw. IV., cap. 4, (1478-9), forbids under severe penalties, any householder to suffer any person to play in his house or garden, " at the closh-keyles, half-bowle, hand-in, hand-out, or quyc boarde," and recites the grounds of other like prohibitions, viz:—to bring in a more frequent use of the bow, because the defence of the land was much then by archers, to prevent the impoverishment of gamesters, and the occasioning of disorders.* The act of 11th Hen. VII. recited above, p. 102, includes cards for the first time among "tinyse, dyce, bowles and other vnlawfull games," and limits the stakes to "meate and drynke," on the sole occasion permitted, and this even was abolished by a later act of the same king in 1503.

By the "Archery Statute" of Henry VIII. in his thirty-third year, (1541-2) which compelled every one of the king's subjects, between seven years of age and sixty, save the clergy and justices, to practice shooting with the long-bow, and keep a bow and arrows proportioned to their strength, always ready for use, no person was allowed for his lucre and living to have any common house, alley, or place of bowling, coyting, closh-cayles, half-bowls, tennis, dicing, tables, or carding, or to haunt places so kept, which have not "placardes" expressing what games shall be used there, and what persons shall use the same. "And none artificer, or handycraftsman, husbandman, apprentyce, laborer, servant at husbandry,

* Vid. Gataker "*Of the Nature and Use of Lots,*" 4to, 1619, p. 203. *Abridgement of the Statutes*, 1542.

iorneyman or servant of artificer, maryner, fysher-
man, waterman, or serving man, shall play at
tables, tennis, dyce, cardes, bowles, closh, coytyng,
logating, &c.," out of Christmas, and then also
any where save in his master's house and presence.
So partial, however, was the operation of this
edict, that it permitted any servant to play at
cards, dice, or tables with his master, or any
gentleman repairing to his house, openly in his
house and in his presence; and every nobleman
or gentleman of £100 yearly income or above,
might license his servants at his discretion to
play at these games within his house, garden or
orchard, as well among themselves, as with others
repairing to the same house.*　Observe also, that
cards are mentioned without any special stigma,
among games of agility and skill, and the scope
of all these ancient statutes up to this time, appears
to be, to correct the bias of the vulgar mind, after
the decline of the military enthusiasm and chival-
rous spirit which characterized so strongly the
middle ages, to relax all meritorious exertions and
warlike exercises, and resort to such games and
recreations as promoted idleness and dissipation.

* This act was revived 2 and 3 Phil. and Mar., cap. 9, and
14 Eliz., and probably fell into disuse when gunpowder superseded the use of the long-bow.

The bishops and clergy of the Roman Church seem to have been peculiarly the objects of satire, in almost all countries, to the Reformed party for their addiction, in defiance of the Canon, to gaming and secular pursuits, and England and Scotland were, old writers say, by no means behind the rest in this respect.

With the Reformation however, came a stricter rule. Queen Elizabeth's "Injunctions," published in 1559, the first year of her reign, admonish the clergy that they " shall in no wise at any unlawful time, nor for any other cause than their honest necessities, haunt or resort to any taverns or alehouses. And after their meats, they shall not give themselves to drinking or riot, spending their time idly by day, and by night at dice, cards, or tables playing, or any other unlawful game,"* and one of the Visitation Articles of John, Bishop of Norwich, in 1561, directs inquiry to be made whether any parson, vicar, or curate, offend in these respects, and if any of them be " dycers, tablers, carders, swearers, or vehementlie suspected thereof." These prohibitions are embodied also in Canon xxv. (1603) with the addition, that no ecclesiastical persons shall give themselves to

* See *Injunctions, &c.*, Sparrow's Collection, No. 7.

any base or servile labour, and are therefore still binding on the clergy.

The laws which regulate the importation and manufacture of cards, up to the time of the Commonwealth, have been already discussed, and the progress of high play, and adventuring large sums of money, does not appear to have provoked the attention of the English Legislature till the reign of Charles II. In France, however, as early as 1565, minors were allowed to institute actions for the recovery of sums lost at play,* and an *ordonnance* dated January, 1628, in the reign of Louis XIII., declared all debts contracted at play, and all engagements and promises to pay the same, null and void, and not recoverable by law.

Probably the followers of Charles II. brought with them from France, the rage for heavy stakes and bets on the event of the game, for in the sixteenth year of that king, an act was passed against immoderate gaming, and the encouragement of professional gamesters, who plundered the younger nobility to the great loss of their time and estates. Any person who should fraudulently acquire any sum of money at cards

* *Ordonnance de Moulins*, art. 59. In 1781, Louis xvi., who hated gaming, renewed the ancient statutes, and added fresh penalties.

or betting, was to forfeit treble the amount, half to the crown, and half to the party losing. Also if any person losing more than £100 at play, should, for want of ready money, enter into any bond for further payment, that bond to be null and void, and the loser not to make good the same, but the winner to forfeit treble the excess over £100, one half to the king and the other to the prosecutor.* In fact, card playing became amenable to the law, from the moment of its ceasing to be an amusement, though the practical effect of its regulations was the creation of what are called *debts of honour*, inasmuch as they have no protection in law—a title, the propriety of which, involving as it does a breach of the law, is very equivocal.

The 9th Anne, c. 14. (1711), was still stricter; all securities for money won at play, or lent at such times were to be void ; and estates mortgaged for gambling debts, were to pass to the heir, as if the grantor were naturally dead. Any person also, losing £10 at one time, might recover it again of the winner by action of debt, and persons cheating at cards, were to forfeit five times the value to the informer, and suffer

* Stat. 16 Car. II., c. 7.   Card playing in the Royal Palaces was exempt from the operation of these Statutes, as were also games played for ready money, and not upon *Tick* or Credit.

corporal punishment as for perjury. This act was repealed in 1844 to protect, it is said, some eminent sporting characters who had become liable to its penalties, to an enormous extent.

Furthermore, by the Stat. 5, Geo. III., c. 24, no gamester was to have the benefit of the acts of bankruptcy, who shall have lost in one day £5, or £100 in twelve months, in play, racing, or betting.

The following present regulations affecting cards are taken, by permission, from McCulloch's valuable Commercial Dictionary, 1859. "By the 9th Geo. IV., c. 18, an annual license duty of 5s. shall be paid by every maker of playing cards and dice. The duty on every pack is to be 1s., and is to be specified on the ace of spades.* Cards are not to be made in any part of Great Britain except the metropolis, nor in Ireland, except in Dublin and Cork, under a penalty of £100. Cards are to be enclosed in wrappers with

* After the 11th of June, 1711, for thirty-two years, the act directs there shall be a duty on each pack of cards made, of sixpence, and one of the cards stamped on the spotted side as the Commissioners of Stamp Duties shall direct, under a penalty of £5. Lenthall's cards, however, which were certainly before 1685, bear a red stamp with a crown, and that sum stamped over the design on the ace of spades; as do also more than one other pack of that period mentioned in the course of this history.

such marks as the Commissioners of Stamps may appoint. Before license can be had, bond must be given to the amount of £500 for payment of the duties, &c. Selling or exposing for sale any pack of cards not duly stamped, subjects a licensed maker to a penalty of £50, and any one else £10. Any person having in his possession, or using, or permitting to be used, any pack of cards not duly stamped, to forfeit £5. Second-hand cards may be sold by any person, if sold without the wrapper of a licensed maker, and in packs containing not more than fifty-two cards including an ace of spades duly stamped, and enclosed in a wrapper with the words 'second-hand cards' printed or written in distinct characters on the outside; penalty for selling second-hand cards in any other manner £20."

To give a corresponding detail of the French regulations, would tax the patience of our readers; but as early as 1581, under Henri III., a duty of one sol, in addition to the usual charges, was levied on every case of cards of two hundred pounds weight, designed for exportation, but this in 1605, was entirely prohibited, and a reduction of the home duty made as compensation. At present, in both countries, cards for exportation are duty free.

In 1583, a tax of one sol parisis was levied on each pack manufactured, and double for tarots. At the Revolution, cards like all other things, gained and then lost their freedom, for while the *cartiers* chuckled over their advantage, the law of the *9th Vindémiaire, An. VI.*, imposed a stamp duty on cards, which has remained ever since. This duty is now 15 centimes for each pack of national or piquet cards, and 40 for tarots, *a dos grisaille*, or any cards which differ from the standard pattern. The only cards free of duty, are the little toy packs sold for children's new year's gifts at a sou a piece, and even with these, there is the condition that their relations do not use them for piquet or *écarté!*

The French company of card-makers was suppressed in 1776, but re-established a few months afterwards. The license of a card-maker in France costs 50 francs, and the act of defrauding the revenue, by manufacturing cards without the excise paper furnished for the purpose, or in other ways, involves enormous penalties, and the forfeiture of their franchise. Foreign cards are still prohibited in France.

II. NOMENCLATURE. Cards, or more properly, Playing-cards, to distinguish them from Cards for wool, and Cards an old name for charts or maps,—

in French, *Cartes a jouer;* in German, *Briefe,*
and *Karten* or *Spielkarten;* in Dutch, *Kaarten* or
Speelkaarten; in Danish, *Kort* or *Spilkort;* and
in Russian, *Kartü;* but in Italian, *Naibi;* in
Portuguese, *Naipe;* and in Spanish, *Naypes* or
Naipes,—are divided into two principal classes,
Tarocchi or tarots, and French piquet cards.

The Tarot class includes two varieties; the
tarots, properly so called, a pack of which
includes seventy-eight cards, twenty-two being emblematic, and called atouts, and having no
corresponding feature in any other European
pack;—to which, in consequence of their Oriental
affinities, we have assigned the first place; and
the so called Trappola packs consisting of from
thirty-six to forty-eight cards only, bearing generally the Southern or Oriental marks of suits
like the numeral cards of the tarot, of which
some consider it the original form. The Italian
and Spanish cards of this kind, have the Oriental
feature of a knight or horseman, in place of a
queen, in which they are followed by the German,
the suits of which, however, are different. The
tarots only have both queen and knight, and the
full number of pips, but the Italian trappola
wants the three upper cards of each suit, and the
Germans generally abjure the aces and the three

low cards after the deuce, and the Spaniards the tens.

Of the French piquet cards, which have in many countries entirely or nearly superseded the others, it will be sufficient here to recapitulate, that the marks of suits, honours, &c., correspond with our own, except that in certain games the low cards are rejected in different proportions.

With regard to the tarots, it is singular that so many of the packs, no matter where manufactured, bear French titles, some of them as we have seen, of very barbarous orthography. A pack, however, in our own possession, inscribed on the deuce of cups "*Fabbricatore Gumppenberg*," and on the backs of the cards, which are *tarottés* in blue, "In Milano," has the titles in Italian, corresponding with those of the French pack of 1500 described in our second chapter :—

MODERN ITALIAN.	FRENCH, 1500.
I. Il Bagatell.	Le Bateleur.
II. La Papessa.	La Papesse.
III. L'Imperatrice.	L'Impératrice.
IV. L'Imperatore.	L'Empéreur.
V. Il Papa.	Le Pape.
VI. Gli Amanti.	L'Amoureux.
VII. Il Carro	Le Chariot.
VIII. La Giustizia.	La Justice.
IX. L'Eremita.	L'Erémite.
X. La Ruota.	La Roue de Fortune.
XI. La Forza.	La Force.

MODERN ITALIAN.	FRENCH, 1500.
XII. L'Appeso.	Le Pendu.
XIII. (Death).	La Mort.
XIV. La Temperanza.	La Tempérance.
XV. Il Diavolo.	Le Diable.
XVI. La Torre.	La Foudre.
XVII. Le Stelle.	L'Etoile.
XVIII. La Luna.	La Lune.
XIX. Il Sole.	Le Soleil.
XX. Il Giudizio.	Le Jugement.
XXI. Il Mondo.	Le Monde.
—— Il Matto.	Le Fou.

Garzoni's description published in 1589, varies the names of the following:—I. Il Pagadello; VI. L'Amore; IX. Il Vecchio; XI. La Fortezza: XII. L'Impicciato; XIII. La Morte; XVI. Il Fuoco; XVII. La Stella; and XX. L'Angelo, also called La Tromba.

The modern French tarots have also Pagad as No. I,; Jupiter and Juno take the place of the Pope and Papess; IX. is called Le Prêtre, or the Capuchin, and XVI. La Maison Dieu.*

The names by which the picture cards and marks of suits in the numeral series are known in various countries, may be best seen in the following table, which also exhibits the relation in which they stand to each other:

* Mr. Chatto mentions a pack inscribed " Cartes des Suisses," manufactured at Brussels, in which No. 2. has a figure with the title "Le'Spagnol Capitano Eraçasse" : No. 5. Bacchus supplies the place of Jupiter, and No. 16. has a *tree* struck by lightning, instead of a tower.

	COURT CARDS.					SUITS.				No.
	King	Queen	Cavalier	Valet	Ace	Bastoni	Coppe	Danari	Spade	
CLASS I. (A.) TAROTS.										
Italian.	Re.	Regina.	Cavallo.	Fante.	Asso.	Bastoni.	Coppe.	Danari.	Spade.	78.
French.	Roy.	Reyne.	Chevalier.	Valet.	As.	Bastons.	Coupes.	Deniers.	Espees.	78.
CLASS I. (B.) TRAPPOLA, ETC.										
Italian. / Silesian.²	Re. / Reh.		Cavallo. / Cavall.	Fante. / Fantell.	Asso.	Bastoni.¹	Coppe.	Danari.	Spade.	40. / 36.
Spanish.	Rey.		Caballo.	Sota.	As.	Bastos.	Copas.	Oros or Dineros.	Espadas.	48.
Portuguese.	Rey.		Cavallo.	Soto.	As.	Paos.	Copas.	Ouros, Oiros.	Spadas.	48.
German.	König.	Ober.	Unter.		Daus.	Eicheln.	Roth.	Schellen.	Grün or Laub.	36-48.
CLASS II. FRENCH PIQUET CARDS.										
French.	Roi.	Reine or Dame.		Valet.	As.	Trèfles.³	Cœurs.	Carreaux.	Piques.	36-52.
Italian.	Re.	Dama.		Fante.	Asso.	Fiori.	Cuori.	Quadri.	Picche or Cappari.	
English.	King.	Queen.		Knave.	Ace.	Clubs.	Hearts.	Diamonds.	Spades.	52.
Spanish.	Rey.	Reyna.		Sota.	As.	Palos.	Corazones.	Ladrillos.	Picas.	52.
German.	König.	Dame.		Knecht.	Asz.	Kreuzen.	Herzen.	Rauten.	Spaten.	52.
Dutch.	Koning.	Koningin.		Knecht.	Aas.	Klaver.	Harten.	Ruyten.	Schoppen.	52.
Danish.	Konge.	Dame.		Knecht.	Es.	Klöver.	Hierten.	Ruder.	Spader.	52.
Latin.						Trifolia.	Corda.	Denarii.	Ligones.	52.

1 The club suit was called in Italy in the 16th century *Colonne*, instead of Bastoni or Mattoni, and *Specchi* or mirrors took the place of money. In the German Trappola pack, mentioned p. 132, the ace of Batons resembles a column, and has Roses instead of money. 2 Breitkopf. 3 Peignot says, that in 1668, *Fleur* was used for Trèfle, and the Valets were called *Fous.*

A comparison of these, sufficiently attests the extent to which the invention of the French has been received, and also shews that England is not alone in her variation of their name of the fourth suit, for the Dutch *schop* (scoop or shovel) can, at any rate, claim no immediate affinity with the knightly *espada* of the Spanish Don. "Clubs" however, with us, is beyond all dispute, an anomaly.

We have already noticed an attempt* to make our card-emblems and their names more consistent with each other, but an earlier and more complete essay in the same direction occurs in a pack, date 1790, by Rowley and Co. Here again, the spade is a kind of dagger, of a clumsy and inconvenient form; the ace of the suit being, however, a regular "duty-card." The ace of clubs is a clover-leaf in an oval, surmounted by agricultural implements. "Diamonds" clearly points to the original conventional form of representing this gem, being a veritable diamond, lozenge-shaped, with the facets of the cutting shewn in relief. This idea of a quadrangular shape is involved in all the names of the diamond suit, whether it be panes of glass, (*Rauten, Ruyten*, &c.), or paving tiles, (Spanish

* *Suprà*, p. 183.

Ladrillos), a sense also given to *Carreaux,* by Menestrier.*

The ace of hearts, in the same pack, is represented by a chalice, with a heart engraved on the front, an irreverent introduction, characteristic of that epoch, for we are left in no doubt as to what is meant, for the oval in which it is contained is surmounted by a mitre, cross and crozier. The Court cards appear to be portraits, and the costumes are of the period.

Apropos of Court cards, it may be well to observe that these were anciently called *Coat* cards;† and Strutt says, "I conceive the name implied coated figures, that is, men and women who wore coats in contradistinction to the other devices of flowers and animals."

* *Suprà,* p. 77. According to Minsheu, *Guide into the Tongues, fol.* 1627, a diamond or *Picke,* at cards is called "because he is picked or sharp pointed as the diamond stone," and a writer in the *Gent's Mag.,* for Jan. 1791, says the common people in a great part of Yorkshire invariably call them by this name; "This I take," he says, "to be from the French word *piques,* spades; but cannot account for its being corruptly applied to the other suit." The true reason, however, as Brand remarks, is to be gathered from the resemblance the diamond bears to a *mill-pick,* as fusils are sometimes called in heraldry.—*Popular Antiquities,* vol. ii., p. 11., 4to., 1813.

† Thus, Sir John Harrington, (1615), in his *Metamorphosis of Ajax,* says, "When Brutus had discarded the kings and queens out of the pack, and shown himself sworn enemy to all the *Coate Cardes,* then crept in many new forms of government."—*Strutt,* B. iv., ch. ii., 23.

As early as 1656, we have seen, the numeral cards were called "peeps," or pips, and up to the time of Charles II., a pack of cards was constantly termed a *pair* of cards, a word used anciently, like the Italian *Paio*, to express collectively, a series of separate articles, as *un paio di carte da giuocare, un paio di Scacchi*, &c., and by our old writers, " a payre of Tables," " a payre of beedes," i. e., a rosary.* The explanation of it as a pair of packs, used alternately, as by modern players, is inapplicable, from the evident application of it to a single pack, by Ascham, in a passage quoted above, p. 146. In Queen Elizabeth's time, a pack of cards was also called a *bunch*, and in some of Shakspeare's plays a *Deck*, a term still in use in Brand's time, in the north of England.

Seven of the cards of the Spanish game, accor-

---

* Vocabolario della Crusca, *in voce.* Also Palsgrave, *Eclair-cissement de la langue Française, fol.* 1530. In an old play, called *The longer thou livest, the more fool thou art*, Idleness desires Moros, the clown, to "look at the booke," and shews him "a paier of cardes," and in another old play, *A Woman killed with Kindness*, a pair of cards and counters are mentioned. Sometimes the pack of cards was called a Stock, as in a passage of the old morality of *Three Ladies of London*, "now all the cards in the stock are dealt about," &c. We have already men-tionedt he epithet, "Books of the Four Kings," which Sir Thomas Urquhart, at the end of his translation of the XXII. chapter of Gargantua, has given to a pack of cards though without any cor-responding French expression, *Suprà* p. 87.

ding to Court de Gebelin, are known by peculiar appellations, the mystic significations of which we shall revert to hereafter. The ace of Oros is *Le Borgne*, or, "the One-eyed;" the trey is *Le Seigneur*; the trey of cups, *La Dame*; the deuce is *La Vache*, or "the Cow;" the nines of cups and money are the great and little nines; and the ace of clubs is *Le Serpent*.*

Some of our own cards have also their *sobriquets*, but of no very evident origin. The nine of diamonds is called the " Curse of Scotland," for which several reasons have been assigned ;—that it is an allusion to the arms of Colonel Packer, (*Gules*, a cross lozengy,) who guarded Charles I. on the scaffold, and was hated for his severities in Scotland afterwards; then a similar reason connected with the Earl of Stair ; a third explains it as a corruption of *Cross of Scotland*, the pips being arranged somewhat in the fashion of a St. Andrew's Cross. In the *Oracle; or, Resolver of Questions*, 12mo, 1770, the reason of the name being given is stated to be that the crown of Scotland had but nine diamonds in it, and they

* The ace of swords in a pack of Spanish cards now lying before us, bearing the arms of Carlos I. (1516-1556), is wreathed round with what might be taken for a large serpent, in the folds of which is a monkey, apparently with his foot on a roundel, on which is the number 16.

were never able to get more.* The more probable explanation is, however, that in the game of Pope Joan, the nine of diamonds is the *Pope*, of whom our Scottish neighbours have an especial horror.

The common explanation of the term, that it was the card on which the " Butcher Duke " wrote a sanguinary order, after the battle of Culloden, is disproved by a passage in Dr. Houstoun's *Memoirs of his own Lifetime*, where he states that the Jacobite ladies nicknamed this card " the Justice Clerk," after the rebellion of 1715, " Curse of Scotland " being a term of reproach, inflicted on the Lord Justice Clerk Ormistone, for his cruelty in repressing it.

The six of hearts is said to have acquired, in Ireland, the name of " Grace's card," from the spirited answer returned by one of that family, to Marshal Schomberg, who sent to tempt him to espouse the cause of William III., " Tell your master," he wrote on the back of the card, " I despise his offer ; and that honour and conscience are dearer than all the wealth and titles a prince can bestow."† The ace of diamonds has an epithet of the " Earl of Cork " in that country, for a very different reason, if we may believe Mr. Carleton, " because it is the worst ace, and

* See Chatto, p. 267-8.   † Chatto, p. 266.

the poorest card in the pack, and is called the
Earl of Cork, because he's the poorest nobleman
in Ireland."* "Hob Collingwood," according to
Brockett, is the North Country title of the four
of hearts, considered an unlucky card at whist
by ancient spinsters; and [the four of clubs is
known amongst sailors as "the devil's bed-post."

In the *Gentleman's Magazine*, for 1791, before
quoted, the replies to the queries on cards state
that in Northamptonshire the queen of clubs is
called "Queen Bess," perhaps because that
queen, as history states, was of a swarthy complexion, and the four of spades, "Ned Stokes."

At the old game of gleek, Mr. Chatto says,
the ace was called *Tib*; the knave, *Tom*; and the
four, *Tiddy*. The five and six appear to have
been respectively called *Towser* and *Tumbler*,
and to have counted double when turned up. At
certain games the knave of clubs is called Pam,†
and at all-fours the knave is Jack.

That "Trump" called by the French *atout*, and
meaning the dominant suit, as determined by the
turned up card, is derived from *triumph* is evident
from Bishop Latimer's sermons "On the Card,"
preached at Cambridge about 1529, where he speaks

* *Traits and Stories of the Irish Peasantry.*

† In Germany Pam bears the nickname of Wenzel (*Wences-
laus*) or *der Treffle-bube.*

of hearts being his triumph card. It was also the title of a game both in France and England.

Lastly, as to the ordinary names of the three first cards of the pack,—ace, deuce, and tray,— the term As, or Asso, by which it is known in the Southern packs, is sufficiently indicative of unity to connect it with the As, the unit of the Roman coinage.

The German Daus is their master-card ; the English Deuce the lowest of all ; and though the card-player, when it falls into his hand, comforts himself with the hope that "there's luck in the black deuce," all efforts to connect it with the Greek δυς, or the Northern sprite, who figures as the spirit of evil in the superstitions of the vulgar, as well in connection with cards, "the Devil's Books," as with everything else, are un- necessary and absurd, as we have in the Spanish *Dos* and *Tres*, a very satisfactory origin, without involving any diabolic identity of

DEUCE AND TRAY.

III. MANUFACTURE, &c. The art of card-making appears as a regular business in the municipal records of foreign countries about 1420, and its introduction into this country took place, in all probability, some years later, though since their importation from abroad was forbidden in 1463, materials must have been already produced at home, for that which was, even then, beginning to be a popular amusement. It is not improbable that the *alluminors* and printers specially exempted in the alien act of 1 Rich. III., cap. 9, *anno.* 1483, from being prevented from dwelling within the realm for the exercise of their occupations, may have been the *form-schneiders* and *briefmahlers* of mediæval England.

It would very desirable to discover information as to their early productions, but little or nothing is known on the subject. Cards, however, sold at two-pence a pack as related by Ascham in 1545, even allowing for the difference in the value of money, could neither be remarkable for their execution or for their durability, and the superior specimens then manufactured abroad, would be coveted by all who were likely to preserve them.

A peculiarity in the construction of the Italian cards which has conduced much to their better preservation, has been already adverted to,* the making the back layer of the card wider than the other two, and then pasting it over the edges to form a border in front. The ancient specimens of Spanish and German cards, are composed of only two layers, which are frequently separated by the effect of age and damp.

The company of the "Mystery of the Makers of Playing Cards," established in 1629, made great efforts to improve the quality of their wares, and the price of a pack in 1684, appears to have risen to fourpence. Mr. Chatto says, that the card-makers in and about London, in Queen Anne's time, numbered about a hundred; and that there were then annually imported 40,000 reams of Genoa white paper for the purpose of making cards. The price to retailers, one pack with another, was only three-halfpence a pack, and their profit not above a halfpenny. Though they were made smaller and thinner than now, the price seems exceedingly unremunerative.

The art of card-making is one of the few remaining trades still regarded as a "mystery." Secrecy in some manufactories is enjoined among the workmen, and some parts of the process are conducted within barred doors. Like other myste-

* *Suprà*, p. 130.

ries, however, all that is important to know, is no longer a secret, and full and excellent accounts of the whole process may be found in the Art-Dictionaries and Cyclopædias of the day.*

The material used in card making, is a pasteboard, composed of several layers, of which, in England four are used, of uniform quality, first enamelled to exclude the effects of the atmosphere, and afterwards brought to a high solidity and polish by pressure. In France, three are used, the middle one being of a grey colour and coarser texture, to prevent transparency; and the paper for the fronts must be procured from the excise, in sheets containing twenty cards, each of which bears the water-mark of an eagle, (formerly a *fleur-de-lys*) to prevent contraband manufacture.

The ordinary process then adopted in both countries, is to print the outlines, &c., of the devices, and then they are filled up with water-colours by the aid of a stencil. Here again in France, the Government interferes, each card-maker being required to deposit his blocks in the office of the excise, and the impressions are struck off there, under the surveillance of the

* See *Ure's Dictionary of Arts, Manufactures and Mines,* 1860; *The Encyclopædia Britannica; Chambers's Encyclopædia;* and *Bradshaw's Journal,* No. 24, 16th April, 1842.

department, on the water-marked paper furnished for the purpose. The English are not so particular.

The cards are divided into *têtes* and *points*, or pips. The latter are printed here in the ordinary letter-press method, from twenty to forty cards on a block; the têtes, by means of blocks for each colour fitting into each other, so as to form the whole device, but used successively, care being taken that the several parts accurately register by means of points in the tympan of the hand-press, or marks in the stones if the litho-graphic process be used.

In 1832, Messrs. De La Rue obtained a patent for certain improvements in the manufacture of playing cards, viz:—printing in oil colours by means of types and blocks—effecting the same by means of lithography; and thirdly, gilding or silvering ornamental details by either of these processes; and they are, we believe, very chary of allowing their method to be known. It is, however, much the same as that used by printers of calicoes, paper-hangings, &c.

The French use two blocks to print their *têtes*, one of which contains twice over the kings and queens, two knaves of clubs, and two knaves of spades. The other block has ten knaves of hearts, and ten knaves of diamonds. The reason of this is, that for the designs of the first block, five colours are required—red, yellow, dark blue, light blue, and black,—while for the colouring of the second set, no black is required.

As some makers in England still colour their *têtes* by means of stencils, it may be as well to give the French method as described in the *Encyclopédie Moderne*,—" The card-makers themselves construct their stencils ; they employ for these, *imprimures*, that is, sheets of paper covered on each side with several coats of oil colour. As many stencils are required as there are colours to impress, five for the sheet which contains the kings, and four for the other. The workman then takes one of these *imprimures*, places on it a pattern sheet of cards properly coloured, fixes the two firmly together, and then with a sharp-pointed knife, cuts out all the pieces which are of the same colour. He proceeds the same with the next colour, laying a fresh *imprimure* under the same sheet, and so on with the rest." The stencils for the pips are punched out, but the English print them, as before observed. " Everything being thus arranged, the stencils are successively placed over the printed outlines, care being taken that the perforation of the stencil corresponds exactly with the design in outline, and that there are no *fenêtres* or gaps in the colouring. The colours used are distemper, and are taken up on a large brush, spread on a plate, and then applied to the stencil in the usual manner. When dry, the cards are polished, cut on the edges, arranged in packs, and put in envelopes containing either single packs or half dozens. The excise reserves the right of printing and delivering to the makers the ace of *trèfles*, and the packs when wrapped in their envelopes, are again brought to the office, and their bands impressed with a dry stamp."

The ace of spades, the English "duty card" is in like manner printed at the stamp-office, and an officer is sent to seal the envelopes and cases for export.

Abroad, the preference is always given to English-made cards, this is partly owing to the perfection of the machinery employed, and the care taken in the different processes,—pasting, pressing, colouring, &c.,—which causes them to be more durable ; and partly, because they are always believed to be honest, that is, without those cheating tricks and secret marks on their backs, which characterize many of the foreign cards : no slight tribute to the good faith of the nation.

As nothing is further from our wish than to

minister even indirectly to the vices of a nation, we shall abstain from a description of those cards of an indecent nature, which at first sight present nothing different to the eye from ordinary cards, but when held up to the light reveal groups of the grossest, and most sensual description. They are largely made in France, Germany, and even Spain, and find their way to this country, though we believe the English are not so far gone in immorality as to manufacture them.

The beautiful patterns observable on the backs of some cards, are printed by the Messrs. De La Rue, from woven wire, for which they have taken out a new patent. It is this firm which exports the largest quantity to the Continent; Reynolds and Sons, to the Colonies. No less than 134,684, and 197,178 packs were respectively exported by these firms in 1859; and 120,700, and 76,882 supplied for the home market. The duty of one shilling per pack on cards produced in 1859-60 the sum of £15,256 shewing that 305,120 packs had been disposed of in England. The qualities of cards are distinguished by their envelopes, which bear respectively a portrait of the Great Mogul, of King Henry VIII., a Highlander, and a Merry Andrew.

The regulations affecting the manufacture

of cards in England, having been sufficiently described in the first section of this chapter, it remains to add a few scattered facts connected with the Continent. For the easier collection of the duty, the manufacture of cards in France is limited to some of the chief towns, and the tax, originally expended in the encouragement of manufactures, was devoted by Louis XVI. in 1751 to the support of the *Ecole Militaire*. The company or guild of card-makers of Paris were suppressed in 1776, but re-established soon after. In their statutes of 1594, they called themselves *Tarotiers*, but when they were first constituted is unknown. The trade in France was carried on in 1847, by 129 makers, of whom 16 were at Paris, who employed 263 men, women, and children. A curious instance of the extent to which real occupation diminishes the propensity for trivial amusement, is afforded by the fact, that the French excise, which stamped in 1847, 5,555,807 packs, of which 1,337,678 belonged to Paris alone, only registered the next year 4,476,723—a diminution to the revenue of 32 per cent. In Russia, where in the long winter evenings, the extent of card playing is unparalleled, the manufacture is a royal monopoly, which is enjoyed by the Foundling Hospital at St. Petersburg, the most richly endowed of all the Russian institutions, and Mr. Chatto mentions a paragraph in the *Literary Gazetteer*, stating that though 14,400 packs were manufactured daily, the supply was unequal to the demand, and that a petition had been presented to the Emperor, praying for a more liberal issue.

PLATE XLIV

Arms of the Card Companies of France.

End of Part I.

PART THE SECOND.

CARD PLAYING AND CARD PLAYERS.

I.

THE GAMES OF THE XVTH. AND XVITH. CENTURIES.

ONCE on a time, there was a king of the North who was impressed with a violent horror of gaming, and prohibited it throughout his dominions under the severest penalties. No play of any kind was permitted to be used—neither cards, nor dice, nor loto, nor anything,—all was done away with. His Scandinavian majesty piqued himself amazingly upon this exhibition of authority, and said to himself every morning, "Certes, thou art a man of might! is it a fact that thou art only a man?" After a day or two, however, the secret police warned him that certain great lords were in the habit of meeting in secret assembly, and there playing away sums beyond all reason. No sooner heard, than an order was issued to discover the place of meeting, and seize the materials of play. Soon they found out that the forbidden spot was a spacious saloon. A spy insinuated himself there forthwith. No one spoke; all was according to the edict— neither cards, nor dice, nor loto. Nevertheless, from time to time, certain of the company manifested emotions of delight, and others appeared correspondingly depressed. Money passed from one to another; evidently play was going on. But the question was, *at what ?* The spy was utterly at fault, and the king from chagrin got the megrims. A long time afterwards, the king learned that his courtiers had hit on the following device; they kept their eyes on the lofty windows of the saloon, each one selecting a pane to observe, and the winner was he, on whose pane, in a given number of minutes, the greatest number of flies had alighted !

This anecdote enables us, at the commencement of the second part of our subject, to dispense with any elaborate discussions upon Gaming in general, and the influence which the passion for play exerts in upsetting the good sense of individuals.

We have before remarked the early cognizance

taken of it by the law. Even the Romans issued edicts against it, for they played desperately in those times, though they had nothing but *tali*, or hucklebones, the tossing of which afforded them it appears, infinite delight, albeit it might well kill us of modern times, with sheer *ennui*. The fathers of the Church and the councils multiplied the prohibitions, and in the eleventh century the Cardinal Peter Damian condemned a Florentine bishop, who had played at a hostel to excess, to recite the entire Psalter thrice, to wash the feet of a dozen paupers, and then give them a crown a-piece!

Gaming was forbidden by Mohammed,* and it is wonderful to what an extent the better sort of Moslems at any rate, have abstained from it.

In India and China, the mania for play is extreme.† The poem of Mahabarata exhibits

* In the chapter of the Koran, entitled "the Cow," the word used in Sale's translation is *lots*, which the commentators take to mean games of chance or hazard, at which anything is played for or betted. This is observed by the Sonnite sect, who moreover eschew even *carved* chessmen, conceiving that the dislike of Mohammed was founded likewise on their resemblance to *images*. The Persians and Hindus are not so scrupulous, and the Moors play at ombre in secret.—*Vide* p. 24.

† "Gaming is the ruling passion of the Chinese. No sooner does the artisan touch his scanty wages, than he rushes off to play, without troubling himself as to whether he thereby risks the necessaries of life. It is with them a perfect mania, which

Judishter and his four brothers, although famous as models of royal wisdom, losing their treasures, and even their kingdom, at a game of dice.

But our concern is neither with the tali of the ancients, nor with the dice of more modern times. Our task is to investigate the history of cards, and to recount the associations immediately connected with it, and for this our space is already all too small; the materials which exist, were they accessible to us, being probably sufficient to form a far more imposing volume than we can pretend to.

We have already, in the earlier part of this work, discussed the Tarots, and their Oriental

presents a curious contrast to their usual sordid avarice. Moreover, it is by no means the lower class of Chinese who are thus imbued with the passion for play. Rich and poor, labourers and merchants, all are gamesters and frantic ones too. No people also, are in possession of such means of gratifying their desires ; with them anything will do for a game, provided there is a chance of winning and losing, so as to keep the balance even. Games which with us are left to children, with them are played with avidity at any age. This does not hinder them from having games like ours, of a more piquant kind, where a stroke of good luck may double one's fortune, or an unlucky turn produce a correspondingly calamitous result. I have seen houses at Amoy quite up to the mark of the most scandalous of our *hells*; and what surprised me much, I discovered in the jargon of these players of the far east the same humorous and figurative expressions which we remark among our own."— MONTFORT, *Voyage en Chine*, 1854.

affinities,—affinities which, while separating them from the category of ordinary playing cards, go far to prove them a connecting link between the latter and their prototypes in the far east.

There are, in the museum of the Royal Asiatic Society, some packs of circular Hindustani cards, one of them alleged to be a thousand years old. Another, similar to this, has for four of its marks of suits, a parallelogram, a sword, a flower, and a vase ; and a third bears the mythic representation of the ten Avatars, or incarnations of Vishnu. True it is, that the temptation in these matter is, to see *too much*, to none more than Orientalists ; true also, that a writer who describes them quotes Cicero to prove that the Brahmins, who invented all things, consequently invented cards ;* yet we cannot help seeing in these facts, on the one hand, a parallel to the allegories of the tarots, and on the other the carreau and espada, the club (*fiore*) and the copa of the numeral European suits. Another pack has something resembling an acorn, and all of them have two honours, a king, and a vizier on horseback, and ten numeral cards in each suit, with pips of no more uniform type indeed than the European, but arranged

* See a review of "Whist, *par Deschappelles*," by B. E. B. Pote in the *Foreign Quarterly*, No. 48, p. 344.

precisely in the same order. In numbers the resemblance ceases, the suits varying from eight to ten.

It is the old Spanish cards, of all others, which retain most traces of an hereditary Oriental type; and from a description of the game played with the Hindustani cards in the *Calcutta Magazine*, (vol. ii., 1815.) Mr. Chatto considers it to present striking points of analogy with the Spanish game of *Ombre à trois.** It is to be regretted that we are in possession of such scanty information respecting the old Spanish games, but they were probably, as we have before observed, of a grave and dignified character, in accordance with the temperament of the nation, (*p.* 41).

That cards of this kind were in use among the higher classes in the south of Europe, in the very earliest times, is evident from the miniature in the MS. *Romance of King Méliadus*, mentioned at p. 57, and now in the British Museum (*Addit. MS.*, 12, 228, *fol.* 313, *V°.*), stated to have been

---

* Chatto, p. 45. The game appears to be called *Gunjeefu*, and the terms employed in it of a Persian or Arabian origin. See also specimens of the Portuguese pack, 1693, copied from the *Jeux de Cartes, Tarots, &c. Ib.*, p. 253, where it is remarked that the *Oros* on those cards much more resemble the *Chakra*, or quoit of Vishnu than pieces of money. The other details also are remarkably Oriental.

executed in the south of France, between the
years 1330 and 1350, and representing a royal
party at cards, on which are plainly marked the
two and four of Oros or money, and the deuce
of Bastos or clubs.*

Akin to these in almost every respect, and
probably contemporaneous, so that they must
needs spring of a common stock, were the Trappola
cards, with which the hot-blooded and hasty
Italians played their earliest games of mere
hazard. The Trappola game was probably extremely simple, and Singer says, was played
with thirty-six cards only. Nine cards were dealt
to each player, which, if four played, consumed
the whole number, but if only two played, eighteen remained in the stock. The cards, and
probably the game, migrated from Italy into
Germany, in the fourteenth century; where some
of the earliest packs bear the Trappola suits, and
were still, in Breitkopf's time, in common use
among the country people in Silesia, their
mutilated names betraying their Italian origin,

* For illustration of this important bit of evidence, see
Singer, p. 68, who, moreover (p. 3), says, that cards make
appearance in the annals of Provence, about the year 1361, and
that the valet was then known by the name of *Tuchim*, the
appellation of a band of robbers then ravaging the Venaissin:
see also the *Art Journal*, (which gives plates of two other
mediæval card parties) for 1859.

—*Reh, Cavall, Fantell,* &c.,—and the suits retain their Italian names.*

The writers of the sixteenth century, who mention Tarocchi as a kind of cards, give an account of them entirely corresponding to the packs still used in some parts of France, Switzerland, Germany, and Italy, consisting of fifty-six numeral, and twenty-two emblematical cards. The comparative antiquity of these two kinds, probably originally distinct, is undetermined; and Garzoni's description of the game, in 1589, as a new invention, had probably, from the context, only a reference to the introduction of the French suits, instead of the Southern; and thus Volaterrano's evidence, which he adduces, may have only related to a change in the form of the game, and not to the first origin of it.† That their combination took place as early as 1393, is evident from the cards executed for Charles VI., by Gringonneur, which are to all intents and purposes tarots, though not yet arranged according to the order of the later packs.

Cicognara states, that the inventor of the game

* Singer, p. 29.

† See above, p. 128, 131. The pack first described on p. 131, was probably of this description, as there was neither 3, 4, 5, nor 6, in it. A very early pack of the kind is also engraved in Breitkopf's work.

was Francis Fibbia, Prince of Pisa, who was an exile in Bologna, and died in 1419, but as Mr. Chatto suggests, there is nothing in his account hostile to the supposition that Fibbia may have merely modified and combined in one pack, for the purpose of playing Tarocchino, two already existent elements, the old series of Atouts, and the Trappola or numeral cards.*

There are two classes of games played in Italy with Tarots, the one *Tarocco*, or *Tarrocchino*, according to Baretti, (*Manners and Customs of Italy*, ii., 217), chiefly prevalent in Piedmont and Lombardy, with seventy-eight cards; the other *Minchiate*, which is most in vogue in Tuscany and the Pope's dominions, with ninety-eight.† In both, the numeral cards, with the exception of the kings, are called *Cartacce*, or *Cartiglie*, and the atouts, which in the Minchiate pack, are increased to forty, with the Matto or Fool— *Tarocchi* or *Trionfi*.   They are also called *Germini*, which his Dictionary renders "terrestrial triumphs."   "Both games also," he says, " may be played by only two or only three people, in several ways, but the most ingenious, as well as

* Chatto, p. 192.

† At Munich, according to Singer, they have increased the number of cards to 103, by doubling the twenty-one Tarocchi, the fool, and the ace, king, and knave of hearts,—p. 30.

the most in use, are two or three games that are
played by four people; and one especially, one
against three, after the ruling principle of ombre;
and another played, two against two, not unlike
whist."

In the Paris edition of the *Maison des Jeux*,
1668, the compiler, after remarking that the Swiss
and Germans prefer Tarocco to any other game,
gives brief descriptions of one or two methods of
playing it. One, which he calls *Triomphe forcée*,
may be played by two or more persons; five cards
are dealt to each; the holders of the fool and the
juggler save their stakes; the player who has
La Force gets double, or if "Death" falls to his
lot, he sweeps the board. The winners, moreover,
continue their game, and the one who makes the
most tricks gains it.

Another is a three-handed game in vogue among
the Swiss, in which all the cards but three are
dealt, which the dealer takes into his own hand,
discarding three inferior cards for the purpose.
He who has made the most points at the expiration of the third deal, is the winner. The cards
count according to a certain scale, the World,
the Juggler, the kings and queens, *five* each; the
Fool only *three*; but he never takes or is taken,
for in case he is covered by a higher card, the

holder is privileged to substitute any card for
him, from the trick he has won; he is of all suits,
and can therefore be played on any emergency,
which is called an *excuse*. A different game is
described by Court de Gebelin, the account of
which we compress from Singer. Here, as before,
five cards are dealt, and the dealer takes up
and discards three, but as only two persons
play, the third hand is kept in reserve. The
first five of the figured cards, (see p. 14), are
called *petits atous*, and Nos. xvi to xxii, the
grands atous. If a player has three of either
of these, he counts five points; if four, ten
points, and fifteen if he has five. Ten of the
atous in a hand of twenty-five counts ten more;
and thirteen are equal to fifteen points, independent of their other combinations. Seven
cards—the World, the Fool, the Juggler, and the
four kings—are called *Tarocchi nobili*, or *Tarots
par excellence*. If a player has two of the three
first of these in his hand, he can call the third,
by saying *qui ne l'a;* and if it is not forthcoming,
he marks five points; but if he holds all three
himself, fifteen; sequences or flushes of four
cards mark also five points. The *role* of the Fool
is the same as in the other game, and may be played
to form a sequence in an *excuse*. The Fool with

two kings, counts five points; with three kings, fifteen points. If the *Pagad,* or Juggler, is taken, the party taking him marks also five points.

The principal drift of the game is to take from your adversary the cards which are of the highest numerical value, and to do all in your power to form sequences; the chief point for the adverse party to attend to is, to save his high-figured cards, and to endeavour to draw them from the other players' hand, by making slight sacrifices of minor cards. The dealer for whom the discarded cards count, is not allowed to throw out *atouts* or kings; he would by this means have too great an advantage, in saving himself from the risk of play. All that he is allowed to do is to discard a sequence, which will count for him, and may form him a renounce, which will be a double advantage.

The game is generally one hundred, as at piquet, with this difference, that it is not he who first arrives at one hundred, when a game is begun, who wins, but he who can reckon the greatest number of points. To count the points which you may hold in your hand, each of the seven *Tarocchi nobili* before named, with a common numerical card, marks five points. The queen and one card marks four; the knight and one card marks three; the knave and one, six; two common cards together, one : this is in showing. The number of points which one player has above the other are all that reckon for him, and the cards are played until the one or the other arrives at one hundred, or till the game is finished.*

An account of the manner of playing the game is also to be found in the edition of the *Académie des Jeux*, published by Corbet, Paris, 1814.

With regard to the Italian game of *Minchiate*, a paper, by Robert Smith, Esq., F.R.S. and F.A.S., was read before the Society of Antiquaries in December, 1803, accompanied by a pack of the cards used for the purpose at Florence, and a small treatise in Italian, on the game, for the museum of the Society. To this, printed in the *Archæologia*, vol. xv. (1806); and to another account, reprinted by Singer from Minucci and Biscioni's notes to *Il Malmantile Racquistato*, an heroi-comic poem, by L. Lippi, we are chiefly indebted for the following brief description.

The number of Tarocchi in the game of *Minchiate* is increased to forty, independently

* *Singer*, p. 237—40.

of the *Matto* or fool, which is reckoned, as usual,
last. The fifty-six *cartacce* or *cartiglie* remain
the same, except that while in the two suits of
bastone and *spade*, the values rise from ace to
ten, and so on to knave, knight, queen, and king,
in the other two, *danari* and *coppe*, the reverse
is the case, and the knave in these is called
Fantina, instead of Fante. Thirty-five of the
Tarocchi are numbered, and five, called *Arie*,
with the *Matto*, are unnumbered. Nos. I to
VI are denominated *Papi*, or popes—pope-ace,
pope-deuce, &c., and bear respectively a Juggler, an
Empress, an Emperor, a Pope, and a Lover
wooing his mistress—a combination perhaps not
wholly accidental. These five are also called
nobili, because they each count a certain number
of points to the holder—the first, five points,
and the other four, three each. Nos. X, XIII,
and XX, count five each, as do Nos. XXVIII,
to XXXV, except No. XXIX, which counts nothing
unless it be either the first or middle card of
a *Verzicola*,* it then counts five points also, as

* A *Verzicola* is a species of sequence peculiar to this game,
and is of greater or less value, according to the quality of each
card separately, and to the whole in combination. A sequence
of 1, 2, 3 ; 2, 3, 4 ; 1, 2, 3, 4 ; 2, 3, 4, 5, &c., is called a *Verzicola* of Popes : 28, 29, 30, a *Verzicola* of thirty ; 31, 32, 33,
Verzicola di Sopratrenti ; 33, 34, 35, *Verzicola di Rossi*, from
the red colour of the cards. A *Verzicola* of *Arie* consists of

PLATE XLV

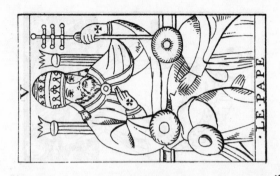

TAROCCHI CARDS.

PLATE XLVI

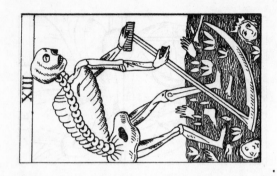

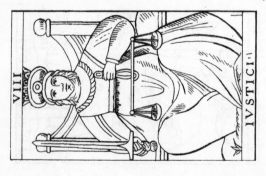

TAROCCHI CARDS.

do the kings which are reckoned among the *nobili,* of which the *Verzicole* are formed. The last five are the *Arie,* and represent *Stella,* a star; *Luna,* the moon; *Sole,* the sun; *Mondo,* the world; a winged and crowned female on a circle, representing Eternity; and *Trombe,* the Trumpet, the same as the Last Judgment, No. xx of the tarots.† Each of these counts ten points, independently of its value in a *verzicola.*

Nos. vi to xii are also called popes, but neither they (with the exception of the ten), nor any of the other numbered cards count anything, and are therefore called *ignobili;* they have on them figures of historical characters, male and female; of beasts and other animals, real and fabulous; emblems of the four elements; the twelve signs of the Zodiac; Youth, Old age, Fortune, Justice, Death, the Devil, and some ludicrous devices without any determinate meaning.

one, two, or three *Arie,* with other cards, counting respectively 20, 25, and 30 points; and an irregular *Verzicola* is three, or four kings, ace, *matto,* and *trombe;* 10, 20, 30; 20, 30, 40; or 1, 13, 28.

† The allegory of this, is said to be—As the stars are overcome by the light of the moon, so is the moon by that of the sun; and as the world is greater than the sun, so is Fame, personified by the trumpets, of more consequence than the world, inasmuch as he who has done noble deeds lives by it, when his connection with the world has ceased.

The last card making the whole number of ninety-seven, bears the *Matto* or fool, which seems to be one of the most important in the game, and counts five points. It has, moreover, peculiar privileges—it is considered to be of any suit, and can never take or be taken, as it may be exchanged with any other *cartaccia*, unless the holder has won no card with which he can effect it.

The game is played by *four* persons at most, and then twenty-one cards are dealt to each; if three persons only play, twenty-five cards are dealt. The treatise above mentioned, which contains an ample description and the rules, speaks of this curious and difficult game as the most noble ever invented with cards. Besides *Minchiate*, there are two other games which can be played with this pack, called *A'sei tocchi* and *Al palio*, described in Biscioni's notes as given in Singer's Appendix, No. xii.

Both *Tarocco* and *Minchiate* are mentioned as early as 1526, by Berni, in his *Capitolo del Gioco della Primera*, published at Rome in that year, in which, after enumerating nine or ten games of cards—*Bassetta, Cricca* (*sup.* p. 91), *Trionfi, Trionfi-piccoli, il Flusso, Trentuno, Noviera, Sestiera, Quintiera*, and *Ronfa* (the

invention of which he attributes to king Ferdinand),—all inferior, in the commentator's opinion,
to *Primero*; he continues, "Another, as more
pleasing, prolonging the entertainment and de-
lighting the company by looking at the paintings,
has found that Tarocchi are an excellent game,
and he seems to be in his glory when he has in
his hand to the number of two hundred cards
which he can scarcely hold, and which, not to
be overlooked, he shuffles, as well as he can,
under the table. Let him look to it who is
pleased with the game of Tarocco, that the only
signification of this word Tarocco is *stupid*,
foolish, simple, fit only to be used by bakers,
cobblers, and the vulgar, to play at most for
the fourth part of a *carlino*, at Tarocchi or at
Trionfi, or at any Sminchiate whatever; which
in every way signifies only foolery and idleness,
feasting the eye with the sun, and the moon, and
the twelve (*signs*) as children do."

Gough calls the game *la Menchiata*, and says
it was invented at Sienna, by Michael Angelo, to
teach children arithmetic, but that it did not
become generally fashionable till the time of
Innocent X., whose portrait is the Pope of these
cards.

It is to a French source we are indebted for

the most complete enumeration of the card-games played in the fifteenth and sixteenth centuries; a period, which although a hundred years subsequent to the first introduction of cards into Europe, or rather, to their assuming a settled method, is fortunately most of all connected with their regular adoption in this country.

The twenty-second chapter of *Gargantua*, one of the productions of coarseness, and deep thought and satire combined, which emanated from the pen of Rabelais, recounts the games at which his lubberly hero* was proficient. The list exhibits no less than 230 games, the investigation of which has plentifully exercised the ingenuity of the learned; but as only the first portion is supposed to relate to cards, we are fortunately spared the recapitulation of the rest, many of which bear titles calculated to shock the modesty of our readers, and may confine ourselves to such, as will fairly exhibit the games of cards known in France in the time of Rabelais, (1483—1553).†

---

* Gargantua is supposed to represent in his youth Henri d'Albret, King of Navarre, who married Marguerite, sister of Francis I., and grandfather of Henri Quatre.

† Supplementary and illustrative lists of French games may be found in the *Voyage de Mc. Guilliaume*, 8vo., 1611, and in the *Veritable Suite du Parlement burlesque de Pontoise*, 4to., 1652. Some of the stalls and painted glass in the French

Le Flux, the Spanish form of our flush or flusse, probably a very ancient game, from its simplicity. In Italy it was called *Il Frusso*. Lorenzo de Medici mentions it with *Bassetta*, in a Canzone printed among the *Canti carnascia leschi*, and says it was in daily use among the common people. These are known to have been youthful compositions of Lorenzo, who died in 1492, at the age of forty-four. Louis XII. played at it in his camp, in the sight of his army,* and Francis I. was also excessively addicted to it. It is still played in the Charente district, the birth-place of that king, about Cognac and Fontenay-le-Comte. Berni, as we have seen, mentions it in his *Capitolo* (1526), and it is also the name of a winning position in the game of Primero, when the cards are all of one colour.

La Prime. Of this game, the Primero of our Elizabethan writers, Duchat, in his note on this chapter of Rabelais, says there are two kinds, the greater and the lesser, the former being played

Cathedrals are full of representations of ancient games,—Rouen, Champeaux, Beauvais, and even at S. Denis. The list of Rabelais, copious as it is, is almost tripled, in imitation of *Gargantua*, by the German Fischart.—Desmarets and Rathery *Œuvres de Rabelais*, tom i., p. 86.

* See Hubert Thomas, *Vie d'Electeur Palatin*, 4to., 1524, p. 24.

with the figured cards, while in the latter, the highest card is the *seven* which counts for twenty-one. According to Singer, *Prime, Primero, and Prima-vista*, are one and the same game, but Mr. Bowle in *the Archæologia*, vol. viii., distinguishes between the two first of these, and Minsheu distinctly calls the two last, "two games at cardes." Taylor also, the water poet, in his picture of the life of a prodigal, 1630, enumerates them separately. From the terms employed in the game, it is generally supposed to be, like most of the early varieties, of Spanish origin. Berni, at the commencement of the sixteenth century, speaks of it as being commonly played in France, and different parts of Italy, as well as in Spain, but with considerable variations in the manner of playing it. The name is doubtless derived from *prime* or *primera*, a point in the playing, which is a sequence of the best cards and a good trump, because, as Minsheu says, "he that can shew such an order of cardes *first*, winnes the game."

According to Duchat, each player has four cards, which are dealt one by one; the next card in value to the seven is the six, which counts for eighteen, and the five, fifteen points. The ace reckons for fifteen, but the deuce, four, and trey

only count for their respective numbers. To
these cards, may be added, if wished for, the
Quinola, for which the knave of hearts is commonly pitched upon, which the player can make
what card and what colour he pleases. Each of
the players shows his four cards, and he whose
cards are all of different sorts wins the *prime*,
and when they are all of one colour he wins the
flush.

This latter point in the game, forms the subject of a painting by Zucchero, to which we have
already alluded at page 142. From Barrington's
description of it in the *Archæologia*, it seems that
each of the players held four cards in his hand,
and eight others were turned over on the table,
their blank sides uppermost. One of the players
exhibits his cards, which are the *knave of hearts*,
with the ace, seven, and six of clubs. As there
were heaps of gold and silver on the table, they
were evidently not playing for what is called a
chicken stake, "and there seems to be little doubt
that Primero was the game the painter attempted
to describe; and that the person exhibiting his
cards has won the flush, for his three clubs are
the best for counting, and his knave of hearts
(*Quinola*) may double the best of these, whilst
it also becomes a club, and thus wins by the

number of points, as well as by the four cards becoming a flush of clubs."*

The account of the game in the Dictionary of the Spanish Academy, resembles in many respects, that given above, but the deuce is said to count for twelve points, the trey for thirteen, and the four for fourteen, and the figured cards are each equivalent to ten. The best hand, and that which wins everything is the flush, the next the *punto* or point, consisting of the Quinola, and seven, six, ace, which count for fifty-five, and then the primera. "From these three principal heads," says Berni, "are deduced all the varieties which daily occur at Primero, as the greater and lesser flush, the great and little prime, and more or less *punto,* which diversity gives rise to numerous controversies and a thousand disputable points." He also says, that at Florence, it is the custom to leave out the seven, eight, and nine, keeping and vying only with the smaller cards ; the *Rest* is made at the second card, and when the first player says

* Vol. viii., p. 33. This picture which had descended to Viscount Falkland, then lately dead, was purchased by Mr. Bird, of Hanover Square, at Greenwood's auction rooms, in April, 1785. Mr. Douce says, that on the table there was also lying the cover of the pack, on which were two lions supporting a shield, charged apparently with a rose, and underneath, but indistinctly marked, the card-makers name, Jehan Licl . . . rer.

Pass, every one is obliged to *discard*, notwithstanding any one may have an ace or a six in
hand; but at Rome there is more liberty, the full
numbers of the suits are preserved, it is allowed
to discard, but not to discard both cards after
Pass is once said, nor can this be done with both
cards of the *Rest* as is usual in other places, (see
also Cardan's account, Singer's Appendix, No. x.)
Among the epigrams of the facetious Sir John
Harington, (4to. 1615), is one which describes
"the Story of Marcus' Life at Primero," and well
exemplifies the Spanish origin of the terms used.

> Fond Marcus ever at *Primero* playes
> Long winter nights, and as long summer dayes ;
> . . . .
> And he ne'er ceast to venter all in *prime*
> Till of his age quite was consumed the prime ;
> Then he more warily his *Rest* regards
> And sets with certainties upon the cards,
> On six and thirty, or on seven and nine
> If any *set his rest*,* and faith and mine ;
> But seld with this, he either gaines or saves,
> For either Faustus prime is with three knaves.
> Or Marcus never can *encounter* right,
> Yet drew two aces, and for further spight
> Had colour for it with a hopeful draught,
> But not *encountred* it availed him naught.

* *El Resto* or the Rest, according to Bowle, is the money
which the player has before him on the table.   Hence the
phrase "to set up a rest," which constantly occurs in the writers
of the early part of the seventeenth century.   See examples in
Singer, from whom much of the above is taken.   *El Encuentre,*

There is also a good illustration of the method of playing primero in the reign of Elizabeth, in one of the dialogues at the end of Minsheu's *Spanish Dictionary.** The game continued to be fashionable, both in France and England, till the period of the Restoration.

La Vole. Of this game Duchat gives no explanation. In Sir Thomas Urquhart's translation of Rabelais, it is rendered " the Beast," i.e. the French game of La Beste, described in the *Académie des Jeux.*

La Pile. This is one of the terms of the next game ; can it possibly have also a separate existence ?

La Triomphe. This game called *Trionfo* by the Italians and Spaniards, is probably the same as Trump or Ruff which was played in England as early as the time of Edward VI. In some dialogues, written both in Latin and French, by Vives, a Spaniard, who died in 1541, there is an interesting one over a card party at *Triumphus*

or Encounter, is the Spanish term for a pair, as two kings or the like.

* See also a dialogue from Florio's *Second Frutes,* 1591, quoted in Halliwell and Wright's edition of *Nares' Glossary,* (*s. v.* Primero), which proves, moreover, that " French Cardes," were used here in the sixteenth century. *Vid. supr.* p. 142. The editors trace a resemblance between Primero and and the French game *l'Ambigu.* Quinola is also a term in *Reversis.*

Hispanicus, containing much information on the different varieties of cards, and the style of play in vogue at the time. The dealer asks for instance, whether he shall deal from left to right in the Dutch manner, or from right to left in the Spanish fashion.* This game is the parent of *écarté*.

Le Cent, in Spanish *Cientos*, or *hundred*, the point that wins the game. It is mentioned in our old writers occasionally as *Saunt*, or *Mount Sant*, of which, in an old play, entitled *The Dumb Knight*, printed in 1608, the queen says, " the name is taken from hundreds." As it is of Spanish original, and has some appearance of having resembled Piquet, the two games may have been to a certain extent identical, especially as Piquet is still called *le Cent* or *la Grande Brisque* in the Charente district. Sir Thomas Urquhart, of Cromarty, in *The Discovery of a most exquisite Jewel, found in the Kennel of Worcester Streets, the Day after the Fight*, 1651, makes use of this game as an illustration: "Verily I think they make use of kings as we do of card kings in playing *at the Hundred ;* any one whereof, if there be appearance of a better game without

---

* See *Bibliographical Appendix*. Singer gives a large portion of the Latin version. For an account of the English game, see our next chapter.

him (and that the exchange of him for another
incoming card is like to conduce more for drawing
the stake), is by good gamesters without any ceremony discarded." Lord North, in 1578, notes
losing fifteen shillings at Saint.—*Archæologia*,
xix., 297.

Le Trente et ung. Enumerated as *Trentuno*
in Berni's list of Italian games, 1526. It was
an old and favourite game in England under the
name of One and Thirty. It is also described in
the *Dialogues* of Barlandus, published at Antwerp
in 1534, the cards employed being a full French
piquet pack. It was possibly the original form of
the family round game of *Vingt-un*, which is constantly played now for winter evenings' amusement.

La Condemnade. This Urquhart trans-
lates "the last couple in hell,"—a title we have
not seen elsewhere. It was played by three persons only : the youngest hand named a card, and
then the cards were turned up all round, one at a
time, and he to whom the card fell, won the stake.
It is constantly alluded to by French and Italian
poets of the early part of the sixteenth century.
A poetical epistle of Clement Marot was staked
and lost, he tells us, at *Condemnade*, against a fair
lady's ribbons. These were truly the days when
romance was not confined to childhood.

La Charte Virade (the turned-up card). Urquhart renders this the *Hock;* but as the French editors make no such suggestion, we are at a loss to know his authority for the statement. *Hoc* is a well-known French game, and is described in the *Académie des Jeux.* We have already alluded to it at p. 193, and it has two varieties, *Hoc Mazarin*, and *Hoc de Lyon.*

Le Maucontent. This, according to some, is the same as *Hère;* but De Brianville, in recommending them, with *Coucou,* another of Gargantua's games, for his *Jeu de Blazon,* on account of their simplicity, speaks of them as distinct.* Another name for it is *le Malheureux de Languedoc.* Rabelais appears to cite in several instances the same games under different names, and this one appears in another place as *la Malheureuse. Le Hère* is described in the *Académie Universelle des Jeux,* Amst., 1721, as a game easy to play—but the description is by no means perspicuous;—and *Coucou* in the Paris edition of 1739.

Le Lansquenet. This is a German game of early date, and, like *Basset* and *Faro,* one of hazard, and, as such, was prohibited in France, Germany, and Italy. There are some who refer *Lansquenet* to the earliest period of cards. De

* See p. 198, *suprà.*

Murr even asserts, that it was known, not only in Germany, but in France, as early as the year 1392.* The modern game is probably different.

12. *Le Gay.* What this game is, is uncertain. The Sieur de Cholières mentions it in his *Matinées*, 1586, p. 162. "They passed two or three hours at playing *Flus*, at *Jay*, at the *Séquence*, at *Condemnade*, at the *Clef*, at *Remuer-mesnage*, &c." The name is believed to be derived from *j'ai*, the exclamation of a player who has got what he wanted to win the game. In Normandy the *Brelan* bore this title.

La Séquence. Besides this there is another game in the list, *Pair et Séquence*, translated by Urquhart "Post and Pair, or Even and Séquence," which, as an English game, we shall take occasion, to discuss hereafter.

La Luette. The seafaring population of Saintonge still play at this on the sands.

Le Torment. "A game at cards," says Duchat; but query what? The title is far from prepossessing.

La Ronfle. Bullet has edified us on the subject of this word. The Celtic etymology he has given us is his master effort. He insists on

* See above, p. 111, and a second notice, p. 279.

ronfle being the *point*,—that is, the cards whose aggregate values surpass those represented by the cards of the rival player. To obtain this is the entire object. They play still at *Ronfle* in the Vosges. It is a very simple game, well fitted to amuse these mountaineers when they are fatigued with their cheesemaking.

Le Glic (mentioned by Villon, 1461). Duchat derives it from the German *glück*, good fortune; Chatto, from *gleich*, which signifies in the same language, *like*. Either derivation is probable: for Gleek signifies at some games, three cards of a sort—aces, kings, queens, or knaves; a piece of good luck for the player, as it counts several points. It is also one of the terms of a game called *Dix Croix*. At Metz it is still played; and the name is well known on the German frontier, where they mispronounce it *glit*. We have alluded (p. 91) to an Italian game called *Cricca;* this is explained in the *Della Cruscan Vocubulary* to have the same signification as Gleek.*

---

* Gleek was played in England by three persons, and with forty-four cards, rejecting the deuces and trays, each hand having twelve, and eight being left in the stock, seven of which might be bought by the players, and the eighth is the turn-up card, which belongs to the dealer. The best account of the game is that given in the *Wit's Interpreter*, 1670.

The *Piquet* which Rabelais mentions further on, is not the ordinary game, which is, as we have said, related to *Cent*, but another of a totally different description. Rabelais quotes also *le Tarau*, so that the tarot game was still in use, although it had long been going out of fashion. Cleland, in his *Institution of a Young Nobleman*, 1607, speaks of them familiarly, as if known in England. We quote the passage as given by Singer, as it tends to modify the opinion expressed at p. 85, though it is still doubtful if the word *tarault*, as applied to cards at this period, included the emblematic atouts.* "His majesty's permission of honest house games, as cardes, French cardes called *Taraux*, Tables, and such like plaies, is sufficient to protect you from the blame of those learned men, who think them hazards; as for myself, I think it great simplicitie and rusticitie in a nobleman to be ignorant of any of them when he cometh into companie : yea, I would wish you to be so perfect in them all, that you may not be deceived or cousened at play."

It is unfortunate that we have in the list we have been quoting, no mention of *Bataille*, and we

* *See Bibliog. App.* In the *Tesoro Espanola*, Geneve, 1661 the word *Malillo*, a term of the game of Ombre, is defined to be the nine of Money in the game of *Taraults or cards*, &c., evidently denoting only the ordinary Spanish pack.

have ourselves only as yet casually alluded to it; but it was, in all probability, the earliest game played with the French pack. Though hardly aspiring to the rank of a game, it is still a diversion with cards, of the class of our "beggar my neighbour," requiring no study, and yet amusing. A simple game of this nature would be just such a one as Charles VI., if he played cards at all, would have been able to delight in.

Lansquenet is peculiar to Germany, as *l'Hombre* is to Spain, from whence they were respectively imported into France. The latter, the title of which is equivalent to "the game of Man," is probably the most ancient of games still in use. Its invention in Spain must have been long anterior to that of Piquet, or even the introduction of cards into France. It is a very natural deduction from the primitive tarot game, and needs both leisure and attention to play it. *Lansquenet*, on the contrary, smacks of the camp. The very name means *soldier;* and Breitkopf derives it from *land* and *knecht*, a peasant-soldier, such as they raised in Germany to defend the country from invasion. The pipe was not then invented to solace their bivouac; and where so likely an origin of a game requiring so little talent to comprehend it, and yet offering

such opportunity for trickery, as a *corps de garde*
of these rough warriors? From them, the soldiers of every land adopted it, and from the
soldiers it became general.

Such is the progress of civilization : what
originates with the upper circle speedily descends
to the lower, and what begins with the latter
sometimes ends with being the summit of all. In
a single century cards had made the circuit of the
whole of Europe.

The French poets of the time speak of them
with rapture. Le Seigneur Villon (1461), no
habitué of the royal palace, in his burlesque
piece *Grand Testament*, bequeaths to his friend
Perrinet,

> " Trois detz plombez de bonne carre
> Et ung beau ioly ieu de cartes."

A few years later, we read in Crétin (1483—1547):

> " Pour les Ecots n'y montent ; si font rage
> Aux dez fonces et cartes lansquenets."

And cards are constantly mentioned as the ad-
juncts of sparkling wine and jovial cheer.

In these times of jollity, when Francis the
First was king, the ladies of the French Court
invented, or rather adopted the game of *reversis*,
so called because its order and construction was
entirely the reverse of those already in use.

Those who made the most tricks, won in other games, but here, to make *none* was an advantage ; the lowest cards are the highest, and the knaves are better than the kings. It is doubtless the Spanish game of *la gana pierde*, " the winner loses," and was perhaps introduced by Marguerite of Navarre. In both, the knave of hearts is called Quinola, and the tens are subtracted for marking, which is strongly confirmatory of the Spanish origin, there being no tens in the Spanish pack. Rabelais calls it *Coquimbert, qui gaigne perd*, which, Cotgrave says, was a game of cards like our " loosing-lodam." Urquhart renders it, " *at losing, load him*," which corresponds tolerably with the Spanish title. Lodam is continually mentioned among old English card games.

The *berlan* or *brelan* was contemporary with bataille, and an old favourite in the provincial districts of France, a very simple game, but one which has become the origin of others. Bullet says, that berlan is a Celtic word for *hazard*, and he may be right, for gaming-houses in France were for a long time called *berlans*.

In the sixteenth century, cards had completely won their position. Francis was remarkable for anything but consistency. He protected tennis

by his letters patent, of Nov. 9, 1527, and declared that what was won at that game was justly
acquired, and no more than the reward of labour ;
but he made no secret of his detestation for cards,
and prohibited (certainly with some reason) all
those who managed the revenues and finances of
the kingdom, from playing at any game whatever,
under penalty of deprivation of office, whipping,
banishment, and confiscation.   This might be
expected from a sovereign who subsidized the
protestants of Germany, and caused the protestants of France to be burnt.   About the same
time, various edicts of Parliament prohibited the
inhabitants of Paris from permitting gaming in
their houses.

Henry VIII. of England was addicted to
martial exercises, and preferred, no doubt, games
which promoted vigour and action, to mere se-
dentary amusements.   Yet Shakspeare speaks of
his playing Primero with the Duke of Suffolk,
and he may have had reasons for doing so.*   His
Spanish consort, as Sir William Forrest tells us,
was an adept at Gleek,† and the privy-purse
expenses of their daughter Mary, afterwards
queen, contain numerous entries—items for the
"playe at the cardes."

* K. Henry VIII., Act v. sc. 1.   *Suprà*, p 141.

In Germany and Italy, the mania which prevailed for play may be easily accounted for in an age of adventures. Games of chance suited well the wild spirits of those days, and card-playing appears to have been carried to an extravagant degree, by all classes, before it was attacked by Luther and the Reformers. Representations of card-playing began to be common in wood-cuts and illuminations, and the writers of the day used argument and satire, both for, and against the practice. Benvenuto Cellini commends the skill of the Venetian players; and the Council of Augsburg, in 1548, refused the communion to any one who had not a pious horror of all games of chance.

The bishops, who drew up the edicts, however, themselves violated the law, and the ministers of justice whose duty it was to put them in execution, were players themselves. "What good Papist" asks the author of a violent attack on the French clergy, "could behold with composure, his prelate lose at play for an after dinner pastime, four, five, or six thousand crowns? See him stake on a rest at Primero five hundred; and lose for an *aflac*, a thousand: or, that nearly all the bishops, and down to the lowest canons hold open table (*berland*) to play at all manner of games, forbidden

and prohibited not only by the canon law, but
also by the *ordonnances* of the king ?"*

William Roy, the author of a satire upon
Wolsey, which was bought up and suppressed by
the Cardinal, but after his death, in 1530, trans-
ferred to the prelacy generally ; after reproaching
them with their " skyll in wynes, better than
of devinite," dislike of preaching, fondness for
field sports, rather than to make a sermon, &c.,
says,

> "To playe at the cardes and dyce
> Some of theym are nothynge nyce
> Both at hasard and mom chaunce."†

Similar charges were brought against the Scottish
clergy, especially by Sir David Lyndsay, in his
poem against Cardinal Beaton.

Henry II. of France (1547), according to
Brantôme, had been an adept at cards. Large
sums began to be risked, and fortunes shattered.
Gaming grew furious in those days. There
was a Captain La Roue, who offered to stake
20,000 crowns against one of Andrea Doria's
galleys ; 20,000 then, would be equivalent to five
times that amount now. A pretty sum to slip

* *Cabinet du Roy de France*, 12mo., 1581. Le Duchat
ascribes it to Nicolas Froumenteau.

† The first edition was printed abroad, *sine anno aut loco*,
144 pp. ; the second at Wesell, in 1546. See *Gent's Mag.* for
1843. Momchaunce was a game of hazard with dice.

over a card—Cut !—Eight of Clubs !—Knave of Hearts !—the galley's mine ! Fancy play in that fashion now-a-days ; an East Indiaman with her cargo dependent on the turn of a card.

Francis II. had barely time to sigh beside Mary Stuart ; Charles IX. was a rhymer; Henry III. played at cup and ball; Catherine de Medicis was engrossed with gipsies, astrology, and divination. If the Court did not make much account of piquet and reversis under her three sons, the queen mother made it up by her devotion to magical cards, and the gipsies who divined their language. The Hotel de Soissons was the scene of more than one mysterious conclave, where the death of the Duke of Guise, or of some other troublesome personage, was the secret attempted to be divined !

This same Duke of Guise, far different from the king, had a right royal way of his own with cards. One time he won of M. D'O, the superintendent of finance, 100,000 livres, which was brought him next morning by one of the *employés* in a leathern bag, 70,000 in silver, and 10,000 crowns in gold. One feels disposed to liberality in the moment of good fortune. The duke took the bag, believing it to contain a sum in silver, and made a present of it to the messenger. The man departed, opened the bag, and found the 10,000 crowns in gold, and suspecting a mistake, which the Duke would regret, he returned to him with it at once. The Duke of Guise replied, that he would by no means balk his luck, and suffered him to keep this magnificent douceur.

Henry of Navarre, the future Henry IV. promised badly as an example to the gentlemen of France; when he joined Henry III. of France in the camp before Paris, with his Huguenots, card-playing was all the fashion with his followers, and the French courtiers not partaking of their master's fondness for cup and ball, accepted with avidity the challenge of the Béarnais. On the evening of the day when Henry III. was assassinated, there was a brilliant card party in his generals' tent. Let the Duc d'Angoulême, son of Charles IX. and Marie Touchet, tell the story. " The king," he says, " ordered us to retire, and M. de Bellegarde, as first gentleman of the bedchamber, after drawing the royal curtains, accompanied me to my quarters, where I found Chemerault, Richelieu, Lavergne, and Renty playing at Primero, with whom I made a fifth. The game lasted till four in the morning, and it being sunrise, I threw myself on my bed, and was just settling off to repose, when one of my footmen arrived with the news of my utter ruin, crying out in tones of amazement, as the occasion warranted, that the king was stabbed."

Henry III. died, and Henry of Navarre was king of France. From his reign, dates a new era for the cards in France. It was from henceforth the royal game—the chief amusement—the most sought after—the most beloved by the court. Louis XIV. made it almost an institution of state.

CARD PLAYING IN THE XVITH. AND XVIITH. CENTURIES.

THE sixteenth century was the epoch of the military type of game. Europe was full of adventurers who, casque on head and sword in hand, pillaged without compunction, for one master or other, towns and villages, and even the territories of the Holy See. Religious differences aggravated this state of contest, and increased the sharp and decisive character which always attends partisan warfare. A few carbine shots settled the question of the booty, and the victors, rich for the moment, betook themselves

amusements proper for a monarch, and says
may after dinner indulge himself with music
otherwise,

> Att tables, chesse, or cardis awhile himself repose,

but adds, that "syttynge pastymes are sel
found good, especially in the day time;" he t
fore advises the pursuit of those that affo
both air and exercise. He condemned more
the practice of card-playing by labouring p
at improper times and places, as producti
idleness.

> "Att ale howse to sit, at mack* or at mall
> Tables or dyce, or that cardis men call
> Or what oother game owte of season dwe
> Let them be punysched without all rescue."

The allusion is to the statute quoted at p.
by which card-playing was only allowed t
working classes at Christmas-tide, to whic
sermon of Latimer alludes, as also He
Epigram:

> "At Post and Paire, or Slam, Tom Tuck would play
> This Christmass, but his want wherewith, sayes Nay
>   *Hesperide*

The misuse of this season, unhappily b
a national custom, was even then deprecat
right-thinking people. Philip Stubbes,

* Perhaps identical with the old French *Jeu de Macao.*—

---

to play. These were the men to set the cards going, and lansquenet, and such like games of a dashing and gambling nature, prevailed everywhere in the camps and hostels. England, less excitable and unsettled, adhered to the Spanish style, at least among the upper classes. As early as 1508, it is true, Barclay, in his translation of Sebastian Brant's *Ship of Fools*, speaks of

> "The damnable lust of cardes and dice,
> And other games prohibite by the lawe."

And the author of an old morality, entitled "Hycke Scorner," of about the same date, has enumerated card players among such characters, as evinces that he had no great opinion of their morals:—

> "Walkers by nyght, with gret murderers,
> Overthwarte with gyle and joly carders."*

But the courtly and dignified Primero continued to be the fashionable game for more than a century, when it began to be superseded by Quadrille and Ombre. Shakespeare makes Falstaff say, "I never prospered since I forswore myself at Primero;" and Zucchero's picture affords proof that Queen Elizabeth's Lord Treasurer took a hand at it. She herself was a cardplayer, and lost her temper, too, occasionally,

* *Vid.* Strutt, *Sports and Pastimes*, p. 328.

John Dewey Library
Johnson State College
Johnson, Vermont 05656

as a correspondence of the period testifies. Trump also, which some consider the parent of whist, was perhaps of equal antiquity with Primero, and was so commonly known, that Latimer, afterwards bishop and martyr, in some sermons "on the Card," preached at St. Edmund's Church, Cambridge, the Sunday before Christmas, 1529, actually used it as a familiar illustration, and thus dealt out an exposition of Christianity :—

> "And whereas you are about to celebrate Christmas in playing at cards, I intend by God's grace, to deal unto you Christ's cards, wherein you shall perceive Christ's rule. The game that we will play at shall be called the *triumph*, which, if it be well played at, he that dealeth shall win; the players shall likewise win; and the standers and lookers upon shall do the same; insomuch that there is no man willing to play at this triumph with these cards, but they shall be all winners and no losers."

"It seems," says Fuller (*Hist. of Cambridge*, p. 103), that he suited his sermon rather to the time than to the text, which was the Baptist's question to our Lord, "Who art thou?" *John* i. 19, taking thereby to conform his discourse to the playing at cards, making the heart triumph (*trump*).

This blunt preaching was in those days admirably effectual, but would be justly ridiculous in our age.

"I remember," adds Fuller, in my time, a

country minister preached at St. Mary's, from *Rom.* xii. 3, "As God hath dealt to every man the measure of faith." In a fond imitation of Latimer's sermon, he prosecuted the metaphor of *dealing*, that men should play *above board*, i.e., avoid all dissembling, not pocket cards, but improve their gifts and graces, *follow suit, &c.,* all which produced nothing but laughter in the audience.* The lower classes at the end of the sixteenth century were very fond of trump. In the comedy of "*Gammer Gurton's Needle*," said to have been first printed in 1551, Dame Chat says, What, Diccon? Come here, ye be no stranger!

> "We be fast set at trump, man, hard by the fire
>   Thou shalt set upon the king, if thou come a little nyer.
> Come hither, Dol; Dol, sit down and play this game,
>   And as thou sawest me do, see thou do even the same.
> There are five trumps besides the queen, the hindmost thou
>   shalt find her
> Take heed of Sim Glover's wife, she hath an eye behind her."

Sir William Forrest, who wrote at the close of Henry VIIIth's reign, and presented a poetical treatise, entitled, "The Poesye of Princylye Practice,"† to his son Edward VI., describes the

---

* *See* Gough, *Archæol.*, vol. viii. *170.
† Forrest's MS. is in the Royal Library, No. 17. D iij., and at the commencement of the poem he is represented as presenting it to K. Edw. VI.

"*Anatomie of Abuses*," printed in 1583, remarks, "especially at Christmas time, there is nothing els used but Cardes, Dice, Tables, Maskyng, Mummyng, Bowling, and such like fooleries. And the reason is, thei think thei have a commission and prerogative that tyme to do what thei list, and to follow what vanitie they will. But alas doe thei thinke thei are privileged at that time to doe evill? The holier the time is (if one time were holier than another, as it is not) the holier ought their exercises to bee."

John Northbrooke also, complains, that "the after part of the Sunday was allotted for the performance of vaine playes and interludes," to which are added, "dice and card-playing, dancing and other idle pastimes."

In a book called *The Pope's Kingdom*, translated from the Latin of Tho. Neogorgus, by Barnabe Googe, and dedicated to Queen Elizabeth, in 1570, the young gallants of this country are described as spending their Sunday afternoons in athletic games, shooting, public spectacles, &c., and,

"Another sort there is, that doe not love abroad to roame,
But, for to passe their time at cardes, or tables still at home."

This state of things, though it was no doubt

surpassed on the Continent, provoked the denunciations of many writers, both moral and religious, some of whom carried away by their zeal, and not content with stigmatizing the abuse, ended by condemning *in toto* all games of chance as an invention of the devil, and contrary to the Word of God.*

In the sister kingdoms also, as we learn from several testimonies, card-playing was freely practised, as might be expected from the intercourse of Scotland with France, and Ireland with Spain. Spenser, in his " *View of the State of Ireland,*" written about 1590, describes certain idle and dissolute fellows, called " Carrows," who wandered up and down to gentlemen's houses, living only by cards and dice. Cervantes, in his *Comical History of Rinconete y Cortadillo*, makes the former of these sharpers boast of gaining

* See Chatto's account of James Balmford's tract on the unlawfulness of playing at cards or tables, dedicated to the Mayor and Burgesses of Newcastle-on-Tyne, in 1593. The learned Thos. Gataker, in his work *On the Nature and Use of Lots*, 4to., 1619, has refuted the extravagancies of these writers. They were not, however, without their effect, for in the 25th of Elizabeth, on the occasion of the fall of the theatre, at the Paris Garden, in Southwark, on a Sunday afternoon, by which many persons were killed and wounded, and which was considered as a judgment from God, a general prohibition was issued of all public pastimes on the Lord's Day.—*Strutt.*

his livelihood in the same manner, *jugando a la veyntiuna*.*

Pinkerton's *History of Scotland*, gives the advice of a Scottish poet to James V. to use rather manly pastimes and chess, than cards and dice, except with his mother or chief lords, as it was a disgrace for a prince to win from men of inferior station, and his gains at any time ought to be given to his attendants.

While there is no doubt that in this country large sums of money changed hands through card-playing, for according to the old saying, "*Sine lucro friget ludus* — No gaining, cold gaming," it was as dust in the balance, compared with the pictures we have of the corresponding period of the annals of the French game.

Henry IV. had passed through the career of an adventurer before he became king, and he could not entirely shake off at the Louvre, the habits of the camp. Surrounded by friends, male and female, the latter the least sincere of the two, the bold and jovial game was his chosen pastime, and with an utter scorn of economy,

---

* Chatto says, this was the same as the favourite Irish game of One and Thirty.—*Facts and Speculations*, pp. 114, 115. We have already, p. 40, given Paschasius Justus' account of the prevalence of cards in Spain, first published in 1560. This is confirmed by the *Invectiva contra los Tahures, Sevilla*, 1557.

he was not the man to draw back at the immensity of a stake.   At each reverse, the prudent Sully* grew pale with rage, but *paid*.   Biron and Bassompierre were the heroes of these occasions.   The former lost in a single year 500,000 crowns (four or five millions of francs). It was his debts which eventually brought him to grief.   He had need of more money than his royal friend could furnish him with, resorted to others, and only obtained it as a bribe to join in their schemes.   In this way, Biron became a conspirator and a traitor.   The evening before his arrest, he was playing once more at primero with the queen, the favourite game everywhere at this time.   Neither of the queens of Henry IV. thwarted him in his pursuits, for both Margot, and the Italian Marie de Medicis joined him in them, and had better luck.

Bassompierre also, though Biron lost his money and himself, could boast of his success. He speaks of gaming as a natural occupation, and one to be preferred before all.†   His win-

* Rosny, Duc de Sully, was the faithful friend and chief minister of Henry IV.; to his memoirs we are indebted for the details of the history of the period.   He always refused to imitate his masters example and turn papist.   The Pope tried hard to induce him, but his answer was, "that he would never cease to pray for the conversion of his holiness."

† *Memoires de Bassompierre.* Coll. Petitot, t. xix. pp. 353—374.

nings were enormous. On one occasion, observing the chagrin of D'Epernon, at losing to him 25,000 crowns, he laid out more than half the money on a coat glittering with pearls and diamonds, and a sword costing 5,000 crowns, and assisted therewith at the christening festivities of the royal infants.

These great French players, however, occasionally caught a Tartar. There were sharks abroad in the shape of Spaniards and Italians of good birth, who appeared everywhere for the express purpose of fleecing whom they could. The *Histoire générale des Voyages*, tells us they were to be found at the courts of the Negro kings and of Indian rajahs. Beaulieu, the traveller, met with one Don Francisco Carnero, who continually managed to break the bank of the king of Achem.

The Portuguese Don Antonio Pimentel seems to have played a game of this sort at the court of Henry IV., who from the moment he saw him, conceived a high regard for him. Bassompierre relates in his Memoirs, that the king sent for him to court, and having piqued him with the alleged superiority of the new comer, they sat down to play, which ran so high, that neither silver nor gold would content them, but counters which went as high as five thousand livres apiece. At the end of the season, Bassompierre had gained 500,000 livres, and Pimentel 200,000 crowns! How they must have shorn the sheep between them! This was in 1608. For all this, Bassompierre died in debt. As for Pimentel, he had the assurance to ask of Sully some favour on the strength of his intimacy with the king, and received a severe rebuff for his pains.

The faithful minister was sorely tried on the score of finance. Witness the annoyance of such letters from the king as this, dated 1609.

"My friend,—I have lost at play twenty-two thousand pistoles; I pray you to remit them incontinently by the hands of the bearer, Feideau, that so he may distribute them among the persons to whom I am indebted, according to my order. Adieu, my friend. "HENRY.

"Monday Morning, this 18th January, at Paris.

"I wish that this sum should be entered in an account."

The necessary funds had of course to be raised instantly to save the king's honour, who did not fail, some days after, to call upon his minister, beg his pardon, and promise (which he never meant to keep) to be less extravagant for the future.

Sully, in a note at the end of his *Économies Royales*, accuses Henry of an inordinate love of the game of hazard, and states that by his example he was the ruin of many wealthy families, and was the indirect cause of the "cheating devices, and damnable tricks," which began then to be used, thus plainly making him an encourager of the ingenuity of these vile "Greeks," as card-swindlers were very early called.*

Following the example of the court, the practice of gaming spread among the citizens; *brélans* or gaming houses were set up, and let for enormous prices; and people subsisted on the proceeds of play. All the poets, or almost all, lived in this fashion, of which Villon had already set the example.

No sooner had the dagger of Ravaillac made an untimely end of this gallant and gambling king, than an immediate stop was put to the former state of affairs.

The preamble of the *ordonnance* of the 30th May, 1611, soon after the accession of Louis XIII., draws a gloomy picture of the general

* Sully adds, that he had taken note of several considerable sums squandered in play by Henry, but these were by no means all. In 1607, Henry writes that certain merchants held him *au cul et aux chausses* for a sum of 9000 livres, which he had dissipated at the fair of St. Germains in trinkets and trifles. He was still worse in succeeding years, one entry is for 22,000 pistoles lost at play, of which 51,000 livres were due to the Portuguese Edward Fernandès; this last sum being equivalent to 6 or 700,000 francs now, yet he only applied to Sully from dire necessity. What a whirlpool!

dissolution of morals and ruin of families caused by the neglect of the laws against gaming, the increase of gaming houses and gamesters, and their consequent and inevitable results, dissipation of patrimonies and hard earned fortunes, borrowing large sums of money, which, being in their turn played away at the gaming tables, caused bankruptcy to the creditors, &c. This law was twice renewed, and put in practice with severity. Two persons named Duméri and Le Mage being detected at cards in the apartments they occupied, were with their partners, and their two landlords, arrested by the police, and finally, by sentence dated 21st April, 1635, were each fined 10,000 livres, one-third to the informer, and the rest to the poor.

This severity deterred the people. At the court, the king's example kept gaming in check.* He cared for nothing but the cross-bow, with which he shot admirably, wherefore he was called Louis le Juste. Richelieu hardly played at all, he had other business in hand.

The queen Anne of Austria, however, a Spanish princess, had a liking for cards, and the

---

* Save and except the queen mother's favourite, Concini Maréchal d'Ancre, who played very commonly a game of 20,000 pistoles (about 600,000 francs of the present reckoning).

to play.   These were the men to set the cards
going, and lansquenet, and such like games of a
dashing and gambling nature, prevailed everywhere in the camps and hostels.   England, less
excitable and unsettled, adhered to the Spanish
style, at least among the upper classes.   As early
as 1508, it is true, Barclay, in his translation
of Sebastian Brant's *Ship of Fools*, speaks of

> " The damnable lust of cardes and dice,
>   And other games prohibite by the lawe."

And the author of an old morality, entitled
" Hycke Scorner," of about the same date, has
enumerated card players among such characters,
as evinces that he had no great opinion of their
morals :—

> " Walkers by nyght, with gret murderers,
>   Overthwarte with gyle and joly carders."*

But the courtly and dignified Primero continued
to be the fashionable game for more than a
century, when it began to be superseded by
Quadrille and Ombre.   Shakespeare makes Falstaff say, " I never prospered since I forswore myself at Primero ; " and Zucchero's picture affords
proof that Queen Elizabeth's Lord Treasurer
took a hand at it.   She herself was a card-
player, and lost her temper, too, occasionally,

* *Vid.* Strutt, *Sports and Pastimes*, p. 328.

John Dewey Library
Johnson State College
Johnson, Vermont 05656

as a correspondence of the period testifies. Trump also, which some consider the parent of whist, was perhaps of equal antiquity with Primero, and was so commonly known, that Latimer, afterwards bishop and martyr, in some sermons "on the Card," preached at St. Edmund's Church, Cambridge, the Sunday before Christmas, 1529, actually used it as a familiar illustration, and thus dealt out an exposition of Christianity :—

"And whereas you are about to celebrate Christmas in playing at cards, I intend by God's grace, to deal unto you Christ's cards, wherein you shall perceive Christ's rule. The game that we will play at shall be called the *triumph*, which, if it be well played at, he that dealeth shall win ; the players shall likewise win ; and the standers and lookers upon shall do the same ; insomuch that there is no man willing to play at this triumph with these cards, but they shall be all winners and no losers."

"It seems," says Fuller (*Hist. of Cambridge*, p. 103), that he suited his sermon rather to the time than to the text, which was the Baptist's question to our Lord, "Who art thou ?" *John* i. 19, taking thereby to conform his discourse to the playing at cards, making the heart triumph (*trump*).

This blunt preaching was in those days admirably effectual, but would be justly ridiculous in our age.

"I remember," adds Fuller, in my time, a

country minister preached at St. Mary's, from *Rom.* xii. 3, "As God hath dealt to every man the measure of faith." In a fond imitation of Latimer's sermon, he prosecuted the metaphor of *dealing*, that men should play *above board*, i.e., avoid all dissembling, not pocket cards, but improve their gifts and graces, *follow suit, &c.*, all which produced nothing but laughter in the audience.* The lower classes at the end of the sixteenth century were very fond of trump. In the comedy of "*Gammer Gurton's Needle*," said to have been first printed in 1551, Dame Chat says, What, Diccon ? Come here, ye be no stranger !

" We be fast set at trump, man, hard by the fire
   Thou shalt set upon the king, if thou come a little nyer.
Come hither, Dol ; Dol, sit down and play this game,
   And as thou sawest me do, see thou do even the same.
There are five trumps besides the queen, the hindmost thou
      shalt find her
   Take heed of Sim Glover's wife, she hath an eye behind her."

Sir William Forrest, who wrote at the close of Henry VIIIth's reign, and presented a poetical treatise, entitled, " The Poesye of Princylye Practice,"† to his son Edward VI., describes the

* *See* Gough, *Archæol.*, vol. viii. *170.

† Forrest's MS. is in the Royal Library, No. 17. D iij., and at the commencement of the poem he is represented as presenting it to K. Edw. VI.

amusements proper for a monarch, and says, he
may after dinner indulge himself with music, or
otherwise,

> Att tables, chesse, or cardis awhile himself repose,

but adds, that "syttynge pastymes are seldom
found good, especially in the day time;" he therefore advises the pursuit of those that afforded
both air and exercise. He condemned moreover,
the practice of card-playing by labouring people
at improper times and places, as productive of
idleness.

> "Att ale howse to sit, at mack* or at mall
> Tables or dyce, or that cardis men call
> Or what oother game owte of season dwe
> Let them be punysched without all rescue."

The allusion is to the statute quoted at p. 103,
by which card-playing was only allowed to the
working classes at Christmas-tide, to which the
sermon of Latimer alludes, as also Herrick's
Epigram :

> "At Post and Paire, or Slam, Tom Tuck would play
> This Christmass, but his want wherewith, sayes Nay."
>
> *Hesperides*, p. 281.

The misuse of this season, unhappily become
a national custom, was even then deprecated by
right-thinking people. Philip Stubbes, in his

---

* Perhaps identical with the old French *Jeu de Macao.*—*Singer.*

"*Anatomie of Abuses*," printed in 1583, remarks, " especially at Christmas time, there is nothing els used but Cardes, Dice, Tables, Maskyng, Mummyng, Bowling, and such like fooleries. And the reason is, thei think thei have a commission and prerogative that tyme to do what thei list, and to follow what vanitie they will. But alas doe thei thinke thei are privileged at that time to doe evill ? The holier the time is (if one time were holier than another, as it is not) the holier ought their exercises to bee."

John Northbrooke also, complains, that "the after part of the Sunday was allotted for the performance of vaine playes and interludes," to which are added, " dice and card-playing, dancing and other idle pastimes."

In a book called *The Pope's Kingdom*, translated from the Latin of Tho. Neogorgus, by Barnabe Googe, and dedicated to Queen Elizabeth, in 1570, the young gallants of this country are described as spending their Sunday afternoons in athletic games, shooting, public spectacles, &c., and,

" Another sort there is, that doe not love abroad to roame,
    But, for to passe their time at cardes, or tables still at home."

This state of things, though it was no doubt

surpassed on the Continent, provoked the denunciations of many writers, both moral and religious, some of whom carried away by their zeal, and not content with stigmatizing the abuse, ended by condemning *in toto* all games of chance as an invention of the devil, and contrary to the Word of God.*

In the sister kingdoms also, as we learn from several testimonies, card-playing was freely practised, as might be expected from the intercourse of Scotland with France, and Ireland with Spain. Spenser, in his " *View of the State of Ireland,*" written about 1590, describes certain idle and dissolute fellows, called " Carrows," who wandered up and down to gentlemen's houses, living only by cards and dice. Cervantes, in his *Comical History of Rinconete y Cortadillo,* makes the former of these sharpers boast of gaining

* See Chatto's account of James Balmford's tract on the unlawfulness of playing at cards or tables, dedicated to the Mayor and Burgesses of Newcastle-on-Tyne, in 1593. The learned Thos. Gataker, in his work *On the Nature and Use of Lots,* 4to., 1619, has refuted the extravagancies of these writers. They were not, however, without their effect, for in the 25th of Elizabeth, on the occasion of the fall of the theatre, at the Paris Garden, in Southwark, on a Sunday afternoon, by which many persons were killed and wounded, and which was considered as a judgment from God, a general prohibition was issued of all public pastimes on the Lord's Day.—*Strutt.*

his livelihood in the same manner, *jugando a la veyntiuna.**

Pinkerton's *History of Scotland*, gives the advice of a Scottish poet to James V. to use rather manly pastimes and chess, than cards and dice, except with his mother or chief lords, as it was a disgrace for a prince to win from men of inferior station, and his gains at any time ought to be given to his attendants.

While there is no doubt that in this country large sums of money changed hands through card-playing, for according to the old saying, "*Sine lucro friget ludus* — No gaining, cold gaming," it was as dust in the balance, compared with the pictures we have of the corresponding period of the annals of the French game.

Henry IV. had passed through the career of an adventurer before he became king, and he could not entirely shake off at the Louvre, the habits of the camp. Surrounded by friends, male and female, the latter the least sincere of the two, the bold and jovial game was his chosen pastime, and with an utter scorn of economy,

---

* Chatto says, this was the same as the favourite Irish game of One and Thirty.—*Facts and Speculations*, pp. 114, 115. We have already, p. 40, given Paschasius Justus' account of the prevalence of cards in Spain, first published in 1560. This is confirmed by the *Invectiva contra los Tahures*, *Sevilla*, 1557.

he was not the man to draw back at the immensity of a stake. At each reverse, the prudent Sully* grew pale with rage, but *paid*. Biron and Bassompierre were the heroes of these occasions. The former lost in a single year 500,000 crowns (four or five millions of francs). It was his debts which eventually brought him to grief. He had need of more money than his royal friend could furnish him with, resorted to others, and only obtained it as a bribe to join in their schemes. In this way, Biron became a conspirator and a traitor. The evening before his arrest, he was playing once more at primero with the queen, the favourite game everywhere at this time. Neither of the queens of Henry IV. thwarted him in his pursuits, for both Margot, and the Italian Marie de Medicis joined him in them, and had better luck.

Bassompierre also, though Biron lost his money and himself, could boast of his success. He speaks of gaming as a natural occupation, and one to be preferred before all.† His win-

* Rosny, Duc de Sully, was the faithful friend and chief minister of Henry IV.; to his memoirs we are indebted for the details of the history of the period. He always refused to imitate his masters example and turn papist. The Pope tried hard to induce him, but his answer was, "that he would never cease to pray for the conversion of his holiness."

† *Memoires de Bassompierre.* Coll. Petitot, t. xix. pp. 353—374.

nings were enormous. On one occasion, observing the chagrin of D'Epernon, at losing to him 25,000 crowns, he laid out more than half the money on a coat glittering with pearls and diamonds, and a sword costing 5,000 crowns, and assisted therewith at the christening festivities of the royal infants.

These great French players, however, occasionally caught a Tartar. There were sharks abroad in the shape of Spaniards and Italians of good birth, who appeared everywhere for the express purpose of fleecing whom they could. The *Histoire générale des Voyages*, tells us they were to be found at the courts of the Negro kings and of Indian rajahs. Beaulieu, the traveller, met with one Don Francisco Carnero, who continually managed to break the bank of the king of Achem.

The Portuguese Don Antonio Pimentel seems to have played a game of this sort at the court of Henry IV., who from the moment he saw him, conceived a high regard for him. Bassompierre relates in his Memoirs, that the king sent for him to court, and having piqued him with the alleged superiority of the new comer, they sat down to play, which ran so high, that neither silver nor gold would content them, but counters which went

as high as five thousand livres apiece. At the
end of the season, Bassompierre had gained
500,000 livres, and Pimentel 200,000 crowns!
How they must have shorn the sheep between
them! This was in 1608. For all this, Bassompierre died in debt. As for Pimentel, he had the
assurance to ask of Sully some favour on the
strength of his intimacy with the king, and received a severe rebuff for his pains.

The faithful minister was sorely tried on the
score of finance. Witness the annoyance of such
letters from the king as this, dated 1609.

"My friend,—I have lost at play twenty-two thousand pistoles; I pray you to remit them incontinently by the hands of
the bearer, Feideau, that so he may distribute them among the
persons to whom I am indebted, according to my order. Adieu,
my friend.   "HENRY.

"Monday Morning, this 18th January, at Paris.
"I wish that this sum should be entered in an account."

The necessary funds had of course to be raised
instantly to save the king's honour, who did not
fail, some days after, to call upon his minister, beg
his pardon, and promise (which he never meant to
keep) to be less extravagant for the future.

Sully, in a note at the end of his *Économies
Royales*, accuses Henry of an inordinate love of
the game of hazard, and states that by his example he was the ruin of many wealthy families,

and was the indirect cause of the "cheating devices, and damnable tricks," which began then to be used, thus plainly making him an encourager of the ingenuity of these vile "Greeks," as card-swindlers were very early called.*

Following the example of the court, the practice of gaming spread among the citizens; *brélans* or gaming houses were set up, and let for enormous prices; and people subsisted on the proceeds of play. All the poets, or almost all, lived in this fashion, of which Villon had already set the example.

No sooner had the dagger of Ravaillac made an untimely end of this gallant and gambling king, than an immediate stop was put to the former state of affairs.

The preamble of the *ordonnance* of the 30th May, 1611, soon after the accession of Louis XIII., draws a gloomy picture of the general

---

* Sully adds, that he had taken note of several considerable sums squandered in play by Henry, but these were by no means all. In 1607, Henry writes that certain merchants held him *au cul et aux chausses* for a sum of 9000 livres, which he had dissipated at the fair of St. Germains in trinkets and trifles. He was still worse in succeeding years, one entry is for 22,000 pistoles lost at play, of which 51,000 livres were due to the Portuguese Edward Fernandès; this last sum being equivalent to 6 or 700,000 francs now, yet he only applied to Sully from dire necessity. What a whirlpool!

dissolution of morals and ruin of families caused by the neglect of the laws against gaming, the increase of gaming houses and gamesters, and their consequent and inevitable results, dissipation of patrimonies and hard earned fortunes, borrowing large sums of money, which, being in their turn played away at the gaming tables, caused bankruptcy to the creditors, &c. This law was twice renewed, and put in practice with severity. Two persons named Duméri and Le Mage being detected at cards in the apartments they occupied, were with their partners, and their two landlords, arrested by the police, and finally, by sentence dated 21st April, 1635, were each fined 10,000 livres, one-third to the informer, and the rest to the poor.

This severity deterred the people. At the court, the king's example kept gaming in check.* He cared for nothing but the cross-bow, with which he shot admirably, wherefore he was called Louis le Juste. Richelieu hardly played at all, he had other business in hand.

The queen Anne of Austria, however, a Spanish princess, had a liking for cards, and the

---

* Save and except the queen mother's favourite, Concini Maréchal d'Ancre, who played very commonly a game of 20,000 pistoles (about 600,000 francs of the present reckoning).

little harmless card parties arranged under her patronage, and that of the king's brother Gaston, re-assured by degrees the lovers of the game.

The Memoirs of La Porte speak of a party at *reversis à quatre*, of which an Englishman, Lord Montague, formed one, and from other collections of the same sort, we gather that the prohibitory statutes had only half remedied the evil. The father of Madame de Maintenon, for instance, ruined himself at play, and the *Mémoires de Grammont* abundantly testify that the profession of gamester was not considered incompatible with the esteem of the public.

Throughout these memoirs, the idea attempted to be conveyed, is "the incomprehensible pre-eminence which in war, love, play, and the various circumstances of a long life, rendered the Count de Grammont the marvel of his age," but they indicate everywhere the character of a determined gamester, combined with that of the fine gentleman.

After the Restoration, de Grammont visited England, where his reputation preceded, and his good luck accompanied him. Charles II., a prince by nature and associations inclined to pleasure, and the nobility lately emancipated from puritan tyranny, welcomed the French gamester as a hero. Invitations poured in upon him from all quarters, and he lacked neither the skill nor the art of a Bassompierre or a Pimentel in easing the *mélancoliques insulaires* of the contents of their purses. Enriched with their spoils, he yet had the want of generosity to leave it on record, that the English players were slow payers.

With regard to card-playing in this country, although owing to the comparatively peaceable habits of the people, it did not partake so much of the reckless hazard which characterised, as we have seen, the continental games, the frequent mention of cards, and controversies respecting them, in the writers of the early part of this century, afforded ample proof that the practice was rife among all classes. It appears from a passage of *The Gull's Hornbook*, printed in 1609, that the spectators at the play-house amused themselves with cards while waiting for the commencement of the performance. James I., though he had prohibited cards in Scotland, was not so scrupulous as king of England, and with his son, the lamented Prince Henry, who died at an early age, in 1612, they were a favourite amusement. In his *Basilicon Doron*, or, rules for the nurture and conduct of an heir apparent to the throne, addressed to this young prince, James expressed himself on the subject of gaming in this manner, "As for sitting or house pastimes, since they may at times supply the roome which, being emptie, would be patent to pernicious idleness; I will not, therefore, agree with the curiositie of some learned men of our age, in forbidding cardes, dice, and such like games of hazard . . . . . . When it is foule and stormie weather, then I say may ye lawfully play at the cardes or tables; for, as to diceing, I think it becometh best deboshed souldiers to play at on the heads of their drums, being only ruled by hazard, and subject to knavish cogging; and as for the chesse, I think it over-fond, because it is over-wise and philosophicke a folly." The king's own favourite game appears to have been Maw, which is alluded to in a passage quoted by Mr. Chatto, from a satirical pamphlet of this reign, called *Tom Tell-troath*, and re-printed in the *Harleian Miscellany;* " They say you have lost the fairest game at Maw that ever king had, for want of making the best advantage of the five-finger, and playing the other helps in time. That your owne card-holders play bootie, and give the signe out of your owne hand, that hee you played withal hath ever been knowne for the greatest cheater in Christendome.[*]

[*] The King of Spain, or his ambassador Gondomar.

Maw is mentioned with other of "the games that have been in request at court;" in another of the epigrams of the facetious Sir John Harington (4to, 1615).

> "I heard one make a pretty observation
> How games have in the court turn'd with the fashion,
> The first game was the best, when free from crime,
> The courtly gamesters all were in their *prime*:
> The second game was *Post*, until with posting
> They paid so fast, 'twas to leave their boasting;
> Then thirdly follow'd *heaving of the Maw*,*
> A game without civility or law,
> An odious play, and yet in Court oft seene,
> A sawcy Knave, to trump both King and Queene.
> Then followed *Lodam,* ————————
> Now *Noddy* follow'd next, as well it might,
> Although it should have gone before of right.
> At which I saw, I name not any body,
> One never had the Knave, yet laid for Noddy.
> The last game now in use is *Bankerout*,
> Which will be plaid at still, I stand in doubt,
> Until *Lavolta* turn the wheele of time,
> And make it come about again to *Prime*."

That Primero was still played appears from the Earl of Northumberland's Letters about the powder plot, which describe Joscelin Percy

---

* *Heaving of the Maw.* This expression looks at first sight, like a play on the stomachic meaning of the word, but Messrs. Halliwell and Wright, in their edition of *Nares' Glossary,* imagine it to be some grotesque action incidental to the game, quoting a passage in support from Turbervile's *Book of Faulconrie.*

> "To check at cheese, to *heave at maw*, at macke to passe the time,
>   At coses or at saint to sit, or set their rest at prime."

playing at it on Sunday, when his uncle, the conspirator, called on him at Essex House; and a game called Gresco is mentioned with it, in Jonson, Chafneau, and Marlowe's comedy of *Eastward Hoe*, printed in that year. Post, or Post and Pair, is said to have been a more perilous game to the purses of players than Primero. It was something akin to Commerce, and was in use before 1563, as bishop Jewel alludes to it in his controversy with Harding: "Touching the Head of the Church, he (Mr. Harding) cometh in only with jolly brags and great vaunts, as if he were playing at Post, and should win all by vying." Bowle derives it from the Spanish *apostar*, to place in the hands of a third party a certain sum of money or an equivalent for the winner—a sense still in use, as in "posting the poney." Urquhart gives it as the English representative of one of Rabelais' games, *Pair et Sequence*. Cotton says the play depends much upon daring or vying. The vye is what you adventure upon your own hand; and if you have the boldness to adventure much, you stand a chance of winning considerably. The ace of trumps is the best card, as at Ruff and Honours. At Post the best cards are twenty-one, viz., two tens and an ace: a pair is two kings, two queens, &c.;

and a *prial*, or pair-royal, three. He who has the
best pair or the best post, is the winner, but a
pair-royal wins all. You must first stake at
post, then at pair; then deal two cards apiece,
then stake at the seat, and then deal the third
card about.

Mawe is described in a unique and curious
tract written by Arthur Hall, about 1580, as " a
playe at cardes grown out of the country, from the
meanest, into credit at court with the greatest."
It is mentioned with Lodam in a satirical tract,
entitled the *True History of Pope Joan*, printed
in 1559, where, speaking of the Jesuits, the author
says, " A certain prince of ours did compare them
unto a game at cardes, in which the gamesters
like Loadam-playe, and bring them for the last
that are of most price, to beat down the adverse
party: or like the *ace of hearts* at *Mawe* (the game
is with us called *Rumstick*)." From this, Singer,
to whom we are indebted for the quotation, infers
that Maw is the same as *Romestecg*, a game
described in the *Académie des Jeux;* but from the
allusions to the " five-finger" and ace of hearts in
Tom Tell-troath and *Pope Joan*, it seems to
present more affinity with the Irish game of Five-
cards, described by Cotton, in which also " the
five fingers (*alias* five of trumps) is the best card

in the pack; the ace of hearts is the next to that, and the next is the ace of trumps."* That Lodam is identical with the French game Reversis is confirmed by Cotgrave, who gives "Coquimbert qui gaigne pert, a game of cards like our Loosing-Lodam." Barrington calls it Saint-Lodam, but does not give the reason.

Noddy, according to Halliwell, is an old game at cards, conjectured to be the same as Cribbage, but he does not state his authority. It appears from the *Compleat Gamester*, that knave Noddy was the designation of the knave of trumps, in playing this game. It was probably a childish pastime, as it is quoted under the name of *Seize-Nody*, with Maw, Jick Jack, and Ruffe, by Strutt, *Manners and Customs*, iii. 147, from a MS. in the Harleian Library, 2057, and entitled "*An enumeration of antient customs in games, used by boys and girles, merrily sett out in verse.*" Carr mentions Noddy-fifteen in his *Craven Glossary*,

---

* *Compleat Gamester*, p. 90. Edit. 1709. The five-finger and ace of hearts are also, according to Chatto, mentioned in connection with Maw, in the inscription beneath a caricature engraving of the period, in the Library of the Royal Society of Antiquaries, representing the kings of England, Denmark, and Sweden, with Bethlem Gabor, playing at cards, &c., with the Pope and his monks.—P. 127. Halliwell and Wright compare it to Commerce.

fifteen being probably the game.* Of Bankerout
nothing is known; the word is probably derived
from the French, and means *bankrupt;* and
Lavolta does not appear to be a game of cards
at all. Knave-out-of-doors is mentioned with New
Cut and Ruff, which is proposed to be played with
honours, in *A Woman killed by Kindness*, a play
by Thomas Heywood, of which the third edition
was published in 1617. "English Ruff and Honours (*alias* Slamm)," and French Ruff, are
described by Cotton;† and there appear to have
been also Wide Ruff and Cross Ruff. The
former, he says, differs little from Whist, and is

---

* Halliwell also describes a game called Niddy-Noddy, a
favourite children's game, which we remember well. Any
number can play. The cards are all dealt out: the elder hand
plays one (of which he hath a pair, or a *prial*,[1] if a good player)
saying or singing "Here's a good card for thee;" the next player
covers it, saying "Here's another as good as he," and passes it
on to the third, who, if he holds a better card of the suit, says
"And here's the best of all the three;" and the fourth crowns
all with "Here's old Niddy Noddee," takes the luck, turns it
down, and begins again. He who is first *out* receives from his
adversaries a fish or counter for each unplayed card.

† *Compleat Gamester.* Slamm is mentioned by Herrick. It
is also a term in Whist, used when one party wins a game before
the other has gained a trick. Of the manner of playing *Knave
out of Doors* and *New Cut* we have no account. The former
may perhaps be the same as *Knaues out of Town*, mentioned in
Poor Robin's Almanac for 1709.

[1] Prial, *i.e.* pair-royal, a term at post and pair. Another term is *pur.*

so commonly known in England that every child of eight years old hath a competent knowledge in it.

These games are also mentioned, with others, in *Machivell's Dogge*, printed in the same year as the above:

> " Cast up the cardes, the trickes together put,
> And leaving Ruffe, lets fall upon New Cut."

And again:

> " But what shall bee our game? Primero? Gleake?
> Or one and Thirty, bone-ace, or New-cut?"

Bone-ace is also one of Cotton's games, who describes it as played by persons of quality, and " a *licking* game for money;" the ace of diamonds is *Bone-ace*, and wins all other cards whatever; afterwards, the nearest to one and thirty wins the game, and he that turns up or draws to one and thirty, wins it immediately.*

The fashionable vices of excess in matters of dress, gaming, drinking, and haunting of taverns, appear to have been carried to great lengths during the reign of James I., and in the first part of that of Charles, and called forth severe

---

* *Compleat Gamester*. Florio, *s. v. Trentune* mentions a game at cards called " One and Thirtie, or *Bone-ace*," as if they were identical, but they probably only bore a common analogy to the foreign game.

attacks from the Puritan party, already incensed by the publication of the celebrated *Book of Sports*, which however gives no countenance to indoor games. But the latter did not always have it their own way. Mr. William Ames, then fellow of Christ's College, Cambridge, having preached at St. Mary's, in 1610, against playing at cards and dice, as being forbidden by scripture, his discourse gave so much offence to persons in authority that he withdrew from the University to avoid expulsion,* and Gataker, in his treatise *On the Nature and Use of Lots*, demolished the more extravagant positions, and demonstrated the lawfulness of card-playing under due restrictions and limitations.

The following picture of a prodigal's life from the pen of Taylor, the water-poet, supplies us with the titles of some more card games of this period ;

> " The prodigall's estate, like to a flux,
> The Mercer, Draper, and the Silkman sucks :
> The Tailor, Millainer, Dogs, Drabs, and Dice,
> Trey-trip, or Passage, or the Most-at-thrice.
> At Irish, Tick-tackle, Doublets, Draughts, or Cheese,
> He flings his money free with carelessnesse :
> At Novum, Mainchance, Mischance (chuse ye which),

* *Chatto*, p. 281. Ames subsequently became Theological Professor at the University of Francker, Friesland. He was also one of Gataker's opponents.

At One-and-Thirty, or at Poor-and-Rich,
Ruffe, Slam, Trump, Whisk, Hole,* Sant, New Cut.
Unto the keeping of four knaves he'll put
His whole estate; at Loadum or at Gleeke,
At Tickle-me-quickly, he's a merry Greek;
At Primifisto,† Post-and Payre, Primero,
Maw, Whip-her ginney,‡ he's a lib'ral hero;
At, My-sow-pigged :§ but (reader never doubt ye)
He's skilled in all games except Looke about ye.
Bowles, Shove-groat, Tennis, no game comes amiss,
His purse a nurse for anybody is;
Caroches, Coaches, and Tobacconists,
All sorts of people freely from his fists,
His vaine expenses daily suck and soake,
And he himself sucks only drink and smoake.
And thus the Prodigall himself alone
Gives sucke to thousands, and himself sucks non."

Taylor's Motto, 12mo., 1622.

Halliwell, in his Dictionary, mentions a juve-
nile game at cards called "Laugh-and-lay-down,"
in which the winner, who holds a certain combina-

---

* Hole, sometimes called "My Lady's Hole," or *Trou Madame,*
from its being played by ladies, not a game at cards, but like
Trunks, by trundling little balls into holes on a bench.

† i. e. *Prima Vista.*

‡ Or *Whip-her-Jenny,* a game at cards borrowed from the
Welsh. Halliwell says it was also a term of contempt.

§ Still played under the name of "My Bird sings." Florio
mentions a similar title, "My Hen hath laid," p. 474. The expression, "My bird sings," is also one in use among usurers.
"My bird would hardly sing to-day, he wasn't in good voice,"
says Mr. Andrew Wylie, in G. H. Lewes's (Slingsby Laurence,
and Pelham Hardwicke) Comedy, *A Bachelor of Arts,* Act i.,
p. 17.

¶ Southey, in chap. 142 of the *Doctor,* p. 356, gives a short
list of games, but containing nothing of importance.

tion of cards, lays them down upon the table, and laughs (or is supposed to do so) at his good luck; and in Dodsley's collection of old plays, Crimp occurs as a game of cards; and again, at a later period (1757), in Clarinda's Diary, *Spectator*, vol. v., No. 323. The exact date of the introduction of Piquet from France is uncertain, but it is not unlikely that the marriage of Charles I. with a French princess, daughter of Henry IV., may have rendered it fashionable at court. It is mentioned with Cribbage by John Hall, in his *Horæ Vacivæ*, printed in 1646. "For cardes," he says, the Philologil of them is not for an essay; a man's fancy would be sum'd up in Cribbidge; Gleeke requires a vigilant memory; Maw, a pregnant agility; Picket, a various invention; Primero, a dexterous kinde of rashness," &c.

If the popular acquaintance with cards furnished the early divines with an apt vehicle of instruction, the pamphleteers of this period availed themselves of it for some telling titles for their productions. We have alluded to one, p. 164, and Chatto mentions another, printed in 1659, *Shuffling, cutting, and dealing in a Game at Pickquet*, being acted from the year 1653 to 1655, by O. P. and others;" and Gayton, in 1645, adopted the title of "*Chartæ Scriptæ; or, a New*

Game at Cards, called Play by the Book," for a quarto volume of miscellaneous poems.* The terms of Gleek especially officiated in this way. In the *Lenten Litany*, a satirical prayer for the Rump Parliament, one of the stanzas runs thus:

> " From Villany dressed in a doublet of Zeal,
> From three Kingdoms baked in one Commonweal,
> From a *gleek* of Lord Keepers of one poor seal,
>   Libera nos Domine."

Another satirical poem, dated 1683, is entitled, *A Murnival of Knaves; or, Whiggism Plainly Displayed.* A murnival was a set of all four cards of a sort, as four aces, four kings, queens, or knaves, as Gleek is of three.

This was nothing, however, compared with the artillery of the Puritans. Every conventicle rung with their fierce denunciations of cards, dice, dancing, and ornament in dress. It is supposed that not a single card crossed with the Pilgrim Fathers to New England, even now re-

---

* In his *Festivous Notes upon Don Quixote*, fol. 1654, p. 14, Gayton tells the following story: " A lady once requested a gentleman to play at Gleek, was refused, but civilly, and upon three reasons, the first whereof, Madam, said the gentleman, is, I have no money. Her ladyship knew that was so material and sufficient, that she desired him to keep the other two reasons to himself."

markable for a scarcity of such things; and their brethren at home, as they got into power, left no means untried to bring them into entire disuse. Books, prints, and pamphlets, on purpose to denounce these " carnal vanities," were written by Prynne, Hall, and others, in profusion. Even Quarles, in his poems, has the customary fling. In the seventh picture to his Second Book of Emblems, the divine Cupid is represented casting away the follies and vanities of this life; and amongst masks, battledoors, balls, and books of love, we find dice and cards; the latter, indeed, are found so frivolous and light that the wind has already blown some far away. A modern writer, in a late work, conjures up a picture of a knot of persecuted Royalists amusing themselves within barred doors and closed windows at a game of cards,—no bad idea of the condition of card-playing during the Commonwealth.

Perhaps one of the most interesting matters in connexion with the effect which the pack of cards has had upon society generally, is the use to which its terminology has been applied in political pamphlets and similar whimsical productions. Two very rare instances of this kind, which have fallen into the writer's hands, may suffice.

The first is entitled : *The Knave of Clubs. Otherwise called, A Game at Cards, and Clvbs Trump. Doe you not see the Knave turn'd up? Rub and lose cards. Play faire* [here a knave of clubs, with the words "*Edward Fryer*" on a band behind the legs of the figure] *and above Boord. London : Shuffled, Cut and dealt faire by* Stysichorus. *Anno Dom.* 1643.

This pamphlet is an allegory, representing the "artful dodges" of early card-sharpers, but having obvious reference to passing events. The characters are *Prometheus, Olympius, Monopoly, Curtius, Decus,* and *Hephestion.*

Curtius, Decus, and Hephestion begin to play cards, with varying fortunes ; and Prometheus looks over Hephestion's hand : little is lost on either side, but Prometheus, being very poor, "a greater griping" is stirred up in him. Hephestion becomes, however, a serious loser in the end ; upon which Prometheus calls upon Monopoly. Monopoly suggests a method of confederacy. "Then they fell to disputing a great while with themselves what signes would be best, whereby they might clearly understand each other ; at last it was resolved, that the best manner of doing it would be by the buttons of his Jerkin, or the joynts of his fingers, according to the Gamuth when we first learn to sing, and having made tryall thereof three or four times, they grew so ready and so perfect therein, that they understood one another as well by their tokens as their tongues."

Hephestion being ruined, Prometheus accepts the challenge of the players Curtius and Decus, feigning at first to be engaged with his *Rosario*, or rosary, and doing it out of complaisance. Prometheus, despite his cunning, loses all before him, and has to draw money from Monopoly, who leaves the room, but is at last begged to remain and snuff the candles. Upon this Monopoly commences the system of private signaling, and the two gamesters are beaten.

This play continues for some time to the advantage of the confederates; but at last the signaling of Monopoly is suspected, and being turned out of the room, Prometheus is made to lose, and ultimately they send him away "like a clean gentleman." Then follows the rhyme:

> "Prometheus fire stole from Heaven,
>   To quicken his Idols vaine;
> The Arian Prelate Olympius
>   For cursing Christ was slaine;
> Monopoly his Country wrackes,
>   By patents most unjust,
> For which good Curtius freely gave
>   His body to the dust.

Hephestion is a Favourite,
But Decies three are blest,
The Father, Sonne, and Nephew eeke,
For Country do protest."

The pamphlet is a whimsical curiosity, but of little farther interest for the present purpose than as employing many of the terms of card-playing.

The second pamphlet is without date, but it refers to the Parliamentary Wars, being one of the publications on the side of the Cavaliers. The title will sufficiently explain its contents.*

The bloody Game at Cards, As it was played betwixt the King of Hearts And the rest of His Suite, against the residue of the packe of Cards, Wherein Is discovered where faire play; was plaid and where was fowle. [Here a representation of the King of Hearts.] *Shuffled at London, Cut at Westminster, Dealt at Yorke, and Plaid in the open field, by the Citty-clubs, the Country Spade-men, Rich Diamond Men and Loyall Hearted men.*

The publication evidently took place after the Battle of Edgehill, in 1642, but before the decision of the struggle between the royal and parliamentary forces.

* The title is here repeated, having been incorrectly and imperfectly quoted on p. 164.

III

CARD PLAYING IN FRANCE DURING THE XVIITH. AND XVIIITH. CENTURIES.

CARD PLAYING AN INSTITUTION OF STATE—MAZARIN—GAMING AN ENGINE OF POLICY—ANNE OF AUSTRIA—CARDS IN THE CAMP—MARIA THERESA—HOCCA—GOURVILLE—DEATH BED OF MAZARIN—THE AGE OF FESTIVALS—CARD SHARPING AT THE COURT—DE LANGLEE AND MADAME DE MONTESPAN—HOCCA SUPPLANTED BY BASSETTE—DANGEAU—THE DUCHESS DE MAZARIN—PROMINENT PLAYERS—GAMBLING AT VERSAILLES—DANGEAU AND HIS CAREER—HIS READY POETICAL TALENTS—ELECTED GRAND-MASTER OF THE ORDER OF LAZARUS—SINGE DU ROI—PRINCESSES SMOKING—DEMORALIZATION OF THE ARMY—CARD BALL—LANGLEE AND THE DUCHESS OF BURGUNDY—BRELAN AND THE DEATH CHAMBER—MONSIEUR AND THE DAUPHIN—THE GAMBLING LADIES—MADAME DE CLEREMBAULT—MADAME DE POLGNAC PRINCESS HARCOURT—FUN FOR AN ELECTOR—CARDS MURDER POLITICAL LIFE.

IT is an apparent, but not a real, exaggeration to say, that the magnificent Louis XIV. almost raised card-playing into an institution of State. Indeed, it is an historical fact hitherto considerably overlooked, and worthy of attention.

It was Mazarin who suggested this course of ideas to Louis. As an Italian, Mazarin was pas-

sionately attached to play; for although his ava-
ricious disposition would apparently have tended
to deter him from gambling, yet he was a "Greek,"
sure of his prey, and played heavy stakes.   Penetrated with a knowledge of the truth, that when
the attention is drawn to trifles, the important
concerns of life and policy pass unheeded, he
introduced play at court to the king and queen-
regent in 1648, the better to veil, nay, to assist, his
own intricate plots.   The example set by the
palace, rapidly spread through all ranks, and even
the peasant's hut became a gambling-house, where
the stakes were only pitifully small instead
of splendidly extravagant.   Out-door games fell
into disrepute ;   men became weaker, unhealthier,
and more ignorant, while a sad effect upon
female morality was perceptible.   This general
degradation of manners had an important political
effect, and aided to complete the task commenced
by Louis XI., continued by Richelieu, and now
forming the problem at which Mazarin laboured.
This task was the establishment of absolute
monarchy upon the ruins of feudalism.   Of
course this purpose was veiled, although sufficiently perceptible to later generations.   Occasionally, even, convictions took place for gambling.
In 1643, Guillaume Ballichard, a blacksmith, was

scourged for keeping a gambling-house; and in 1655, cards, dice, and billiards were interdicted, although the parliament subsequently removed the interdiction from the last game.

Anne of Austria played much, and loved cards passionately, although her lady-in-waiting, De Motteville, says of her, that "she played like a queen, without passion or greed of gain."

In 1649, at the time of the Fronde, on the day of Kings, just before the flight, the courtiers adhered to their usual pursuit of card-playing. The Duke of Orleans and Condé played that night at Marshal Grammont's house; and as to Mazarin, "he continued where he was, amusing himself with play, while his confidential servants packed up his valuables and took them away."[*]

So general was the passion for cards, that when Condé, Conti, and Longueville were consigned to the Bastille in the following year, finding no beds provided, they procured cards, and passed the whole night in that occupation.

The young king, no doubt, as a contemporary writer, La Porte, states, found a ready preceptor in card-playing in the person of Mazarin; and anecdotes told by La Porte prove that he was

[*] Madame de Motteville.

in the habit of paying somewhat dearly for his lessons.

During the war of the Fronde and the Spanish campaigns, cards were the pastime of the victors and the consolation of the vanquished. Bussy Rabutin, who, in 1657, was fighting in Flanders and Artois, thus narrates the passion for card-playing which prevailed in the army : *

" From Malsy, we came to Lusoir, near La Capelle, and according to the intelligence we had received respecting the enemy we altered our posts : however, we were in the greatest condition of idleness, which compelled us to play from morning till night. For my part, I had surprising luck : if I lost once, I won ten times : all my friends pressed me to let them go shares with me—halves, thirds, or quarters, and I considered that I was giving my own money to those persons with whose requests I complied. This good fortune was so famous that it came to the ears of the cardinal (Mazarin), and when I sent a gentleman to him to beg for payment of the thousand crowns with which the king was accustomed to pay the lieutenant-generals serving the campaign, he answered my messenger, that he was rejoiced to hear I had gained so much money, and that Talon would bring the supply to the army. And Talon did, indeed, come, but he gave to every one, except to myself, telling me that the cardinal had taken my part as his share of my gains. I said to Talon, that I would not have it so, that when I took leave of his eminence, he had positively promised me one thousand crowns as soon as I arrived at the army, and that we had not agreed that I should play halves with him during the campaign —that, indeed, I did not ask for the money from the need I had for it, but rather from the annoyance it caused me to see others preferred. Talon assured me that he would press him hard, and, indeed, he succeeded so well, that I obtained my thousand crowns."

* Edit. 1704, vol. ii., p. 400.

Upon the re-establishment of peace, and the marriage of Louis XIV., the cardinal gave full license to his passion. Formerly he had played privately; he now played publicly, without check upon himself, and enormous sums were won and lost. The king, upon his return down the Garonne, played openly all day long, and the Abbé de Garde lost fifty thousand crowns in one hour, — a sum equivalent to £12,500 at the present day. The young queen, Maria Theresa, also played deeply, but with great illfortune, losing all before her, and getting into debt besides. The cardinal had little mercy upon unfortunate gamblers. He expected all to win: to "make use of their advantages," as he phrased it; and when, upon one occasion, the queen applied to him for funds, he would not hear of her card debts, answering, that if "she knew whence the money came, and that it was the life blood of the people, she would not be so liberal of it."

This magnificent speech, however, was as false as it was apparently highsouled. Madame de Motteville indignantly bursts out about the matter. "This man to say so ! he who every day gambles away three or four thousand pistoles; he who has all the wealth of France in his coffers, and who permits his niece, the Countess of Soissons, to play away immense sums every day !"

Mazarin, in his eagerness for play, even went so far as to seek out and introduce new games into France. Among these is an Italian game, known as *Hocca*, or Hoc.* Some have attributed the invention of Hoc to Mazarin, but this was not the case. So much evil had been wrought by these games in Italy, and so many wealthy families had been reduced to beggary, that Urban VIII. and Innocent IX. expelled the professors of the game from their dominions. Four of the exiles made their way to Paris, and established themselves publicly there. *Hocca* worked its usual ruin, and was met by severe Parliamentary decrees. On the 18th of December, 1660, a royal order, more rigorous still, was published; yet, while the public was being overawed into terror-stricken obedience, Mazarin was urging on the fever of gambling at the court with all his might.

The finance-superintendent Fouquet, who was very prosperous, emulated the prime minister, but surpassed him in the elegant way in which he was hastening on the ruin of France and of himself. On the very eve of his ruin, at the festival

* See page 193 of this work. That Mazarin could not have been the *inventor* of the game of *hocca* or *hoc* is sufficiently proved by the fact that it is included by Rabelais in the list of games played by Gargantua (Book i., c. xxii., vol. i., pp. 171-2). In Urquhart's translation it is specified as " the hock."

of Vaux, this immaculate chancellor of the exchequer presented each of his guests with a purse of gold, that play might amuse all and afflict none.

At this great festival was performed Molière's comedy of *Des Facheux*. Molière depicts the gambler in Alcippe, and makes him relate the points of a game of piquet played with thirty-six cards.

In the early days of the reign of the Grand Monarque, while the court was yet fresh and young, the most successful and skilful player of the time was Gourville, a native of the Angoumois. This district was famous for producing games and gamesters. In his own memoirs, Gourville has devoted some pages to the history of his exploits, which show that the games in vogue at the time were chiefly games of chance, in which but little skill was necessary. The year was 1660, the first year of his visit to court. He says :*

"I proposed to these gentlemen (de Vardes, d'Herval, and de La Basinière) to play at *trente et quarante;* that having never played it, I should be glad to learn. I won, on the first occasion, seven to eight hundred pistoles. A short time afterwards, *M. le Surintendant* being at Saint Mandé proposed to M. d'Herval and others to play. M. d'Herval having told M. Fouquet that I was a player, and that he had played with me, he said that I must be of the party. I won seventeen

* *Collection Petitot,* vol. lii., p. 332.

hundred pistoles. I gave one hundred for the cards, being unaware of the custom on the occasion. There was great play at M. Fouquet's almost every day. Madame de Launay Grancé, afterward Marquise de Piennes, usually played there with other ladies, and sometimes even with gentlemen ; I was one of the party on every occasion of my visits. M. le Comte d'Avaux being once present, sat down to play, and as I felt in a fortunate vein, I played heavy stakes, especially when I won. At the end of the sitting, M. d'Avaux owed me eighteen thousand livres. These games were played without any money being staked on the table, but upon leaving off, a writing-case was brought, and each person wrote upon a card the amount of his debt, and upon presentation of that card, the money was paid. M. d'Avaux gave me his card, and begged me to visit him on the next day to receive the sum due to me, which I willingly did. Jewellery of price, Venice lace of great value, was frequently staked, and one day, as well as I can remember, point-lace ruffles of seventy or eighty pistoles each, were played for.

"One day, M. Fouquet, wishing to make up a party of great players,* begged M. de Ricourart to give a dinner in a house he had near Paris. M. d'Herval was always one of the first to be bidden to these parties of play : he was the most unfortunate player in the world. M. de la Basinière, who was attacked with the same malady to almost as great an extent, was also present. I do not remember the others, with the exception of Marshal de Clérambault, who often sought an occasion to play with these gentlemen. The company had arrived a little while before the dinner hour. Cards were brought, and I won four to five hundred pistoles before dinner was served.

"After dinner, M. Fouquet set himself against me, and staked such large sums at a time when I held the cards, that his marks, which were on a piece of cut card, were often worth a hundred pistoles each : this annoyed him exceedingly, and the

* Colbert mentions his magnificence. "He has been seen to play away twenty to thirty thousand pistoles in one night, without reckoning his expense in buildings, fountains, furniture, women, or the ordinary charges of his house, carrying luxury and feasting to a point which many wealthy persons deemed madness." MS. of Colbert on the finance of France. See P. Clement, *Pièces Justificatives.*

company was astonished at everything he said. Seeing, however,
that the time to recoup himself had arrived, he made such a
great stake of the marks that were on his cards, that he,
having dealt thirty-one and I forty, won back by that one stroke
more than sixty thousand livres he then owed me. Hereupon
he grew merry, and I was greatly rallied by these gentlemen at
not having known how to withdraw myself with the larger
portion of the great winnings I had made. I replied, laughing,
that in my country good breeding demanded that the winner
should not leave the cards. Every one rose to go, and M.
d'Herval, having gathered up the cards from the floor, where
they lay in great multitude, challenged me to stake something.
I staked five hundred pistoles—all I intended to lose. Having
won, I took the cards: he pressed me so hard two or three
times in succession, that in a very short time he owed me five
thousand pistoles. Upon this I threw down the cards, and
declared I would no longer play after the fashion of my country,
at which every one fell a-laughing and got into their coaches to
depart. I also remember that one day on which fireworks were
to be let off on the shore, M. de la Basinière invited M. the
Superintendent and his wife to supper, together with many
others, including myself, the house being opposite the place
where the fireworks were to be exhibited. M. the Duke de
Richelieu, who was there, said to me that he had heard I was a
great and fine player, and took up a pack of cards which were
on the table, the others not thinking of playing. In the course
of a few minutes I won of him fifty-five thousand livres ; but
the fireworks beginning, I remembered the advice which had
been given me, and took my leave with a great bow, at which he
was surprised, and not a little annoyed. That did not however
prevent my being paid by means of an estate he had in Saintonge,
which he sold to the Marshal d'Albret. My great profits
always arose when I held the cards, and the other piquetted
to recoup that they had lost. When others held them, I never
played high stakes : I had made it a rule never to lose more
than a thousand pistoles of my own money. Once in my life,
having in my turn piquetted, I lost twenty thousand livres."

Such was the rage of Mazarin himself for play,

that he almost died with the cards in his hands. Paul de la Roche painted a picture of the cardinal upon his death bed. He is there represented as being unable to play himself, but is employing others to play for him. His eyes sparkle, and he seems as it were to be playing again. The painting is no fiction. Contemporary persons testify to its fidelity. Brienne says, in his Inedited Memoirs,* "Among the last incidents of the cardinal's death, of which I was witness, I may mention that they played in his chamber, by his bedside, even to the day on which the papal nuncio—informed that he had partaken of the viaticum—came to confer the indulgence upon him, after which the cards disappeared. Colonel de Souvré held his cards when I was there; he made a lucky stroke, and hastened to inform his eminence of it, thinking to please him. 'Commander,' replied he, with great justice, 'I lose more in my bed than I win or could win at the table at which you hold my hand.' "

After the death of Mazarin, Louis XIV. reigned without any prime minister; he in person presided over all the magnificence, pomp, and vanity of the Century of Ceremony. The age of festivals had arrived.

* *Mémoires inédits de Brienne,* chap. xv.

Play, forbidden to the mob, was not only permitted, but enjoined, at Paris, Fontainebleau, and St. Germain, and subsequently at Marly and Versailles. It must ever be esteemed a grievous fault on the part of the king that he encouraged and fostered the passion of gambling; and amid the hollow frippery of the age, there were not wanting those who protested loudly against the vice of gaming, and in a few vigorous lines, sadly at variance with the feeble tone of French thought during the period in which it was written, Madame Deshoulières vehemently stigmatised card-playing.

Those, who, from their position, dared not openly indulge in their love for gambling, adopted disguises for the purpose—abbés dressed themselves as women, and went to the play-tables masked or painted, that recognition might be impossible.

The excessive love of cards has, unfortunately, the same tendency to deprave morality as a passionate pursuit of any other species of gain. Consequently the *noblesse* of France, without the excuse of the needy card-sharper, of whom it will be our duty to speak in a future chapter, speedily found themselves, in the modern French phrase, *capable de tout. Mais! vous le voulez, Georges Dandin!* and the ineffable Georges Dandin, who

reigned and gambled, looked, as his predecessor
Mazarin had done, with an unfavourable eye
upon the gambler who, to cover his losses, used
skill and sleight of hand to recoup them. Madame
de Sévigné says, writing in March, 1671, that the
common talk of Paris in that month was the
degradation and banishment from the metropolis
of a certain M. de S———. He had cheated at
cards—had made the worse the better fortune,
and won five hundred thousand crowns with
prepared cards (*des cartes ajustées*). The king,
anxious to do justice, himself interrogated the
culprit, who met the charge at first with a flat
denial. However, his majesty, getting curious,
promised him a pardon, and he then avowed that
he had carried on his practices for a long time,
and it was even elicited that certain excellent
families were furnished by him with packs of
cards so arranged as to determine the issues.
Here was a great man who was an habitual thief!
and his case was soon not without a parallel. A
street-row shortly afterwards occurred, between
two gentlemen, M. de Langlée and M. Dangeau,
as to the settlement of a debt of honour thus
incurred. Amidst threats and recriminations
they avowed, that they each were in the enviable
positions of the pot and the kettle ; and, though

the affair was settled, the card-bullies continued to pursue their business. Langlée was very free and familiar in his manners, and during a game of *brelan* he was playing with the Count de Grammont, he used some very coarse expressions, which the latter met with the remark : "M. de Langlée, keep those familiarities for occasions when you play with the king!"

Thus it is all the world over, when a king's favorite vice is the passport to his presence for a sharper and a cheat. Langlée, by extraction, was the son of a footman; a parentage which, with honest courses, could not have failed to have preserved him in the paths of virtue and obscurity : he preferred to be a rogue, and thus became the guest and companion of a king prouder than any the world ever saw, and the donor of costly gifts to the king's "friend," Madame de Montespan. One incident is worthy of mention, from its whimsicality as well as its extravagance.

Langlée had a magnificent robe of cloth of gold, embroidered with gold, and further adorned with gold lace and some other trimmings of gold prepared : it was, of course, committed to the care of the lady's tailor, to whom her measures were necessarily known. It was desirable the

gift should be as unexpectedly received as
lavishly bestowed. The tailor of the monarch's
"friend" brought a garment she had ordered, but
had designedly made it a ridiculous misfit. It
was wanted in a hurry, as all ladies want everything, and the scolding was, no doubt effectively
executed. The tailor trembled, slouched, cringed,
and apologised, but the storm continued. At last
the unlucky workman humbly proffered another
robe, with the timorous manner of a man in fear:
"It was the only one he had; might it not do, just
as a makeshift?" Madame de Montespan agreed
to look at it. "Oh! what beautiful material! what
splendid stuff! It comes from heaven!" The body
was tried on—it fitted like a glove, marvellous!
Just then the king came in, and the tailor, with
a bow, said, "Madame, it was made for you."
But who could be the donor? "It is Langlée,"
said the king. "Langlée, most assuredly," said
the lady; "no one but Langlée could have
imagined so costly and magnificent a gift." So
the outside world—the lesser fowls in the royal
chicken-yards—clucked, "It is Langlée!" and the
brilliant and witty Madame de Sévigné, from whom
we derive the anecdote, concludes her letter to
her daughter,—"And, my daughter, I say to you,
to be in the fashion, it is Langlée!" Verily, 'tis

a good thing to be born of a footman, live by
gambling, be exposed at the corner of the Rue
des Jacobins by a "pal," and to have all the world
aghast at the splendour you exhibit towards a
king's mistress! "*C'est Langlée!*" and dearly
she paid for her whistle, no doubt!

The game at which Mazarin generally seems
to have played was *hocca* or hock, mentioned
several times in the course of these pages.
Fashion is imperious, and as variable as an
English spring. Hocca recedes from view and
gets out of date in the days of Louis XIV.—
perhaps he remembered the cash lost at it to his
eminent and clerical preceptor. Bassette took its
place. An Italian game, it partook of a similar
character, and, indeed, the games known as
fiorentini and *pharao* together with *bassette* and
hocca are all the offspring of *lansquenet* or *Lands-
knecht*. That *bassette* obtained the supremacy,
is plain from the use Madame de Sévigné makes
of its terms in letters to her daughter.

If Langlée were supreme in robe-making,
Dangeau, his rival, was the arbiter of the *bassette*
table, as he had previously been of *hocca* and
manille (or the comet), a game attributed to the
invention of Louis Georges Dandin himself.
Respecting Dangeau, a *bon mot* of the first water,

and which caused his own mouth, no doubt, not
to be without moisture, is recorded. Some one
said of him that, " If the peace only lasted ten
years, Dangeau would be marshal of France."

Such was the attraction of the gaming table,
and of the game of bassette especially, that the
noble youths who were about the court even
abandoned their mistresses. Among these, was
the Marquis de la Fare, who had previously been
deeply enamoured of Madame de la Sabliére.
His punishment soon came in the form of great
losses, alluded to by La Fontaine, to whose retirement even the rumours of La Fare's ruin had
penetrated.*

New games were the fashion at the court, and
the old games soon became the unfashionable
pastime of the country, where alone they were
held in esteem. Even in Madame de Sévigné's
retirement, she mentions that they had three
tables constantly going, one of trictrac, one of
hombre, and one of reversi. But bassette became
the most popular method of reducing oneself to
the condition of the cynical philosopher who
reckoned all superfluity as the curse of mankind.
The Duchess of Mazarin, the niece of the cardinal, who resided in England, grew so mad

* *Lettres à divers*, xix. (1678).

with it as to terrify all her friends. Of twenty-five millions of livres left her by her cardinal uncle, the beautiful Hortensia Mancini had managed to make such respectable ducks and drakes, as to die insolvent,* as well as insane.

In the memoirs of the Marquis de Sourches, some interesting details of the court life are given, worthy to be noticed. Among the prominent players of the age, were the Marquis de Sessac, once the Abbé de Clermont, the Count d'Aulonne (who died in 1686), the Count d'Auvergne, the Marquis de Béringhen, and the master of requests, Chamillard. The last three often held a hand for the king.

In November, 1686, the king returned to Versailles, and instituted a regular system of play in the evening, at which the principal players were the king, Monseigneur, Monsieur, Dangeau, and Langlée, the footman's son, fit boon companions for a king of France! Even when engaged in necessary business, play proceeded; the king deputing some one of his courtiers to hold his cards and continue the game. Gambling went on in the day when a reception was held; but in the winter time, at Versailles, the hours of play were from six in the evening till ten at night. A short

* *Works of Saint Evremont*, vol. vi. p. 261.

concert preceded the evening's business; after which, there was a rush to the tables, draped with green velvet, and embroidered with gold. The players took their places where it pleased them; and when the king was not himself playing, he walked up and down among the tables, watching the progress of the games. All salutations to the king were suppressed on these occasions.

While the king appeared pleased to see his do-nothing aristocrats engaged in losing their money, or winning that of others, it is perhaps to his credit that he disliked to see his generals or other officers of merit at the play-table. He was too well aware of the influence of habitual gambling not to discourage them. The Count de Forbin, on one occasion was playing at Versailles, and had won two thousand louis, "much," he remarks, "to my satisfaction; but," adds he, "I soon had reason to regret it—for the king, well informed of all that was going on, asked Bontemps why he allowed me to play such high stakes."* At this time, however, Forbin was yet very young, and under the pupilage of Bontemps.†

* *Collect. Petitot*, vol. lxxv., p. 19.

† In 1691, Louis issued an order prohibiting Pharaoh, Bassette, &c., under penalty of fine and imprisonment. The host was to be fined 6,000 livres for each offence. Gaming was forbidden under pain of death to the cavalry.

Another great advantage the king derived from thus causing his courtiers to become passionate gamblers, consisted in the true knowledge he was able to obtain of their characters, knowing well, that, in moments of unguardedness —as the life of a gambler reveals his character fully—he should see the flatterers and time-servers by whom he was surrounded in their true colours. Himself despicable, he employed yet more despicable means for the detection of his worthless, but involuntary, associates. La Bruyère bitterly says that play equalises all ranks, and experience fully bears out the moralist's statement.

We have already mentioned the name of Dangeau on many occasions, and we may allege an excellent excuse for the iteration. In what book, save a history of cards and card-players, is it ever likely to find mention of a man distinguished for nothing but being the best player in France? St. Simon* gives a portrait of him.

"Dangeau," he says, "was a gentleman of Beauce, and in his youth a Huguenot—like the remainder of his family. He was not wanting in a certain kind of intellect, especially that applying to the world and to conduct. He had much honour and probity. Card-playing, by which he pressed his way at court, at that time occupied entirely with love and feasting,

* *Memoirs*, vol. i., p. 392.

brought him into better company. By it he won all his property, and had the good fortune never to be suspected; he lent
willingly; made friends—and the certainty of his wares won him
true and useful friends. He paid his court to the king's mistresses. Play brought him into their society; they treated him
with familiarity, and procured him that of the king."

To those of the readers of this volume whose
poetical talents are considerable, the following
mode of obtaining free quarters in a palace may
furnish a not unwelcome hint.

Being very desirous—like all gamblers, who
know how uncertain their income may be—to
economize, Dangeau asked his majesty to give
him apartments at St. Germain, where the court
then was. The grant was difficult, inasmuch
as there was but little accommodation. "The
king's reply," says Fontenelle, in the Academical
eulogy pronounced by him at the Academy in
memory of Dangeau, "was that he would grant
him the favour, provided that he asked it in one
hundred verses to be made during the time of
play: but they were to be *one hundred* lines exactly, not one more nor one less. After the ordinary play of the evening, at which he (Dangeau)
seemed to have been as little engaged as usual,
he recited the hundred verses or lines to the
king." Accordingly he was lodged at St. Germain
free of cost! What days for playing poets!

This *jeu d'esprit* appears to have been the complete fortune of Dangeau; he filled the post of reader to the king, and afterwards those nameless offices with which the complaisance of a time-server only permits himself to be invested. Next we find him colonel of the royal regiment of infantry. He was once sent upon a diplomatic mission to England, and on his return, as "everything had its price," he bought the government of Touraine, and the post of "*chevalier d'honneur*" to the Dauphiness. Winnings at cards and dice furnished him with the means of paying Richelieu, who sold it to him in order to raise money to pay his own gambling debts. In 1688, he was decorated with a royal order, and, at the death of the Dauphin, received further promotion. Being a widower, having previously married the daughter of the Jew gambling-house keeper Morin, he now took to wife Mlle. de Löwenstein, of the Palatinate family; and such was his bombast that he imagined himself Elector Palatine, at least so went the story. The height of absurdity crowned his efforts,—he, the veriest Lazarus in real labour, was fitly elected Grand Master of the Order of Saint Lazarus,—investing him with the kind of sovereignty best merited by so surpassing a genius. The Academy, to its shame, upon some mathematical quips being brought forward in proof of his ability as a mathematician (master of the doctrine of probabilities, if anything), elected him a member of its own body. Other equally ridiculous appointments, before and since, have been made. Dangeau's nickname was "*Singe du Roi*" (king's chimpanzee), to wit. His wife was a lady of the palace.

A strange fascination induces us to linger over the shabby-grand details of the Great Monarch, but we cannot avoid doing so. Fancy a scene for a princess's *boudoir* in the most ceremonious court of the Most Christian King, such as this reported by Saint Simon. Time 1696.

"Monseigneur played late in the *salon*. Returning to his own apartments, he looked in upon the princesses, and found them smoking pipes which they had sent out to borrow from the Swiss Guard."*

Delightful little princesses!

Things had come to a pretty pass, it will be believed, when, at Meudon, at the Dauphin's, the Prince de Conti and the Grand Prior of Vendôme, over a game of cards, began to abuse each other like lackeys!† The Grand Prior

* *Saint Simon*, vol. i., p. 328.

† *Saint Simon*, vol. ii., p. 190, and *Memoirs of Dangeau* (28th July, 1698).

found his way to the Bastille for his share in
the wrangle.

Thus went the evil rolling on, growing like
a snowball, which the fiery wrath of the Revolution was at last to melt. Play began to destroy
manners. Its effects were worse—demoralization
in the army followed—officers deserted because
their play-debts could not be paid. Reineville,
lieutenant, one of them, was lost for fifteen years,
and turned up full private in a Bavarian troop.
Permillac, says Saint Simon, did worse, for he
" killed himself one morning in bed, by a pistol
shot through the brain, for having lost all that
which he had not, nor could possibly have, being
throughout his life a large and devoted gambler."*
Sometimes repentance struck these gambling
lords, and they turned monks, having exhausted
every other disreputable position, and failed in it.
St. Simon mentions a Seigneur du Charmel who
did this; "a man," says the writer, "who always
was the first to throw himself headlong into
what he thought was the best thing to be done."
The Duke de Caderousse, in the veins of whose
present representative, a recent law-case shows
a similar love of betting (in the present case on
horses and newspaper editors) to flow, followed

* *Saint Simon*, vol. ii., p. 289.

the example of the immaculate gambler, du Charmel, who found the world too wicked for him —*bien entendu, mieux instruit.*

The beginning of the eighteenth century was marked by a card-ball, which took place at Marly, on the 19th February, 1700. At this ball, a special dance was provided for the amusement of the spectators, consisting of four kings, four queens, and four knaves,—all of a pack. This was a success, for a good reason—Marly was the holy of holies—the adytum of gambling in those days.

The sister-in-law of Louis XIV. supplies us with some important details as to the inner court life, and the frankness of her letters certainly vouch for her unhesitating revelations.

Let a letter literally translated be some proof of the way things went on.

"Marly, 6th August, 1700.

" I never see Monsieur here ; we do not dine together. He plays all day, and, at night, we are each in our own apartment. Monsieur [evidently getting into the fatilistico-superstitious mood] has the weakness to think that one [*on*, the writer] brings him misfortune, so that I do not witness his play. He has caused us some terror because he has had two attacks of quartan fever : to-day is the day for its recurrence ; but, God be praised [they do praise God, even in Catholic countries, ye Puseyites !], he has yet felt nothing, and is in the salon at play."*

* *Nouvelles lettres*, 1853, p. 24.

Arcades ambo. Having attempted to do
justice to Dangeau, let us return to Langlée,
that meek mutton, somewhat lost and a little high.
It would seem that the Duchess of Burgundy,
like all the rest of the world, got into trouble by
play, and lost money to an enormous amount.
She admitted to Madame de Maintenon that she
was insolvent, and at length the king consented
to pay her debt—committing the arrangement of
the accounts to Langlée. He seems to have ac-
quitted himself of his charge much to his own
advantage, for Saint Simon falls foul of him with
carping words in reference to his honesty, &c.
His moral character, even for that age, was as
bad as could be, if we may trust his critic.

It would be tedious to continue the recital of
all the extravagance and waste of time, money,
and health brought on by this reckless gambling
at the court of Louis XIV. Two or three more
anecdotes must suffice.

The Count de Grammont even, in a quiet way,
reproved the king. On one occasion, the Grand
Monarque was playing at backgammon. Having
a doubtful throw, a dispute arose, and the sur-
rounding courtiers, uncertain how to act, remained
prudently silent. De Grammont happened at this
moment to enter, and the king desired him to

settle it. He instantly replied: "Sire, your majesty is in the wrong." "How," said Louis, "can you decide without knowing the question?" "Because," answered the count, "had there been any doubt, all these gentlemen would have given it in favor of your majesty."

On the day of the death of the king's brother, after dinner was over, the Duke of Burgundy, on rising from table, asked the Duke of Montfort if he would not play at brelan. "At brelan!" cried Montfort in a horror; "do you not remember Monsieur is still warm!" "Pardon me," replied the prince, "I remember it very well; but the king will not have anyone feel bored at Marly. He has commanded me to make everybody play, and, for fear that no one will dare to begin, to set the example myself." And they therefore sat down to brelan, and the *salon* was soon full of players.

The king, who had thus ordered his court to gamble on the occasion of his brother's death, did precisely the same when his grandchildren died in 1712, as Saint Simon reports. "The king," he says,* "went to Marly on Wednesday, the sixth of April, where, although the Dauphin and Dauphiness were not yet buried, he resumed

* *Saint Simon*, vol. x., p. 285.

his play at Madame de Maintenon's on the Friday after, and directed the *salon* to be set out as usual, and that M. and Madame the Duchess de Berry should publicly play at lansquenet and brelan ; play-tables of different games being provided for all the court."

Yet at the very moment that the court was so deeply engaged in gambling, some poor players at pharao were being expelled Paris, not for the crime of gaming,—a non-existent crime,—but for daring to advocate a game which had recently been considered unfashionable, and so condemned.

The ladies of the court were as bad, or even worse than the men. Here are a few brief notices of several of these female gamblers.

Madame de Clerembault at Pontchartrain, one fine morning, on her return from mass, placed herself on the bridge leading to the gardens, and turned slowly round in every direction, after which she addressed the company, and said : " Well ! I have walked enough for to-day; let us have no more said ! let us sit down and play cards at once !" And so they did, without interruption except for their meals, and she thought it very hard even to leave off at two o'clock in the morning. She lived to over eighty, and this was her daily life !* Madame de Caylus was another passionate player, but in her memoirs she omitted all mention of it.

Madame de Polignac played until she ruined herself; and Le Bordage, her lover, took opium on hearing of it, but recovered and played on, and was still a gambler at the age of seventy.

Among the oddities of the time was a certain Princess Harcourt—the wife of a swindler, and herself an open cheat, with manners like a fish-wife. She was considered fair game for practical jokes in the court of Louis XIV., at which every one laughed. The Duke of Burgundy once put a petard under her chair while she was playing piquet,† and there was great difficulty in dis-suading him from lighting it. The Princess Palatine, whose apartments were below those of the other lady, mentions, writing in 1721, that she often heard the princess beating her servants, and sometimes the stick fell out of her hand and rolled on the floor. On one occasion the princess got a sound thrashing in return, which made her give up her mode of correction and diverted the whole court.

* She practised geomancy and other arts, which obtained her a certain reputation.

† *Saint Simon*, vol. vi., p. 233.

The Duchess de Lorges, the third daughter of Chamillart, died passionately devoted to play—in a violent consumption ; and when, in a dying state, she continued playing, she was asked how she could enjoy any pleasure in that condition, she answered, in an almost inaudible voice, that she enjoyed the greatest pleasure from it. After this she soon died. But what can be expected in a court where the Duchess of Burgundy played all the night through until daylight returned ?

When the Elector of Bavaria visited France, the only entertainment devised for him was to set him down to bassette and lansquenet at Marly, at St. Cloud, at Antin's gaming house, and where not.

Louis XIV. continued a gambler to the end. In 1715 he was seventy-seven years of age, and near his end. Still he played at brelan to celebrate the Feast of Kings : and in May, he concluded his terrible career by a last and fearful scene. He caused the Duchess of Berry, in defiance of all private sorrow, to lay aside her deep mourning, and forced her to the play-table in the *salon*. Four months after this he expired.

As the Princess Palatine writes in one of her

letters,—in describing the condition of the court,
—play had superseded everything—" conversation was no longer the fashion."

The deep laid scheme of Mazarin had succeeded; frenzied gambling had deprived the nobility of any interest in France or its welfare; cards had killed conversation, and murdered political life.

IV.

LOUIS THE GRAND TO LOUIS THE LOCKMAKER.

LOUIS' LEGACY—THE REGENT'S INTERDICT—THE POLITICAL
GAME OF PIQUET—LAW, KING OF GAMBLERS—ENORMOUS
STAKES—BONEUIL MURDERED—LETTRES PERSANES—VOL-
TAIRE—CANDIDE'S EXPERIENCE—VOLTAIRE NO GAMBLER—
A LULL—CIRCE DUBARRY—JE SUIS FRITE!—VINGT-ET-UN
—WHIST, HORACE WALPOLE'S MENTION OF IT—ELECTRESS
OF SAXONY—SOVEREIGNS CHEAT ONLY FOR CROWNS—
THE TIMES OUT OF JOINT.

EVERY dog has his day; and a very long day
goodman Louis the Great Monarch had enjoyed.
Borne to his rest, he bequeathed to France a
legacy which it would not "willingly let die."
Yet every new government, like every new
broom, likes to show its efficiency by poking into
holes and corners, and effecting extraordinary
reforms. It might be impossible to banish cards
—it was possible to render high stakes unfashionable; and with this the Regency commenced its
career. Player Dangeau pathetically says, writing
the 25th of October, 1715: "Every day play
goes on at the Luxembourg and the Palais
Royal alternately, but *always for small stakes*."

Two years afterwards, St. Simon says that the Duke of Orleans acted usefully in the publication of the severe interdict against bassette and pharao —" without distinction of persons." Such was the pitch to which this insanity had risen, that the marshals of France had determined at their tribunals that it was not obligatory on any one to pay debts incurred at such games.

As policy had dictated the encouragement of card-playing in the late reign, so custom fostered it during the Regency. Despite the strict ordinances of the duke, his own duchess disregarded them ; indeed, so passionate was her devotion to play (lansquenet was her favourite game), that she actually played in bed, and often played all day without rising. The Duchess de Berry seconded by her efforts the ladylike example of the Duchess of Orleans ; and they jointly continued the traditions of Versailles.

Though play was thus carried on by the court, the severe regulations of the Regent were carried into effect among the general public. Dangeau mentions a case : *

" Some days since, M. de Machault, having been warned that pharao was played at Madame de Péau's, sent officers thither to take down the

* *Memoirs*, 22nd July, 1718.

names of all the players, and cause them to pay the fine prescribed by the edict. M. de Marolles, captain of cavalry, who dealt that day, tried to leave the house. One of the officers stopped him, and gave him a bayonet wound, of which it is believed he will die."

Among those players whose death is recorded at this period we may mention de Lauzun, who died in 1723, after having stripped the majority of players in England and France, and left not a doit behind him.

So engrained had play become in French society, that—as we have seen in the case of the English pamphlets the titles of which have been given—the terminology of cards was used in squibs and similar fugitive productions. Among others, here is a specimen duly translated :

THE GAME OF PIQUET (1716).

THE KING.—I play not without counsel.

THE DUKE OF ORLEANS.—I hold all the hearts, and besides a very good game.

THE PARLIAMENT.—A king had spoilt my game ; it is beginning to get very good.

THE DUKE OF MAINE.—Who leaves off, loses.

THE PRINCE DE ROHAN.—I played with more luck than wisdom ; I won with a wretched hand ; a queen (*dame*) I lost* has made my game very bad.

FATHER LETELLIER.†—I have shuffled the cards well, but I have no longer a good game.

THE SOCIETY.‡—My game is lost by a storm.

THE CONSTITUTION.‖—My game is getting ugly. I wish the cards were burnt, as well as those who made me play.

THE BANISHED.—A 14 king§ had spoilt our game; a 15 king¶ makes it better.

THE CARDINAL DE NOAILLES.**—By playing well, sooner or later one triumphs over fortune.

M. DESMARETS.††—I had gamed the game and my revenge; but I lose all.

MADAME DE MAINTENON.—I have played the greatest game possible; I will retire upon my losses.

THE PEOPLE.—In changing the cards we have

---

* Madame de Maintenon.

† A Jesuit, confessor to Louis XIV.

‡ Of Jesus. The storm is Letellier.

‖ The Bull Unigenitus, so hostile to the Jansenists, had, under Louis XIV., become the Constitution of the State.

§ Louis XIV.   ¶ Louis XV.

** The Archbishop of Paris, suspected of Jansenism, in disgrace under Louis XIV., subsequently in favor, and admitted to the Council of Conscience.

†† Minister of France, who had succeeded in maintaining his position, and finally relinquished it to Marshal Villeroy and the Duke de Noailles.

a better game; if the tens and heads (*têtes*) are thrown out, all will go well.

MADAME DE VENTADOUR.*—Though my game looks like a child's game, it is good. I hold a king, which is the best of my game.

THE TOWN.—I am ready to play as long as some one pays.

BORROWING FUND.—I have played too much on credit.

THE INTENDANTS OF FINANCE.—We are (*capot*) ruined.†

The Duchess of Mazarin, of whose infatuated play mention has already been made, did not escape the scourge of satire for her folly, and she was made to figure in a satirical comedy entitled *Le Tailleur de Bassette*, together with the Jew Morin and M. de Saint Evremond. The contents of this piece are unworthy of quotation; but the fact is significant, as implying considerable press-freedom.

But, as time progresses, so also do men outvie each other either for good or for evil. Langlée, Dangeau, and the Grand Monarque who had hobnobbed with them, having passed away, a greater and more reckless personage stepped upon the

* Governess of the young Louis XV.

† The harpy contractors were about to be made to disgorge.

stage to enact the part of a commercial Attila,
and prove a scourge in another sense. Wonderful was the character of the celebrated Law.
A gambler,—he daringly and openly cheated; a
commercial speculator,—he unscrupulously failed.
Appearing in Paris, about 1716, he stormed that
nation by the suddenness of his attack upon its
weak point, so nurtured by Louis XIV., and became the King of Gamblers. Duclos was a
famous female tragedian of the day, and at her
house did Law set up his pharao-bank, by the
proceeds of which he was rendered one of the
wealthiest of the wealthy. In manners he was
most winning, and his society was eagerly sought
by the noble and fashionable of the land. His
magnificence even caused him to assume another
regal attribute. Not content with using the cur-
rency of the country for the purposes of the play-
table, he caused, as Duhaut-Champ tells us, medals
of the intrinsic value of eighteen louis to be struck,
with which to pay his losses, when he had any.
For be it understood, that his luck was as great as
his effrontery, and failed not in the end to procure
for him the distinction of expulsion from Paris
by the inexorable voice of M. d'Argenson. Yet,
in an incredibly short space of time, he had won
sixty-seven thousand pounds sterling

Suddenly the financial system of Law became an accepted fact, and his commercial kingdom was established. As in every case when sudden wealth falls upon a multitude, extravagance and excess of every kind was the result. Duhaut-Champ mentions that some speculators played at piquet with bank notes of one hundred thousand livres, "as if they were only ten-sous pieces." The Duchess of Berry at this time lost in one night the enormous sum of one million seven hundred thousand livres at pharao. In 1720, the fury was at its height, and all ranks were alike infected, or rather steeped, in gambling. The advocate Marais records in his journal that nothing went on except eating, drinking, and gambling with fearful stakes, and all the business that was done was the hanging of a criminal or two here and there. One of these criminals was that Count Horn, who had turned thief and murderer after living a life of low gambling and profligacy.*

The Princess Palatine gives an account of the murder of an abbé—the Abbé Boneuil—who, together with his servant, were barbarously assassinated in his lodgings, for the purpose of obtaining four thousand francs. They lived over

* *Saint Simon*, vol. xviii., p. 162.

a shoemaker's, and the blood having found its way through the ceiling, led to the discovery of the bodies. He had returned in the night from the play-table, and met his death at the hand of some assassin who knew what his night's winnings had been.

The author of the *Persian Letters* has thus caused his traveller to write home: " Play is very much in vogue in Europe; to be a gambler is to hold a position; this title alone stands in the stead of birth, wealth, or probity. The person who bears it is placed by it in the ranks of honest men, without question, although no one is unaware that in judging thus deception is frequent; but it has been agreed to be incorrigible in the matter. Women are especially devoted to gambling. 'Tis true they do not pursue it in their youth, except for the means of indulging a still dearer passion; but as they grow older, their passion for play seems to be rejuvenated, and this passion takes the place of every other." *

Voltaire, rich as he is in materials for the history of the manners of his time, does not furnish us with many allusions to gambling in his day. Where, however, he does speak of it,

* *Lettres Persanes*, Letter lvi.

he speaks without anger, without regret, and even seems grimly to approve of the evil it was working in the upper classes.

A chapter in *Candide*, worthy of quotation here, displays the interior of a gaming-house, as depicted by the satirist : *

"Candide, who was naturally inquisitive, permitted himself to be conducted to the lady in the Faubourg Saint Honoré. Pharao was the occupation of the evening. A dozen sad punters held in their hands small books—the well known registers of their misfortunes. Profound silence reigned, pale were the brows of the punters, anxiety sat upon the wrinkles of the banker, and the lady of the house—seated beside that pitiless banker— watched with lynx eyes all the *parolis*, the *sept-et-le-vas* of the campaign, at which each player doubled down his cards. She caused them to be undoubled with close attention, though politely, and exhibited no anger, for fear of losing her customers. The lady was called the Marquise de Parolignac. † Her daughter, a girl of fifteen, was among the punters, and by a glance gave notice of the cheating of those poor people, who thus sought to repair the cruelties of fate.

"The abbé, Candide, and Martin entered. No one rose, no one saluted them, or even looked up. They were all profoundly occupied with their cards. 'Mme. the Baroness of Thunder-ten-Tronckh was more civil,' said Candide.

"Meantime the abbé whispered to the Marquise, who half rose, honoured Candide with a gracious smile, and Martin with a most noble gesture. She had a seat and a pack of cards furnished to Candide, who gaily lost fifty thousand francs in two deals. After which they had a very merry supper, and every one was

* *Candide*, chap. xxii.
† No doubt the Marquise de Parolignac alluded to the well-known female gambler Madame de Polignac, of whom we have already caught a glimpse.

astonished that Candide was not cast down at his loss; the servants whispering each other, 'He must be an English milord.'"

Although Voltaire could describe the interior of a gaming saloon, it would appear that he was only an idle spectator there, in attendance, perhaps, upon that charming Marquise du Chatelet, with whom his private life was indissolubly connected, and who was herself, like most worthless women, infatuated with play.

The fashion changed for a time towards the middle of the eighteenth century. Exhaustion succeeded fever; and love, of the French sort, resumed its sway. Madame de Pompadour did not play like Madame des Montespan, and a few old harridans only remained to preserve the traditions of a time long banished to a most deserved limbo. Among these might be mentioned Madame de Tallard, who had been governess to the royal family. But for one unfortunate circumstance, the lull might have been succeeded by a torpor, perhaps by an atrophy. This, however, was not to be. A Circe rose up once more to turn men into spiritual swine. In this wise:

Jane Vaubernier, a young damsel in the gaming-house of the Marquise du Quesnay, in the Rue de Bourbon, and no doubt an ornament to

the establishment, made one evening an eligible
acquaintance.   It was the Count Dubarry, who
wooed and won her, and then, full of pride and
vainglory, wore her, like his heart, "upon his
sleeve."   He paraded his acquisition, and, at last,
his most Christian Majesty Louis XV., King
of France and Navarre, had the honour of
making his obeisance to the Countess Dubarry—
qualified enchantress to the royal person.

Her mother had been a cook, and the early
associations with the platter and the stewpan
could not be eradicated.   At *pharao* one day,
perceiving that a card fatal to her interests
had turned up, she exclaimed, "Ah! I am well
done *(je suis frite)!*"   "You cannot be wrong,
madam," was a reply; "you are an authority
as to that!"

It was the king who, one night, gave a fresh
impulse to play by calling for a *vingt-et-un*
party to amuse Madame Dubarry, that being a
favourite game of the countess.   In this Madame
de Havacourt joined, with Marshal Richelieu,
while the king played whist.   At this time, then,
pharao, *vingt-et-un*, and whist, were the prevalent games, and the last game receiving royal
favour, made a triumphant entry.

Horace Walpole, writing in 1767 from Paris,

remarks that the French had adopted the two dullest things the English had — whist and Richardson's novels.*

Fond as Madame Dubarry was of gambling, however, she cared little for winning, and asked amusement, not victims. Her brother-in-law, Count John, cost more than she did, in play, to the coffers of "La France," as she playfully called the monarch. For indeed the count used the king's purse as his own. He was, however, not popular at the court, and few visited him.

His reply to the dowager Electress of Saxony deserves repetition here from its readiness. He was acting as the banker, and, vigilantly watching over his interests, appeared to have some suspicion of the noble lady's play, at which she expressed her surprise. "A thousand pardons, madam," cried the count, "my suspicions could not fall on you. Sovereigns cheat only for crowns."

The times were "out of joint," and everything was getting vulgarized; royalty was growing coarse, the nobility gross, and the magistracy venal. The growing evil was beyond arrest; and though a justiciary ordinance was published in 1760, fixing the limit of losses at one hundred

* *Walpole's Letters*, vol. v., p. 66.

pistoles, it was generally disregarded. Charles
II., in our own country, had already determined
the limit at one hundred pounds; but, just as is
the case in our modern clubs, high play and
great losses continued the custom.

V.

CARD PLAYING IN FRANCE FROM LOUIS THE
LOCKMAKER TO LOUIS NAPOLEON.

MARIE ANTOINETTE—WHY M. POINÇOT GOT A CHAIR—PROFITS
OF M. DE CHALABRE—LOUIS LOSES LOUIS D'ORS—MARLY EN
POLISSON — CARD-SHARPING — REVOLUTIONARY GAMBLING
—BIRIBI, THE GAME OF THE MOB—THE PALAIS ROYAL—
GAMBLING GENERAL—BARERE'S HOUSE AND THE SUIT OF
CLUBS—BOUILLOTTE A REVOLUTIONARY GAME—NAPOLEON
A WHIST PLAYER—JOSEPHINE—MARIE LOUISE—NAPOLEON
PREFERRED VINGT-ET-UN—M. DE TALLEYRAND INVENTED
FOR WHIST — JUNOT — NAPOLEON'S OPINIONS ON CARD-
PLAYING — CONVERSATION WITH LAS CASES — GAMING-
HOUSES LICENSED—PAOLI—GAMING IN CORSICA—NAPO-
LEON'S NINE OF DIAMONDS—GAMING DISREPUTABLE—THE
CODE NAPOLEON — ITS PROVISIONS—SUPPRESSION OF THE
HOUSES—STATISTICS OF GAMING—EXPENSES AND PROFITS
— MASSENA — THE ISLAND OF AMATHONTE — RUSSIAN
GAMING.

KING Louis the Lockmaker was of a homelier
cast of mind than his predecessors on the French
throne. Gaming was his abhorrence; and had
not Marie Antoinette upheld it by example, and
fostered it by encouragement, card-playing as a
fashionable vice might have fallen into disrepute.
The court festivals always comprised in their

programmes a pharao-bank and other similar
amusements. Of the former game, the queen
was passionately fond, and M. de Chalabre, the
son of the famous gambler, always presided at
the queen's table. Bachaumont, in his memoirs,
gives an amusing picture of the state in which
the court was.* It would seem that the queen's
banker being overdone with work, represented to
her majesty that he absolutely required an assistant at his duties, and the queen then desired
him to select whomsoever he liked. There was
at the court a certain M. Poinçot, a Knight of
St. Louis, but of minor rank in the army. According to etiquette, no officer could be seated
in the presence of royalty unless he bore a
colonel's commission. Therefore, when her majesty entered, she found the new croupier standing
—a position of the greatest inconvenience. Her
majesty seeing this, and possessing but small
awe of gold-sticks-in-waiting and such fry, desired
a chair to be given to M. Poinçot, to the great
disgust of the punctilious courtiers of Versailles,
who saw that the world was evidently about to
come to an end. Play went on at Marly every
evening, as also at Fontainebleau, and M. de
Chalabre, like a prudent man, reaped great

* *Mémoires de Bachaumont*, vol. xii., p. 140.

profits from his position as banker. In the year 1779, he gained no less than twenty-three thousand louis d'ors during a single progress of the court. Poor Louis the Lockmaker on this occasion was forced to join in the general pastime, and, losing five hundred louis d'ors, made a great moan, and button-holed everybody to tell them, over and over again, how unfortunate he had been, and how foolish it was. He always spoke of it as a piece of folly of which he was determined never again to be guilty.*

It would not seem, that, in the face of the prevailing passion, etiquette could make much head. A simple introduction by some known court official, and a decent coat, was enough to admit any aspirant to the royal gambling saloon. This saloon was of octagonal form, very extensive, decorated in the Italian style, and surmounted by a cupola containing balconies, in which ladies not presented at court were permitted to see the brilliant spectacle. The gentlemen who were admitted in the manner above mentioned, were allowed to solicit one of the ladies seated at the pharao and lansquenet tables to stake such gold or notes as they might present. Madame Campan tells us, that the chief

* *Bertrand Barère*, vol. i., p. 357.

gamblers in Paris never failed to frequent the
gaming saloon of Marly on every play-evening,
when the sums which changed hands were
always of very considerable extent. The unquestionably free and easy style of Louis the
Lockmaker's court is best seen by the phrase
usually employed by visitors to Marly: they used
to say, that "of course they only went there *en
polisson*."

Mixed society such as this proved very dangerous. The knavish instincts of human nature
soon showed themselves; and Bachaumont reports, that it became necessary to surround the
table with a ribbon before beginning play, and
only those sums staked beyond the ribbon were
regarded as really risked; many disputes and
sharp encounters having previously taken place
about these matters. Card-sharping was rife,
and many were the devices adopted by the
"wise" to ensure success. The back of an important card was rubbed with pumice stone, or
a little hair or straw was fixed to it, known
only to the person having so marked the
card. A fugitive piece of the time, *Diogenes at
Paris*, records these and other tricks. A judicious method of setting up your polished gold
or silver snuffbox revealed to your anxious

gaze the course of the game by reflection; and sometimes, a card slightly bent proved an almost imperceptible sign. Of these tricks we shall speak more at length in a future page.

When any of these immaculate gentry were found out, Louis XVI., good honest man, was very angry and annoyed, and took advantage of the occasion to complain of the light conduct of the queen and court, and especially of the way in which the Count d'Artois, the leader of the band, went on. Play was the rage, and continued the rage even when the Bastille was being thundered down, and the baker, his wife, and the baker's boy, were forced back to the Tuileries from Versailles.

But the rage for blood and revenge aroused by the Revolution, did not extinguish the older passion. The populace opened gaming-houses in every street, and gambled furiously until they each in turn came to peep through the national window into eternity. Political use was again made of card terminology. In 1791, we find a caricature representing the king playing at cards with a *sans culotte*, and Louis is saying, "I have lost hearts—he has the spades (pikes); I am lost!" (*J'ai écarté les cœurs—il a des piques; je suis capot!*)

The popular passion for gambling sank deep into the hearts of the sovereign people, and, at the street corners, and in the gutters, by night, the ragged kings, by the glare and flare of burning houses, and amidst the angry growl of cannon, staked their miserable *liards* at *biribi*, the favorite game of the poor. The police were always too late when they did come to disperse the gamblers. A dealer in earthenware at the Palais Royal, named Sourig, grew wealthy by pandering to this miserable vice—he was the principal street-banker of the time—and the workmen got deep in his debt.

Gradually Paris became a nest of gambling-houses, and from morning till night and night till morning play continued without intermission. The Palais Royal became the capital of gambling; and the chief games played were *creps*, *passe-dix*, *trente-et-un*, and *biribi*. In the Palais Royal alone there were no less than thirty-one gaming-houses, and the total number of such establishments was estimated at four thousand.

There were establishments suited to every condition of life, possessing the common feature of ruthless rapacity. Dumoulin, formerly footman to the Count Dubarry, kept No. 33, in the Palais Royal, where high play was the rule. Strangers

assembled in the Rue des Petits Pères, at Rue
Richelieu, No. 18, or at the tavern of Lafare,
who sold excellent cold breakfasts of roast beef
and tea in the English manner. The lawgivers
of the nation played at the house of Madame
Tallien, once an actress at the Italian comedy.
It was at the house of the Baroness de Lisembac,
an actress also, that Mirabeau was robbed of a
gold casket full of assignats. *Rouge et Noire*
was played at the house of Madame Lacour,
where young folks could always find numbers of
delightful ladies and plenty of sparkling wine.
It were indeed needless to extend the list, for the
grades and distinctions of houses were as numerous and varied as their frequenters were alike
infamous. Perhaps, however, the most terrible
of these haunts of passion was one in the Rue
Richelieu, where the miserable gamblers might
stake as low as six *liards*, and where the refreshments consists of coarse beans and lard, while
the benches served as beds for the hapless ruined.

The events which happened at these vile re-
sorts were of the ordinary character well known to
the imagination,—avarice, murder, suicide, and
nameless horrors were rife in these dens. Those
whose honour had yesterday been spotless, were
to-day flying from justice to escape the penalties

of some frenzied crime, some sudden assassination perpetrated under the influence of this terrible delusion. Lost to every other emotion, many lived precariously upon the proceeds of the gambling table, and, with hideous glee, partook of the orgies of the more fortunate. From the great, wild-hearted, magnanimous Mirabeau, down to the most tiger-hearted assassin, all, all were gamblers! Gaming was godlike and demoniacal at once, at that sad time.

Sometimes the revolutionary authorities, in their mad anger against the insignia of the hated monarchy, came across the emblems of cards, and played havoc with them. In Barère's memoirs,* he mentions that the avenue leading to his house was ornamented with marble slabs, into which were let smaller stones representing hearts, diamonds, spades, and clubs. The three first he thinks they would have overlooked, but the clubs bore too near a resemblance to the hated lily, and a formal decree had confiscated all property and objects upon which that emblem had not been effaced. The revolutionary committee of Tarbes became informed of it, and Barère's house was accordingly confiscated. " Thus," he says, " being in the midst of revolu-

* Vol. ii., p. 191.

tion, I gathered great benefits therefrom." A sly
dry touch of satirical humour in this, truly!

Even to the revolution, there is due the
honour of adding fuel to the fire, and inventing
new games. *Bouillotte* was contrived at the
Luxembourg, in full conclave of the Directory.
Madame Tallien once said of the Luxembourg
folks, " There are five kings up yonder who are
sweating blood and water to make a gleek of
knaves."

With their revolutionary livery off and their
human dressing-gowns on,—their moral slippers
being very much down at heel, no doubt,—these
noble legislators puzzled themselves under the
red night-cap of liberty how best to disguise and
modify pharao and bassette.

At this time, also, the noble English game of
whist, introduced in a preceding century, was
making its way in France, and when Napoleon
was first consul he played sparingly at the game.
Perhaps the example of moderation set by that
remarkable man has not been without influence
upon society. When Morellet was summoned
to the Tuileries in 1803, he found Napoleon
installed there with his wife, the illustrious
Josephine, and engaged in whist. This unhappy lady, and, subsequently, Marie Louise,

had their favourite games; they were whist and, sometimes, *vingt-et-un.*

It is on record that Napoleon preferred *vingt-et-un* to any other game of cards; and from the social, mirth-creating nature of the game, we may deem him to have been right. While whist might be an excellent game for M. Talleyrand, respecting whom, it is difficult to say, whether whist were invented for him or he for whist, the active discursive mind of the chief of France demanded something more stimulative and more easily abandoned. Junot, soldier and general, with dash and *verve*, but very little power of combination, characteristically preferred the easy but daring game of lansquenet, the soldier's game *par eminence.*

Napoleon, like all great rulers, and as Louis the Grand had done before him, did not like his active men to be gamesters. Years afterwards, during the melancholy, but necessary, exile, which confined that great spirit to the narrow limits of a tropical island, he was conversing with his friend and companion Las Cases, and, upon Las Cases owning that he had himself been a gambler, during the byegone days in Paris, he broke out with: "Ah! how glad am I that I knew it not! I should have deemed you lost in my own mind; you would never have done anything. It proves to me that we do indeed know ourselves little, and that you could not have given umbrage to any one, for there would have been plenty of charitable folks about me to tell me of it. My dislike to gamblers was well known in those days ; they always were ruined in my estimation. I had no leisure to learn whether I was right or wrong, but I never relied upon them any further."

Baron de Meneval tells us, that the emperor thought of suppressing the gaming-houses, as the tax levied upon them seemed to him immoral. In 1811, a commission was charged with the duty of an enquiry into the matter, but this commission determined to adjourn the consideration of their report. Finally, these houses were licensed. No doubt, the decision was wise, for it was plainly impossible to put a period to the passion for play.

Lord Holland relates an anecdote of somewhat doubtful authority, wherein Napoleon, in 1796, is represented as having placed in the hands of Junot the gross total of the sums he had collected together, and sent that officer to a gambling-house to augment it or lose it, that funds might be furnished for the Italian campaign. Junot won largely; but this apocryphal story further says, that Napoleon told him it was not enough, and sent him back to brave the goddess Fortune in her lair once more.

In Corsica, Napoleon must have seen his countrymen constantly gaming, for the vice was cardinal in that island as elsewhere.

To this, Pascal Paoli, himself no player, bears testimony. He said of the Corsicans, that "play was not only a pastime, but a passion among the Corsicans." "The Corsican gambles, it is said," continues Paoli, "because he knows not how better to occupy his leisure. This was my opinion also, but reflection and a more profound study of his habits soon caused me to alter my view." The true cause of this frenzied taste for gaming arose, he found, partly from the necessity of some aliment for the restless activity of the Corsican mind, and partly from its affording an opportunity of exercising and trying his intelligence doubly, by studying the rules of the game, or the diverse combinations from which arise favorable chances. "Therefore, I am not afraid of avowing," he concludes, "that there are few countries in Europe where a greater number of good players exist among the working class. Love of gain would not be a sufficient motive for retaining them so long around a table."*

* Arrighi : *Histoire de Paoli,* vol i., p. 28 ; vol. ii., p. 381.

Though Napoleon had disdained cards in the days of his glory and power, they became a pleasant solace in the period of his captivity. His chief games were whist, *vingt-et-un*, and piquet, and almost every evening was beguiled by play. Napoleon usually limited his loss per night to ten or twelve Napoleons, though he occasionally passed this limit. There is still preserved, the writer believes in the possession of Napoleon III., who derived it from Mr. John Sainsbury, the diligent collector of the Napoleon Museum, a nine of diamonds, which the emperor had covered with short phrases in English, at a time when he was endeavouring to acquire some facility in that language.

Gambling has fallen into much greater disrepute since the era of Napoleon, although its influence still prevails. Kings and princes amended the error of their ways, and left to the eccentric and the vicious only, what once was a pardonable fault in all classes. Gaminghouses, where card-playing still goes forward, of course exist; but a gambler, as such, is no longer a courted companion, but usually a needy sharper, or an incurable fool. Of course, as is well-known, the Second Empire has afforded another outlet for the passion of

gaming; the Stock Exchange, with its Eldorado
of paper and its convenient system of time
bargains, has completely, with respectable people,
superseded the " four aces." It looks more respectable to game in the guise of business, than
to stake a fortune upon the turn of a card, or
the hazard of a pair of dice.

The days which France spent under the
rulers who followed, in rapid succession, that
brilliant man of whom it is yet even difficult,
with all our resources, to form a satisfactory
opinion, furnished an example of the wisdom
of the licensing system he had initiated, although
ultimately, gambling-houses were treated much as
he would have treated them himself, had the
venomous gathering been ripe for puncture—
they were suppressed. The only mention made
in the *Code Napoléon* of games of cards or play,
is as concise, or even conciser than its expressions
usually are. It defines in brief the nature of a
gambling debt, as a reciprocal contract, the effect
of which both as respects the parties to it, and as
touching loss and gain, depends upon an uncertain
event. * It provides that no action can lie for a
gaming debt, or for the recovery of money lost in

* *Code Napoléon*, No. 1964, confirmed by No. 1104. Each
Article in the Code has a distinct number.

a wager. * Military games, foot and horse racing,
chariot racing, tennis, and similar games, demand-
ing personal agility, are alone excepted.† Should
a loser, however, voluntarily pay such a debt, he
cannot recover it from the winner unless there
has been wrongdoing, cheating, or swindling.‡
Such is the curt, summary settlement, from which
very properly there is no appeal.

With all the suppression, persecution (as the
"persecuted" might call it), and general bedevil-
ment to which the children of the painted pack have
been put—despite police visitations, fines, and imprisonment, still there are persons daring enough,
not only to continue to keep such "hells," as they
were at last called in England, but contrive to keep
them handsomely, being handsomely supported by
their profits in return. A few anecdotes, selected
from the general mass of material, may here suffice,
and we shall then leave this part of our subject.

Before the final suppression of the gaming
saloons, the Ministry of Police, with the immaculate M. Fouché at its head, managed to make nice
pickings out of the doomed vice. The right of

* *Code*, No. 1965. In English law, any trader who can have
been proved to have lost sums of money at play is thereby de-
barred from obtaining a certificate in bankruptcy.

† *Code*, No. 1966.

‡ *Code*, No. 1967. See Nos. 1109, 1116, and 1235.

keeping open these houses was farmed in succession to Perrin, Bernard, Chalabre, Boursault, and Bénazet, who all made snug fortunes out of the affair. In the concession were comprehended all the considerable gaming-houses of Paris ; and the farmer of these establishments paid a gross sum, in monthly payments, of 5,550,000 francs per annum. To carry on business, it was necessary that the general bank should always contain at least 1,291,000 francs for current outgoings, without counting the expense of refreshments, wages, &c. The farmer deposited 500,000 francs caution money as an earnest of his power to carry out his contract.

The following table, extracted from a work of considerable authority, will give some idea of the enormous sums which annually changed hands at these public establishments, to the shame of France, and the enrichment of the gaming-house contractors.*

Years.	Sum.		Years.	Sum.	
	fr.	c.		fr.	c.
1819	7,682,533	42	Brt. forwd	40,269,011	45
1820	7,801,752	27	1824	8,222,339	72
1821	8,724,504	27	1825	9,008,628	51
1822	8,651,376	76	1826	7,349,411	32
1823	7,408,844	73	1827	7,213,264	23
Card. forwd.	40,269,011	45	Card. forwd.	72,062,655	23

* *Mémoires d'un bourgeois de Paris*, vol. i., p. 386. It is right to mention that the writer has corrected the total, wrongly stated in the work cited.

Years.	Sum.		Years.	Sum.	
	fr.	c.		fr.	c.
Brt. forwd.	72,062,655	23	Brt. forwd.	105,043,570	69
1828	7,387,545	94	1833	6,138,479	14
1829	7,080,139	62	1834	6,546,319	30
1830	6,403,029	90	1835	6,630,383	71
1831	6,055,100	00	1836	6,115,792	47
1832	6,055,100	00	1837	6,841,838	35
Card. frwd.	105,043,570	69	Total	138,316,381	66

Thus, in less than twenty years, nearly one hundred and forty millions of francs (£200,000) were taken from Parisian gamblers, and paid over to government by the farmers of the gaming-houses. This, it must be remembered, does not include the proceeds of the state lotteries. It will thus be easily understood that the public were considerable gainers by the suppression of both these establishments.

The following account of the expenses and profits of a Parisian gambling-house, about the period to which the above table refers, is interesting as showing the enormous profits of such establishments.*

"Under the present administration there are :

       7 tables of Trente-et-un,
       9 tables of Roulette,
       1 table of Passe-dix,
       1 table of Craps,
       1 table of Hazard,
       1 table of Biribi.

* *Bibliothèque Historique*, 1818.

Twenty tables distributed in nine houses, four of which are in the Palais Royal.

"To serve the seven tables of Trente-et-un, there are :

28 Dealers	at 550 fr. a month .	fr.	15,400
28 Croupiers	at 380 fr. ,, . .		8,640
42 Assistants	at 200 fr. ,, . .		8,400

"Service for the nine Roulettes and one Passe-dix :

80 Dealers	at 275 fr. a month . .	22,000
60 Assistants	at 150 fr. ,, . .	9,000

"Service of the Craps, Biribi, and Hazard :

12 Dealers at 300 fr. a month . .	3,600
12 Inspectors	1,800
10 Assistants	1,000
6 Chefs de Parties at the principal houses	4,200
3 Chefs for Roulette . . .	1,500
20 Secret Inspectors . . .	4,000
1 Inspector General . . .	1,000
130 Waiters at 75 fr. a month .	9,900
Cards, a month	1.500
Beer and Refreshments . . .	3,000
Lights	5,500
Refreshments for the Chief Salon, two dinners a week included . .	12,000

Expense per month . . .	fr.114,440
Multiplied by 12 is . . .	1,872,800
Rent of 10 houses . . .	130,000
Expenses of offices . . .	50,000
Total per annum	2,052,800
Estimate the privilege at . .	6,000,000
If the bonus of a million is given for six years, the sixth part, for one year, would be . . .	166,666
Total expenditure . . .	fr.8,219,466

Estimate profits per month 800,000,
  per annum 9,600,000
Deducting expenditure . . . 8,219,466

Net annual profits fr.1,380,534

Which produces at the expiration
  of the lease of six years . . fr.8,283,204

The gambling-houses, while they lasted, had each their separate set of customers—their "regulars," "irregulars," and their "eccentrics." Dr. Véron relates in his memoirs,* that there was a person, named Masséna, always to be met with at No. 129, Palais Royal, who each night played only for a single quarter of an hour, and within that time, he either lost three or four thousand francs, or won twelve or fifteen millions.

In 1837, however, the suppression of the houses caused an emigration; and our Knights of the Green Cloth were forced to march "bag and baggage" in search of happier climes. Véron tells us that, in 1849, he visited all the gambling-houses on the Rhine, and found within their walls many faces familiar to him—especially amongst the professionals : there were the dealers of 1818, the punters, the bonnets, and the rest of the crew, in high feather.

Contemporaneously with the gaming-houses,

* Vol. i., p. 284.

flourished establishments of an humbler kind, known as *maisons de bouillotte* and *baccarat*. These were tolerated by the police, and strictly watched. The French mind is ambitious of equality, and therefore it would have been hard to have denied — as a paternal government might have done—the luxury of ruination to the poor. Here, for all practical purposes, you might easily take lessons in the school of want, and grow as poor as Job, with very little exertion. Having, perhaps, enjoyed the minor pleasure of being cleaned out at Frascati's of all your gold, you might yet, for a few francs, revel in the major enjoyment of being completely ruined,— and then depart homewards with the calm satisfaction of a philosopher who has nothing to lose. Ecarté was the principal game at these humble temples of ruin.

Despite the strict surveillance of the police, gambling has not, however, been effectually checked in the French metropolis. The *Presse* newspaper of the 25th of June, 1854, contains an amusing instance of the stratagems both of the gambling-house keepers and the police.

One of that fair sisterhood whose charming and open behaviour has procured them the honour of the peculiar attention of the French police, had hired a delightful villa on one of the islands of the Seine, near Asnières, where she carried on the business of a gambling-house. Every evening, and especially after the public balls, ladies and gentlemen were seen to embark in an elegant canoe, and land, at the island,—which had received the romantic name of Amathonte,—and here, hidden from the impertinent gaze of the vulgar and the scrutinizing glance of the police, they enjoyed themselves at *trente-et-quarante, lansquenet,* and other prohibited games.

However, the police soon smelt a rat; and Messieurs Boudrot and Hébert, whose talents lay greatly in such enterprises, were confided with a mission of disturbance. Arrived on the river-bank, these gentlemen found themselves in a hobble. The canoe of Madame B——, the proprietrix of the house, was safely moored to the island ; and no boat was to be obtained. As they gazed wistfully at the scene of the gambling, luck provided them with the means of transport. A long and broad raft at this juncture came down the river ; and by traversing this, they gained, first the boat, and then the islet.

Amathonte was full of excellent company— chiefly consisting of actresses, *lorettes*, artists, and students. Names, when demanded, were refused ; and the police had to content themselves with seizing the gaming apparatus, the furniture, and Madame B—— herself.

Very different was this to the jolly times at the beginning of the century, when lansquenet, écarté, whist, and bouillotte, were openly played everywhere. The game of whist, which has been justly regarded as noble, has never found as much favour in the eyes of our volatile neighbours : they abhorred the restrictions of silence under which it placed them, and had not the patience for its grave combinations. Yet the French are far from insensible to the charms of a complex game ; they have ever held a good position as chess-players, and at this latter game have shone with great brilliance. Perhaps one of our best modern amateurs is M. Louis Blanc, formerly of the provisional government of 1848.

Yet how absorbing is the preoccupation of a true lover of whist ! To address conversation to such a person is as much waste time as to seek to engage the ear of Mr. Babbage with the gentle strains of a street band. In the club of the Boulevard Montmartre, twenty-five whist-tables are constantly going, and the eminently aristocratic game finds numerous supporters.

One of the later French kings was solemnly

playing at whist one night, when, by some accident, he let a louis d'or fall from the table. The monarch stooped to pick it up, when an ambassador, eager to aid the king in his search, took up a note of a thousand francs and lighted it to serve as a flame by which the king could see to find his coin. Whist had become a habit, and the king played because all his predecessors had played. Charles X. was playing at whist while the battle was raging which tumbled him off his throne.

Germany for many years has been famous for its gaming establishments ; but at these places games of hazard are rather the rule than cards. Russia, when at home, in dressing-gown and slippers, plays chiefly at *preference :* and it is a singular custom among the Russians to make the visitors pay for their cards. A pack of cards is never used more than once, and the player, on taking a second pack, pays the servant presenting them for the first. The money is put into a box, and subsequently divided among the servants. Rumour, however, asserts, that in the great houses, where the receipts thus obtained amount to something considerable, the money finds its way into more aristocratic pockets.*

* Léouzon le Duc : *La Russie Contemporaine*, p. 152.

As we have previously remarked, the reign of the present emperor is marked by a singular devotion to gambling on a larger and apparently more justifiable scale. We doubt, however, whether the questionable schemes of a Mirés are much to be preferred to the combinations of the crafty gambling-house keeper. If it be nobler to be open in what you profess, then we apprehend the monarch of the four aces would bear away the palm of nobility.

Alas ! however, for poor humanity ; even in vice men must shine pre-eminent, or else hide their diminished heads under the bushel of obscurity : and as it was inevitable that a Beau Brummell should swagger, and patronise his king, so also it becomes a matter of course that some sharper of pre-eminence should attain the highest pinnacle of infamy, whence his fall would the more certainly lead him to destruction.

Perhaps the most remarkable as well as the most recent case of card-sharping is that of Signor Garcia, of Parisian notoriety. In February, 1863, there were assembled at the house of Madame Julia Barucci, in Paris, some thirty of the more numerous than unquestionably respectable class of pleasure-hunters, who had come together for the express purpose of celebrating the fact of Madame Barucci's tenancy of a new domicile. Over the antecedents of the fair hostess, aged twenty-five, it may, perhaps, be as well to throw the veil of prudence. It will be enough to say that her society was, in a certain sense, charming; and her knowledge of her own loveliness had so far melted her sense of decorum as to induce her to lend no unfavourable ear to the impassioned vows of her train of ardent and liberal-pursed lovers. Among the guests present on this interesting occasion was a certain Signor Garcia, a gentleman who had gained fame by rising the winner of seventy-five thousand pounds in two seasons, at Homburg and Baden, but generously losing the whole of it a short time after. Garcia was not friendless nor alone at Madame Barucci's; his intimate associate was present, being no less than Signor Calzado, the director of the Italian Opera at Paris. Calzado was not popular; his reputation as a " Greek" was more than suspected, and a wide spread distrust of him existed in the minds of the *gandins*.

Calzado had "done a thing or two" in his life time. His card-sharping was bold and original. On one occasion, he effected an " operation" of great magnitude. Going to Havannah, he bought up every pack of cards in the place, and then quietly awaited the arrival of a vessel he had previously freighted with marked cards. The trick told: Calzado "went in a buster,"— as the knowing ones say,— and played enormously, with corresponding certainty of winning, until the discovery of his manœuvre.

At Madame Barucci's, there was not quite such scope for his daring genius; however, fate favours the bold, and on the evening of the party, a Signor Miranda, of good family and well-filled purse, was present. He had about him, for purposes of play, a cool hundred thousand francs, —no bad provision.

A *rouge-et-noir* table was opened with Signor Garcia as its presiding genius. Calzado and Miranda played, and the latter won thirty thousand francs very soon. Supper put a temporary stop to this amusement, but after that meal, when the guests had taken a sufficient quantity of wine, they returned to the play-table. Baccarat was substituted for *rouge-et-noir*, and the fun, temporarily interrupted, soon recommenced. Garcia made an excuse, and went away for a time. After half-an-hour's absence, he re-entered the room with several packs of cards disposed about his person. He joined in the excitement and the amusement, playing for very high stakes. Soon Garcia won one hundred and forty thousand francs from Signor Miranda, and Calzado was a considerable winner also. This run of luck drew close attention to Garcia, and it was discovered that the cards with which he played were some of his own providing, properly " doctored." He was charged with cheating. He admitted that he had brought cards of his own, but declared that he was playing fairly, and that he brought the cards from a belief in their lucky qualities. He offered, provided the affair were settled, to refund, and produced fifty thousand francs ; but the " pigeons" would not accept one third of their losses in lieu of the whole. Hereupon, Garcia endeavoured to escape, but failing to get out of the house, he was hunted from room to room, and finally stripped of the money in his possession. Thieves all, without honour ! Calzado fell under suspicion also, but they were not so fortunate with him. Garcia and Calzado were finally allowed to leave, and even then carried off forty thousand francs.

Cited before the court, Calzado appeared in person, but Garcia had " evaporated." They were tried and convicted ; Garcia being condemned in his absence to five years imprisonment, and Calzado to thirteen or fifteen months, and both were fined severely. Garcia is not likely to return to Paris, it is thought, for some time, as the air of the French metropolis disagrees with his sensitive constitution. Madame Barucci was not visited with any punishment, though she will no doubt be careful as to allowing prohibited games to be played in her house. M. Calzado remains in " durance vile," though he has been kindly permitted to pass a portion of his sentence in a *maison de santé*, which it is to be hoped for his own comfort, is better managed than Mr. Charles Reade is at present depicting the private asylums of our own land, and for the reformation of which we trust the public will lend him a hand.

VI.

CARD PLAYING IN ENGLAND IN THE XVIIth. CENTURY.

POLITICAL CARD SQUIB AT THE CLOSE OF THE COMMONWEALTH
—THE RESTORATION—CARDS AND DICE RAMPANT—LADY
CASTLEMAINE — LEGISLATIVE ENACTMENTS — PEPYS AT A
GAMING-HOUSE—THE ROYAL REVELS—VENETIAN GAMBLING
—DE GRAMONT — THEOPHILUS LUCAS — MOLL DAVIS —
COLONEL PANTON — NELLY GWYNN — THE DUCHESS DE
MAZARIN—ETHEREGE—TOM D'URFEY—CLANCY—"NAILING
YOUR MAN"—INVENTION OF WHIST—DEATH OF CHARLES
THE SECOND—JAMES THE SECOND—ANNE.

WE have now to return to our own island and
watch the progress of, and changes in, the fashion
respecting card-playing. Having already, in the
first part of this work, sufficiently narrated the
history of the pack itself, our office here is rather
to gather up the quaint and characteristic notices
of the social historians of the times, as displayed
in their gossiping diaries and chatty correspondence.

But it is first worth while to stay a moment,
and examine a political squib, which made its

appearance in the year after the death of the great Protector. It is entitled, "*Shufling, Cutting, and Dealing, in a Game at Pickquet: Being acted from the Year* 1653 *to* 1658. *By O. P. and others; with great applause. Tempora mutantur et nos*—. *Printed in the Year* 1659."

Oliver P. himself opens the game with the remark, "I am like to have a good beginning on't: I have thrown out all my best cards, and got none but a company of wretched ones, so I may very well be capetted." Lambert, Laurence, Fleetwood, Fiennes (Fynes), Musgrave, succeed with various observations. The last promising to play whatever game his Highness pleased—"especially now I see you play so well when you loose." Bernard succeeds with a determination not to bet, and then Vane says, "One had better sometimes play with a good gamester than a bungler; for one knowes not where to have him. If Cromwell had discarded, as he ought to have done, I had won my stake at it: as it is, I shall save myself; which I fear he will hardly do, though he juggles the cards well when he deals himself, and hath excellent luck in cutting when another deals."

In the copy before the writer, there are a few manuscript additions in a contemporary hand.

Lenthall is introduced as saying, "My Lord, I lost dealing twice together, because you interrupted me." Sir George Askew is also put in by the annotator: "They will not let me play, they think I play too well for them." The Trustees for delinquents' lands say: "I owe you for the last game, gentlemen, dowble or quitt." Richard Cromwell: "I'll play my game in the country." Henry Cromwell: "I play my father's cards here, but I feare I discard a wrong sute; those I keepe are leading cards at another game, but nothing at this." Claypole: "I have but one court card, and shee lyes bare, so that shee'll be snapt quickly." Ludlow: "If I play, I'll push; I care not what I fling out,—kings, queenes, or knaves." Such are the MS. additions, worthy of note as displaying the opinions of the day.

The pamphleteer represents Harrison as playing the fool and going in for a fifth king, "when there was but four in the stock." Lawson throws up his cards, because the Protector took the game which was not dealt to him. Noell makes his fortune by lending the gamesters money. Monk says: "My Lord, when you came to play, your stock was none of the greatest; but since I see your good fortune, I am resolved still to play as you do; especially, since you have made me master of one of your great playhouses : but, above all things, if you can keep the bone in your hand, the doggs will follow you : if you can keep the treasure, the gamesters will all crowd to you." Pride and Baxter are "at the old foolish Christmas game with honours." The dissenting army-members refuse to play, because Cromwell juggles. The Law Courts complain ; and the Commissioners for Excise and Customs say, pithily, " Gentlemen, pay the box." Then the parsons make moan, and Papist winds up the whole with the remark, " If you all complain, I hope I shall win at last." Which brings us to Charles and the Restoration, and rids us of the incongruous idea of " Old Noll " ever having held a hand at cards, a proceeding somewhat inconsistent with his general reputation.

The Puritan abhorrence of cards, which we have already noticed, and which has indeed continued to the present day, was by no means entertained by the roystering blades who, having shared the foreign fortunes of the second Charles, trooped to their native land, full of French fashions, and by no means " for their country's good."

As we are not here writing a history of manners or aiming at political history, we may well be excused for passing over the periods under review in the most cursory manner.

Charles and his train, so long expatriated, upon their return, were made welcome,—for the reason that the nation was glad to obtain any rule in place of that of a number of factious generals,—and Charles, like the prodigal son, was pardoned all that had gone before, and the court, with its magnificence, gaiety, and novelty, blinded all eyes to the recklessness of its proceedings.

Cards had been greatly put down in stern Oliver's time, both from his own religious views, and because his military strictness, aided by the fanaticism of the army, discouraged their use. When the Cavaliers, however, had again obtained footing in England, and the Puritans had fallen, the repression under which all classes had lain led to great excesses, in the usual course of things. No wonder, then, that legislative enactments regulating card-playing should have been passed, as already mentioned in another chapter of this work.* It would not seem, however, that all the intended restrictions were carried out.

* Part i., chap. xii., p. 224.

We find the French ambassador, Count de Comminges, in February, 1662-3, writing to M. de Lionne, that it was proposed in the Lower House to pass an Act against the playing of Ombre, or at least to limit the stakes to £5. But he reports that the proposition was received with ridicule. Another Act he then mentions as being in contemplation, was one by which all persons under thirty-one years of age were to be exempted from the payment of debts incurred at cards. This, however, appears also not to have been the ultimate form in which the Act became law, other provisions in the law having been finally settled.

The great and the wealthy, however, laughed at the law, and cards resumed, with other kinds of gambling, their usual popularity as means of ruin. It is on record that Lady Castlemaine, afterwards Duchess of Cleveland, one of Charles's mistresses, won £15,000 one night, and lost, in February, 1667, £25,000 in another single night.* Perhaps the great number of dramatic entertainments, which commenced at three, may have tended slightly to check this, yet, from what is recorded, this interference could have been but slight, from the early hour at which the play-

* *Pepys' Diary*, vol. iv., p. 357.

houses were closed. The popular games were gleek, lansquenet, pharao, and the like.

Amidst the many card-players of the great vagabond era of Charles II., it perhaps will please more than one, that Samuel Pepys, whose diary gives, more than any known book, the habits of his time, was no great gambler. Though here and there he refers to playing at cards, he does not seem to have had much passion for them. Sometimes, to please an old lady, or a visitor, or to wile away some hour that might have been passed in contention with his wife, we find him sitting down to cards; and then he manifests so little interest, — contrary to his uncommonly bombastic, though honest, nature,— that we never learn whether he was wise or foolish, winner or loser, nor even what he played at. Probably some such games as gleek or ombre. He gives a good account of his opinion of a gaming-house.

"Captain Ferrers," says Pepys, writing the 11th of November, 1661, "carried me, the first time that ever I saw any gaming-house, to one entering into Lincolne's Inn Fields, at the end of Bell Yard, where strange the folly of men to lay and lose so much money, and very glad I was to see the manner of a gamester's life, which I see is very miserable, and poor, and unmanly.*"

The reason which caused Pepys to keep his amusing diary appears, from its contents, to have been partly want of memory, not unusually apparent in the course of it. After the account already quoted, he is found thus recording another visit: †

"By and by I met with Mr. Brisband; and having it in my mind this Christmas to do what *I never can remember that I did*, go to see the gaming at the Groome-Porter's,—I having in my coming from the playhouse stepped into the two Temple-halls, and there saw the dirty prentices and idle people playing; wherein I was mistaken, in thinking to have seen gentlemen of quality playing there, as I think it was when I was a little child, that one of my father's servants, John Bassum, I think, carried me in his arms thither. I did tell Brisband of it, and he did lead me thither, when, after staying an hour, they begun to play at about eight at night, where to see how differently one man took his losing from another, one cursing and swearing, and another only muttering and grumbling to himself, a third without any apparent discontent at all: to see how the dice will run good luck in one hand, for half an hour together, and another have no good luck at all: to see how easily here, where they play nothing but guinnys, £100 is won or lost: to see two or three gentlemen come in there drunk, and putting their stock of gold together, one 22 pieces, the second 4, and the third 5 pieces; and these two play one with another, and forget how much each of them brought, but he that brought the 22 thinks that he brought no more than the rest: to see the different humours of gamesters to change their luck, when it is bad, how

* *Pepys' Diary*, vol. i., p. 294.
† *Pepys' Diary*, vol. iv., p. 309.

ceremonious they are to call for new dice, to shift their places, to alter the manner of their throwing, and that with great industry, as if there was anything in it: to see how some old gamesters,* that have no money now to spend as formerly, do come and sit and look on, and among others, Sir Lewes Dives,† who was here, and hath been a great gamester in his time: to hear their cursing and damning to no purpose, as one man being to throw a seven if he could, and, failing to do it after a great many throws, cries he would be d—d if ever he flung seven more while he lived, his despair of throwing it being so great, while others did it as their luck served almost every throw: to see how persons of the best quality do here sit down, and play with people of any, though meaner; and to see how people in ordinary clothes shall come hither, and play away 100, or 2 or 300 guinnys, without any kind of difficulty: and lastly to see the formality of the groome-porter, who is their judge of all disputes in play and all quarrels that may arise therein, and how his under-officers are there to observe true play at each table, and to give new dice—is a consideration I never could have thought had been in the world, had I not now seen it. And mighty glad I am that I did see it, and it may be to find another evening before Christmas be over to see it again, when I may stay later, for their heat of play begins not till about eleven or twelve o'clock; which did give me another pretty observation of a man, that did win mighty fast when I was there. I think he won £100 at single pieces in a little time. Which all the rest envied him his good fortune, he cursed it, saying, it come so early upon me, for this fortune two hours hence would be worth something to me, but then I shall have no such luck. This kind of prophane, mad entertainment they give themselves. And so I have enough for once, refusing to venture, though Brisband pressed me hard, and tempted me with saying that no man was ever known to lose the first time, the devil being too cunning to discourage a gamester; and he offered me also to lend me ten pieces to venture; but I did refuse, and so went away."

* Not, Mr. Hughes, of the true Berkshire species!

† Of Bromham, Bedfordshire. Now apparently become Lazarus.

And so, honest Clerk of the Acts, will we, an ye please, being satisfied to emerge from Pandemonium with an unscathed conscience and whole skin.

While Pepys appears to have carefully abstained from gambling at the Groom Porter's, his contemporary and acquaintance, Mr. Evelyn, seems to have witnessed the royal revels occasionally. On the 6th January, 1661-2, the king opened the revels by throwing the dice himself in the privy chamber, "where was a table set on purpose," and lost "*his*" £100—an allusion to the act of limitation passed by his parliament. Evelyn mentions that the year before he won £1,500, and he adds that the ladies played very deep. He departed when the Duke of Ormond had won about £1,000, and they were still at cards. This evening he seems to have devoted to gadding about, for he proceeds: "At other tables, both there (the palace) and at the Groom Porter's, observing the wicked folly and monstrous excess of passion amongst some losers; sorry am I that such a wretched custom as play to that excess should be countenanced in a court, which ought to be an example of virtue to the rest of the kingdom."

That gambling, both here and on the Continent, had a fatal hold upon all classes is well proved by another passage of Evelyn, when at Venice, where he mentions (*s. d.* 21st October, 1644, more than fifteen years before Pepys visited the Groom Porter's) that "here was a tent where any idle fellow might stake his liberty against a few crowns, at dice or other hazard; and if he lost, he was immediately chained and led away to the galleys, where he was to serve a term of years, but from whence they seldom returned: many sottish persons in a drunken bravado, would try their fortune in this way."*

Among the more prominent men of pleasure at the court of Charles the Second was the witty, wayward, and versatile Count de Grammont. "A fellow of infinite humour," it is, perhaps, a pity that Shakspere had not lived to paint him; still, in the memoirs of him published by Count Anthony Hamilton, we have a vivid picture of himself in that rare repertory of scandal, humour, and merriment. Arbiter, we have already seen him, of the royal backgammon-table at St. Germain. At Charles's court, he, perhaps, held not so prominent a position, as far as we can judge; for the strange compound of honesty and vagabondism which rejoiced in the nickname of " Old

* *Evelyn's Diary*, vol. i., p. 91.

Rowley," saw through his vanity, and permitting him to fool himself to the top of his bent, gave him the run of Whitehall, and no more. De Grammont (or Gramont, as it should properly be), used such opportunities as he had, and won when he could, to meet his extravagance in presents to ladies. Not even the feeling that an acquaintance was about to go to prison could check his friendly enthusiasm for his amusement; for on the night that Talbot, afterwards Duke of Tyrconnell, was committed to the Tower, the worthy count exerted himself to entertain his friend, to such a degree, that—he won three or four hundred guineas of him.

While the more considerable of the king's mistresses won and lost their money at basset, the others laudably imitated their example, and won and lost too. Moll Davis, who was one of king Charles's actresses, seems, on occasion, to have won what she could ! A good anecdote is preserved regarding her, in a queer quaint book about Gamesters, of which, first, a word.

The author must have been an oddity, like some others, if what he says is to be deemed (which it can scarcely *be* deemed) true. In his preface, he states himself to have once been a man of considerable property, and that he had lost an estate of £2,000 per annum by gambling. *Ex dono Dei*, our worthy Theophilus Lucas proposes to confer on the world, not the benefit of his sad example personally, but his experience of gamblers and gambling in *their* persons, by, Grub-street-like, collecting together the histories of gentlemen who, being exalted at Tyburn, were subsequently delivered to the affiliates of Surgeons' Hall for anatomy, unless they had interest enough to bribe the hangman for their own bodies. A nice book, and one full of warning to worthy Lucas's nephew (probably a creature of the imagination, endowed with a *chateau d'Espagne*), "who is the very next heir to £1,500 per annum by the death of his uncle." Let us hope that the book paid, and that the nephew "took pattern" in an inverse ratio by his uncle's friends.

A lady, however, is waiting to be introduced. Moll Davis encountered Colonel Panton, a gentleman of "fortune," as he might truly be called. They sat down to basset, and Moll Davis produced a bag containing some £1,500 : they played a game, Moll staking one hundred and fifty guineas, and Colonel Panton—with an eye to the bag—politely lost the first game. He was all expectation for the second, when Moll *drew* the stakes, and pleaded that she never played more than one deal. Colonel Panton was annoyed, but could not object.

They, however, soon met again ; and Panton placed Miss Moll with her back to a looking glass, and speedily won £1,100 by inspecting her hand that way. By play, this Colonel Panton ultimately won a large fortune, and realized it in an estate near Leicester-square. Little do the needy rogues who, for gambling, swindling, and worse purposes, congregate there, know that their haunts of Panton-street and Panton-square were built from a gambler's gains. It is scarcely possible to avoid feeling, that places won by easy and unjustifiable means are thenceforward cursed with a squalid and sordid destiny, when we look round at the dens which stand, like Panton-street and Drury-lane, upon the haunts of the gay court of Charles. Colonel Panton retired from the profession of gambler, on the results of his exertions, and died in 1681.

While Lady Castlemaine won and lost at cards enormous sums, it was not extraordinary that others of Charles's lady companions should give way to the fashionable vice. "Pretty witty Nelly"—to whom all honour for founding Chelsea Hospital, and for innumerable graceful warm-hearted acts—kept her basset table both at Pall Mall and at Burford House in Windsor. She came into contact with the lovely and half frantic Duchess of Mazarin, and, to her, lost in one night the sum of fourteen hundred guineas,—as much as five thousand pounds of our present money.*

Of the Duchess of Mazarin, the lovely niece of the gambling cardinal, the worthy Grub-street—now Milton-street—writer is good enough to say:

"She would play as fair as any person, when she found her gamester played only upon the square; for she played so well that scarce any one could match her; but when she had a sharp gamester to deal with, she would play altogether upon the sharp at any game upon the cards, and generally came off a winner." †

Whether the Countess de Cruchecassée would do otherwise with a benighted Englishman of the nineteenth century, would, the writer surmises, very much depend upon the length of his purse and—his ears. Madame de Cruchecassée could perform the part of Titania to perfection—except that Titania had no wrinkles.

Basset was the theme of Etherege's songs;

* Cunningham's *Story of Nelly Gwynn*, p. 128; a graceful and gentle book, stored with pleasant facts and flowing English.
† Lucas's *Memoirs of Gamesters*, p. 250.

and he, with Lady Mary Wortley, celebrated its attractions and its snares. Tom D'Urfey, in one of his plays, has condemned this game, which was, no doubt, the prevalent mode.

Another famous sharp of the age of Charles, was one Clancy, who combined in himself the king's commission of a major, the tastes of a swindler, and the presence of mind of a jester. Such a congeries of talents conferred upon him the distinction of a noose in the fashionable neighbourhood of Tyburnia, but before enterprising builders had created a town, from nothing, by the ingenious aid of mortgages. He at one time resided in Saint Martin's-lane, which must then have been no unfashionable spot. Like other worthy men, he was troubled for a little money—probably to "oblige a lady." Looking out of the window, he saw a varlet opposite, of whom specimens are extant in our days, and have been painted by Mr. Dickens in *Bleak House*, as "Coavins's:" he was a bailiff's man, a "follower." Patience is the badge of all their tribe, conjointly with ardent spirits ; yet, weary with waiting, and no doubt aware of the noble captain's unwillingness to emerge from his lodging, this bailiff's man was sitting on a joiner's stall. Clancy sent the servant across, to bid the joiner's apprentice

come to him. He came, and was promised a
crown if he could manage to nail the bailiff's
man, by his leathern belt, to the stall. The
apprentice soon found means to fuss about the
stall, and managed to "nail" the gentleman.
A coach rattled up to Clancy's door, and forth
rushed Clancy, and up rose my worthy and
patient officer to "nail" his man with as much
despatch as he had been nailed himself. My
efficient bailiff's man, however, found that the
whole structure upon which he had been resting
came clattering down with him, and, as Lucas
tells us, down came cabinets, coffins, tools, and
all else upon the stall, with a mighty clatter,
amidst which Clancy disappeared, not to emerge
for us until hanging time, in 1666, when he
"danced upon nothing," *ætatis* thirty-nine.

Several worthies of the same era might briefly
be named. Perhaps they are not worth the type
the printer sets for their miserable biographies, so
that one must serve for the rest. Let us be brief.

Sir John Johnson, of Kirkcaldy, in Fife-
shire, kingdom of Scots, was a gambler, knave,
and bully. He used the slip at put, and pegged
forward at cribbage. For these two virtues, and
some trifling error in his knowledge between what
was, and what was not, criminal in jurisprudence,

he was hanged on the 23rd December, 1690; being then forty-two years old, and a child of king Charles's time. Men and women of England, who see, every day, in London numberless children starving, and gambling, and cheating, in filth and squalor, which lead to crime, to the dock, and the hulks, could you not interpose to prevent one of them from having such a biography and such an epitaph?

To the period of Charles II. may most probably be referred the invention of the game of Whist. Founded upon the game known as *Ruff and Honours*, it was originated between 1664 and 1680; for though not mentioned in the first edition of the *Compleat Gamester*, published in the former year, it is named amongst the generally known games in the second edition which appeared in the latter. There was at first an additional stake called *swabbers*, and these stakes the holders of particular cards swept off the board. The term originated from the nautical implement used in that maritime age by sailors to clear and " swab " the decks. Like some other games, the kitchen was its first home, and, " born in a kitchen," it made its way to the saloon, in company, very likely, with some of the gay damsels who rose so high in those days.

Whist, however, became first scientifically cultivated in 1730, when a club of gentlemen, among whom was the first Lord Folkestone, met to play it at a coffee-house known as the Crown, in Bedford-row.

The noble and single minded Evelyn, in recording the last few days of Charles Stuart the restored, gives a strange, almost painful, picture of a winter Sunday at Whitehall. "I can never forget," he says, "the inexpressible luxury and profaneness, gaming and all dissoluteness, and, as it were, a total forgetfulness of God (it being Sunday evening), which this day se'nnight I was witness of : the king sitting and toying with his concubines, Portsmouth, Cleveland, Mazarine, &c.; a French boy singing love songs in that glorious gallery; whilst about twenty of the great courtiers and other dissolute persons were at basset round a large table, a bank of at least £2,000 in gold before them; upon which two gentlemen who were with me made strange reflections. Six days after, all was in the dust." The king was fatally seized on the Monday morning, and though he lay in a flickering state until the following Friday, the powers above knew that the hour had struck, and the awful moment when life, in its most intensified horror,

rushes through the memory in the guise of evil
deeds, was there to sear the tremulous conscience,
or to brand the eternal memory of one, who,
called to a high office, neglected its duties for
personal gratifications, was too idle not to be
popular, as turning aside to the merest boor who
amused or bored him, and too wise not to see
that kingship as a personal divine inheritance
had cropped out. Had Charles survived to old
age, James would not have abdicated,—William
would never have reigned.

After the death of Charles II., and when the
reaction perceptible in social manners, as well as
historical events, began to set in, the minds of
men became concentrated upon other matters
than cards. Yet it is singular that the rebellion
of Monmouth, and the "Popish Plot of 1679,"
should both be found directly illustrating our
subject. Shortly after the disastrous defeat of
that "spoiled darling" of Charles the Vagabond,
a pack makes its appearance, of which some few
remaining cards have been kindly shown the
writer by Mr. Quaritch, in whose possession
they are.

So far as it can be understood, they give an
outline of the Monmouth Rebellion, though in no
especially favourable light.   The cards of 1679

illustrate the events of the Spanish Armada, and were quiet reproofs to the mendicant priests who haunted England previous to the abdication of the king to whom his brother, himself a king of England, said, "Never mind, York, they will never shoot *me* to make a way for you." When said York was, perhaps, anxious to make an illicit way to the throne, please the Pope, satisfy the Presbyters, and otherwise cool down the Nonconformists to a reasonably tepid point. No, no, vagabond Charles was, perhaps, not the most moral, but inconfutably the best, of the later Stuarts, and he saw through York's "diminutive game."

Of the age of William, who caught a cold in the dark waters of the Boyne, little is preserved, save the deeds already familiar to every Englishman in the brilliant, but factitious history of Macaulay, first Baron of English Literature. In passing lightly over these times, we cannot either afford the reader hope of extricating such a small matter as card-playing from the enormous stir of events, nor think to illustrate it by anecdote.

There was a most certain lull in all matters connected with cards. The great American continent had gradually been draining off the best of the men who lived by cards. They eagerly sought,—as every desperate man does,—not only an outlet for themselves, but an opportunity of displaying their energy and, practically, retrieving their positions and characters.

Cards, therefore, were to them merely a pastime for the desert or the plain, when camp-fires had been lit, and the prowling panther of America kept off. There, upon rude blocks of wood, in the midst of the primeval forest, these sons of sin and Adams of adventure scored their quarrelled points. Cavaliers by nature, King Charles's death and King James's abdication had expatriated them; and, lords of a new soil, they were introducing to a new country the vices, the licence, of the old. In the forest glades of Virginia, these men rested and died—the founders of a Southern nation, which, as did the Cavaliers, possesses the quality of courage, the generosity of the Englishman, and the fierceness of a race which feels itself misrepresented and oppressed by a faction in the country, which dares to say that it—composed of slavetraders and promoters of despotism—shall alone be the arbiter, not only of property, but of freedom.

Turn we rather to the reign of Queen Anne, of whom the demise has been more frequently asserted than believed.

It was then that the chaplain crouched on week-days, and was glad of a mess of pudding—if asked to stay—when slinking off to the society of the still-room maid. On Sunday, Boanerges-like, he was at liberty to beat the pulpit-cushion, so long as the squire's stertorous breathing was not interrupted. And a hand at whist, or a dish of tea, was the reward of the much-enduring pastor. It was then, especially at Christmas, that the squire brought down the cards from that country bank of sociality—the mantleshelf. Then the chaplain cringed and fawned, and joined the game with ardour—haply winning a sixpence, and having to drink much small ale in the morning to allay his thirst.

Small were the joys, and rude indeed, of the good times ere Queen Anne was kind enough to give an opportunity for a statue to her memory. Simple country boors perpetuated the fanaticism of cards in the humble form of *Beat my Neighbour out of Doors*, which, in a more practical manner, it is not beyond the bounds of belief was their custom.

VII.

CARD PLAYING IN ENGLAND DURING THE XVIIIth. CENTURY.

THE GEORGES—ADDISON ON GAMBLING—OMBRE—POPE'S DE-
SCRIPTION OF BELINDA'S GAME—A GAMING-HOUSE STAFF—
A CHILD STAKED AT CARDS—NEWMARKET—OSTERMAN—
FREDERICK, PRINCE OF WALES—BUBB DODDINGTON—THE
DUKE OF CUMBERLAND—PLAY IN WALPOLE'S TIME—LOO—
SIR WILLIAM BURDETT AND LORD CASTLEDURROW—LORD
RODNEY—O'BIRNE—"DOCTOR, YOU ARE TO DEAL!"—FARO
—A STRANGE WHIST PARTY—WILBERFORCE—"ROBBING
THE MAIL!"—SELWYN—MISS VERNON—COUNT ADHEMAR—
CARICATURE CARDS.

On the accession of the Hanoverian dynasty, a
heavier and graver tone pervaded society. Yet
the sway of cards continued. The elegant Addison, in that rare repertory of moral sermonizing,
The Spectator, muses upon the singularity of the
gambler's taste. In the ninety-third number, he
says:

"I think it very wonderful to see persons of
the best sense passing away a dozen hours together in shuffling and dividing a pack of cards,
with no other conversation but what is made up
of a few game phrases, or no other ideas but

those of black and red spots ranged together in different figures. Would not a man laugh to hear any one of his species complaining that life is short ? "

It cannot be doubted, however, that whatever sobering influence the Commonwealth, in the first instance, might have exercised, the licence of Charles's time had continued to sway the gay and thoughtless of later times. Gambling in England had grown statelier, and the quaint fashions of the time invest with an indescribable tinge the amusements of the day. Frolic was dead, and though no one will dispute the completeness of Pope's description of the game of Ombre in the lines which follow, it is difficult to realize any enjoyment in a pursuit such as that in which Belinda is depicted as engaged.

" Belinda now, whom thirst of Fame invites,
    Burns to encounter two advent'rous Knights
At Ombre, singly to decide their doom,
And swells her breast with conquest yet to come.
Straight the three bands prepare in arms to join ;
Each band the number of the sacred nine.
Soon as she spreads her hand, th' Aërial guard
Descend, and sit on each important card :
First Ariel perched upon a matadore,
Then each, according to the rank they bore ;
For Sylphs, yet mindful of their antient race,
Are, as when women, wond'rous fond of place.
    Behold, four Kings in majesty rever'd,
With hoary whiskers, and a forky beard :

And four fair Queens, whose hands sustain a flower,
Th' expressive emblem of their softer power ;
Four Knaves in garb succinct, a trusty band,
Caps on their heads, and halberds in their hand ;
And party-colour'd troops, a shining train,
Drawn forth to combat on the velvet plain.

The skilful nymph reviews her force with care ;
Let Spades be trumps, she said ; and trumps they were.

Now move to war her sable matadores,
In show like leaders of the swarthy Moors.
Spadillia first, unconquerable lord !
Led off two captive trumps, and swept the board.
As many more Manillia forc'd to yield,
And march'd a victor from the verdant field.
Him Basto follow'd, but his fate more hard,
Gain'd but one trump, and one plebeian card.
With his broad sabre next, a chief in years,
The hoary Majesty of Spades appears ;
Puts forth one manly leg, to sight revealed ;
The rest in many colour'd robe conceal'd.
The Rebel-Knave, who dares his prince engage,
Proves the just victim of his royal rage.
Ev'n mighty Pam, that Kings and Queens o'erthrew,
And mowed down armies in the fights of Lue ;
Sad chance of war ! now, destitute of aid,
Falls undistinguish'd by the victor Spade.

Thus far both armies to Belinda yield ;
Now to the Baron, fate inclines the field.
His warlike Amazon her host invades,
Th' imperial consort of the Queen of Spades.
The Club's black tyrant first her victim dy'd,
Spite of his haughty mien, and barb'rous pride !
What boots the regal circle on his head,
His giant limbs, in state unwieldly spread ;
That long behind he trails his pompous robe,
And, of all monarchs, only grasps the globe.

The Baron now his Diamonds pours apace ;
Th' embroider'd king who shows but half his face,

And his refulgent queen, with powers combin'd,
Of broken troops an easy conquest find.
Clubs, Diamonds, Hearts, in wild disorder seen,
With throngs promiscuous strew the level green.
   The Knave of Diamonds tries his wily arts,
And wins (O shameful chance!) the queen of Hearts.
At this the blood the virgin's cheeks forsook,
A livid paleness spreads o'er all her look;
She sees and trembles at th' approaching ill,
Just in the jaws of ruin, and Codille.
And now (as oft in some distemper'd state)
On one nice trick depends the gen'ral fate;
An Ace of Hearts steps forth: the King unseen
Lurk'd in her hand, and mourn'd his captive Queen;
He springs to vengeance with an eager pace,
And falls like thunder on the prostrate Ace.
The Nymph exulting, fills with shouts the sky;
The walls, the woods, and long canals reply."

What *would* be thought of any modern damsel
so excited over a game of cards, as to fill "with
shouts the sky?" In an age like our own, when
to be natural is to be essentially vulgar, such
resounding "shouts" would be the height of
ill-breeding in every way.

While Belinda was satisfactorily strengthen-
ing her lungs and vanquishing her adversaries,
rascaldom, like the poor, ever present with us,
was not less active than it ever is. Gaming-
houses were kept up at great expense, and with
corresponding commercial success. If ten per
cent. hangs to the tail of a vice, there ever will

be men ready and willing to take the ten per cent. and supply the meretricious enjoyment.

In 1731 the following officials formed the regular establishment of an English gaming-house : a commissioner, usually a proprietor himself, who, with two other proprietors, audited the accounts weekly, and gave general attention of an evening to the house ; a director, who specially attended to the room ; an "operator," whose business it was to cheat at pharao ; two croupiers, who watched the cards and gathered in the money ; two "puffs,"—in modern phrase, "bonnets,"—to act as decoys ; a clerk, who acted as a check on the "puffs," to prevent their pocketing the money given them to play with ; an under-puff, to act the tyro ; a "flasher," to swear how often the bank had been broken ; a "dun," whose office was to receive the money lost at play ; a waiter, to fill up wine glasses, snuff candles, &c.; a Newgate "attorney ;" a fighting captain ; an usher, to light up the guests ; a porter, usually a private in the Foot Guards ; an orderly man, to watch and give the alarm ; an out-door spy, to watch justices' meetings, &c.; and, finally, a tagrag and bobtail of common bail, affidavit men, ruffians, assassins, and "people in general."

Into such haunts, alike in all ages, we may well decline to penetrate.

Strange stakes were sometimes made at cards in the early days of the eighteenth century; and among these, one mentioned by Sykes is perhaps the oddest. In Durham, at Chester-le-Street, at the sign of the Salmon, in October, 1735, a child of James and Elizabeth Leesh was played for at cards—four shillings being staked against the child—by Henry and John R. Trotter, Robert Thompson and Thomas Ellison, and won by the latter, being duly delivered to them. It does not appear what the father and mother thought of the transaction, but as the child was handed over to the parties, we must presume that the parents consented.*

Gaming, however, was sufficiently rife all over England. On one occasion, we learn, that at Newmarket, about the middle of the century, some one staked a bank bill, and then carelessly left the gambling-table. Some slight question arose as to the ownership, but no one claimed it; so, to settle the affair, the bank bill was given to a man standing by, and the matter ended.

During the reign of the Empress Anne of Russia, Osterman, her grand-chancellor, learnt

* Sykes's *Local Records*, p. 79.

that the court of Versailles proposed to send a polished gentleman, whose *forte* was cards, to tempt and attack her favourite, the Duke de Biran, on his weak side, that of gambling, and thus gain some advantage over him which might be turned to political use. The chancellor thereupon called at the minister's house, but the duke feigned, from caprice, to be from home. Pretending sickness in turn, Osterman wrote to the empress that he had important matters to reveal, and the duke was therefore ordered to wait upon him. Affecting great pain, the chancellor, amidst the apparent agonies of gout, stammered out that the " French were sending a gamester."

At this the duke was enraged, and represented to the empress that Osterman was delirious, and had sent for him on a fool's errand. However, in due time, an elegant, fascinating marquis made his appearance, whose easy and graceful dissipation stamped him a " sensation" in society. The duke was charmed, disembarrassed of his cash, forthwith, and put at his wit's end how to foil and discomfit his delightful foe.

At the city of Moscow about this time there resided a midshipman named Kruckoff, whose reputation as a " young man from the country not easily got over," had spread to the capital   An adept at cards, he was great at their "management," and especially at the game of *Quizze*, at which the duke had been worsted. The chancellor sent for Kruckoff.

Like M. Poinçot, he was not fully qualified to play at cards at court, and therefore they were obliged to give him military rank—the only rank recognised in Russia then, as now. After losing largely to the marquis, he began to retrieve his losses, and speedily wound up the Frenchman to a pitch of desperation. He at last proposed an enormous stake, and prepared his cards so as to effectually control the result. The marquis already appeared on the point of winning, when, by a master stroke, Kruckoff "buzzed" him, and won the game—*swallowing* a card among some sweetmeats.

After this, Osterman again went to see the duke, and restoring him the money he had lost, advised him to pay more heed to the advice of gouty people, telling him plainly that this whole business had been a plot. The ensign, Kruckoff, was allowed to keep the balance of the money, but warned that another game at cards would send him to Siberia for life.

During the Georgian era, however, though gambling might still be a passion among all classes, it seems to have partaken of the heavy lumpishness which the German sovereigns imported. Elegance and grace departed with the Stuarts, and hence we have little to tell respecting this time. Ombre, as we have already seen, was Belinda's passion, and there can be little doubt that the general *ennui* visible in those days, was the result of the unintellectual lassitude caused by the licence of former reigns.

Gambling, however, prospered, as all vagabondish pursuits must for a time, thriving until detection puts an end to the illusion.

An English prince, for whom his contemporaries devised the following epitaph, was one who reckoned gambling and card-sharping among desirable accomplishments :

> " Here lies Fred,
> Who was alive and is dead.
> Had it been his father,
> I had much rather ;
> Had it been his brother,
> Much better than another ;
> Had it been his sister,
> No one would have missed her ;
> Had it been the whole generation,
> Still better for the nation ;
> But since 'tis only Fred,
> Who was alive and is dead,
> There's no more to be said."

We have quoted this epitaph upon Frederick

Louis, Prince of Wales, partly from its inherent merit, and also from its great fitness as applied to gamblers in general.

In his lifetime, in common with his royal relatives and progenitors, Frederick was a card-player. As Eliot Warburton observes of him, "He had had the credit of a taste for trickery, even from a child." * Once, on an occasion when he had obtained from the wealthy and fantastical Bubb Doddington the sum of five thousand pounds, he came chuckling home to Charles Hedges, his secretary, and pointing out Doddington, exclaimed, "That man is reckoned one of the most sensible men in England, yet, with all his parts, I have just *nicked him* out of five thousand pounds!" Not that Bubb Doddington was alone in his sufferings, Frederick favoured many others in the same way.

On the news of Frederick's death, which occurred somewhat suddenly, in March, 1757, being brought by Lord North to the king his father, George II. was sitting at cards; and in reply to the intelligence merely remarked, "*Il est mort!*" Whether he went on with his game is doubtful, but he was very little moved by the news. George IV., the grandson of Fred "who

* *Walpole and his Contemporaries*, vol. i., p. 262.

was alive and is dead," proved worthy of his grandfather, and finely "nicked" the Bubb Doddingtons of his day.

George II., however, was no gambler, as we can see from a letter of Horace Walpole to Montagu, dated in January, 1752. He tells us that on Monday, being the Twelfth-day,—a day by the way called All Gamesters' Day,—"his majesty, according to annual custom, offered myrrh, frankincense, and a small bit of gold; and at night, in commemoration of the three *kings* or *wise men*, the king and royal family played at hazard for the benefit of a prince of the blood. There were above eleven thousand pounds upon the table; his most sacred majesty won *three guineas*, and his royal highness the duke *three thousand four hundred pounds*." * Moderate play for a monarch in good sooth, to win but three guineas. Cumberland, the winner on this occasion, did not always come off so well.

"If you are acquainted with my Lady Barrymore," writes H. Walpole to his friend Montagu, "pray tell her that in less than two hours t'other night, the Duke of Cumberland lost four hundred and fifty pounds at loo; Miss Pelham won

* *Walpole Letters*, vol. ii., p. 275.

three hundred, and I the rest. However, in general, loo is extremely gone to decay; I am to play at Princess Emily's to morrow for the first time this winter, and it is with difficulty she has made a party." * This was in December, 1761.

Princess Emily was that daughter of George whom the king supposed to be so attached to him, but who seems, by all accounts, to have been far more devoted to her own amusements than anything else. She frequently expressed her disgust at her father in unmeasured terms, acting hypocritically enough, at the same time, in his presence.

The condition of card-playing in the upper classes, described by the same writer a few years before, is very different. In 1759, he mentions that loo "is mounted to the zenith; the parties last till one and two in the morning. We played at Lady Hertford's last week, the last night of her lying in, till deep into Sunday morning, after she and her lord were retired. It is now adjourned to Mrs. Fitzroy's, whose child the town calls *Pam-ela*. I proposed, that instead of receiving cards for assemblies, one should send in a morning to Dr. Hunter's,

* *Walpole Letters*, vol. iii., p. 470.

to know where there is loo that evening.
. . . . . The invasion is not half so much
in fashion as loo." *

Among the notabilities of the time who were
"wise in their own generation" at cards and
dice, was a certain Sir William Vigors Burdett—a Carlow man, we find, from Dunmore.
Of this worthy, Walpole relates an exploit,
in which Admiral Rodney, then a junior, was
concerned.

"About two months ago," gossips Walpole,
"he met at St. James's a Lord Castledurrow, a
young Irishman, and no genius, as you will find,
and entered into conversation with him : the lord,
seeing a gentleman, fine, polite, and acquainted
with everybody, invited him to dinner for next
day, and a captain Rodney, a young seaman who
has made a fortune by very gallant behaviour
during the war. At dinner it came out, that
neither the lord nor the captain had ever been at
any Pelham levees. ' Good God ! ' said Sir
William, ' that must not be so any longer; I beg
I may carry you to both the duke and Mr.
Pelham : I flatter myself I am very well with
both.' The appointment was made for the next
Wednesday and Friday : in the meantime, he

* *Walpole Letters*, vol. iii., p. 229.

invited the two young men to dine with him the
next day. When they came, he presented them
to a lady, dressed foreign, as a princess of the
house of Brandenburg : she had a toadeater, and
there was another man, who gave himself for a
count. After dinner, Sir William looked at his
watch and said, 'J——s ! it is not so late as I
thought by an hour ; princess, will your highness
say how we shall divert ourselves till it is time to
go to the play ?' 'Oh !' said she, 'for my part
you know I abominate everything but pharao.'
'I am very sorry, madam,' replied he, very gravely,
'but I don't know whom your highness will get
to tally to you ; you know I am ruined by
dealing.' 'Oh !' said she, 'the count will deal to
us.' 'I would, with all my soul,' said the count,
'but I protest I have no money about me.' She
insisted : at last the count said, 'Since your
highness commands us peremptorily, I believe
Sir William has four or five hundred pounds of
mine, that I am to pay away in the city to-
morrow ; if he will be so good as to step to his
bureau for that sum, I will make a bank of it.'
Mr. Rodney owns he was a little astonished at
seeing the count shuffle with the faces of the
cards upwards. In short, my lord (Castledurrow)
and he lost about a hundred and fifty apiece, and

it was settled they should meet for payment the next morning at breakfast, at Ranelagh. In the meantime, Lord C. had the curiosity to enquire a little into the character of his new friend, the baronet; and being *au fait*, he went up to him at Ranelagh, and apostrophized him, 'Sir William, here is the sum I think I lost last night; since then I have heard that you are a professed pickpocket, and therefore desire to have no further acquaintance with you.' Sir William bowed, took the money, and no notice; but as they were going away, he followed Lord Castledurrow and said, 'Good God, my lord, my equipage is not come; will you be so good as to set me down at Buckingham gate?' and without staying for an answer, whipped into the chariot, and came to town with him. If you don't admire the coolness of his impudence, I shall wonder." *

Lord Rodney, who was in this case bitten by Sir William Burdett, himself became an inveterate gambler, and lost much money. He was not, however, the only admiral whose love for gambling prompted him to desperate courses. It is difficult, of course, to separate one species of gambling-infatuation from another, so that a cast with the "bones" is not to be excluded from our

* *Horace Walpole's Letters*, vol. ii, pp. 141-3.

gambling chronicle. In 1780, the Cocoa Tree was set in a flare of excitement by one of these gaming campaigns. A young middy had then just inherited an estate by the death of his brother; his name was Harvey, and he subsequently fought at the battle of Trafalgar, being finally an admiral. The difference at hazard had amounted to one hundred and eighty thousand pounds; and the adversary was a Mr. O'Birne, an Irish gamester. The latter had won one hundred thousand pounds of Harvey, and told him that he could never pay him. "I can," said the youth,—"the estate will sell for the debt." "No," answered the Irishman, "I will win ten thousand; you shall throw for the odd ninety." They did so, and Harvey won. Admiral Harvey might well have been known to many still living, as his death was as recent as 1830.

Basset, ombre, loo, and pharao were not, however, the only popular games at this time.

Of tredille, Horace Walpole tells an amusing story against himself. "I was playing at eighteen-penny tredille with the Duchess of Newcastle and Lady Brown, and certainly not much interested in the game. I cannot recollect nor conceive what I was thinking of, but I pushed the cards very gravely to the duchess and said, ' *Doctor,*

you are to deal.' You may guess at their astonishment, and how much it made us all laugh."*

Gaming, however, was not in a flourishing
way, the same authority tells us, "for want of
materials," in the year 1774. " Want of materials," rendered into the vulgar tongue, is " want
of cash."

At this time duels were common, even in the
streets. Gaming often led to various encounters.
Pall Mall was the scene of one among a number
in 1782. Two officers squabbled over an E.O.
table, at the house of the notorious quack and
gaming-house keeper, Graham, and, adjourning
to the street, one of them, Captain Lucas of
the Guards, was severely wounded, and carried
into a neighbouring house.

" Lateness of hours," writes Walpole, in the
middle of 1781, "is the principal feature of the
times, and certainly demands no stress of invention. Every fashionable place is still crowded;
no instance of selection neither. Gaming is yet
general; though money, the principal ingredient,
does not abound. My old favourite game, faro, is
lately revived."† Mr. Fox is mentioned as a great
gambler in this letter. Faro (or pharao), however,

* *Walpole Letters*, vol. vi. p. 125.
† *Ib.*, vol. viii., p. 41.

we learn, in a letter immediately succeeding the above, had a very short reign,* though it was still played at court by Princess Amelia.

Horace Walpole writes in December, 1781, to one of his constant correspondents: "I was diverted last night at Lady Lucan's. The moment I entered, she set me down to whist with Lady Bute; and who do you think were the other partners?—the Archbishopess of Canterbury and Mr. Gibbon. I once saved Lady Suffolk at the Dowager Essex's from playing at the same table with Lady Yarmouth. I saw Lady Suffolk ready to sink, and took her cards from her, saying, ' I know your ladyship hates whist, and I will play instead of you.' "†

The odd collocation of partners has been humorously commented on by a writer in the *Westminster Review* for July, 1863, who suggests how odd it would seem for Mrs. Longley and Bishop Colenso to be found amicably engaged in such a pursuit. But the positions of the two countesses must have been worse, intellectually and morally.

" The first time I was at Brookes's," writes Wilberforce,‡ " scarcely knowing any one, I

* *Walpole Letters*, vol. viii., p. 47. † *Ib.*, vol. viii., p. 125.
‡ Life, vol. i., p. 16.

joined, from mere shyness, in play at the faro-
table where George Selwyn kept bank. A friend,
who knew my inexperience, and regarded me as a
victim decked out for sacrifice, called to me,—
'What, Wilberforce! is that you?' Selwyn quite
resented the interference; and, turning to him,
said, in his most expressive tone, 'O, sir, don't
interrupt Mr. Wilberforce; he could not be better
employed!'"

White's had preceded Brookes's in popular
favour; and before Selwyn habitually frequented
the latter, he was often a visitor at the former.
He walked into White's Club House (now Arthur's) one November night in 1752, and saw
James Jeffries playing at piquet with Sir Everard
Falkener, who at the time was Joint Postmaster
General. "Oh!" quoth he, "now he is robbing
the mail!" *

Brookes's was a favourite haunt of Selwyn's;
and many of his jests have been preserved. Once
a picture of the Beauties of England was hung up
opposite Brookes's Club House in St. James's-
street. The subject was oddly selected. The
Princess Royal, with all the court beauties around
her, was depicted in the character of the daughter
of Pharaoh finding Moses. This picture had

* *Walpole Letters*, vol. ii., p. 315.

been painted as a companion to some other work then the fashion. Selwyn remarked that he could recommend a better companion to it in the *sons* of *Pharaoh* over the way at Brookes's. Great *beauties*, no doubt!

The ladies, sometimes, were as sharp as any of the men, and performed very queer tricks upon their opponents. One of the maids of honour, Miss Caroline Vernon, lost one night the sum of two hundred pounds at pharao, and bid her opponent mark it up. The gentleman intimated his preference for a draft on her bankers. "Most willingly," she replied, and gave him one on Drummond's. Off went the lucky recipient early next day, in case all the lady's money should be drawn out.

"Sir," said the clerk, "would you receive the contents immediately?"

"Assuredly!"

"Why, sir, have you read the note?"

The winner took the note, and read,—"Pay to the bearer two hundred blows, well applied."

The lady told the story over town with great glee, and the gentleman was pleasantly "buzzed," and had to keep his counsel.

In the *Memoirs of Mrs. Hannah More*, we find a singular instance of the love for gambling which pervaded all classes of society. She is writing to her sister, and thus narrates the circumstances:

"I believe I mentioned that a foreign ambassador, Count Adhemar, had a stroke of palsy, and that he was to have had a great assembly on the night of the day on which it happened; it is shocking to relate the sequel. It was on a Sunday. The company went—some hundreds. The man lay deprived of sense and motion; his bedchamber joins the great drawing-room, where was a faro-bank held close to his bed's head. Somebody said they thought they made too much noise. 'O, no,' another answered, 'it will do him good; the worst thing he can do is to sleep.' A third said, 'I did not think Adhemar had been a fellow of such rare spirit; palsy and faro together is spirited indeed; this is keeping it up!' I was telling this to Mr. Walpole the other day, and lamenting it as a national stigma, and one of the usual signs of the times I had met with. In return, he told me of a French gentleman at Paris, who, being in the article of death, had just signed his will, when the lawyer who drew it up was invited by his wife to stay supper. The table was laid in the dying man's apartment; the lawyer took a glass of wine, and, addressing him-

PLATE XLVII

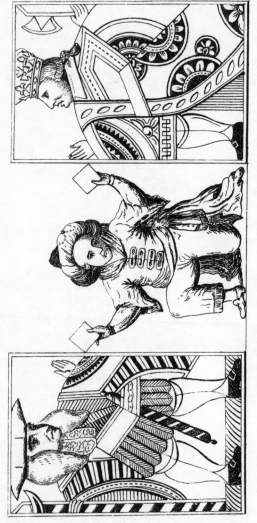

COURT CARDS the beſt to deal with.

self to the lady, drank, *à la santé de notre aimable agonisant!* I told Mr. Walpole he invented the story to outdo me; but he protested it was literally true." * And Walpole told the story on a return from Paris, as a truth, some years before.

The Georgian era was further signalized by the common application of the pencil of the caricaturist to playing-cards. One of these political squibs represents an Indian potentate, in full costume, kneeling and presenting diamonds to the king (who has no suit), and the knave (the prime minister). As a curiosity, we have had it copied for the reader, on a smaller scale.

But even so late as the time of George III., cards were still manufactured in England with the ancient devices of cups for hearts, swords for spades, &c.; and a well-preserved pack of these may be seen in the Library of the British Museum.† Here, however, the ace of cups is represented with a heart upon the outside; no doubt, as it has been supposed, this referred, somewhat sacrilegiously, to the cup used at the communion. It is certainly a singular device, and worthy of passing notice.‡

* *Memoirs*, vol. ii., p. 396.   † Press-mark, 7913. a.
‡ See p. 232, *antè*.

Later on, we find other packs of caricature cards published in Great Britain, of a less grave kind. One of these packs has fallen into our hands : the devices on the cards are very varied, and less gross than might be expected. As giving an accurate view of the costumes of the time, they are very interesting. In the suit of hearts, King George is represented on his throne, with Cupid kneeling before him bearing a basket full of hearts for his acceptance. This pack appears to have been issued in the time of George IV. The publisher was Mr. Fores of Piccadilly, whose relatives still carry on a well-known business as print-sellers, though they have abandoned the branch of caricatures, for which their house was renowned at the beginning of the century.

Some of the cuts at contemporary manners are very good. The deuce of diamonds portrays two Italian posture-masters, one standing upon his hands, while the other supports him in the well-known fashion. Another tumbler is depicted in the four of clubs, where the figure supports itself upon the two lower clubs with his hands, and balances the other two upon the tips of his toes. One very significant card is the knave of clubs, where an individual, dressed in the height of the then fashion, stands, bearing a wand at

the top of which is the ordinary club, and four
labels hang down, respectively inscribed "Hazard,"
" Rouge et Noir," " Whist Club," and " Trou-Ma-
dame." His right hand grasps a dice box, and in
the background a crow is plucking a pigeon,
standing upon two books, marked " Art of Plucking," and " The Compleat Rook."

The queen of clubs represents a virago admin-
istering a sound thrashing to her husband with a
rolling pin, holding him by the hair of the head
during the operation. The knave of spades is a
sexton; the knave of hearts, Cupid; the knave
of diamonds, "Simon Sham, dealer in Bristol
stone, Dovey's Paste," &c. The king of diamonds
is an Indian king; and the king of spades, a gar-
dener. Venus is represented as the queen of
hearts, and a gorgeously attired damsel as the
queen of diamonds. A drunken harlequin, surrounded by the watch, is the five of clubs; and
the four of hearts is portrayed as a butcher's shop,
with the dogs stealing two bullocks' hearts from
the ground. The six of spades is also represented
as a tumbler, " The celebrated Signior Pietro
Francisco Joseph Andrea Balanca, First Equili-
brist to His Catholic Majesty," an important
and stagey-looking personage, reminding one of
the circus-sawdust, and the lamps of the prosce-

rium. These cards are creditably executed, although the points of humour in them are somewhat dull at the present day.*

Our common address and message cards derived their origin from the practice (mentioned in the *Spiritual Quixote*, a novel of George III.'s time) of writing messages on the backs of playing-cards. Lord Orford, in one of his sketches, shows that they were amazingly in vogue, as he there playfully proposes a tax upon such message-cards.

Cards had permeated English society at this time, and every one, old and young, high and low, joined in the time-destroying pastime. As Cowper says in the *Task* :

> " E'en misses, at whose age their mothers wore
> The backstring and the bib, assume the dress
> Of womanhood, fit pupils in the school
> Of card-devoted Time, and night by night,
> Plac'd at some vacant corner of the board,
> Learn ev'ry trick, and soon play all the game."

Moralists and poets of all ages have alike agreed in censuring this fatal devotion to gambling. The wise though gruff old Doctor Johnson says, in the tenth number of the *Rambler :* " My business has been to view, as opportunity was offered, every place in which mankind was to

* See p. 182 *antè*.

be seen; but at card-tables, however brilliant, I have always thought my visit lost; for I could know nothing of the company but their clothes and their faces."

Yet Dr. Johnson in private life spoke differently. He had never learnt to play; but one day, expressing his regret about not knowing any game, he gave as the reason for his regret: "It is very useful in life; it generates kindness, and consolidates society." Such are the inconsistencies sometimes noticeable in eminent men!

We may conclude this record of English card-playing with some judicious observations of the gentle Southey, who was a rank Tory, and characteristically summarized the whole matter in a few pithy sentences.

"It is quite right," he remarks, "that there should be a heavy duty on cards; not only on moral grounds; not only because they act on a social party like a torpedo, silencing the merry voice, and numbing the play of the features; not only to still the hunger of the public purse, which, reversing the quality of Fortunatus's, is always empty, however much you may put into it; but also because every pack of cards is a malicious libel upon courts, and on the world, seeing that the trumpery with number one at the head is the best part of them, and that it gives kings and queens no other companions than knaves."

John Locke adhered to his opposition to cards; in his Treatise on Education, he says: "As to cards and dice, I think the safest and best way is never to learn any play upon them, and so to be incapacitated for those dangerous temptations and encroaching wasters of useful time."

"Who shall decide when doctors disagree?"

VIII.

CARD NOTABILIA IN OUR OWN DAY.

WHEN Horace Walpole, in 1792, became the Earl
of Orford, Mrs. Epictetus Carter was delighted,
and proposed to the new peer that he should get
an Act of Parliament to put down pharao. He
somewhere exclaims: "As if I could make Acts
of Parliament! and could I, it would be very consistent in me, too, who for some years played more
at pharao than anybody!"

What Horace Walpole confessed himself unable
to do, time has effected, so far as England is concerned, in a most signal manner. Within the
last reign gambling became an inexcusable folly,
punishable both by social enactments and legal
penalties. Yet, lingering on in a modified

manner, we may here and there see a little knot of players who play for play's sake; but, as a rule, Lord Herbert's advice has been followed, to "play not for gain but sport:"

"—— who plays for more
Than he can lose with pleasure, stakes his heart,
Perhaps his wife's too, and whom she hath bore."

The world has at length agreed with old Burton, that "sports and gaming, whether pursued from a desire of gain, or love of pleasure, are as ruinous to the temper and disposition of the party addicted to them, as they are to his fame and fortune." No one can deny the truth of Lavater's observation, that "it is possible that a wise and good man may be prevailed on to game; but it is impossible that a professed gamester should be a wise and good man."

To look back at the early part of our century, and see how dire was the final madness for gambling; to see how the "hells" of St. James's-street and Jermyn-street drew crowds to destruction and death, is terrible indeed. The evil had risen to its zenith in the days of the Prince Regent, and the social condition of the country was threatened with a lasting disease. A reaction then fortunately set in. Books exposing the horrors of gaming became frequent, such as the *Greeks*, the *Pigeons*, and the *Gaming Calendar*. In these works were registered the names and careers of many of these desperate and deluded gamblers; and it would seem almost incredible to think that such a state of society should have existed so near our time. Fox, Sheridan, Canning, and all the most eminent men of the day, followed in the footsteps of the prince's crew; and even the Church, custodian as it is of public morality, was powerless to discourage and interfere. Clergymen are well known as good and steady whist-players; and much as cards have been blamed by many, others have not scrupled to commend them. Archdeacon Butler, in a sermon on Christian Liberty, preached before the Duke of Gloucester and the University of Cambridge, on the occasion of the duke's installation as chancellor, June the thirtieth, 1811, referred to the "harmless mirth and innocent amusements of society;" and, in a note upon this point, the archdeacon quoted a passage from the eminent and pious Jeremy Taylor, who says, "That cards, &c., are of themselves lawful, I do not know any reason to doubt. He can never be suspected, in any criminal sense, to tempt the Divine Providence, who, by contingent things, recreates his labour. As for the evil appendages, they are all separable from these games." Arch-deacon Butler remarks upon this : " Such are the sentiments of one of the most truly pious and most profoundly learned prelates that ever adorned any age or country; nor do I think that the most rigid of our disciplinarians can produce the authority of a wiser or a better man than Bishop Jeremy Taylor."

No history of card-playing would be complete without the well known fragment of popular ingenuity called "*Cards Spiritualized; or, the Soldier's Almanac, Bible, and Prayer Book,*" which, in the form of a half-penny broad-sheet, is still circulated among the poorer classes of our population.

"RICHARD MIDDLETON, a soldier, attending divine ser-vice, with the rest of the regiment at a church in Glasgow, instead of pulling out a Bible, like his brother soldiers, to find the parson's text, spread a pack of cards before him. This singular behaviour did not long pass unnoticed, both by the clergyman and the serjeant of the company to which he belonged; the latter in particular requested him to put up the cards, and on his refusal, conducted him after church before the Mayor, to whom he preferred a formal complaint of Richard's indecent behaviour during divine service. 'Well, soldier!' (said the Mayor) 'what excuse have you for this strange scandalous behaviour? If you can make any apology, or assign any reason for it, it's well; if you cannot, assure yourself that I will cause you, without delay, to be severely punished for it.' 'Since your honour is so good,' replied Richard, 'I will inform you. I have been eight days on march, with a bare allowance of sixpence a day, which your honour will surely allow is hardly sufficient to maintain a man in meat, drink, washing, and other necessaries that consequently he may want, without a Bible, Prayer Book, or any other good book.' On saying this, Richard drew out his pack of cards, and presenting one of the aces to the Mayor, continued his address to the magistrate as follows :

" ' When I see an Ace, may it please your honour, it reminds me that there is only one God ; and when I look upon a Two or a Three, the former puts me in mind of the Father and Son, and the latter of the Father, Son, and Holy Ghost. A Four calls for remembrance the Four Evangelists, Matthew, Mark, Luke, and John. A Five, the five wise Virgins who were ordered to trim their lamps; there were ten, indeed, but five, your worship may remember, were wise, and five were foolish. A Six, that in six days God created heaven and earth. A Seven, that on the seventh day he rested from all that he had made. An Eight, of the eight righteous persons preserved from the deluge: viz., Noah and his wife, with his three sons and their wives. A Nine, of the nine lepers cleansed by our Saviour; there were ten, but one only returned to offer his tribute of thanks. And a Ten, of the ten commandments that God gave Moses on Mount Sinai, on the two tables of stone.' He took the Knave and put it aside. ' When I see the Queen, it puts me in mind of the Queen of Sheba, who came from the furthermost parts of the world to hear the wisdom of Solomon, for she was as wise a woman as he a man, for she brought fifty boys and fifty girls, all clothed in girls' apparel to shew before King Solomon, for him to test which were boys and which were girls,—but he could not until he called for water to wash themselves; the girls washed up to their elbows, and the boys only up to the wrists of their hands, so King Solomon told by that. And when I see the King, it puts me in mind of the Great King of Heaven and Earth, which is God Almighty ; and likewise his Majesty King George the Fourth, to pray for him.' ' Well,' said the Mayor, ' you have given a good description of all the cards except one, which is lacking.' ' Which is that ?' said the soldier. ' The Knave,' said the Mayor.

" ' If your honour will not be angry with me,' returned

Richard, 'I can give you the same satisfaction on that as any in the pack?' 'No,' said the Mayor. 'Well,' returned the soldier, 'the greatest knave that I know is the serjeant who brought me before you.' 'I don't know,' replied the Mayor, 'whether he be the greatest knave or no; but I am sure he is the greatest fool.'

"The soldier then continued as follows: 'When I count the number of dots in a pack of cards, there are 365,—so many days as there are in a year. When I count how many cards are in a pack, I find there are 52,—so many weeks are there in a year. When I reckon how many tricks are won by a pack, I find there are 13,—so many months are there in a year. So that this pack of cards is both Bible, Almanack, and Prayer Book to me.'

"The Mayor called his servants, ordered them to entertain the soldier well, gave him a piece of money, and said he was the cleverest fellow he ever heard in his life."

This amusing sketch, in the copy from which it is transcribed, is surrounded by rude cuts of a suit of cards, in black, and was printed at Newcastle.

The Chevalier de Chatelaine, well known for his humorous French versions of English poets, some two years since, privately printed a versified account of this story; but he was perhaps unaware that he had been preceded in his own language many years before in an *Anecdote curieuse et interessante, sous le nom de Louis Bras-de-fer*, printed at Brussels in 1778; and also at Paris, in 1809, a similar flying sheet appeared. Mlle. Lenormand also published it in her *Souvenirs Prophétiques*.

In another chap-book, entitled *A new Game of Cards, between a Nobleman in London and one of his Servants*, we find a variation of this story. The servant, denounced as a gambler, denies the charge; a pack of cards is found in his pocket, and he defends himself similarly by stratagem. He is reminded of his allegiance by the King and Queen; the Ten is the ten commandments; Nine refers to the nine muses; the Eight, of the eight altitudes, and the eight saved in the ark; the Seven, of the seven wonders of the world, and the seven planets; the Six, of the six petitions in the Lord's Prayer; the Five, of the five senses; the Four, of the four seasons; the Three, of the three graces, and the three days and nights Jonah was in the whale's belly; the Two, of the two Testaments, and the two contrary principles, virtue and vice; and the Ace, of the worship of the One God. The knave is the person who informed against him.

There are several synonyms of this story, but it is scarcely necessary, from their obvious sameness, to quote them.

Great as has been the worship offered by enthusiastic and infatuated gamblers to playing-cards; as there is always a "deep below a deep;" so, in this particular, a singular instance of card-

idolatry exists, though perhaps in an unexpected
quarter. The learned Orientalist, Dr. Sprenger,
whose erudite and interesting work on Mohammed
is now in course of issue, supplies us with the
incident, new in every way. Sprenger is describing and commenting on the idols worshiped by
the Arabs anterior to the promulgation of Islam,
and he continues thus :*

" I spent the summer of 1850 in the Tibetan district of
Kanaur, on the other side of the first snowy range of the
Himalayas ; and, although the inhabitants are denominationally
Buddhists, their worship reminded me very forcibly of what I
had read and thought upon the religion of the ancient Arabs.
Every village possesses one or more idols, having the most
fantastic shapes. The temple either stands in the village, or in
the most beautiful situation of the neighbourhood, and I was
usually permitted to pitch my tent beside it. Every object of
colour and interest which the inhabitants discover is placed in
it. Round about the building there are generally set up a
multitude of the antlers of rock-deer (*cerambyx cervicornis*),
and other animals of those magnificent mountain ranges. Over
the doorway of the temple of Sunnam (in Gerard's map,
Soognum) were pasted gilt show cards of English shirting
pieces, and in the temple I found *a couple of old playing-cards*
stuck up. Some German antiquary may, at a future time,
find in this an opportunity for imaginative research, as to how
the *knave of hearts* or the *ace of acorns* arrived at divine honours,
as also into the possible dissemination of the worship of these
two divinities, and as to whether its origin may not be traced
to Tibet."

No apology is needed for the length of this

* *Das Leben und die Lehre des Mohammad*, vol. ii., pp. 13 sq.
Berlin, 1862.

citation, as it affords us a lively and forcible picture of perhaps the only temple in the East where advertising and playing-cards have alike been deified. In the West, both of these have long since received the eager worship of the discerning multitude ; and it is satisfactory to perceive that, slowly but surely, the civilization of Europe, as evinced in the idolatry of advertising and gambling, is penetrating to the remote corners of the globe. The inhabitants of Sunnam are highly to be praised ; and it might be advisable to encourage such devotion by sending out a cargo of Messrs. Moses's show cards, and a few copies of such notions as insurance-office placards, pill and potion wrappers, and the like.

While this rage for play is greatly to be condemned, there is no reason, however, why the diversion of cards should ever cease to exist. The misuse of the amusement is no reason for its extinction. Who can look upon a party of old ladies (male and female) engaged in their evening game without a feeling of satisfaction, that they have at least one enjoyment left, more dignified and less harmful than scandal ? Stout old Sarah Battle, beautifully depicted by that gentlest of essayists, Charles Lamb, has a right to her tussle at whist, and ought not to be blamed

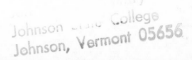
Johnson State College
Johnson, Vermont 05656

for insisting on her rights, and "sticking out" for her points like a trump. He would, indeed, be an ignoble personage who would stand in the way of the whist-player of mature age. Talleyrand, whose own devotion to whist was extraordinary, remarked of some one who confessed his ignorance of it, that his want of knowledge was preparing for him a miserable old age. Even Southey, with whose opinion we concluded our last chapter, invented a game of cards. Here it is for whoso desires to learn and play it.

"Last night, in bed, before I could fall asleep, my head ran upon cards, at which I had been compelled to play in the evening, and I thought thus of making a new pack.

"Leave out the eights, nines, and tens, as at quadrille.

"In their place substitute another suit, ten in number like the rest, blue in colour, and in name *balls*. The pack then consists of fifty. Add two figured personages to make up the number—the emperor and the pope.

"Play as at whist. Balls take all other suits except trumps, which take balls. The emperor and the pope are superior to all other cards, and may either be made equal and so capable of tying each other, and so neutralizing the trick, or to preponderate according to the colour of the trump,—the emperor if red, the pope if black; and, belonging to no suit, they may be played upon any. If either be turned up, the dealer counts one, and balls remain the only trumps.

"The emperor and pope, being led, command trumps, but not each other. Trumps, also, in default of trumps, command balls. If the emperor and pope tie each other, the tier has the lead."[*]

There is a certain similarity between this imagined game of Southey's, and the game already mentioned in a former chapter, in which the extra stakes of "swabbers" occurs. Indeed, it seems a compound between Whist and Tarocchi.

At the present day it is satisfactory to observe the general moderation existing among players—the fierce and furious gamblers are few and despised—and even at the clubs, where play still holds its undisputed sway, a perceptible improvement is evident. There are, however, peculiarities in club-players worthy of notice. One of these consists in the fact of their invariably preferring to play with cards of the same colour and fashion.

[*] Southey's *Common Place Book*, Fourth Series, p. 517. Aug. 10, 1814.

One of the large card-makers in London told the writer, that many years ago, his brother, the head of the firm at that time, introduced a scarcely perceptible modification in the colour of the knave's garter. Cards were supplied, as usual, to the customers; but very soon the steward of one of the considerable clubs came rushing down in a great hurry to the shop. "The Committee can't think what you have been doing to the cards! All the members are complaining that they keep losing! What have you done?" At first the card-maker said, "Done? why nothing!" not thinking the trifling change of any importance; but on further inquiry it was found that the indescribable something the clubbists had detected, confused them, and he was obliged to take back all his cards, and supply those of the former old fashioned sort. Such is the influence of a trifle!

Since that time, however, many alterations have been introduced, and not a few improvements. Messrs. Reynolds and Sons have patented a card, the corners of which are rounded off, thus preventing the dog's-earing sometimes seen in much-used packs. These packs are very handsome, and the public have welcomed them with great satisfaction.

Another useful improvement recently brought before the public, consists in cards, the spots on which are slightly raised, so that a blind person can discover his cards by the touch. These raised cards were originally devised for a member of the royal family, who had unfortunately become blind: they are also made by Messrs. Reynolds, but only to order.

A newspaper correspondent, a short time since, described an odd pack as appearing in New York.

" A new pack of playing cards has been invented; it is called the 'America.' They are sold by A. Dougherty, 26, Beekman-street. The heads of the four kings are Lincoln, Buchanan, Pierce, and Fillmore (all alive!). The heads of the queens are the Secretary of the Navy, General Dix, and two other old women of note. For the four knaves we have Mayor Opdyke and the other prominent shoddy contractors."— Manhattan's letter in the *Evening Standard* of Saturday, November 14, 1863.

As but little allusion has been made to card-playing in America in its proper place, we take this opportunity of recording that the American game of Poker is our old English "Post and Paire." The game of Euchre, Euka, or Youka (for it is variously spelt), largely played by the rowdies, is simply *Ecarté*. The game known as Forty-fives, played in Ireland, and by the Celto-Americans, is the old game of Maw.

We have now arrived at the close of this portion of our subject, and in the next part have to draw the attention of the reader to a very different series of facts and speculations— the subject of fortune-telling by cards in various ways.

End of Part II.

PART THE THIRD.

FORTUNE-TELLING, CONJURING, AND CARD-SHARPING.

I.

FORTUNE-TELLING.

EARLY HISTORICAL CARTOMANCY—PHILIPPE LE BON—MARCO-
LINI—IL BAGATELLO—GALASSO—BACON—CUFFE—LENT-
HALL'S FORTUNE-TELLING CARDS—METHODS OF USE—
THE SYBIL'S LEAVES.

THE art of cartomancy, or divination by playing cards, dates from an early period of their
strange history. There is so great a faculty of
wonder in the uneducated—so infinite a longing
for some knowledge of the events to come—that
high and low alike sought oracular responses
from the adepts in the art, and rejoiced greatly if
the replies were only vague enough to give countenance to the hopes they entertained.

Kings did not disdain to consult old women
as to the mysteries of the future; and a picture

has been engraved in the *Magasin Pittoresque*,* in which Philip the good is represented as consulting a woman who is revealing the future by the means of cards. This picture has been ascribed to Van Eyck, though it is certain that he was not the artist. The costume is that of the reign of Charles VIII., and therefore between 1483 and 1498. Philippe le Bon, Duke of Burgundy, died in 1467, and John Van Eyck had passed away some twenty years before, so that at best it can only be ascribed to his school. Proof, at any rate, is thus furnished of the use of cards in Europe, for fortune-telling purposes, before the close of the fifteenth century.

The earliest book expressly treating of car-tomancy would seem to be *Le Sorti*, by Francesco Marcolini, who printed it at Venice in 1540. It may however be doubted whether this author was seriously inculcating an art by which the veil of the future was to be lifted : his own term for his system is "*piacevole inventione*,"—that is, pleasant invention. The cards directed by him to be used were the king, knight, knave, ten, nine eight, seven, deuce, and ace of *deniers* or money. His book contains a number of woodcuts, some of which are little more than an inch long.

* 1842, p. 324.

Between the time of the appearance of Marcolini's work and the beginning of the seventeenth century, only two works of any importance seem to have appeared, both apparently by professional jugglers. The first of these was by Francesco di Milano, " *nominato in tutto il mondo il Bagaletto* " (named throughout the world the conjuror), published about 1550, and professing to instruct in the art of foretelling the future. The other was by Horatio Galesso, and taught " admirable games of cards and memory," issued at Venice in 1593. However, fortune-telling proper seems here to have been confused with games of skill in various ways. It is singular that the great Francis Bacon, when a boy, had his attention roused by observing the tricks of a juggler at cards ; and his biographer, Basil Montagu, thinks it not improbable that to this fact we owe the subsequent researches which the philosopher instituted into the nature of the imagination.*

A remarkable story is told by Rowland, in his *Judicial Astrology Condemned*, of Henry Cuffe, the celebrated Greek scholar, and secretary of the unfortunate Earl of Essex. Twenty years

* *Life of Lord Bacon*, p. 5. See Bacon's own account in his *Sylva*, p. 245.

before his death, it happened that Cuffe, one day, calling at a friend's house, accidentally, found a cartomancer exercising his mysterious art, and severely ridiculed such an absurd practice. The fortune-teller, however, speaking up in defence of his profession, dared Cuffe to draw three cards from the pack. He did so. The first card represented himself a prisoner, surrounded by men bearing bills and halberts; the second, he was before a court of justice, apparently undergoing a trial; and in the third, he saw a place of execution. Cuffe laughed at the trick, but long after, when, for complicity in the treason of Robert, Earl of Essex, he was taken prisoner, tried, and brought to the gallows at Tyburn, he remembered and declared the prediction to his friends. It is evident that the cards used by the cartomancist on this occasion were tarots. The first drawn, was in all probability an atout, called the Traitor, which in some old Italian packs held the place of the Devil; the second could be no other than Justice; and the third would be sufficiently shadowed forth by the Hanged Man. The Traitor, *Il Traditor*, is mentioned in an ancient Italian poem, printed in 1550, and entitled *Invettina contra il Gioco de Tarocco*. The passage may be translated thus:—

Again, what signifies the female Pope,
The Chariot, the Traitor, the Wheel, the Fool;
The Star, the Sun, the Moon, and Strength,
And Death, and Hell, and all the rest
Of these strange cards?

A still darker story, of the same period, is told in allusion to the death of Queen Elizabeth. Two ladies waiting on the Queen, in her chamber, discovered, in the bottom of her chair, a queen of hearts, with a nail of iron struck through the forehead, which they durst not pull out; remembering that the like thing was reported to be used to others for witch-craft.

But our limits will not permit us to give a great space to the early history of cartomancy, therefore we shall content ourselves with a brief description of an early English pack of semi-astrological fortune-telling cards already referred to in a former chapter.* As the most intelligible method of using them, we transcribe the directions of the publisher.

"THE USE OF THE CARDS.

" WHEN any person is desirous to try their fortune, let them go to one of the four Kings, and chuse what question they please, and carry in their mind, the Number and words set down before the question, and let them go to that sphere marked with the same word and number—then let them draw a card after they have been shuffled and remember the number drawn—the

* See Part I., chap. ii., p. 209.

knave standing for eleven, the queen for twelve, and the king for thirteen, then look in the lower ring of the sphere for the same number you have drawn, and above that number you will find a word and number. Then go to the queens and knaves, for that Book under which you will find the same word and number set down, look into that Book and it shall send you to that Card that hath the very same word and number. Then look on the line that answers that number drawn, and you shall read your answer.

"Example. Suppose you take the question which demands whether the party is beloved or not : over that question you will find the letter or word A and figure 1, which signifies that you must goe to that sphere marked with the same letter A and figure 1. Then lay that sphere on the table. Then draw any Card out of the pack after they are well shuffled, observe the number which that Card bears. Let us suppose nine of clubs, then look for figure 9 in the lower ring of the sphere, and above that number in the two other rings you will find '*falls* 29,' then look among the books supported by the queens and knaves for that which is denoted by the same word and number, which you will find in Hewsen the knave of Clubs— look in that Book in which you will find Europea and number 50 which shows that you must go to the Sybile Europea at number 50, then read that line marked with the same number with the Card you draw, which was supposed the nine of Clubs and their (*sic*) you will find your answer, thus : *The Stars foretell, they love you well*."

This pack of cards belongs to a period as already stated, shortly succeeding the era of the Restoration : and it is singular that the person selling them should bear the name of the famous speaker, Lenthall, of whom he said he was a relative.

We can say but little for the intellectual resources of the time, if these exceedingly dull cards proved laughter-moving to the gay ladies of the court of Charles the Second. It is, however, worth while noting down for the reader's edification a few of the odd collocations found in the names at the head of this pack. In the suit of hearts, we find Hermes Trismegistus, leading the van with St. Shiptonica (probably a relative of Old Mother Shipton), Averoes, Zoroaster, Jamblicus, Friar Bacon, Cupid (!), Semiramis, and Herod,—the last three being knave, queen, and king. Spades is headed by Ptolomye, followed by Copernicus, Tycho Brahe, Cornelius Agrippa, Dr. Dee, Wat Tyler (knave), Dido (queen), and Holophernes (king).

Diamonds begin with Albumezar, succeeded by Nostradamus, Cardan, Sosipater, Erra Pater, Mahomett (knave), Proserpina (queen), and Nimrod (king). Finally, Clubs is represented by Merlin, Dr. Faustus, Anaximander, Apollonius, Artemdiorus, Colonel Hewson the Cobbler (Cromwellian parliamentary knave), Clytemnestra and Pharaoh, as queen and king. We have omitted the names of the saints, as they are all imaginary, and imagined in the dreariest way—St. Shiptonica being the only name suggesting any association worth remembering.

John Lenthall's cards, however, were not the only fortune-telling oracles extant at the time of Charles. In 1663, there was published a poor black letter book in sixteens, entitled a *Merry Conceited Fortune Teller*.* Those who have been in the habit of "gambling" among what may be called stifled literature, will readily appreciate the dreariness with which we approach any work of that era, bearing on the title page the fatal word "merry." "A right merrie jest" makes us only more despondent.

Many systems of fortune-telling cards have been published from time to time, but none approaching in complexity and beauty of design the ancient Tarot cards, specimens of which are given on plates XLVI. and XLVII. Nevertheless, we must not, before ending this historical sketch of fortune-telling cards, omit to notice a pack, now somewhat rare, issued a good many years since, and called *The Sybil's Leaves, or a Peep into Futurity*. It was published by Ackermann of the Strand, and consisted of sixty lithographic verses on as many cards, in a case bearing an engraved representation of a party in high humour consulting the cards. Of these, thirty bear inscriptions designed for ladies, and thirty for gentlemen :

* The Press-mark at the British Museum is 12,316.

a lady is to hold the gentleman's pack, and *vice versa*. The consultant draws a card containing the "infallible" prediction. This, in point of fact, was nothing but another form of the cards we have just described.

In the olden time most serious subjects were accompanied by burlesques or comic representations. Death had his dance; and the sacred mysteries of the Old and New Testament were exhibited in dramas, which must have been as mirth-provoking as our modern pantomimes and farces. It is not strange, therefore, to find that the ingenuity of mankind should have been exerted to produce comic fortune-telling cards. It will be sufficient, bearing in mind that comicality of a more or less pungent nature is necessarily a "badge of all their tribe," to cite two instances of such cards, before we pass on to the more delicate task of teaching young ladies how to tell their own fortunes.

As polite Englishmen, we will give the *pas* to a foreign country, and without further preface introduce the reader to a humorous German pack in our possession. Humour from Germany is somewhat of the cumbrous, yet it must be admitted that the dreamy artists of that happy land have done their best.

The pack consists of thirty-two cards, and each represents some phase of fun according to "Deutschland." In the first card we behold King Gambrinus, the jolly monarch of a "schoppe Bairisch," or a measure of sour Bavarian beer. Tendering it to others he seems, with hospitable intentions, not disposed to drink before his guest the consultant, and he represents the king of diamonds. The next card displays a very unhappy set of people in a sailing boat, determined not to turn their faces, but resolved to represent the seven of spades. A knock-kneed monarch succeeds; unlike the present reigning sovereign of Prussia, he is the king of hearts, which is hoisted as a target behind him. Another card represents a balloon. The ace of spades alludes to a locality which Herr Von Bismarck Schönhausen will ever remember with feelings of political satisfaction. On the tenth card Death is represented as tendering (sad consolation!) a "stange" (rod) of *weissbier* to an individual on the verge of leaving this, for a better world. As to card the twelfth, the minute book which accompanies the pack, attempts a trifle of satire truly Teutonic. "The imprisoned bird holds good faith to thee only so long as it is in the cage. Leave him free to go, and he will flit to others with his songs. The truth of this card," concludes the profound cartomancer, "lies in the warning, not to be imprudent in what you do with—several species of birds."

Card fourteen represents a sensitive German lady—on the verge of romance, according to the Countess Ida Hahn Hahn—confessing the sins she might have committed, to a fox with a high coat collar, who apparently knows all about them. The attitude of the lady, and the rectitude of the Father Confessor are full of spirit As to number nineteen, we only regret that we are unable to reproduce it for our readers. Those who judge of the German female character by the meek pictures displayed to us by poets, dramatists, and romancists, would be somewhat astonished by this portrait of a high-stepping lady (queen of clubs) in a homely dress and short petticoats, a broom over the right shoulder, and a toasting fork of a formidable kind in the left hand, crowned,—as all regal personages should be,—but like a good but recalcitrant housewife, crowned with a saucepan, and on her face—ruddy as the orient sky when the sun approaches the dawn—*such a sneer!* Away with the romantic ideas about meek German maidens, after such a sample!

Turn we from this card rather to the thirtieth in the series, which represents a lady (one who "has been born,") nurturing with tender hands and watering-pot the gentle musings of her affections, springing in the form of blossoms,—in number, two; in shape, a Prussian and an Austrian officer. Undecided are the thoughts upon her brow; she knows not which to choose, being in the position of Captain Macheath, able to be happy with either, embarrassed by the presence of both.

It is scarcely necessary to say that German "proclivities" to fun induce them as a matter of course to "lug in" the sun and moon; no great effects, however in this instance. The minute instruction book, alluded to before, informs us that card thirty-three (for some numbers are omitted), which portrays a harlequin and king of clubs is the many hued chameleon of the modern world—the philanthropist, the disinterested patriot, the noble benefactor to his species, the unselfish administrator of his time and his advice to others, the statesman, the pension dispenser and holder,—in fact, the diplomatist. Holding in his hand a key, he skips about with equanimity; the fool's bauble in his other hand, smiling with self-gratulation that his shifty hands have retained it so long. We can well trace in the bubbling and heavy jests of Germany some attempt at satirizing the rulers they have lived beneath so long. Indeed the last card in the series displays, as the ultimatum of all gratifications in Teutonic existence, the right to wear epaulettes and the insignia of a not very illustrious order.

A highly amusing pack of English cards of a comic kind was published a few months since by Messrs. Reynolds, of whose other improvements we have spoken in a previous chapter. The writer was informed by the firm, that on its suggestion to them they were half afraid and half ashamed of issuing the pack. But that portion of the public willing harmlessly to be amused, eagerly availed themselves of these new comic fortune-telling cards, and the firm speedily disposed of a large impression. Their price is so moderate, and the fun so genial and unexceptionable, that we take a pleasure in recommending them as vehicles of innocent amusement to all who like a hearty laugh.

We must, however, abandon the humorous for the descriptive portion of our subject. We have yet to say a little about modern fortune-telling by cards, on either side of the channel.

The stormy period of the first Consulship of Napoleon and that of the Empire which followed it, was especially characterized by cartomantic practices in France. At this time, there lived in Paris a famous woman, whose renown as a prophetess will probably not soon pass away. This person was Mlle. Lenormand, whose influence with the empress Josephine, and even Napoleon himself, was said to be considerable.

Whether we are to give any credence to the general predictions made by her, is doubtful; yet it cannot but be conceded that some of her prophecies are couched in such plain and straightforward language, that they seem unmistakeable. In a work published by her in 1820, after a prediction relating to Napoleon the First, we find the words: "And the nephew will accomplish that which the uncle was unable to perform."* If we regard the astonishing rise of the present emperor, we cannot but be struck with the truth of the prediction. It is more than suspected that Napoleon III. is himself a believer in such matters, as was his renowned uncle.

It is unquestionable that Mlle. Lenormand for more than half a century was a respected and accredited prophetess. Even from the early age

* "*Et fera le neveu ce que l'oncle n'avait pu faire.*"

of seven, she was in the habit of foretelling future events. She was brought up in the Benedictine abbey of Alençon, and she made many predictions in 1779 respecting the events about to happen to that place, which were subsequently verified.

In person she was stout and tall, but intolerably ugly; in speech she was emphatic and commanding, fond of metaphor : but in her writings she was turged and dull. In the memoirs of the empress,* there is preserved a short correspondence between Josephine and the sybil, in which the empress compliments the cartomancer, and begs an explanation of an enigmatical note found under her dinner napkin, as follows :

"Who tempts the Lord will become himself subject to temptation. The bow over bent will break in the hands of the hunter. Ice is no better for the game than fire. Let him beware of 23 and 31, it is a series of misfortune. Happy his companion should she exchange seven pebbles for three branches of fern and straw. Thus saith the prophet."

On receiving this, Mlle. Lenormand explained it somewhat haughtily to refer to an expedition which the emperor was warned thereby not to commence without due preparation. The hunter was Napoleon. Syria and Holland were alluded to as fire and ice. She declined with contempt

* _Mémoires sur l'imperatrice_, 1828, vol. ii., p. 355.

to explain the numbers, adding, "Cagliostro himself would have offered no solution. The *star* of the emperor, or rather his genius, must divine this." The seven pebbles allude to the palace of stone, and the fern and straw was meant to indicate that poverty was preferable to the greatness enjoyed by Josephine.

Mlle. Lenormand, whose character was vain and arrogant, positively attended the congress of Aix-la-Chapelle, deeming her presence there of the utmost importance. She actually moved all her goods to Aix, to the infinite disarrangement of the custom-house officers, who were thus forced to pay her some attention. On her return, she actually published her impressions on the political crisis, and headed them with a vignette picture, on which she was represented as the centre of the group of sovereigns and powers, who were tremblingly listening to her oracular utterances !

A couple of anecdotes about Marianne Lenormand will fitly dismiss her. On one occasion, Joachim Murat, when king of Naples, went to consult her. She received him with her usual haughtiness, and the cards were speedily produced. He cut them. The king of diamonds appeared. In some systems, this card is considered to be of the utmost ill-fortune, and is called the *Grand*

Pendu, or the great hanged person. Mlle. Lenormand told him that prosperous as he might then be, an execution awaited him. He laid ten napoleons on the table, and begged for another trial, The sybil granted it, and he again cut the king of diamonds. Once more he laid a similar sum on the table, and once more the king of diamonds was turned up. The king then drew forth fifty napoleons, and with pitiless iteration, the fatal card again appeared. He then offered the prophetess one hundred napoleons for a final chance ; but she angrily threw the cards at his head, telling him to begone, turning him out with the consolation that his fate was the gallows or the musket-shot. All persons know that Murat met his fate by military execution in Calabria, in 1816.

But Mlle. Lenormand sometimes predicted good as well as evil fortune. In the life of Bernadotte, the king of Sweden, an anecdote is told which unquestionably refers to the sybil of the Rue de Tournon.

One of Bernadotte's *aide-de-camps*, Gerard, afterwards marshal of France, was entertaining his chief with anecdotes of this proficiency of the cartomancer, and invited Bernadotte to accompany him to her house. This was in January, 1804. The latter consented, and away they went. The colonel presented his general as a rich merchant, who was anxious to learn the result of certain commercial speculations that he was about to commence in different parts of Germany. "Sir," replied the prophetess, "you are no merchant, but an officer, and an officer of very high rank." She was assured that she was wrong; at which she shook her head and continued, "Well, sir, if you go into commercial speculations you will be unsuccessful and forced to re-enter the career pointed out by destiny." She again examined the cards, and pursued her discourse :—" Sir, not only are you of high military rank, but you are or will be related to the emperor."   "What emperor?" cried Bernadotte and Gerard.   "I mean the first consul, but you will soon see him emperor." Then with her fingers slowly tracing the mystic signs, she exclaimed in a solemn and inspired tone, "Yes! he will be emperor; but here are some clouds dividing you." Bernadotte looked significantly at Gerard.   The sybil went on :— "There is no separation however; you are attached to him—Ah! how his star is rising!" She stopped a moment, as if in surprise.   "Sir," she added, "be careful not to break with him; he will be very powerful; the world will be at his feet; and you, you, far away from him, will be a *king*. Yes," she repeated, "yes, you will be a *king*." She said no more. "Good," said Gerard, "what follows." "I can see no more, and can add nothing."*

The mode of fortune-telling used by the English "card-cutters," as they are familiarly termed, has now to be described. A man of very fair complexion is represented by the King of diamonds; a woman by the queen of the same suit. Persons of less fair complexion, according to sex, by the king and queen of hearts. A man and woman of very dark complexion, by the king and queen of spades; while those not quite so dark are represented by clubs. If a married woman consults the cards, the king of her own colour represents her husband, whether he be fair or dark, and *vice versa* if the cards be consulted by a married man. Lovers, whether in *esse* or *posse*, are always represented by cards of their peculiar colours; and all cards when representing persons, lose their normal significations. There are exceptions, however, to all general rules. A widow, no matter how fair she may be, can be represented only by the queen of spades; while a

* Sarran's *Histoire de Charles Jean XIV.*, 1845. Vol. i., p. 50.

man wearing uniform, even, if a negro cymbal-player in a regimental band, may be represented by the king of diamonds—the dress of a police-man is not considered as uniform. The ace of hearts denotes the house of the person consulting the decrees of fate. The ace of clubs, a letter. The ace of diamonds, a wedding ring. The ace of spades, sickness and death. The knave of diamonds is a selfish and deceitful friend. The knave of hearts, an unselfish sincere friend. The knave of spades is a lawyer, a person to be avoided. The knave of clubs is a sincere friend, but of very touchy temper. In all instances, however, the knaves signify the thoughts of their respective kings and queens; and, consequently, the thoughts of the persons whom those kings and queens represent, in accordance with their complexion; and when doing so, lose their normal signification. Generally speaking, diamonds and hearts are more fortunate than spades and clubs. Several diamonds coming together, signify the receipt of money; several hearts denote love. A concourse of clubs foretells drunkenness and debauchery, with their consequent ill-health; and a number of spades together, indicate disappointment, with its accompanying vexation.

The kings and queens, besides representing

persons, according to colour, have private significations of their own, that may be of interest to the physiognomist. Thus, the king of diamonds is quick to anger, but easily appeased; while the queen is fond of gaiety, and of rather a coquettish disposition. The king of hearts is slow to anger, but when put in a passion, is appeased with great difficulty; he is good-natured, but particularly obstinate; his queen, however, is a model of sincere affection, devotion, and prudence. The king of spades is so ambitious, that in matters of either love or business, he is much less scrupulous than he ought to be; while his queen, is a person not to be provoked with impunity, never forgetting an injury, and having a considerable spice of malice in her composition. The king and queen of clubs are everything that can be desired; he is honourable, true, and affectionate; she is agreeable, genteel, and witty.

The interpretations of the minor cards are as follows:—

DIAMONDS.

Ten.   Wealth.   Honourable success in business.
Nine.   A roving disposition, combined with successful adventure in foreign lands.
Eight. A happy marriage, though perhaps late in life.
Seven. Satire.   Scandal.

Five.   Unexpected, though generally good, news.

Four.   An unfaithful friend. A secret betrayed.

Trey.   Domestic quarrels, trouble, unhappiness.

Deuce. A clandestine engagement. A card of caution.

HEARTS.

Ten.   Health and happiness, with many children.

Nine.   Wealth, and good position in society.

Eight. Fine clothes. Mixing in good society. Invitations to
          balls, theatres, parties.

Seven. Good friends.

Six.   Honourable courtship.

Five.   A present.

Four.   Domestic troubles caused by jealousy.

Trey.   Poverty, shame, and sorrow, the result of imprudence.
          A card of caution.

Deuce. Success in life, and a happy marriage attained by virtu-
          ous discretion.

SPADES.

Ten.   Disgrace, crime, imprisonment. Death on the scaffold.
          A card of caution.

Nine.   Grief, ruin, sickness, death.

Eight. Great danger from imprudence. A card of caution.

Seven. Unexpected poverty, through the death of a relative.

Six.   A child. To the unmarried, a card of caution.

Five.   Great danger from giving way to bad temper. A card
          of caution.

Four.   Sickness.

Trey.   Tears. A journey by land.

Deuce. A removal.

Six.   Early marriage, succeeded by widowhood.

CLUBS.

Ten.   Unexpected wealth, through the death of a relative.

Nine.   Danger through drunkenness. A card of caution.

Eight.   Danger from covetousness. A card of caution.

Seven.   A prison. Danger from the opposite sex. A card of caution.

Six.   Competence by honourable industry.

Five.   A happy, though not wealthy marriage.

Four.   Misfortunes through caprice or inconstancy. A card of caution.

Trey.   Quarrels. It also has a reference to time, signifying three years, three months, three weeks, or three days ; and denotes that a person will be married more than once.

Deuce.   Disappointment, vexation.

The general mode of operating is simple enough. The person consulting fortune, after shuffling the cards, cuts them into three parts. The seeress, then, taking up the parts, lays them out one by one, face upwards, on the table, in rows, nine in each row, save the last. Nine, in fact, is the mystical number. Every ninth card bearing a portentous import, while each nine consecutive cards forms a separate combination, complete in itself; yet like a word in a sentence, no more than a fractional part of the grand scroll of fate. Moreover, every card, something like the octaves in music, has a peculiar bearing on the ninth card from it, and these ninth cards form in themselves peculiar combinations of nines, though parts of the general whole.

After the cards are thus laid out, then comes the reading of this strange book, which we may attempt to describe from a fanciful disposition of the cards in our minds eye, be it remembered. The young lady, who is examining the future, being fair, but not too fair, is, as the card-cutters express it, of a heart colour, and represented by the queen of hearts. Sad to say her fair lover (the king of diamonds) is found flirting with a widow (the queen of spades) rich in this world's goods, being accompanied with the ten of diamonds. But, her lover's thoughts (the knave of diamonds) are directed towards her house (the ace of hearts) ; a letter (the ace of spades) and a wedding ring (the ace of diamonds) are in close combination ; evidently signifying that though the lover is actually flirting with the widow, he is thinking of sending a letter with an offer of marriage to the young lady herself. There is a legacy (ten of clubs) in store, for the seeker after fortune ; but a lawyer (the knave of spades) stands between her and it, who will cause some vexation (the deuce of clubs) and disappointment. A sincere friend (the knave of hearts) will assist to put matters right. The unfaithful friend (the four of diamonds) will find both satire and scandal (seven of diamonds) helpless to injure our interesting queen of hearts. A present (five of hearts) will soon be received by her, honourable courtship (six of hearts) will lead her to a happy marriage (deuce of hearts), the reward of her virtuous discretion; health and happiness, and troops of children (ten of hearts) will be her enviable lot. Do this young lady's thoughts, represented by the knave of hearts, ever stray far from home? Yes, look, there they are far away with the old, hot-tempered, dark-complexioned lover (king of spades) who, as is plainly shown by his being accompanied by the ten of diamonds, is prosperously engaged at the Australian diggings, or elsewhere. Does he ever think of his old flame, the heart-complexioned young lady now consulting the cards in England? No. His thoughts (the knave of spades) are fixed on that very fair but rather gay and coquettish lady, (the queen of diamonds): they are only divided by a few good hearts, one of them (the six) representing honourable courtship. Count now from that six of hearts to the ninth card from it, and lo! it is a wedding-ring (the ace of diamonds)—they will be married in less than a year.

The nine of hearts is known as "the wish card," for there is always a secret something, an aspiration of some kind or another, lying in the lowest depth of the human heart, that even general good fortune, health and happiness, cannot gratify. So, after the fortune has been told, as we have described, *secundem artem*, the grand question arises, will this particular wish be gratified ? To solve this important problem, the cards are well shuffled, and cut, the cut card being particularly remembered. The pack is again well shuffled, and cut into three heaps, each of which are taken up and examined separately. If the wish card, the nine of hearts, be found in any of these heaps near the representative card of the person, whose fortune is being told, the wish will be gratified, sooner or later, according to the relative positions of the cards. If the nine of spades, deuce of clubs, or other very unlucky card be in the same heap, the gratification of the wish, according to the number of the unlucky cards is doubtful, or will be greatly delayed. But, mark, if the card first cut be in the same heap, the evil effect of the opposing unlucky cards, will be greatly, if not entirely, modified.

Card-cutting, as practised among the lower

classes in England, not only foretells the certain
future, but also warns against dangers that may
be avoided. In an able article on this subject,
in that valuable compilation, Chambers's *Book of
Days*, the author says: "Unlike the witches of
the olden time, the fortune-tellers are generally
esteemed and respected in the districts in which
they live and practice. And it will not be difficult
to discover sufficient reasons for this respect and
esteem. The most ignorant and depraved have
ever a lurking respect for morality and virtue ;
and the fortune-tellers are shrewd enough to know
and act upon this feeling. They always take
care to point out what they term ' the cards of
caution,' and impressively warn their clients from
falling into the dangers those cards foreshadow,
but do not positively foretell, for the dangers may
be avoided by prudence and circumspection. By
referring to the preceding significations of the
cards, it will be seen that there are cards of caution
arising from drunkenness, covetousness, inconstancy, caprice, evil temper, illicit love, clandestine
engagements." Consequently, the "card-cutters"
really exercise a considerable effect of a most bene-
ficial kind, on the moral conduct of the poorer and
more ignorant classes dwelling in the crowded
unhealthy houses of our large towns and cities.

CARD-CONJURING AND CARD-SHARPING.

THERE are two principal methods used to perform conjuring tricks with playing cards; one is
by calculation, generally according to a pre-
arranged formula of words; the other by dexterity
of manipulation, commonly termed sleight of
hand. The first of these methods has for centuries supplied interesting problems to the mathematician and other students of the exact sciences;
while the second has afforded equal facilities to
the wonder-working conjuror, and the cheating
sharper. As very curious and little known
exercises of human ingenuity, the first of these
methods demands an early notice, and a trick
called the ten duplicates furnishes a good example.
The problem is this, twenty cards being arranged

in pairs, face upwards on the table, to tell whatever pair any of the bystanders may think upon. Any twenty cards may be taken at random out of the pack, and being placed in ten pairs, the person who performs the feat, asks the company to select, mentally, any pairs they may individually choose, warning them to pay particular attention to the cards forming each pair thought upon, as they would next be seen in a different arrangement. The company having made their selection, the performer takes up the pairs indiscriminately, taking care, however, to keep the two cards which form each pair invariably next each other, and then proceeds to arrange them face upwards on the table as shall presently be described, according to the letters of the following words, which must previously have been committed to memory.

N	O	M	E	N
M	U	T	U	S
D	E	D	I	T
R	O	R	I	S

The performer places the first pair of cards on the table in similar positions, and to represent the two letters N N in nomen; of the next pair, he places one to represent the O in nomen, and the other the O in roris ; the next pair, he places one for the M in nomen, the other for the M in mutus ; the next pair represents the E in nomen, and the E in dedit ; this arrangement is continued till all the ten pairs of cards are placed in the positions of, and to represent the ten pairs of letters of the same kind in the four words. The performer then asks a bystander, who has thought on a pair, to say in which of the four lines, leading from left to right, the cards are. If the reply is "both in the first line," the pair thought on, must inevitably be those representing the N N in nomen ; if in the first and fourth lines, they must be the representatives of the O in nomen, and the O in roris : if in the second and third line, they must be the T in mutus and the T in dedit. Further explanation must be unnecesary; as the reader will at once perceive that the twenty letters in the four words, are composed of ten duplicate letters, which will always point out the positions of the ten duplicate cards, if they are arranged in the places of those letters. Any number of the bystanders may select pairs, and to make the feat appear still more mysterious, the pairs may be selected and placed on the table back upwards, the performer not seeing or turning them, until he places them according to the duplicate letters.

In another feat of a similar description, the performer commences by relating a story of

TURKS AND CHRISTIANS.

A ship's crew being in great distress for want of provisions, held a council, at which it was unanimously determined that, as all could not be saved from the horrors of a lingering death by starvation, out of thirty men, the full number, fifteen should be thrown overboard, to save the lives of the rest; every ninth man being selected as the victim. Fifteen of the crew were Turks, the other half were Christians; and an astute Christian, who was on board, arranged the thirty so, that all the Turks were thrown overboard, and all the Christians were saved. The performer, then, taking the cards, red to represent Christians and black for the Turks, arranges them according to the numerical value of the vowels in the following line, thus—

Populeam virgam mater regina ferebat
4 521   3 1   1 2 2 3 1 2 2 1

Commencing with the red cards, o, being the fourth in numerical order of the vowels, four red cards are placed first; u, being the fifth vowel, calls for five black cards; e, the second vowel, has two red cards; a, being the first, has one

black, and so on, red and black alternately, till
each vowel has its complement of cards, according to its numerical position, thus—

a	e	i	o	u
1	2	3	4	5

Of course the above words have no recondite
meaning of their own, yet there can be no doubt
that many ancient myths and mysteries, of an
exactly similar kind, have come down to us with
the reputation of being powerful charms and in-
vocations, to puzzle the weak brains of fruit-
less consumers of the midnight oil. Intelligent
readers, however, will readily conceive that similar collocations of meaningless words have served
to conceal and design the proportions of sub-
stances necessary in certain chemical combinations; and they will also recognise the fact that,
during the mediæval period, the different forms
that may be taken by syllogism in argument,
were indicated by barbarous Latin verses.

An unintelligent person, however, could scarcely
be made to believe that the preceding feat was
performed by the respective position of the vowels
in the words. He would seek for its explanation
in the meaning of the words, and absurdly establish some mysterious relation between the art of

divining and the above Latin line, which may be translated—A branch of poplar held by a queen and a mother. Nor could any argument, less than complete demonstration, cause them to believe that the arrangements of the vowels in the following English lines, would answer quite as well.

From numbers aid and art
4   5   2   13   1   1
Never will fame depart
2 2   3   1 2   2 1

The cleverer and more intelligent of the cheats, who assume to tell fortunes by cards, work upon this tendency of the human mind in a rather curious manner. When they perceive persons doubtful of their power to foretell future events, they will say, " I can prove to you by a simple experiment in five minutes, that I possess the art of divination by cards." The natural reply is, " Proceed then, and convince us of your power." The fortune-teller demurs to this brusque mode of proceeding. His feats are serious matters, not to be lightly performed, without fit and proper occasion. But, reckoning up the strength of his visitor's pockets, by their general appearance, he will do it for a guinea or five, just as he may estimate their want of discretion and their plentifulness of money—two Napoleons is the sum generally charged in Paris. The visitors soon raise the sum required among them, stipulating, however, that they must be convinced of the fortune-teller's power of divination by cards before they pay it, to which the rogue smilingly agrees, Three articles are then selected, say a coin, a ring, and a key, and placed upon the table; the fortune-teller then takes twenty-four cards, and giving one to one of the persons, two to another, and three to a third, places the remainder on the table. He then says, I am about to leave the room, let one of you in my absence take the coin, a second the ring, and a third the key; let him, who takes the coin, take also as many cards as he already has; he who takes the ring, take twice as many cards as he has; and he who takes the key, take four times as many cards as he has; on my return to the room, by consulting the remaining cards, I will be able to divine who has taken the coin, who has the ring, and who has the key. He then leaves the room; in a few moments he returns, and after pretending to consult the remaining cards, at once points out who has taken the various articles. The visitors, being unable to comprehend the mystery, pay the sum agreed upon, and sneak off in a rather humiliated kind of manner.

The fellow manages the matter thus. He
mentally terms the coin *a*, the ring *e*, and the
key *i* ; he also, in the same manner, distinguishes
the three persons by certain numbers. The person to whom he gave one card being 1; the one
to whom he gave two cards being 2; and the one
who received three cards being 3. Long previously, he has committed the following line to
memory, which forms a key to the whole.

1	2	3	5	6	7
Salve	certa	animæ	semita	vita	quies.

On his return into the room, the fellow pretends to consult the cards, his real object being
to count the number left. The number whatever
it may be, having an intimate connection with the
words of the preceding line. Thus, if only one
card be left, the number refers to the word salve,
in which the first vowel is *a* the second *e ;* and,
consequently, the person mentally distinguished
as 1 has the coin represented by the vowel *a*,
while 2 has the ring represented by the vowel *e*,
and so 3 must have the key. Again, if there
were seven cards left, the word referred to is quies,
and consequently 1 has the key *i*, while 2 has
the ring *e*, and 3 must have the coin *a*. It should
be observed that in no instance can there be a

remainder of four cards; and that the first vowel
in each word invariably represents the person
mentally distinguished as 1, the second vowel him
who is similarly regarded as 2. This ingenious
feat is founded on the permutations of the three
articles, or their representative vowels, which can
only be placed in six different positions, and the
corresponding numerical arrangement of the
cards, thus:—

1.	*a*	*e*	*i*	salve.
2.	*e*	*a*	*i*	certa.
3.	*a*	*i*	*e*	animæ.
5.	*e*	*i*	*a*	semita.
6.	*i*	*a*	*e*	vita.
7.	*i*	*e*	*a*	quies.

The three vowels in their different positions
are made easy of recollection, by being united with
consonants, and formed in their regular succession
into the above Latin line, or into the following
similarly constructed French one:—

1	2	3	5	6	7
Par fer	César	jadis	devint	si grand	prince.

This very ingenious feat is said to be the invention of the celebrated mathematician Ozanam,
and it need scarcely be observed, that though
always exhibited as a proof or example of divina-

tion by playing-cards, it really has no connection with cards whatever, as it might, equally as well, be performed with twenty-four counters, or any other small articles readily reckoned.

Another trick rendered easy, though not actually performed, through means of a prepared formula of words, by which any card of the pack, their backs only being visible, may be picked out, at the request of a spectator, is conducted in this manner. The pack being laid out on a table faces upwards are picked up in suits, one by one in the following order, the six, four, ace, seven, five, king, eight, ten, three, knave, nine, two, queen. For which purpose these words will be found useful, as an *aide memoire*.

6   4   ace

The sixty-fourth regiment repulsed the

7   5   king

seventy-fifth; the Kings' army consisted of

8   10   3 knave   9   2

eight thousand and three men, and ninety-two

queen.

women.

Each suit having been taken up according to this formula, and the performer must keep in memory the order in which he takes up the suits, which is easiest accomplished by always taking them up in the same order: the pack is given to the spectators to be cut, which may be done in the usual manner, as often as they please. The performer then takes the pack, and having slyly peeped at the bottom card, proceeds to lay them down on the table in thirteen heaps. That is to say, having laid down thirteen cards separately, he covers them with thirteen more, so when he has finished there are thirteen heaps, of four cards each, on the table. Each heap consisting of four cards of a similar denomination, placed over each other, in the exact order in which the suits were taken up. The card at the bottom of the pack, which the dealer took care to see, forming the key to the whole. For instance—if this, the last card, be a five, the first heap must consist of the four kings, the suits lying over one another according to the order they were taken up; and the series proceeds thus eight, ten, three, knave, nine, two, queen, six, four, ace, seven. Or, counting the reverse way from the five, the series will be seven, ace, four, six, queen, two, nine, knave, three, ten, eight, king. And thus the performer may readily pick out any card, of any suit, that may be demanded, to the no little surprise and wonder of the bystanders.

Some feats performed by calculation alone, without any prescribed formula of words, are curious and worthy of notice. For instance, the amount of the numbers of any two cards, drawn from the pack may be readily told in this wise. The small cards must be reckoned by their amount of pips, but each coat card should be considered to represent the number ten. Any person having drawn two cards, the performer tells him to take as many cards from the pack, each card counting only one, as will make each of the numbers selected amount to twenty-five. This being done, the performer, pretending to consult the remaining cards, counts their number, which will be the amount of the number of pips on the two cards drawn. For example, suppose the person drew a ten and a seven, then he must add fifteen cards to the former, and eighteen to the latter, to make their respective numbers amount to twenty-five. The two cards drawn, and fifteen and eighteen others being added amount altogether to thirty-five; which, being deducted from fifty-two, the number of cards in the pack, leaves a remainder of seventeen, being inevitably the number of pips on the two cards drawn.

The principle of the feat being known, it

may be varied thus, by the performer not requiring to see or touch the remaining cards. The
person having drawn two cards, the performer
tells him to deduct the number of each from
twenty-six, add the remainders together and tell
the amount. This the performer mentally deducts from fifty-two, and the remainder is the
number of pips on the two cards. For example,
let the cards be ten and seven as before; ten
deducted from twenty-six leaves sixteen, and
seven in like manner affords a remainder of
nineteen, these two being added together make
thirty-five; which, deducted from fifty-two, leaves
a remainder of seventeen, the numerical amount
of the two cards as before.

A person who performs feats of any kind,
should always be prepared for any pertinent—in
such cases impertinent—remark or objection that
may be made. He who drew the cards, if of any
acuteness, though utterly ignorant of the principle of the feat, may say, "You desired me to
deduct the number of both the cards from twenty-
six and that is the number of cards in half of the
pack, there may be something in that, though I
cannot exactly see it." "Nonsense," the performer replies, "try it again." This time the
drawer is told to substract the numbers of the

two cards from twenty, the performer taking care
to add twelve, for the two sixes, to the amount.
For, supposing the drawer took ten and seven as
before, these numbers deducted from twenty
would leave ten and thirteen, to which twelve
being added, would make thirty-five; leaving
when deducted from fifty-two, the sum of seventeen, being the numerical amount of the pips on
the two cards as previously shown. And it will
now appear clear to the reader, that the performer
may vary the feat, giving it a greater air of mystery, by changing the number, from which the
cards are to be deducted. As any number less
than twenty-six or greater than ten will equally
answer his purpose ; taking care, however, to add
mentally to the remainder, double the difference
between the number selected and twenty-six.

The amount of the numbers of any three
cards drawn from the pack, may also be told in
a somewhat similar manner. After the party has
drawn his three cards, the performer draws one
for himself, it being necessary that the number
of the remaining cards be divisible by three,
which they certainly will not be in a pack of
fifty-two cards, if only three be drawn from them.
The performer, however, does not explain this
simple fact to the spectators ; on the contrary, he

terms it his confederate card, pretending that by its aid alone, he can discover the amount of the others. He then tells the drawer to add as many cards to each of those he has drawn, as will make its number sixteen, which is the third part of the remaining forty-eight cards. Therefore, supposing he drew a ten, a seven, and a six, he must add to the first six cards, to the second nine, and to the third ten, which together make twenty-five, and with the four cards drawn, amount to twenty-nine. The performer then, taking the pack and counting them over, finds a remainder of twenty-three, which must be the amount of pips on the cards drawn.

This feat may also be performed, without touching or looking at the cards. If the drawer deducts the number of each of his cards from seventeen, and tells the amount of the several remainders. The performer, adding one for the card he drew, subtracts the amount from fifty-two, and finds a remainder of twenty-three the number required. For, supposing the three cards drawn to be a ten, a seven, and a six, as before, then each of these numbers being taken from seventeen, the remainders will respectively be seven, ten, and eleven, which added together with the single card drawn by the performer, make twenty-nine, and that number deducted from fifty-two, leaves twenty-three as before.

There is little reason to imagine any one will discover, why the number seventeen is selected in working this feat; but any other number less than seventeen and more than ten will do just as well, provided the performer adds to the amount of the remainders the double of what the number selected is less than seventeen. For, suppose the number selected be twelve, and the three cards drawn be the same as in the preceding examples, the remainders will be two, five, and six; these added together make thirteen, which with the addition of ten, double the difference between twelve and seventeen, amount to twenty-three, the number required.

Feats or tricks performed with playing cards, by sleight of hand or manual dexterity, may and have been used for purposes of cheating, to which they are peculiarly applicable. A good story is told of the elder Matthews and the late Mr. Yates, who, when travelling together, once found themselves at a provincial inn, without any means of amusement for themselves; though no persons were more highly calculated to amuse others. A game of whist would suit exactly, but where were they to obtain partners. On consulting the landlord, he knew of one person, a good player, who was then actually in the house. A polite invitation being sent through the waiter, the stranger joined the two comedians; preliminaries were at once settled, and they sat down to play, the stranger taking Dummy. There never was such bad luck on one side, and good on the other. Dummy won every game; till at last the stranger, consulting his watch, said that he must cease playing, as he had an important engagement to attend. "But," exclaimed the others, "you surely will give us our revenge,—some chance of regaining our losses." "Certainly, gentlemen," replied Dummy. "I will either at a later hour to night, or to-morrow, give you full opportunity of regaining what you have lost; nothing but important business could induce me to leave you now." "And pray," said Yates, "what pressing business can you have now, at seven o'clock in the evening?" "Oh!" replied the stranger, with a shrewed twinkle in his eye, "I am a professional, like yourselves, gentlemen; I am G——the conjuror, and am now going to perform in my booth near the market house. I wish you a very good evening; and I shall be happy to wait on you again, whenever you may require amusement." The stranger bowed himself out of the room; and though neither Matthews nor Yates, could detect any mal-practices in his play, they unanimously agreed to waive any further proceedings, regarding winning their money back from the conjuror.

We have in previous chapters, dwelt largely upon the legitimate uses of cards as a pastime, and as a feature of national manners. We have now to look upon the reverse of the picture, and to consider in what manner unscrupulous and evil men have turned great talents to base uses, by concentrating skill, invention, and great patience upon modes of entrapping fortune, and making a living by what was intended merely as an amusement. In all times and ages, there has been no lack of such idle persons; and while deception may be the harmless adjunct of the professor of legerdemain, the guilty arts of the card-sharper—not always to be found in the lower ranks,—merit the strongest reprobation and the severest punishment.

It has been seen in the chapter devoted to an account of the legislation upon card matters, that the natural impulse, which leads men to risk all upon chance, demanded and met with prompt and wise measures of repression; the fertility of men's brains, however, enables them to evade law, and to substitute adventitious contrivances, in place of the simpler combinations of skill in play. The card-sharper's golden rule is well given in the following lines:

> He who hopes at cards to win,
> Must never think that cheating's sin;
> To make a trick when'er he can,
> No matter *how*, should be his plan.
> No case of conscience must he make,
> Except how he may save his stake;
> The only object of his prayers,—
> Not to be caught, and kicked down stairs.

Even a more summary mode of ejectment than kicking down stairs, seems to have been not unfrequently practised in the olden times,—the sharper ingloriously making an unwilling exit out of a window. A fellow so served, it is said, once went to a solicitor for advice, when the following dialogue took place:

> Says the lawyer—"What motive for treatment so hard?"
> "Dear Sir, all my crime was but—slipping a card."
> "Indeed! For how much did you play then, and where?"
> "For two hundred; up two pair of stairs, at the Bear."
> "Why, then my good friend, as you want my advice,
> T'other guinea advance, it is yours in a trice."
> "Here it is, my dear sir."—"Very well: Now observe,
> Future downfalls to shun, from this rule never swerve,—
> When challenged upstairs, luck for hundreds to try,
> Tell your frolicsome friends that you don't play so *high!*"

We are glad to have it in our power to introduce the reader to a large and influential

PLATE XXVII

PLATE XLVIII

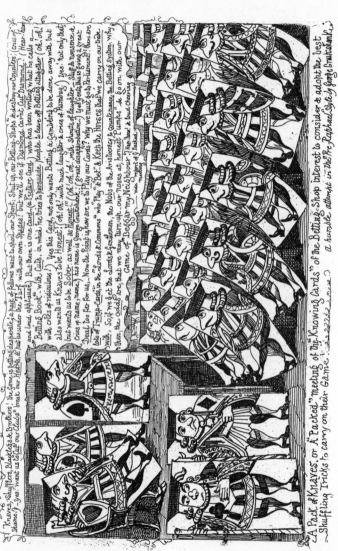

A Pack of Knaves, or A "Packed" meeting of the "Knowing Cards" of the Betting-Shop interest to consider & adopt the best Shuffling Tricks to carry on their Game. A humble attempt in the Pre-Raphael Style by George Cruikshank.

assemblage of "knaves," as depicted by the
graphic pencil of Mr. George Cruikshank, (in
Plate XLVIII). Mark the lazy vacuity of the
noble chairman, the expostulatory and terrified
expression of the speaker on the platform, and
the general fear and trembling exhibited by the
crowded assemblage, whose sacred rights are in
danger of being attacked. No doubt, since the
publication of this engraving some time since,
much has been done to destroy the influence of
the "knowing cards" about town; yet many a
young unsuspecting flat is still caught and
"rooked" of his money, as the daily police
reports plentifully show.

Sometimes, however, the "biter gets bit;" as
the following veritable anecdote will show. In
many games of chance, the cards are skilfully
trimmed and cut previous to play. By cutting
away the sides of certain cards, in such a way as
to present a slight convexity or concavity, the
sharper is able at will to cut himself court cards,
without his adversary knowing it, and immense
sums have thus been fraudulently obtained from
the "gulls" or "pigeons." In the case now to
be mentioned the tables were turned. A person
who had long pursued the occupation of a "leg,"
was engaged in cutting and filing down a pack,

for the purpose of playing at the gambling game of " Blind-hookey," and winning at will. Enter to him just as this was completed and put away, a brother " leg," rather seedy from last night's potations, and indisposed for anything too serious.

Leg B proposed to leg A—first, a hair of the dog that had bitten him, and next a game of cards, it then being somewhere about high noon. Now leg A, who had finished his pack, cared little for cards by day, and put his companion off; however, B persisted; so down they sat,—B unconsciously hitting upon the very game, and proposing blind-hookey. Now A had lost some £15 or £20 the night before to B, so the idea came into his head of getting it back, and consequently played altogether " on the cross." B found the cards against him, and betted furiously; at last, after a long time, he lost his temper, on which the other coolly threw the pack in the fire (of course to prevent his being detected) and declared that for his part he had had enough, and would not play with a man in a passion. He had, it should be added, lost a pound or two towards the last, designedly, in order to have a pretext for burning the cards. Mr. B never found out how his companion had cheated him, and had he done so, would probably only have been laughed at. " Doing the yokels," as cheating the countrymen is called, is of ancient date enough, as we all can well imagine.

An exceedingly common dodge, for extricating money from the pockets of the unwary, is that generally known as the card-sharping trick. We may meet it in steam-boat or railway car; it is not confined to the race-course and the towered city, like the old thimble-rig, which it has almost superseded; but we may find it among solitary ruins, and the grander scenes of nature, wherever tourists in their season most do congregate. Scotland, for several years, has been overrun by these card-sharpers; and the writer actually saw them last summer, labouring in their vocation of picking up flats, close to the sacred shrine of Roslin Chapel, and within hearing of the roar made by the falls of Clyde. It is differently managed, but the principle is in all instances the same. The general mode is for the sharper to take three cards between the fingers of his right hand. He shows the faces of the cards, one of them, say, is the king of hearts, and then throws them down back upwards on a table, bench, crown of a hat, according to the conveniences the place may afford, saying, "I'll bet a wager, that no one finds the king of hearts out of these three cards." And however confident a bystander may be that

he can point out that card, he will inevitably lose.
It is simply impossible to win at this game, and
it is really a curious and not uninteresting fact,
that however dexterously a sharper can perform
it himself, he will most certainly lose, if he bets
against another practitioner in the art.   The
rapid motion of the hand confuses the eye, leading it to fix on a wrong card; besides, there is a
peculiar difficulty in estimating the positions of
the cards on the table, in this wise. The victim
may feel satisfied, the card that fell first on the
table is the one he wants, but is it the centre or
one of the side ones; and if one of the side ones,
which of them is it ?   Even with actual demonstration, it is almost impossible to explain how
this trick is performed.   Indeed there is no secret
or trick in the affair, more than this—in throwing down the cards, the sharper endeavours to
make another, as it were, represent the particular
card that is the subject of the bet. No one can
tell, not even the sharper, how it is done, and the
main thing for a stranger is to avoid being *done*
by it.   A person, not unknown to the writer, once
formed an ingenious speculation to win at this
curious game, by selecting the card, apparently
the most unlikely to be the one required. And
though he had two cards to one against him, suc-

ceeded in pointing out the card required several times. But the sharper perceiving this, at once changed his tactics, and the clever speculator gave up the losing contest, a sadder if not a much wiser man.

Another remarkably successful card-sharping dodge is known as the "King and queen trick." In the evening of a fair or race meeting, when there is a pretty large assemblage of not very scrupulous persons in the smoking-room of a tavern or country inn, a pack of cards is by some means introduced. Immediately, an impudent, rude, and apparently very ignorant young country-fellow seizes the pack, saying that he will show the company a clever conjuring trick. Having thus attracted attention, he takes, say the king and queen of spades, places one at the top, the other at the bottom of the pack; then asking some one to cut and place the cut on the top of the pack, he again takes the cards, and, going leisurely over the pack, shows that he has brought the king and queen together again, asserting that he can repeat the extraordinary feat as often as he pleases. It is then clear to the company that the fellow is the stupidest of simple-tons, as well as a boorish, boasting braggart, as he talks largely of the money he possesses, and

the large sums he will bet, that he can perform
the same wonderful trick as often as he pleases.
He commences to show the trick again; and when
the cards are cut, a person, sitting near the table,
takes an opportunity of placing some of the cut
cards on the top of the pack, when the bragging
fool has turned round to challenge the company
to bet. A person observing the displacing of the
cards, accepts the challenge for five pounds, that
the king and queen of spades will not come
together again, and of course wins, to the apparently great disappointment of the young fellow,
who innocently declares he never failed in the
trick before, but he will try it again. Exactly the
same performance is repeated, the knowing cus-
tomer, who moves the cards, betting five pounds
on the result; and the company, whose sympathies
are all against the blustering simpleton, thinking
they may as well have some of his money as
anybody else, bet freely against the king and
queen coming together again. But to their very
great surprise and astonishment the cards are
found together, and their money is lost; no one
seemingly more confounded by the result than
the man who displaced the cards. While the
company are wondering how, on earth, such a
result could take place, not daring to discuss the

question openly before the man, whom they believe they are cheating; the fellow, now elated by his success, ten times noisier and more bouncible than before, will perform the trick again. This time, however, the man who previously displaced the cards, seems fully determined not to be done. He, watching his opportunity, takes the king of spades away from the pack altogether, and furtively showing it to the company, puts it in his breast-coat pocket, and, buttoning up his coat with a determined air, makes a bet of ten pounds with the young fellow. The company, whatever doubt or distrust they may have had from the result of the previous transaction, are now satisfied of the utter impossibility of the cards coming together again, and once more bet freely against the young fellow, but to lose. He produces the king and queen of spades together as before; and quickly seizes and pockets the bets, which, with careful foresight, he had caused to be posted on the table before him, previous to his performing the trick. We need scarcely say, that the noisy young simpleton is an expert conjuring card-sharper, and that the fellow who displaced the cards, as well as the one who made the first bet, are his confederates. If the company remonstrate, the black-legs will laughingly recriminate, by saying you attempted to cheat us; and the non-betting portion of the company, looking on the whole affair as an excellent joke, will rather be inclined to take the sharper's side of the question. If it comes to a scuffle, the swindlers will soon fight their way out of the room, being not altogether unused to such contingencies.

The principal games played in England are Whist and Cribbage; the former by the higher and upper middle class, the latter, generally, by those of lower station. Whist is too tedious a game for the professional gambler; it is peculiarly a game of skill, and thoroughly unsuited for cheating purposes. A person, it is true, may, by making the pass, manage to hold one good honour each time he deals, but this advantage is not equivalent to the risk of detection; the play, as a' Frenchman would say, is not worth the candle and this a silly old nobleman, a few years since' discovered in a most lamentable manner. Gamblers are consequently thrown upon their ingenuity to devise a speedy means of winning at whist,—a game, be it remembered, which by its very nature seems to disarm suspicion, and a very clever *coup* is executed in the following manner. The writer, indeed, may as well relate a circumstance that fell

under his own notice, speaking of himself as
Simple, his antagonist as Sharp. Some thirty
years ago, Simple and a friend were passing a few
days' holiday at a well-known watering-place on
the South coast, when a sudden shower of rain
drove them to take shelter in an adjoining tavern,
where they were joined by two strangers, namely,
Sharp and Co. The weather, as a confounded
bore, being at once alluded to, a conversation
commenced ; and the important question was
started, how to pleasantly spend the wet evening.
Sharp proposed a game of whist, but his friend
said cards were not kept in the house. However,
the bell was rung, a pack of cards ordered and
brought in by the waiter ; and then Sharp's friend
objected to play for money, it was contrary to his
principles, besides it spoiled the pleasure and
interest of the game ; and so they commenced to
play a rubber for glasses of something to drink
and cigars, Simple and friend, of course, being
partners against Sharp and his companion.

Nothing particular occurred, till the adversaries were a game each, when it became Sharp's
turn to deal, which he did, apparently, in the
usual manner, turning up the deuce of hearts as
trump. Simple taking up his hand, with all the
eagerness of a very young man, found, to his

agreeable surprise, that he held the ace, king, queen, knave, nine, and ten of trumps; the ace, king, queen, and knave of clubs; and the ace, king, and queen of spades. The dealer, who had not looked at his cards, being engaged in taking snuff and pleasantly handing the box round, now rubbing his hands, laughingly proposed a bet on the odd trick. "I have looked at my cards," was the reply, "and you have not lifted yours yet." "O never mind that," retorted the other; "I am in the humour for a little speculation, and if you like to bet on the odd trick, I will take you for a couple of sovereigns." Simple had already tele-graphed, with the tail of his eye, to his friend the excellence of his hand. It was not in human nature to resist such an offer, but then Sharp's companion insinuated something about two sove-reigns being too much for the young men to lose, it would spoil their holiday; and the result of this and other chaff was, that a bet on the winning of the odd trick was made for twenty pounds; and at this moment the landlord *hap-pening* to come into the room, the money, on the proposition of Sharp, was deposited in his hands.

We have seen Simple's cards, let us have a look at those held by Sharp; which were the eight, seven, six, five, four, three, and deuce of trumps; the ace, king, queen, knave, ten, and nine of diamonds. How the twenty-six cards, comprising the rest of the pack, were distributed in the hands of the other two players, it matters not; the hands of Simple and Sharp were alone the seat of war. Simple, confident of winning at least twelve tricks, led off with his trumps, and of course won the first six tricks; he then boldly led off his ace of spades, which fell to Sharp's last paltry deuce of trumps; and then Sharp, bringing in his diamonds, inevitably won the last seven tricks. The landlord, who stayed in the room to see the hand played, at once passed the money over to Sharp; who, then, suddenly recollecting an important engagement, departed with his accomplice, leaving Simple and his friend in a state more easily imagined than described. Their holiday was truly spoiled. At first they could scarcely believe they had been cheated, imagining that Simple had played his hand badly. But, on their return to town, going over the game in the quiet solitude of their chambers, they found it impossible for them, under any circumstances, to have gained the odd trick. For, if Simple had adopted the less obvious plan of forcing the dealer, by playing spade or club, the latter would have trumped the trick and forced the leader, in turn, by playing diamond. Of course, Mr. Sharp knew better than to return trump, for then his number of trumps being reduced to six, the same as that held by Simple, the latter would then take out all the trumps, and win all the remaining tricks. And from this point of view the cheating stratagem affords a good whist lesson; fully exemplifying the value and importance of the last trump, however insignificant, to bring in a long suit, and the peculiar action of what is not inaptly termed forcing.

How was it managed? Easily enough. Sharp had a pack of cards, with backs exactly resembling those used in the house, and these he had prepared — *stocked* he would term it — beforehand, ready for any chance customers that the blind goddess might send him. In a small pocket, made for the purpose, in the inside skirt of his frock coat, he kept his prepared cards ready, till they were required, when they were, in a moment, dexterously substituted for the cards that had previously been used.

The French periodical *Le Palamede*, though principally devoted to Chess, gives the following very curious instance of a "slam," or the whole thirteen tricks having been won at Whist, as having occurred in actual play. A and B, we

shall say, are partners, and having already scored
nine to their antagonists' three, only require the
odd trick to win the game triumphantly. A deals,
and having turned up a heart as trump, finds his
hand constituted as follows :—

HEARTS (trumps)—King, knave, nine, seven, five.
DIAMONDS—King, queen, knave, ten.
SPADES—Ace, king, queen.
CLUBS—King.

With such cards, A felt certain of making the
trick; but when the hand was played out, A and
B not only lost the trick but the game; their
adversaries, C and D, actually winning the whole
thirteen tricks, and consequently the game. And
this, moreover, without any very bad play on the
parts of A and B; on the contrary, the game is
not absolutely forced through the preponderating
weight of the cards alone, but through the excellent play of C and D, who are thus made to
destroy themselves, *secundem artem*, in the most
scientific manner. There are several modes, by
which the desired result may be obtained, but
only one need be given here, as an example. We
have seen the cards of A, let us look at those of
C, his left-hand adversary, which are as follows :—

TRUMPS—Ace, queen, ten, eight, and six.
DIAMONDS—Nine, eight, seven, six, five, four, two.
CLUBS—Eight.

D, the partner of C, holds—

TRUMPS—Four, three, two.
DIAMONDS—Ace.
CLUBS—Ace, ten, nine, seven, three, two.
SPADES—Nine, eight, seven.

B, the partner of A, had, of course, the remaining thirteen cards, which need not be more particularly specified, than as being a very indifferent lot. Let us see, now, trick by trick, how the hands were played out.

1. A, as we observed before, having dealt, C leads off with his solitary club, B plays queen, D ace, and A the king.

2. D, having won the trick, naturally returns club, his partner's lead, A ruffs with the five of trumps, C over-trumps with the six, and B follows suit with the four of clubs.

3. C leads nine of diamonds, B plays the three, D the ace, and A the king.

4. D, who won the last trick, again leads club with the nine, A trumps with the knave, C over-trumps with the queen, and B drops the five of clubs.

5. C, keeping to his diamonds, plays the eight, B throws the four of spades, D cuts in with the two of trumps, and A lets fall the queen of diamonds.

6. D having again to lead, again leads club with the seven, A plays king of trumps on it, C wins with the ace of trumps, and B disconsolately drops the six of clubs.

7. C cautiously leads off the seven of diamonds, B plays the three of spades, D ruffs in with the three of trumps, and A plays knave of diamonds.

8. D, sticking to his text, leads three of clubs, A cuts in with nine of trumps, C again over-trumps with the ten, and B plays his useless knave of clubs.

9. C, knowing the ten of diamonds is yet in hand, boldly plays the six, B follows with the six of spades, D cuts in with the four of trumps, and A sheepishly drops his last diamond.

10. D leads two of clubs, A trumps with the seven of hearts, C over-trumps with the eight, and B plays the five of spades.

11, 12, 13. C leads and makes his three remaining diamonds, all the trumps being played.

Such hands, however, seldom occur in actual play; few persons are aware of the immense number of deals a person may have at the game of whist, without ever holding the same cards twice. As there are fifty-two cards used, and thirteen are dealt to each player, the sum represented by the figures 635, 013, 559, 600, is the different ways thirteen cards may be taken out of fifty-two, and consequently the number required.

Cribbage, being a quicker game than whist, is better adapted for the gambler's purpose; besides, as it is generally played at taverns, and among a lower class of society, strangers can more readily gain admission. The advantage of possessing fives at this game being great, several devices are used to accomplish so desirable a consummation. One termed "handing the cards" is effected by the cheat securing two fives, and any other two cards, in the palm of his right hand. First an indifferent card, then a five, next another card, and lastly a five. It is the cheat's turn to deal, but he says to his antagonist in a careless manner, "Please shuffle the cards for me, while I light my cigar." Simple duly shuffles and cuts; and then the cheat, putting his hand containing the four arranged cards on the top, commences to deal, and thus gives himself two fives without any great exercise of dexterity whatever. Or the four fives are marked, so that

Sharp, when dealing, may not only avoid giving them to his adversary, but secure them for himself. Less dexterous cheats manage, when shuffling, to get the fives at the bottom of the pack, and thus drop them into their own hands, when dealing. Cards, too, are sometimes secured between the knee and the table, so that the cheat has the advantage of changing bad cards, received in dealing, for good cards, previously abstracted from the pack. Sometimes, just within the coat collar at the back of the neck, is selected for this purpose. At the Licensed Victuallers' Ball, a few years ago, a person in the card-room was observed to scratch his neck rather more frequently than the usages of good society warranted; he was suspected, watched, and detected having a card receptacle inside his coat collar; he was given over to the police, subsequently prosecuted, and severely punished. Anthony Pasquin thus interestingly describes the *modus operandi*, as practised at Cribbage—

"The method of doing this, is to select out three or four extraordinary good cards, while your adversary is marking his hand or crib, and placing the same behind your head. This being done, and the cards properly dealt, you take up your own cards, which you take care to examine

pretty quick, and after laying out any two you
think proper for the crib, you immediately with
one hand put your other remaining cards upon
the pack, and with your other take down the cards
which have been secured; then in lieu of very
bad cards, which you possibly might have had,
you have the best which can be got."

Cards are also prepared for cheating at cribbage; the sixes, sevens, eights, and nines being cut
slightly shorter than the others; while the fives,
together with the tenth cards, are cut rather
narrower. So if Mr. Sharp should want a six,
seven, eight, or nine to turn up, he cuts the pack
by lifting at each end, and one of the cards he
requires, they being shorter than the others, will
be sure to be uppermost. But if a five or tenth
card be required, he cuts by taking hold of the
cards at each side, and the card he requires being
narrower than the others, will infallibly be uppermost.

The "old gentleman," or long card, is also
used to cheat with at cribbage. For, by fixing any
card under it that may be thought eligible, Sharp
can always have that card for a start by cutting at
the long card when his adversary has the deal. Or,
by selecting two fives, with any other ordinary card
between them, and placing them under the long

card, Sharp, by cutting at the long card, compels his adversary to deal him a couple of fives.

Tricks indeed may be improvised at cribbage, without any previous preparation, before the parties sit down to play. In the course of a couple of deals, the sixes, sevens, eights, and nines may be bent in the middle lengthways, with the sides downwards; by which means it is easy for the black-leg to have one of these important cards for a start, when he requires it, by cutting where he perceives a card bent in that manner. Always, however, taking care to leave the bent card on the top, that it may be turned up according to his wish. Or two or three small cards may be abstracted from the pack altogether, which not being known to the dupe, causes him to play throughout the game at a very great disadvantage; while the knowledge of the fact enables the sharper to conduct his game with a completely commensurate superiority. The simple and only method of frustrating this and other tricks of a similar description is to count the pack frequently, so as to make sure of there being the normal fifty-two cards in it.

A common method of cheating at Cribbage, Ecarté, and probably other games, cannot be passed over without mention, is what is termed

the telegraph. A confederate sharper, looking
over the honest player's shoulder, under pretence
of taking an interest in his success, and probably
under excuse of a trifling bet on his play, tele-
graphs to the antagonist black-leg the state of the
dupe's hand. This can be done without a word
spoken or a finger moved, by an almost imperceptible elevation of the eye-brows, a more or less
opening of the mouth, a protrusion of the tongue,
as if to lick the lips, and other very obvious
means, previously agreed upon to designate
various cards, by the confederate sharpers.

As we have already given a curious example
of what might occur in actual play at Whist, we
now proceed to show how two partners at Four-
handed Cribbage may win the game in one show,
without any one of the four players holding a
single point, either in hand or crib. Let us say,
then, that A and B are partners, having the deal,
against C and D. A deals, giving each person
a three, four, six, seven, with any tenth card; and
all four, being pretty good players, lay out the
tenth card for crib. The turn-up being a knave,
the dealer makes two points, "for his heels," and
so commences the score. C, having to lead,
avoids playing his six or seven, lest a fifteen
should be made, and so leads his four, which

B pairs, marking two points; D plays another four, marking six points for a "pair-royal;" and then A comes in with his four, scoring twelve points for the "double-pair-royal." It is again C's turn to play, and he leads off with a three, B pairs making two points, D throws down the third three, scoring six for the "pair-royal" as before, and then most fortunate A comes in with his fourth three, scoring thirteen, twelve for the "double-pair-royal" and one for the "go." C having again to lead, plays his seven; this is paired by B gaining two points, D in turn gets six points for his "double-pair-royal," and then A plays the fourth seven, making thirteen holes, being twelve for the "double-pair-royal," and one for the "go." The last round produces exactly similar results, A scoring thirteen, as before, namely, twelve for the "double-pair-royal" and one for the last card. Let us now sum up, and see how the game stands.

C and D score in the first round, .	6
in the second, . .	6
in the third, . . .	6
in the fourth, . .	6
Total, . . .	24

A and B score by turning up knave,   2

	in the first round, .	14
	in the second, . .	15
	in the third, . . .	15
	in the fourth, . .	15

Total, ... 61

Thus winning the game in play without the assistance of either hand or crib.

Conjuring tricks, performed either by cards or any other manner, present very little variety. They run in classes, as it were, a great number of various feats depending upon one single principle. A naturalist would say that in conjuring tricks there were a great variety of species, but very few genera. The main principles upon which almost all sleight-of-hand card tricks, either for conjuring or cheating, depend, is the feat called the Pass—probably, however, better known by its French denomination, *sauter la coupe;* another, termed the Slip,—in French, *filer une carte;* to these must be added the Force, and the Change; when these can be readily performed, the whole art of card conjuring may be said to be at a person's finger ends. The pass, when employed for cheating purposes, simply consists in dexterously placing the cut cards on the top, instead of the bottom of the pack. The object is obvious. By arranging the cards when shuffling, the cheat can manage to *stock* or place them, so as to be most advantageous to himself and useless to his adversary ; or he may, at least, secure a high honour at the bottom of the pack for himself, if the game be whist. In short, by making the *sauter la coupe*, he is enabled to effect all the knavish devices which the law of cutting has been enacted to prevent. The general mode of doing it may be described thus. The cheat first takes up in his right hand the cut cards, and places them in his left, so that the palm is under the cards, the thumb on one side and the fingers on the other. He next takes up the cards that the cut has been taken from, by placing his thumb at the bottom of the cards and his four fingers at the top, so as to hide them from view as much as possible, and puts them in his left hand on the top of the cut, but prevents the two divisions from uniting, by thrusting in the tip of the little finger of his left hand between them. With the same motion, he glides the right hand towards the left shoulder, the thumb of the left hand being lowered beneath the pack out of the way, while simultaneously the cards in the left hand are glided towards the right shoulder, till the edges of each heap pass each other, and then the action is reversed, the cut or lower heap being by this time on the top. In this motion the right hand covers the cards of the heap cut from, while the cut is covered partly by the four fingers of the left hand and the right wrist. This covering of the cards from the eyes of the bystanders is aided by their being held, not in a flat or horizontal position as at first, but by their right edges being lowered as the pass is in the act of being made. So many words has it taken to describe the act of an instant; but it must be remembered, that it is not a simply isolated act, but one composed of several minor consecutive actions. Some persons are so expert as to perform the pass with one hand only, pushing the top heap to one side with the thumb, till they can catch it between the second and third fingers of the same hand and draw it underneath. There are books in existence, which profess to teach the feat of making the pass by description, with the aid of diagrams. The idea is absurd; a man might work seven years at it and not acquire it from a book. But almost any teacher of conjuring will teach it in half-an-hour, and a good card-trick besides, for half a sovereign. I may just add, that by eyesight alone it is utterly impossible to detect the pass when deftly made; but it can be detected by ear, if not very expertly done; for there is a slight tell-tale sound, made by the edges of the two heaps of cards, when passing each other, that is very difficult to prevent, though it may be *drowned* by a cough, as a certain noble lord, who was detected in cheating by this means, used to do. To the amateur conjuror, however, the noise is of little moment, he having command of the pack can do as he pleases with it; and the more noise and gestures he makes in flirting the cards about, the more nonsense he talks to the spectators, the better he conceals his tricks. But, with the cheating gambler the case is very different; he can in handling the cards only follow prescribed rules, and the slightest symptom of eccentricity causes him to be suspected at once.

The Slip is merely a simpler kind of pass; any person that can perform the latter will find no difficulty in the first; it is used to place any particular card at the top, bottom, or middle of the pack, as may be required.

The Force requires more notice; by forcing, a spectator is compelled to draw any card from the pack that the conjuror pleases, and, as may be supposed, it is a most important aid to his

art. No feat on the cards is more puzzling to the
uninitiated than this, yet none is really so simple,
or so ready of acquisition. It is thus performed:
—The conjuror holding the cards spread out, face
downwards, in both hands, says, "Pray draw a
card, sir," rapidly or slowly moving the cards
from left to right, or from right to left, with
either thumb, so that when the person reaches
out his hand to draw a card, the card required to
be forced is just ready to be taken. If the card
be passed either to right or left of the hand of the
drawer, the conjuror shifts them all back again at
one movement, and commences shifting them over
again. The feat depends on the swiftness or
slowness with which the conjuror shifts them, as
may be required, with the readiness of the drawer
to take one. So certainly does the conjuror
manage his cards, that the right card and the
drawer's hand comes together at the same instant,
as the shooter, pointing his gun, pulls the trigger
and kills the flying bird, at the only moment
when it could be killed, eye and finger working
together in complete unison. As already observed,
this feat is of a simple character, and easy of
acquisition. From what is written here, any one
may learn it with a very few minutes' practice.
The intelligent reader observing that the conjuror

does not, in one sense of the word, force the drawer to take the card required to be drawn, and yet he does so, in another, by preventing him from taking any other card.

The Change is also easy to perform, and can soon be learned from the following directions. The performer holds the pack in his left hand, the thumb on top, the first, third, and little fingers at the bottom, the second finger extended downwards beneath all, is quite detached from the pack, and, being covered by it, is unseen by the spectators, the arm hanging down carelessly by the left side. The card to be changed is held between the second and third fingers of the right hand, and the card it is to be changed into, as the vulgar idea goes, is immediately under the thumb of the left hand on the top of the pack, a little in advance, that is to say, to the right of the others. The performer then holding up the card that is to be changed, asks a person, who has just previously drawn a card, "Is this your card, sir?" and, of course, the reply is, "No, decidedly not." The performer, feigning disappointment and surprise, generally says, "No, sir? pray be certain, do not deceive me!" or words to this effect, while he actually makes the change, by dexterously placing the card held between the second and third fingers of the right hand between the bottom of the pack and the second finger of the left hand, at the same moment taking the card off the top of the pack with the forefinger and thumb of the right hand. Then holding the substituted or changed card up again to the drawer, but in a horizontal position, so that he may not see what card it is, the performer again asks, "Are you still certain that this is not the card you drew?" to which question there is simply the confident reply, "Yes!" "Pray blow on it," says the performer, and at that moment turns up the card, to the astounded eyes of the drawer, who then, with wonder, sees and acknowledges that it really is the very card he drew.

With these directions carefully followed, the change may readily be performed after ten minutes', at most, practice, or rehearsal, as one might say. But they must be implicitly followed, or the feat is impossible. The card to be changed must be held between the second and third finger of the right hand, so as to allow the forefinger and thumb of the same hand to take, at the same instant, the substituted card from the top of the pack. So well is every movement managed to work together, the upper card covering the other from the eye of the bystander, that a conjuror may be excused for saying that it is a beautiful trick. Some conjurors, when performing it, sway the body slightly to the left to partly cover the operation; others, when the drawer denies the card, say, "Well, there may be dirt upon it, preventing you from seeing it, probably, which I will soon rub off," and make the change, when partly stooping to knock the card against their right knee, as if to remove the dust. Or again the conjuror, in a defiant manner, will walk up to the drawer, saying, "Do you presume to tell me this is not the card?" making the change, when close to the person of the latter, under his very nose, as one might say, when it is utterly impossible for him, even if he had the eyes of Argus, to see it done.

It must ever be kept in mind, that in any kind of conjuring, but particularly that with cards, the performer must never look at his hands; for, if he does, the spectators will most certainly do the same, a consummation most devoutly to be avoided. In all instances, the performer must keep continually talking to the bystanders, looking them full in the face, so that they may do the same, minus the talking, to him.

Having detailed the various leading feats performed with cards, we shall now describe a trick, of what may be termed a representative kind, as it comprises all these various feats, and is probably one of the best, and most wonder-creating tricks connected with playing cards.

In a large company, the performer will ask a person to draw a card; this first one need not be forced, but it must not be lost sight of. On the drawer replacing the card in the pack, it may be brought to the top by making the pass, then passed or slipped to the centre, and then forced on a second drawer. Or when the card is being replaced in the pack, the performer, by holding the upper division of the cards a little in advance of the lower, will find the card on the top of the latter; and then by catching its end next him between the ball of his thumb and the palm of his hand, the rest of his hand and out-stretched four fingers completely covering it, he can draw it out and place it on the top of the pack totally unseen by any of the bystanders, from whence it may be again passed to the centre and forced as before. Or, better still, when the card is replaced in the pack, the performer, placing the second finger of either his right or left hand on the face of the card, commences to shuffle the pack, holding it horizontally face downwards. The detective finger, however, never leaves the card,

either in shuffling or forcing; if the position of
the cards compel the left hand finger to relinquish
its post, the right hand finger takes the vacated
place, and so the performer may shuffle and force
a card twenty times, without actually knowing,
according to its technical denomination, what card
it really is. Moreover, this extraordinary advantage is gained, without the least suspicion on the
part of the spectator, the fingers beneath the pack
being completely hidden by the cards. Skilful
conjurors laugh in their sleeve, when they hear
people speaking of marked cards and long cards.
What necessity can there be for a marked card,
when the performer, unseen and unsuspected, can
literally hold it at his finger's end ? According to
the number in company, the same card may be
forced on from six to a dozen persons, the performer always taking care they are sufficiently
apart from each other, that no two can know that
they have both drawn the same card. After this
the performer, placing the cards ready for the
change, takes any indifferent card, and asks each of
the audience, one by one, is not that the card,
he drew. Of course, the reply is in the negative :
but the change being made, the card (the substituted one at least) is acknowledged; and the
question is asked, and the change made, before

each drawer in succession, to the very great wonder of the spectators; who, surprised by the apparently miraculous change, are at last astounded by finding that all of them have drawn one and the same card.

We need scarcely observe to the reader, that the above trick may be varied, at least, a dozen different ways; and must say, in conclusion, for to that complexion we have unwillingly come at last, that in the Pass, Slip, Force, and Change, are comprised all the tricks used by card-conjurors; and from our previous explanations, any intelligent person may at once see through a card trick, and with a very little practice be able to perform any one himself.

Card-Playing in the xiv. Century.

Other TUT BOOKS available:

TO LIVE IN JAPAN by Mary Lee O'Neal and Virginia Woodruff

THE TOURIST AND THE REAL JAPAN by Boye de Mente

TOURS OF OKINAWA: A Souvenir Guide to Places of Interest compiled by Gasei Higa, Isamu Fuchaku, and Zenkichi Toyama

TWO CENTURIES OF COSTUME IN AMERICA by Alice Morse Earle

TYPHOON! TYPHOON! An Illustrated Haiku Sequence by Lucile M. Bogue

UNBEATEN TRACKS IN JAPAN: An Account of Travels in the Interior Including Visits to the Aborigines of Yezo and the Shrine of Nikko by Isabella L. Bird

ZILCH! The Marine Corps' Most Guarded Secret by Roy Delgado

Please order from your bookstore or write directly to:

CHARLES E. TUTTLE CO., INC.
Suido 1-chome, 2–6, Bunkyo-ku, Tokyo 112

or:

CHARLES E. TUTTLE CO., INC.
Rutland, Vermont 05701 U.S.A.

688.754 T213hc1   AAO-0448
Taylor,   060101 000
The history of playing cards,

0 0003 0195362 6

Johnson State College